King Edward VIII

King Edward VIII

an american life

TED POWELL

OXFORD
UNIVERSITY PRESS

OXFORD
UNIVERSITY PRESS

Great Clarendon Street, Oxford, OX2 6DP,
United Kingdom

Oxford University Press is a department of the University of Oxford.
It furthers the University's objective of excellence in research, scholarship,
and education by publishing worldwide. Oxford is a registered trade mark of
Oxford University Press in the UK and in certain other countries

© Ted Powell 2018

The moral rights of the author have been asserted

First Edition published in 2018
Impression: 1

Published in the United States of America by Oxford University Press
198 Madison Avenue, New York, NY 10016, United States of America

British Library Cataloguing in Publication Data
Data available

Library of Congress Control Number: 2018942362

ISBN 978-0-19-879532-2

Printed and bound in Great Britain by
Clays Ltd, Elcograf S.p.A.

For Alison, who married one Edward, and found herself living with two

Acknowledgements

I have incurred many debts of gratitude in the course of writing this book. In the early stages I was fortunate to receive helpful advice on planning, structure, and possible publishers from David Cannadine, Tom Penn, Andrew Rose, Ruth Scurr, Catherine Clarke, Caroline Burt, and Richard Partington. Throughout my research I was greatly helped by the expert assistance of archivists and staff at the National Army Museum, the Imperial War Museum, the Cumbria Record Office, the Churchill Archives Centre, the Glenbow Museum in Calgary, Alberta, the London Metropolitan Archives, and the Parliamentary Archives. A happy reunion with my old editor Robert Faber led to a renewed working relationship with Oxford University Press. In Alberta, my wife and I enjoyed the generous hospitality of Jennifer Bartlett as she showed us the wonderful restoration work that she and her husband Curtis are carrying out on the EP ranch; Andrew Wood supplied me with valuable information on Edward's interest in aviation; Charles Metcalfe provided fascinating information on his grandparents, Edward 'Fruity' Metcalfe and Lady Alexandra Curzon; while Katherine Mann provided inspiration on marketing and promotion. Thanks also to my editors at OUP, Matthew Cotton and Kizzy Taylor-Richelieu for all their patience, diligence, and good humour.

The book has been substantially written over the last two years, while I was taking part in the Guardian/University of East Anglia Masterclass on the New Biography, led by Professor Jon Cook. Jon has read virtually the entire book in draft, providing guidance and constructive criticism at every stage of production. He has truly been the 'midwife' in the delivery of the book. My fellow students on the course, Liza Coutts, Diana Devlin, Carrie Dunne, Monique Goodliffe, Lyn Innes, Jo Rogers, Barbara Selby, Ann Vinden, David Warren, and Hephzi Yohannan, have given me tremendous support and encouragement. This is only the first of many published works which will emerge from the class in due course.

My greatest debt is to my family. My father, the late Ray Powell, first awoke my love of history, and I like to think he would have enjoyed reading the book. My mother, Avril Powell, shared with me reminiscences about Edward from her childhood, and provided a very congenial working environment when I went to stay with her. My daughters, Helena and Juliet, have helped me more than they know. I have often benefited from Helena's encyclopedic knowledge of Queen Victoria's family, while Juliet provided insights into Edward's fantasies of escape, and Wallis's identity as a Southern belle. My wife Alison has lived with Edward day-to-day for more than five years. There have been three of us in the marriage (to coin a phrase), so it has been a bit crowded. She has tolerated my obsession patiently, as the house filled with Edward memorabilia, books, busts, china, photographs, and bric-a-brac. She has read all the chapters in draft, and offered penetrating comment. The book could not have been written without her, and I dedicate it to her.

Contents

List of Illustrations

Introduction
An American Love Affair

On 4 April 1970 President Richard Nixon welcomed the Duke and Duchess of Windsor as guests of honour at a dinner in the White House. As the visitors' limousine pulled up, Nixon, looking unexpectedly elegant in white tie and tails, walked down the steps of the entrance to offer assistance to his elderly guests. The Duchess took his arm but the Duke managed with his walking stick. Inside about a hundred guests were waiting, mostly celebrities, film stars, and sportsmen: Fred Astaire, the golfer Arnold Palmer, and the Apollo 8 astronaut Frank Borman.[1] There were also a few of the Duke's contemporaries whom he had known as Prince of Wales, such as John Coolidge, the son of President Calvin Coolidge, the aviator Charles Lindbergh, and Alice Longworth, the 86-year-old daughter of Theodore Roosevelt. The dinner was not a state occasion but rather a private party. The Nixons were repaying a debt of hospitality. In 1964 the Windsors had entertained the Nixons to tea at the Waldorf-Astoria in New York, and in 1966 they had given a dinner party for the entire Nixon family at their Paris mansion. The White House dinner had been laid on partly for the benefit of the Nixons' daughter, Julie Nixon Eisenhower, then a college senior and keen historian. Julie was a self-confessed fan of the Duke. In a well-intentioned but tactless gesture, she presented him with a commemorative mug made for his coronation as King Edward VIII—an event which had not taken place owing to the Abdication in 1936. In another jarring note, the first course was a mousse of sole and shrimp shaped in the form of a royal crest, surmounted by cold salmon. Described by the newspapers as 'La Salmon [sic] Froid Windsor', it served as an inadvertent reminder of how the Duchess had been frozen out by the British establishment and denied royal status.[2]

Figure 0.1. President Nixon entertains the Windsors at the White House, April 1970

Nevertheless it was a convivial occasion. The photographs show the Windsors basking in the limelight of the President's attention while Nixon, whose parents had named him after the medieval English king Richard the Lionheart, savours the faded glamour of the ex-king. It was an intriguing encounter between the only British monarch voluntarily to abdicate the throne and the only US president to resign the office. Nixon had a vivid memory of listening to Edward's Abdication speech on the radio with his college friends, and later claimed that it had made more impression upon him than President Roosevelt's 'fireside chats' of the same era.

The American President's admiration for Edward was nothing new: the close relationship between Edward and the USA was of long standing. He had first visited Washington more than half a century earlier in November 1919, while on an official tour of North America as Prince of Wales. The occasion could not have been more different. Then he came as a guest of President Woodrow Wilson, and he arrived in the middle of a political crisis. The President was forced to welcome the Prince from his sickbed in the White House, his health broken by the protracted negotiations at the Versailles Conference after the Great War and his unsuccessful efforts to persuade the Senate to ratify the Peace Treaty. Edward spoke with Wilson for only a few minutes, and afterwards remarked that he had 'the most disappointed face that I had ever looked upon'.[3]

Edward's meeting with President Wilson came at the end of a year of frequent encounters with Americans. 'I'm liking the Americans more than ever,' he wrote excitedly after visiting American troops in January 1919. 'I'm just longing to go to the States . . . but we just must be closely allied with the USA, closer than we are now, and it must be lasting and they are very keen about it.'[4] He was captivated by the energy, confidence, and raw power of the USA as it strode onto the world stage at the end of the Great War. Edward's tours of North America only served to strengthen that affinity. Fifteen years later, as war threatened Europe again, he told an American journalist:

> The peace of the world depends upon the friendly association of the two great English-speaking peoples. Only the United States and Great Britain working together and in perfect harmony can prevent the world from drifting into helpless anarchy and barbarism.[5]

Edward was not just a fervent advocate of the 'special relationship' between America and Britain. Like the thousands of immigrants welcomed to New York by the Statue of Liberty, Edward, weary of the constraints of the Old World, was 'yearning to breathe free'. He was seduced by American culture, language, music, dancing, consumerism, and, of course, by American women.[6] It was his tragedy that, as heir to the throne of the British Empire, he was himself the embodiment of the old order.

This book offers a fundamental reassessment of the life and reign of King Edward VIII by viewing it through the lens of his lifelong fascination with the United States of America. Such an approach throws new light on important aspects of Edward's career as Prince of Wales and later as King: his innovative approach to the performance of his royal duties; his democratic style and impatience with the rigidities of court life; his love of modernity; and his choice of friends and lovers. In particular the events leading up to Edward VIII's Abdication in 1936 come into clearer focus when viewed with an understanding of the impact upon Edward of his experience of American culture and power during his twenty-five years as Prince of Wales.

Edward's personal experience was reflected more broadly in the prevailing trends in British society after the Great War.[7] Few Britons had the opportunity to travel to the States as Edward did. Nevertheless they encountered

American culture and society at home in the powerful form of Hollywood cinema. This cultural Americanization was accompanied by the flood of American consumer goods into Britain and the invasion of US companies such as Ford, Hoover, and Woolworths. American influence was rapidly internalized in Britain through the use of American language: jazz, movie, radio, hoover. In the 1920s, for Edward, Prince of Wales, and for British society in general, America was the template of modernity.[8] For better or worse, America was the future.[9]

From 1918 onwards, in an effort to reconcile the demands of his princely duties with his desire for personal fulfilment, Edward developed two distinct personas. They even had different names. The public persona was the quint-essentially British 'Edward' the Prince (and later King); the private, genuine persona was the informal, Americanized 'David', David being the name by which he was known to his family and his lovers. The period between 1918 and 1924 was especially important for the development of this split identity. In those years Edward discovered America, and at the same time he embarked on his first serious love affair—with Freda Dudley Ward, the half-American wife of a British Member of Parliament. In the final year of the Great War he frequently met detachments of US troops in Europe, and later enter-tained them at the London victory celebrations in the summer of 1919.[10] He was impressed by the American forces, admiring their self-confidence and determination. He soon adopted their slang expressions: one of his favourites was 'jazzin' around'.[11] Immediately after the war Edward was sent on a goodwill tour of North America. The tour attracted unprecedented publicity for the young prince. Within a few months he was projected from the comparative anonymity of military service into the blinding glare of international celebrity. Separated for several months from his lover, he wrote passionate, anguished letters to Freda, sharing his daily experiences and impressions. It was an extremely stressful period for the diffident young prince, but also a revelatory one. In the course of his American tour Edward was greeted wherever he went by enormous, excitable crowds, and pursued by the press and newsreel cameras. He discovered his ability to communi-cate with ordinary people, both en masse and individually. His intuitive understanding of the expectations of royalty in a democratic society led him to reinvent the performance of modern monarchy.

At the same time Edward was transfixed by the experience of America. Being one of the few places he visited which was not part of the British Empire, America gave him a special sense of freedom. He was greeted by a tickertape welcome in New York, admired the engineering miracle of the Panama Canal, and made a speech for the first time with loudspeakers in San Diego. On his journey through western Canada he was so impressed with the grandeur of the prairie that on impulse he bought a cattle ranch in Alberta.[12] On a stopover in Hawaii on the way to Australia in 1920 he took up surfing. In America he caught a tantalizing taste of a life of freedom, opportunity, and modernity which was denied to him by the accident of his birth. As he wrote in his memoirs, 'America meant to me a country in which nothing is impossible.'[13] By contrast, Britain was a place where many things were impossible for Edward, Prince of Wales, not least his wish to marry the woman he loved. His encounter with America was one of the formative experiences of his life, and it shaped his destiny.

On his departure from New York in November 1919 Edward promised to return to America, and described himself as proud to be a New Yorker.[14] Given the opportunity, he would certainly have made regular visits to the States in the 1920s, as he did after his Abdication. After completing his Empire tours, he managed to fit in a holiday trip to New York in 1924 on the way to his Canadian ranch.[15] On this visit Edward's reputation as a party-loving playboy was truly sealed, generating the famous banner head-line, 'Prince Gets In With The Milkman'.[16] That was to prove Edward's last visit to the US for many years. A projected tour of the industrial cities of the American Midwest in 1926 failed to materialize, probably because of the opposition of Edward's father, King George V.[17] The King was unsympa-thetic towards Edward's love for the USA. He disapproved of what he saw as the undignified way in which Edward behaved in America, and was appalled at the effrontery of the American press in pursuing the Prince so aggressively. For the remainder of his life he blocked attempts by Edward to return to the USA.[18]

Edward responded with a form of 'inner emigration', reinforcing the dichotomy which existed between Edward the Prince and David the private man.[19] He withdrew both physically and emotionally from the rest of the royal family, setting up a weekend retreat at Fort Belvedere, near Sunningdale in Berkshire. He cultivated American friends and took American lovers. He adopted American modes of speech and acquired American products.[20] Edward's first serious affair with an American lover was with Thelma Morgan, Lady Furness, the twin sister of Gloria Vanderbilt and the wife of a wealthy British shipping magnate.[21] The Chicago-born London society diarist Chips Channon blamed Thelma for modernizing and Americanizing the Prince, although in fact their relationship was a symptom rather than a cause of the process:[22] Edward had been attracted to American women since his first encounters with them. It was through Thelma Furness that Edward met Wallis Simpson. Forceful, irreverent, and sassy, Wallis personified everything that he admired about modern America. Their love affair completed the process of Americanization which Edward had begun fifteen years before. The divide between the public and private personas, between 'Edward' and 'David', widened until it became unbridgeable. In the two years before King George's death in January 1936 the Prince's isolation from his family and the royal court became almost total.[23]

The central question which every biographer of King Edward VIII must face is simply put: why did he abdicate? The straightforward answer is summarized in one of the Duchess of Windsor's best *bons mots*: 'Darling, you must understand, you can't abdicate and eat it.'[24] On this analysis Edward abdicated purely for love of Wallis Simpson. Faced with the stark choice of remaining on the throne or marrying Wallis, he chose the latter. This was Edward's own explanation, eloquently expressed in his Abdication speech, 'I have found it impossible to carry the heavy burden of responsibility and to discharge my duties as King as I would wish to do without the help and support of the woman I love.' Few commentators have accepted the romantic simplicity of this version of events, which begs the question as to why Edward could not have retained the throne while marrying Wallis. Edward's two leading biographers, Frances Donaldson and Philip Ziegler, are broadly in agreement that he abdicated in part because he was temperamentally unsuited to the role of king, and could not or would not accept the demands and constraints of his royal position. For Donaldson, Edward's decision to abdicate was 'partly inspired by a deep longing to escape the terrible responsibilities of the role he had inherited'.[25] Other writers have suggested that it was not just a question of Edward's temperamental unsuitability. His poor political judgement and pro-Nazi sympathies raised serious constitutional issues. In the words of Alistair Cooke, 'he had not merely been a lover defied but a constitutional issue of shattering importance'.[26]

An alternative version of events, powerfully argued by the author Compton Mackenzie shortly after the Abdication and frequently restated, is that 'Edward the Martyr' was the victim of a conspiracy by the British Establishment to remove him. According to this view, Edward promised to be a radical and modernizing monarch who had to be ousted because he threatened the vested interests of the old order.[27] Edward's reign was, of course, too short to allow him to implement any proposals he might have had for the reform of the British monarchy. In his memoirs he said that he had no desire to go down in history as Edward the Reformer, although he did want to be king 'in a modern way'.[28] However, there are signs that Edward envisaged a more assertive, populist—even presidential—form of monarchy which was influenced by his Americanized ways of thinking. In 1935, for example, he appears to have intervened directly in diplomatic negotiations regarding the Anglo-German Naval Agreement.[29] He felt that his modernizing approach was in tune with the changes that were taking place in British society, and he saw his proposed marriage in precisely the same light. In a revealing discussion with the Cabinet Minister Duff Cooper, Edward dismissed the suggestion that he might keep Wallis as his mistress, contrasting the hypocrisy of the old European convention of keeping up appearances with the honesty of the 'modern American system' of accepting the reality of divorce.[30] A recent study by Susan Williams suggests that, contrary to the Establishment view, there was widespread support for Edward's stance among his subjects. During the Abdication crisis Edward received thousands of sympathetic letters from ordinary citizens, many of them happy that he should marry Wallis and remain as king.[31]

'The Abdication was a strictly English affair', wrote the historian A. J. P. Taylor. 'The question of Edward's marriage was discussed solely in English terms, related to the English established Church.'[32] Taylor's assessment continues to represent the consensus among historians and biographers. Ever since 1936, Edward VIII has been judged from an overwhelmingly Anglocentric perspective. For both Donaldson and Ziegler, and for Colin Matthew in the *Dictionary of National Biography*, Edward's life was an essentially British tragedy, and the Abdication a fierce little domestic drama played out behind closed doors at the heart of the British Establishment.[33] None of those biographers appreciated the extent of Edward's Americanization before 1936, beyond acknowledging the influence of his American mistresses Thelma Furness and Wallis Simpson. The role of the American press during the Abdication crisis has been recognized, but only as 'noises off', remote from the main drama. In fact the American dimension was crucially important in the unfolding of the crisis. The questions which it posed about Britain's identity and self-image reflected the challenges which the shock of America posed to British society between the wars.[34] Edward's espousal of American values and ways of thinking, combined with the pervasive influence of America on British society since the Great War, helped to define the cultural and social context of the Abdication crisis.[35] Moreover, it was the American press which broke the news of Edward's intention to marry Wallis, thus bringing the crisis to a head, at a time when Fleet Street was still maintaining a self-imposed silence. As events unfolded, the American public avidly followed developments, and on 11 December 1936 the USA, along with Britain, came to a standstill to hear Edward's radio broadcast announcing that he had resigned the throne to marry 'the woman I love'.[36]

The root causes of the Abdication go all the way back to Edward's first years as Prince of Wales. His early training for his royal duties, based on the Victorian concept of monarchy, was permanently disrupted by the Great War. By 1918 most of the European monarchies had been swept away, and it was clear that if the House of Windsor was to survive in the post-war world it had to become more modern and democratic. Much of the burden of presenting the new face of royalty fell on Edward's shoulders, in part because his personality was well suited to the emerging media of radio and newsreel. His wartime encounters with American troops and his visits to the USA after the war had a powerful impact on him, and this growing affinity with America helped to shape his innovative approach to his royal role. In the process he developed a more informal, democratic style of monarchy better suited to the post-war age.

Paradoxically, he was almost too successful. His populist appeal and Americanized lifestyle represented too radical a departure from the backward-looking conservatism of King George V. In 1936 his romantic obsession with Wallis Simpson outweighed his desire to implement the modernization of the British monarchy. Because of his determination to marry an American divorcee he was unable to articulate the case for change in the face of the conservative forces of Church and State arrayed against him.

I

Edward VIII and the Birth of the American Century

In 1894, the year in which Edward was born, Britain remained the world's dominant Great Power, as it had been for most of the nineteenth century. Since the defeat of Napoleon in 1815, Britain had enjoyed worldwide naval supremacy which enabled it to build a global trading network and to project its industrial power to expand its growing Empire. Edward's great-grandmother, Queen Victoria, nominally governed twelve million square miles of land and around a quarter of the world's population. By the 1890s, however, Britain's international dominance was being challenged across the globe, both by traditional rivals such as France and Russia, and more seriously by rising powers such as Germany and the United States. It became increasingly clear that the British Empire was overstretched.[1] In the words of Joseph Chamberlain, the Colonial Secretary at the turn of the twentieth century, Britain was 'the weary Titan, staggering under the too vast orb of its fate'.[2] What the British giant needed was a trusted and like-minded ally, a fellow Titan with whom to share the burden of world leadership. It turned to America.[3]

At first sight America was not a promising ally. There was a long history of antagonism towards Great Britain in the USA. Britain was the traditional enemy, the oppressive colonial power from which Americans had won their liberty through armed struggle. There were more recent grievances as well. The cause of the Confederacy attracted sympathy in Britain, which had antagonized the Union side with covert support for the South during the American Civil War. By the late nineteenth century, however, there were powerful forces for convergence between the two countries. They were brought closer together by rapid improvements in transport and communications. As the USA followed the UK down the path of industrial revolution, the structure of American society became more like that of Britain. Conversely, as the British political system became more democratic through a series of nineteenth-century reforms, it resembled more closely the American system. Large-scale immigration into the United States, mainly from Central and Eastern Europe, prompted the Anglo-Saxon governing elites to reassess their links of ancestry, language, and law with the old country. The prevailing racial theory of 'Anglo-Saxonism' asserted the superiority of the English-speaking nations and their common destiny to rule over 'lesser peoples'.[4]

The Spanish-American War of 1898 was a crucial event in the process of rapprochement. The USA took advantage of the rebellion in Cuba to expel Spain from the last remnants of its American empire and also to destroy its power in the Pacific through the occupation of the Philippines. The British provided logistical support to the American forces, and their victory was celebrated with great popular enthusiasm in Britain. 'All London burst out into the rainbow hues of the American national colours,' wrote an eyewitness, and that summer the British joined in the Fourth of July festivities for the first time.[5] In the aftermath of the war Great Britain made a series of diplomatic concessions to the USA which recognized American strategic dominance of the Western Hemisphere. The British accepted that war with the United States was unthinkable and that it was better to work with it as an imperial partner. Britain also facilitated American expansion into the Pacific, first by acquiescence in the US annexation of Hawaii in 1897, and in 1901 through the Hay–Pauncefote Treaty, which conceded to America the exclusive right to build and control a canal across the isthmus of Panama.[6] 'The United States should hold the iron keys of the gate of two oceans,' commented the London *Fortnightly Review*. 'We ought not to be found in America's way where our interests are secondary and hers are supreme.'[7] In the decade between 1895 and 1905 several Anglo-American friendship societies were founded, including the American Society of London (1895), the Anglo-American League (1898), and the Atlantic Union (1901). The most influential one was the Pilgrims Society, founded in London in 1902, which formed a sister organization in New York the following year. Pilgrims dinners were regularly attended by the respective ambassadors of the UK and the USA, and the Society attracted the patronage of the Duke of Connaught, the brother of Edward VII.[8]

American power was not confined to the Western Hemisphere, however. By the beginning of the twentieth century the USA had far outgrown Britain as the world's largest manufacturing nation. American goods were flooding into Britain, and American companies were starting to buy up British businesses. The scale of the American 'invasion' provoked anger and alarm in the UK. At the turn of the century the British magazine *The Review of Reviews*, edited by the campaigning journalist W. T. Stead, published a regular supplement called 'Wake Up, John Bull', which documented the American threat and catalogued the decline of British industry. Typical articles in the 1902 edition included 'Why the Americans are Beating us', 'How London Loses Trade', and 'The Crisis in British Industry'.[9] In the same year Stead published a book, *The Americanization of the World, or the Trend of the Twentieth Century*. Stead argued that Britain had been overtaken as the leading Anglo-Saxon nation by the USA, which was destined to dominate the globe in the coming century. In Stead's view Britain faced a simple choice between merging its empire into a union with the US, or 'reduction to the status of an English-speaking Belgium'.[10] A series of takeover battles in 1901–2, in the transport, shipping, and tobacco industries, raised fears that America would simply buy up the British economy wholesale. The *Daily Mail* raised the spectre of the complete Americanization of the British way of life. 'The average citizen wakes in the morning at the sound of an American alarum clock, rises from his New England sheets and shaves with his New York soap and a Yankee safety razor. He pulls on a pair of Boston boots over his socks from North Carolina...'[11] In New York, *Life* magazine printed a prophetic view of Trafalgar Square showing Nelson's column surmounted by a giant statue of Uncle Sam.[12] At the same time, however, the American commercial invasion was an indicator of the extent to which the economies of the US and Britain were converging. On the other side of the scorecard Americans could point to the large interests which British investors had built up in the course of the nineteenth century in US industries such as railroads, mining, and ranching.

During the same period the British public experienced for the first time the force of American cultural exports, foreshadowing the Americanization of mass culture in the United Kingdom in the twentieth century. In 1887, the year of Queen Victoria's Golden Jubilee, Buffalo Bill's Wild West Show toured Britain for the first time as part of the American Exhibition at Earl's Court. In media terms the direct ancestor of the western movie genre, the Wild West Show was a huge open-air production with hundreds of performers, together with wild animals such as elk and bison. The show typically lasted for over three hours and included set-piece re-enactments of historical events such as Custer's Last Stand, displays of sharpshooting by stars like Annie Oakley, mock bison hunts, and rodeo events. The show created an immediate sensation. Buffalo Bill (William Cody) was showered with invitations from London society. He had lunch with the Lord Mayor of London and was invited to a soiree by Oscar Wilde. The former Prime Minister William Gladstone visited the Exhibition site and toasted Anglo–American relations over lunch with Cody.[13]

The success of the Wild West Show was assured when it attracted the patronage of the Prince of Wales, the future Edward VII. He attended a special preview on 5 May 1887 with his wife and daughters, and enjoyed the show so much that he urged his mother, Queen Victoria, to see it. She ordered a private command performance at Earl's Court. At the beginning of the show a horseman rode into the arena carrying an American flag. The Queen stood and bowed, and the rest of the audience followed her lead. As Cody recalled: 'All present were constrained to feel that here was an outward and visible sign of the extinction of that mutual prejudice, amounting sometimes almost to race hatred, that had severed two nations from the time of Washington and George the Third to the present day. We felt that the hatchet had been buried at last and the Wild West had been at the funeral.'[14] A few weeks later the Queen ordered a second performance, as part of her Golden Jubilee celebrations. Most of European royalty was in attendance, and at the climax of the show the Kings of Belgium, Denmark, Greece, and Saxony joined the Prince of Wales aboard the Deadwood Stagecoach. Buffalo Bill took the reins of the coach and drove round the arena while the Indians staged a mock attack. Afterwards the card-playing Prince joked to Cody, 'Colonel, you never held four kings like these.'[15] The Wild West Show took London by storm: 28,000 spectators attended the first performance, and by the time the American Exhibition closed in October 1887 more than a million people had seen it. From London the show went on tour to Birmingham, Manchester, and Hull. It returned to Britain for a longer tour in 1891–2 and finally from 1902 to 1904.[16]

Alongside the American commercial and cultural invasion, a social invasion of the British upper classes had been taking place since the 1870s. As W. T. Stead commented, 'among the influences which are Americanizing the world, the American girl is one of the most conspicuous and the most charming'.[17] In the generation before 1914 there were over one hundred marriages between British aristocrats and wealthy American heiresses.[18] The 'buccaneers', as they came to be called, included Jennie Jerome, the mother of Winston Churchill, who married Lord Randolph Churchill;

Consuelo Vanderbilt, who married Lord Randolph's nephew, the Duke of Marlborough; and Consuelo Yznaga, who married the Duke of Manchester. Such alliances integrated American families into the highest levels of British society, giving them access to members of the royal family. Indeed, the first Anglo-American marriages probably would not have taken place but for royal encouragement. In 1873 the Prince of Wales (later King Edward VII) was instrumental in persuading Lord Randolph's parents to approve his marriage.[19] Edward VII enjoyed the company of American women, and many were included in his social set. His mistresses reputedly included Jennie Churchill and Consuelo Yznaga. The King's favour ensured the acceptance of the 'buccaneers' into British high society, and his death in 1910 was seen as a setback for them. 'Prestige of American Peeresses Faces Grave Crisis' was the headline in the *Oakland Tribune*.[20] The new King and Queen were thought to be much less sympathetic to the American interlopers.[21]

The eagerness with which the USA's wealthiest families married their daughters into the British aristocracy revealed that, despite the egalitarian, republican values of America, the New World continued to be fascinated by the traditions and social hierarchies of the Old. The same ambivalence was evident in American attitudes towards the institution which stood at the apex of British society, the monarchy. While deriding monarchy as obsolete and outdated, many Americans nonetheless admired the individual monarchs themselves. Andrew Carnegie, the Scottish-American steel magnate, who was an acute observer of Anglo-American relations, neatly summed up the paradox: 'they are prepared to throw up their hats and cheer lustily for the British republic as soon as you like, always provided it does not come while the Queen [Victoria] lives. At the mere mention of "the Queen" every American hat is off in a moment.'[22] By the end of her reign Queen Victoria was indeed popular in the USA, reflecting the cordial relations which had developed between the two countries in the dying years of the nineteenth century. At her death in 1901 there was widespread public mourning in America. President McKinley lowered the White House flag to half-mast, the first time this had been done for a foreign head of state. The *Los Angeles Times* reported that 'Americans have received the news of the death of Queen Victoria as a bereavement of their own, and commented upon it in terms such as they would employ in the case of an honoured President dying in office.'[23]

Queen Victoria's great-grandson, Prince Edward of York, was born just before 3 p.m. on Saturday, 23 June 1894, at White Lodge, Richmond, just outside

London. He was the first child of the Duke and Duchess of York (later King George V and Queen Mary), who had been married less than a year before. The announcement made the front pages of the American press from coast to coast.[24] Even before the birth the press interest was intense. The *New York Sun* reported that a newspaper artist had been discovered lurking in the laurel bushes in the garden of White Lodge in an attempt to sketch the Duchess during her afternoon walk.[25] The first images of the baby prince appeared in August 1894, shortly after his christening. With halftone printing of photographs still in its infancy, these were engravings of the royal family groups taken by the court photographer. The most famous was the 'Four Generations' group, showing baby Edward on the lap of his great-grandmother Queen Victoria, with his father and grandfather (the future Edward VII) standing behind.[26] For the first time in history four generations of British sovereigns were living at the same time. The future of the royal house had never looked more secure.

With the passing of Queen Victoria in 1901 four generations became three, but during Edward VII's reign the young prince's succession was still a distant prospect. His uneventful childhood drew little attention outside Britain. Tutored at home with his brother Albert until the age of 13, in 1907 he was sent to naval college, first at Osborne on the Isle of Wight and then at Dartmouth.[27] In 1910, however, Edward VII died, and the 16-year-old prince became heir to the throne of Great Britain on the accession of his father as King George V. The event which brought Edward to worldwide attention was his investiture as Prince of Wales in July 1911, shortly after King George's coronation. Dressed in period costume, Edward was invested with the insignia of his Principality by the King, and then 'presented' to the people of Wales from the battlements of the medieval castle of Caernarvon.[28] Lloyd George even taught Edward a few words of Welsh with which to greet his people.[29]

The investiture was widely reported in the USA, and prompted commentators to offer first impressions of the prince's appearance and personality. 'A typical Anglo-Saxon lad is Prince Edward,' reported the *Charlotte News,* 'he is fair-haired, blue-eyed and sturdy of limb.' Noting Edward's obvious physical immaturity, the *Salt Lake Tribune* was less complimentary: 'the young Prince of Wales is a schoolboy, thin-faced, weakly, given to overmuch cigarette smoking'.[30] As to his personality, the *Brooklyn Daily Eagle* accurately identified the 'modesty and painful nervousness' that he displayed as a very young man, while the *New York Sun* noted his solemnity: 'he seems to realize the burden of future kingship'.[31] Other observers thought they detected similarities between the young prince and his pleasure-loving grandfather, Edward VII. It was reported that Queen Mary had banished the old king's favourites from the court to protect the heir to the throne: 'she detects in her son a number of the tendencies towards laxity which the Prince's grandfather exhibited in a marked degree'.[32]

Following Edward's investiture as Prince of Wales, and his coming of age in 1912, the question inevitably arose as to his future bride. Heirs to the throne tended to marry young in order to secure the succession and promote dynastic alliances. Before the Great War it was generally assumed that Edward would follow the tradition of centuries and marry a foreign princess. The visits of European royalty provoked press speculation of an imminent engagement. As early as 1909 the presence of the Russian imperial family in England for a summer holiday prompted rumours of a match between Edward and one of the Tsar's four daughters, while the Kaiser's visit to Britain in 1911 accompanied by his only daughter, Victoria Louise, led the press to the false conclusion that her marriage to Edward was under negotiation.[33] On his trip to Germany in 1913 he did form an attachment to his cousin Princess Caroline Matilda of Schleswig-Holstein, and if the war had not intervened it is likely that he would have married her or another European princess.[34]

For a great republican nation America showed a surprising degree of interest in the marital prospects of the young prince. In the years leading up to the outbreak of the Great War, articles appeared regularly in the US press reporting marriage rumours and reviewing potential brides. 'England Now Engaged in Choosing Future Queen' was a typical headline, from the *Washington Herald* in July 1911. Apart from the daughters of Tsar Nicholas and Kaiser Wilhelm, popular candidates were Princess Eudoxia of Bulgaria, and Edward's cousins Princesses Elizabeth and Marie of Romania.[35] None of the reports appears to have had any foundation. In 1912 Edward went up to Magdalen College, Oxford, where for the next two years he lived an uneventful undergraduate existence until the outbreak of the Great War.

Prince Edward celebrated his twentieth birthday in June 1914. In the photographs and portraits of the time he looked much younger—more like 15 than 20.[36] He was about five feet six inches tall and was physically slight, weighing little more than a hundred pounds. He had a girlish face, pink cheeks, and soft golden hair. At Oxford Edward and his ever-present tutor, Henry Hansell, were nicknamed 'Hansell and Gretel'. He compensated for his puny physique by an addiction to strenuous exercise: he loved long walks and cross-country runs and his favourite sport was squash rackets. He was painfully shy and self-effacing. One observer remarked, 'He cannot get in or out of a room except sideways and he has the nervous smile of one accustomed to float.'[37] Although serious-minded, he was not an intellectual. After two years at Oxford it was obvious he had no interest in academic studies. 'Bookish he will never be,' declared his college tutor.[38] Even if the war had not broken out he would probably not have returned to Oxford for a third year, but would have joined one of the Guards regiments of the British army.

A few days before he turned 20, Prince Edward carried out his first solo public engagement. On 13 June 1914 he laid the foundation stone of the new church of St Anselm's in Kennington, London, which was part of his Duchy of Cornwall estates. A silent newsreel of the occasion shows the boyish prince carefully tapping each corner of the stone with a little mallet, in gloved hands. He looks stiff and uncomfortable in his old-fashioned formal dress—top hat, wing-collar, and frock coat: he is not yet the stylish dresser of the 1920s.[39] With obvious nervousness he reads out a short speech from a piece of paper. According to the *Times* report he was largely inaudible against the buzz of the watching crowd.[40]

Two weeks after the ceremony at Kennington, Archduke Franz Ferdinand was assassinated in Sarajevo, and Edward's leisurely education in the traditional duties of royalty was abruptly terminated.

On 3 August 1914, the day before Great Britain declared war on Germany, Prince Edward spent the afternoon on his own, batting a ball against the blank wall of a squash court.[41] The loneliness and frustration he felt that day were to be repeated all too often in the next four years. Although he volunteered immediately for military service, as heir to the throne his life could not be put at risk by fighting on the front line. The experience was deeply humiliating for him and reinforced his sense of unworthiness.[42] One consequence of the war was that the process of training Edward as a future monarch was put on hold. If he had been older he could have been appointed to a senior military post, like his 32-year-old cousin, Crown Prince Wilhelm of Prussia, who commanded the German Fifth Army. As it was, the Prince of Wales struggled to find a meaningful wartime role.

By contrast, Edward's father did have a clear-cut part to play. No English king had led his troops in battle for almost two hundred years. Instead he served as a symbolic figure, embodying national unity and purpose. Throughout

Figure 1.1. Prince Edward lays the foundation stone of St Anselm's Church, Kennington, June 1914

the war King George V and Queen Mary devoted themselves to promoting the war effort, raising charitable funds, visiting the wounded, and making tours of industrial areas. In four years the King held 450 military inspections, visited 300 hospitals, and conferred 50,000 decorations. He visited the Grand Fleet seven times and made five extended tours of the war zone in France.[43]

Despite this constant effort, the war threw up many challenges for the monarchy. From the outset the royal family's close German connections were a source of acute embarrassment to the King. 'I wonder what my little German friend has got to say to me,' said the future Prime Minister David Lloyd George on a summons to Buckingham Palace in 1915.[44] Apart from the Kaiser himself, the King's cousins included two German princes who held British dukedoms: Charles Edward of Saxe-Coburg, Duke of Albany, and Ernest Augustus of Hanover, Duke of Cumberland. Throughout the war an Irish Member of Parliament, Swift MacNeill, pursued a campaign to have these 'traitor dukes' stripped of their British peerages.[45] The campaign attracted attention in the United States and drew unsympathetic comment about the British royal family. 'Considering the historic fact that it is a German dynasty that rules over Great Britain,' noted the *Indianapolis Star*, 'it seems doubly unwise to make such a fuss over certain Teutonic princes who are alleged to be "traitors" to the British cause.'[46] Despite the King's resistance, in 1917 Parliament passed the Titles Deprivation Act, which expelled the Dukes of Albany and Cumberland from the House of Lords and deprived them of their British titles and honours. Later that year, in an effort to remove all taint of Germanness from the royal family, King George changed the name of the dynasty from the House of Saxe-Coburg to the House of Windsor. At the same time he announced that his children would be allowed to marry into English families.[47] Minor royals with German surnames were required to swap them for British titles; for example, Prince Louis of Battenberg became Louis Mountbatten, Marquess of Milford Haven.[48]

In the spring of 1917 two events occurred which fundamentally altered the course and nature of the war. In March the Tsarist regime in Russia collapsed. King George's cousin Tsar Nicholas II abdicated and a republican government took power in Petrograd. On 6 April, following the resumption by Germany of unrestricted submarine warfare in the Atlantic, the US Congress declared war on Germany. The war changed from being a struggle for mastery among the Great Powers to a crusade to liberate the oppressed peoples of Europe from autocracy and tyranny. President Woodrow Wilson's avowed aim on entering the war was 'to make the world safe for democracy', and in his vision there was little room for monarchy. As the old regimes of Europe crumbled before the forces of nationalism, republicanism, and revolution, the foundations of the British throne suddenly began to look precarious. On 21 April 1917 the London *Times* printed a letter from the writer H. G. Wells advocating the establishment of republican associations in Britain to show solidarity with the nation's allies in France, Russia, and the United States: 'these ancient trappings of throne and sceptre are at most a mere historical inheritance of ours...our spirit is warmly and entirely against the dynastic system that has so long divided, embittered and wasted the spirit of mankind.'[49]

Wells stopped short of calling for the outright abolition of the British Crown, but the implication was clear. The monarchy was an outdated relic of a past age. The subtlety of Wells's argument was lost in America, where his letter was widely reported. 'Overthrow of King Urged by H. G. Wells' was the headline in the *Washington Herald*.[50] His was not the only republican voice. The Labour Party greeted the Tsar's abdication with great enthusiasm, holding rallies in the Royal Albert Hall and elsewhere to celebrate.[51] It dawned on the King and his advisers that the monarchy faced an uncertain and potentially hostile future after the war. It would need to 'democratize' and become more relevant and responsive to the ordinary citizen. 'We stand at the parting of the ways,' advised the courtier Lord Esher, 'the Monarchy and its cost have to be justified in the future in the eyes of a war-worn and hungry proletariat endowed with a huge preponderance of voting power.'[52]

Here at last was a task for which the Prince of Wales could be usefully employed. The very first biography of the Prince, published in 1915, when he was only 21, stressed his impatience with ceremony and his determination not to be given special treatment because of his status.[53] Despite serving in non-combat roles Edward had made repeated efforts to reach the front line and had frequently come under shell-fire. On one occasion he returned to his car to find that his chauffeur had been killed by a shrapnel blast.[54] In order to get closer to the troops he frequently used a bicycle to travel between units, and became a familiar figure on the roads behind the front lines. Edward's rejection of the privileges of life as a staff officer, and his determination to get as close to the front as he could, won him the respect of British troops. As stories of his experiences filtered into the newspapers in Britain and America, Edward came to be presented as a 'democratic' prince eager to share the hardships and dangers of the ordinary soldier.[55]

For example, the *Wichita Beacon* carried a glowing tribute to the Prince in March 1918 under the headline 'Prince of Wales has Known Hardships of War'. It related how Edward would often stop his staff car to give lifts to weary soldiers. 'He has endured all the dangers and discomforts of war-time,' the article went on. 'Many stories of his good nature and democratic manners are told.'[56] Such a narrative fitted in very well with the attempts of the King and his advisers to present a more progressive style of monarchy in response to the threat of republicanism. The Prince's role as the modern democratic face of British royalty in the post-war world was beginning to take shape.

Edward's initiation into his new role came early in 1918, when he was sent on an intensive three-week tour of the industrial areas of Britain. This included a visit to 'Red Clydeside' in Glasgow, which was regarded as a stronghold of Bolshevik socialism. He was well received in the city, where he toured the naval shipyards and tried his hand at riveting. In south Wales he went six hundred feet below ground in a coal mine and exchanged a few words in Welsh with the miners at the coal face. At Woolwich Arsenal in London he charmed hundreds of munitions girls by saluting them as he left the factory.[57] By the end of the war Edward had come to appreciate the enormity of the task which he and his family faced. In November 1918, as the German and Austrian monarchies were collapsing, a shocked Prince wrote to his father: 'Our [monarchy] is by far the most solid, though of course it must be kept so and...this can only be done by keeping in the closest possible touch with the people...I'm out the whole of every day seeing and visiting *the troops* ie *the people*!!!!'[58]

While Edward was in London in March 1918 he paid his first visit to the American officers' club established and run by the Pilgrims Society, the Anglo-American friendship association.[59] By this time there were thousands of US troops in Britain and France, although they had as yet done little fighting. General John Pershing, the commander of the American Expeditionary Force, had arrived in Britain in June 1917. Stepping onto the dock at Liverpool, Pershing was welcomed by a guard of honour from the Royal Welch Fusiliers, a regiment which had fought at the Battle of Bunker Hill in the American War of Independence. He immediately travelled down to London, where he paid a visit to the King at Buckingham Palace. King George urged Pershing to attach American troops to units of the British army in order to bring them into battle as soon as possible, but Pershing had to explain that his orders from President Wilson were to build up a separate US army as a distinct component of the Allied forces. In his address to Pershing's staff, the King emphasized the close links between Britain and America: 'It has always been my dream that the two English-speaking nations should one day be united in a great cause, and today my dream is realized. Together we are fighting for the greatest cause which peoples could fight. The Anglo-Saxon race must save civilization.'[60] The US entry into the war alongside Britain was the culmination of a process of political and cultural rapprochement which had taken place over the previous twenty-five years. The strengthening of political, economic, and social ties had brought the two nations closer than ever before. American heiresses had married into the highest echelons of British aristocracy. It was unthinkable that English princes should continue to marry German princesses. Had the time come for the Prince of Wales to marry an American bride, and so seal the alliance of the two great Anglo-Saxon powers?

Although it might have seemed a remote possibility in 1917, the idea of such a marriage had already been imagined in fiction. *His Royal Happiness*, a novel by the Canadian author Sara Jeannette Duncan, was published in the USA in October 1914 and in Britain in 1915. The hero is Prince Alfred, the younger brother of King John of England, and a descendant of Queen Victoria. At the beginning of the novel, Alfred, like his real-life counterpart, is an undergraduate at Magdalen College, Oxford. He has suffered poor health since childhood but is progressive and democratic in outlook, and chafes against royal protocol. On a tour of America Alfred meets and falls in love with Hilary Lanchester of Baltimore, daughter of the US President. Exhausted by the exertions of his trip, Alfred suffers a severe attack of tuberculosis. His English doctors despair of his life, but an American specialist effects a miracle cure which transforms the invalid prince: 'Dr Morrow...cured me. He did more than that...he made a man of me, who had been, I am afraid, very little more than a Prince.'[61] Convalescence in the Adirondack Mountains, accompanied by Hilary, completes the Prince's recovery. He dreams of settling in America and buying a ranch in Colorado. In order to frustrate the dynastic matrimonial schemes of royal relatives, Alfred persuades Hilary to marry him secretly before he departs for England. Soon afterwards a disaster at sea causes the death of his two elder brothers and Alfred becomes king. Duty separates the lovers for several years, until, following the agreement of a great arbitration treaty between Britain and the USA, Alfred and Hilary are able to reveal the secret of their marriage and to consummate the diplomatic union of their two nations.

Duncan's novel, published just after the beginning of the Great War, has a remarkably prophetic quality. The sickly English prince, whose illness implicitly stems from the stifling constraints of the Old World, is made whole by the genius of American science and the love of an American woman. The union of the two great Anglo-Saxon peoples is symbolized in the marriage of an English King to the daughter of an American President. Although the book must have been completed before the outbreak of war, it foreshadows the Anglo-American alliance against Germany and the regenerative power of the American intervention in the war alongside the Allies in 1918.[62] More specifically, Duncan sketched out the political and cultural implications of Anglo-American rapprochement and the role that a young and democratically minded Prince of Wales might play in it.

2

The Prince and the
Doughboys, 1918–1919

'The Yanks are coming, the Yanks are coming...'—but would they arrive in time? At the beginning of 1918 there were fewer than 200,000 US troops in France. The American Expeditionary Force, under the command of General Pershing, had only just begun to build up its military presence. Pershing's plan was to assemble an independent army, ready to fight alongside the French and British in late 1918 and 1919. The Allies were overtaken by events. On 21 March 1918 the German army launched a wave of offensives on the Western Front in a final attempt to smash the Anglo-French armies, drive the British into the sea, and march on Paris. They almost succeeded. Within days the Germans had advanced several miles, breaking through the Allied lines of trenches which had held for almost four years. After a week the German forces were only fifty miles from Paris, and the British were falling back on Amiens, the gateway to the Channel ports. In this desperate situation the British Prime Minister, David Lloyd George, appealed directly to President Woodrow Wilson to order Pershing to brigade American troops immediately with French and British forces, rather than waiting for reinforcements to form an army of their own. On 27 March five hundred US railway engineers were thrown into the front line before Amiens in an attempt to save the city.[1] The following day, Thursday 28 March, Pershing visited the Supreme Allied Commander, General Foch, at his headquarters at Clermont and assured him that in view of the gravity of the crisis he was willing to send him any troops he had. Speaking in French, Pershing said, 'I have come to tell you that the American people would consider it a great honour for our troops to be engaged in the present battle. The American people will be proud to take part in the greatest battle of history.'[2] Winston Churchill later regarded this as one of the turning-points of the war, and considered that Pershing's words should take their place beside Lincoln's Gettysburg Address in the annals of American history.[3] A few days later Field Marshal Douglas Haig, Commander-in-Chief of the British armies in France, issued his famous Special Order of the Day: 'With our backs to the wall and believing in the justice of our cause, each one of us must fight on to the end.'[4]

Somehow, the line held and the Germans failed to break through. American forces in Europe grew rapidly throughout the year. By July there were more than one million US troops in France, with thousands more arriving every day. The Americans' arrival had a significant impact, both psychologically and militarily. Vera Brittain, the British writer who chronicled the anguish of the young generation that fought the war, described her first encounter with American troops at the base camp near Étaples where she was working as a volunteer nurse.

> I pressed forward... to watch the United States physically entering the War, so god-like, so magnificent, so splendidly unimpaired in comparison with the tired nerve-racked men of the British Army. So these were our deliverers at last, marching up the road in the spring... sunshine. My eyeballs pricked, my throat ached, and a mist swam over the confident Americans going to the front... With the knowledge that we were not after all defeated, I found myself beginning to cry.[5]

The effect on the French was just as invigorating. As the Americans helped them to hold the line east of Paris, a French officer noted: 'Life was coming in floods to revive the dying body of France.'[6] As for the enemy, the growing weight of the American presence was the final blow. In September 1918 the German commander, General Ludendorff, admitted ruefully: 'We cannot fight the whole world.'

On the home front the benign invasion by large numbers of American troops, nicknamed 'doughboys', was met with great popular enthusiasm. In November 1917 the Pilgrims Society, the Anglo-American friendship association, established the Anglo-American Officers' Club in London. Its president was the King's uncle, the Duke of Connaught, and soon after its opening the club was visited by the King and Queen in person.[7] On 4 July 1918 a celebration of the Independence Day of the United States of America was held in London. The Stars and Stripes flew alongside the Union Jack, fluttering above Buckingham Palace, the Houses of Parliament, and outside St Paul's Cathedral. Detachments of troops from across the Atlantic surged like adrenalin through the grey streets of the exhausted city. In bright summer sunshine American soldiers strolled down the Strand, some wearing roses, some with flowers twined round their slouch hats. Street vendors did a brisk trade in badges showing the twin flags, and as the day passed thousands of people wore the Stars and Stripes in miniature.[8] At Westminster Central Hall, Winston Churchill, then Minister of Munitions, addressed a Liberty Day meeting for Anglo-Saxon Fellowship. With his acute sense of history, Churchill grasped the significance of the moment:

> Deep in the hearts of the people of these islands...lay the desire to be truly reconciled with their kindred across the Atlantic ocean...to stand once more in battle at their side, to create once more a union of hearts, to write once more a history in common. It seemed utterly unattainable, but is has come to pass.[9]

The highlight of the day's celebrations was an exhibition baseball match between the US Army and Navy at Stamford Bridge, the home of Chelsea football club. A capacity crowd, estimated at 50,000, attended. Women from the munitions factories, still in their brown overalls, acted as ushers. As well as large numbers of US soldiers and sailors, rooting for their teams, there were thousands of 'Britishers' enjoying a day out. The symbolic importance of the occasion was emphasized by the presence in force of the royal family: King George V, Queen Mary, their children Prince Albert and Princess Mary, and even Queen Alexandra, the aged widow of Edward VII. The US newspapers reported that the King had been limbering up at Buckingham Palace in preparation for pitching the first ball. In the event, however, he merely came down from the stand to meet the team captains, and auto-graphed a baseball as a gift for President Wilson.[10] The newsreel coverage shows the King in military uniform, smiling and chatting with the players. The atmosphere was boisterous but good-humoured. The Navy 'rooters' yelled blood-curdling chants through megaphones, and British spectators were alarmed by traditional calls to kill the umpire. There was even some good-natured joshing of royalty. 'What's the matter with King George? He's all right!' chanted the American servicemen, much to the King's amusement. In a close-fought match the Navy secured a 2–1 victory over the Army, their star pitcher, Herb Pennock, striking out fourteen batters. At the end of the game the crowd surged onto the field, as the victorious Navy team snake-danced exuberantly among their supporters. Amidst the cheering, the band of the Welsh Guards struck up the 'Star-Spangled Banner'. Immediately, as the London *Times* reported, the crowd fell silent:

> Hats came off. Soldiers and sailors stood to attention, saluting...The meaning of this most significant of all ball games was carried along the air...The crowd

awoke to consciousness that the afternoon had passed into the history of two great nations.[11]

One member of the royal family was not present at the ball game that day. Edward, Prince of Wales, was serving with British forces in Italy. Edward, now just 24, had recently been promoted to major, and had a desk job on the general staff, safely away from the front line.[12] Nevertheless he would surely have regretted missing the game, if only because his beloved mistress, Freda Dudley Ward, was in the crowd.[13] It was in Italy that Edward had his first encounter with US troops. One of his nominal duties was liaison with foreign forces, and on 11 August 1918 he drove to Verona for lunch with Colonel William G. Everson, commander of the newly arrived 332nd US Infantry Regiment. This detachment of 1,200 men was a token force sent to boost the flagging morale of the Italians on the Austrian front. 'They are a cheery crowd of d——d good fellows', wrote Edward to Freda, 'and keener than I ever imagined...when I asked them what leave arrangements they had, their reply was the last verse of a very good one-step tune, "We won't go back till it's over over there!!!" Made me feel very small...'[14] Later in the year the 332nd was attached to the British XIV Army Corps, and helped chase the Austrians back across the border at the Battle of Vittorio Veneto, shortly before the Armistice.[15]

By September 1918 the war was turning decisively in the Allies' favour. The final German offensives in July had run into the ground, and from early August the Allied forces rolled the Kaiser's depleted armies back across France and Belgium. The American Expeditionary Forces played an important role in breaking the German lines, notably at the Battle of the Argonne Forest north of Verdun. With the sudden improvement in the military situation, the King decided it was time for Edward to return to France to pay official visits to Imperial troops, in particular the Canadian and Anzac (Australia and New Zealand) Army Corps. Much to the Prince's annoyance, this meant cancelling a three-month staff course he was due to attend at Cambridge, which would have afforded him plenty of opportunity to visit his mistress.[16] After a brief spell of leave in England, including an ecstatic night with Freda on 7 October, Edward found himself back in France, first with Field Marshal Haig at GHQ and then with the Canadian Corps near Cambrai as they advanced into Belgium.

The Prince spent a month with the Canadians and got on well with them; he warned Freda that he would return home with a Canadian accent.[17] He was still with them when the war finally ended on 11 November 1918. On the day itself Edward had lunch with Field Marshal Haig and the visiting Japanese Prince Yorihito. Haig discussed the terms of the Armistice and outlined plans for the Allied occupation of the Rhineland. Edward, however, was more interested in getting back to the Canadian Corps HQ near Mons, where a celebration ball had been arranged, with Canadian nurses invited over from Boulogne. The dance was obviously a success, as it went on until four in the morning, and the following day Edward drove some of the nurses back to Boulogne.[18]

For the rest of the winter of 1918–19 the Prince was kept busy with a programme of visits to Imperial and Allied troops, giving him a foretaste of his future role travelling the globe as the ambassador of Empire. After the Canadians he met the Australians and New Zealanders, as well as Scottish, Welsh, and Irish divisions. All were 'damned good fellows', infinitely preferable to the foreign Allies, especially the Belgians and Italians, whom Edward loathed.[19] In turn Edward was well received by the troops he visited. They warmed to his shy charm, affability, and lack of pomposity. For the Canadians he was 'every inch the gentleman and sportsman, so simple, so charming and so genuine.'[20] A correspondent from the *New York Tribune* noticed his shyness and modesty in public. Attending the liberation of Valenciennes with US and Canadian commanders in November 1918, the Prince slipped away from the platform after the ceremony and vanished into the crowd, his khaki uniform providing welcome camouflage: 'His work was done and he dreaded to be the centre of more ovations.'[21]

Back in England the visit of President Woodrow Wilson, on his way to the Paris Peace Conference, was eagerly awaited. Wilson's Fourteen Points had set out a framework for peace based upon democracy, self-determination, and free trade, which offered the prospect of a new world order free from the threat of war. On his arrival at Dover on Boxing Day 1918 the President was welcomed by the King's uncle, the Duke of Connaught. As he stepped ashore the band played the 'Star-Spangled Banner', while little girls wearing stars-and-stripes frocks strewed roses in his path.[22] King George had even sacrificed his traditional Christmas holiday at Sandringham in order to entertain the President and Mrs Wilson at Buckingham Palace. Everywhere he went Wilson was met with cheering crowds waving American flags. He rode through the City of London, with a Sovereign's escort of Life Guards, to a reception given by the Lord Mayor at the Guildhall. Later he travelled up to Carlisle to visit his mother's birthplace. There in the Congregational Church he spoke movingly of the values taught him by his English grandfather and mother, which now inspired his work for international peace.[23]

At a political level, Prime Minister David Lloyd George was keen to impress Wilson, and to forge a close relationship with him before the Peace Conference commenced. Quite apart from managing the $4 billion of debt which Britain owed to American banks, Lloyd George dreamed of a new Anglo-American alliance which would dominate the globe in the post-war era.[24] Although Wilson himself was keen to stand above the fray in Europe without taking sides, it seemed that in America Lloyd George was pushing at an open door. The great swell of pro-American sentiment which had risen in Britain during 1918 was matched by an equally strong surge of pro-British feeling in the USA. On 7 December 1918 'British Day' was celebrated throughout the nation to pay tribute to British sacrifice and achievements in the War. Organized by Judge Alton B. Parker, the defeated Democratic candidate in the presidential election of 1904, British Day was marked in thousands of towns and cities across the country. Fifth Avenue in New York was decked with British flags, while in Fresno, California, a pageant was held followed by dancing in the streets. In Louisiana, Governor Robert G. Pleasant called upon all Louisianians to celebrate the day 'in recognition of the splendid work the British people have done in defending France and Belgium and safeguarding civilisation'.[25]

Amidst this mutual lovefest, the British press drew the logical conclusion. On New Year's Day 1919, shortly after Wilson's departure for Paris, the London *Daily Express* carried a front-page article which suggested that the Prince of Wales should marry an American bride. 'Enthusiasm on both sides of the Atlantic would be unbounded,' argued the *Express*.[26] The article was widely reported, with varying degrees of enthusiasm, in the US. The *Daily Ardmoreite* extended a warm invitation: 'Come to Oklahoma, Prince...there are Indian queens and paleface queens in Oklahoma by the hundred.' The *Wichita Daily Eagle,* a keen follower of the Prince's activities, was more sceptical. 'Who wants to be a queen?' it asked. 'His job is the worst thing about him, and if he really loved you he might be willing to give it up and buy a farm in Kansas.'[27] In Canada the *Toronto Globe* responded rather peevishly, 'Our girls would not take too kindly to an American Queen at a time when there are so few vacancies on thrones worthwhile.'[28]

Interest in the Prince had therefore increased considerably in the US press by the time Edward paid a visit in early January 1919 to the HQ of the 3rd American Army in Koblenz, part of the Army of Occupation of the Rhineland. He was treated to a flight over the Rhine with the American fighter ace Billy Mitchell, and narrowly avoided being shot at when his convoy drove into a village where American machine-gunners were conducting some over-enthusiastic target practice. A German villager raised the alarm in the nick of time.[29] Not surprisingly most of the press attention focused on the dance given in the Prince's honour at the Officers' Club. Since there was no fraternization with German girls, US Army and Red Cross nurses were bussed in to provide dance partners. Nonetheless they were heavily outnumbered by the officers, and there was much 'cutting in' during dances. 'US officers take royal heir's girls' ran the headline in the *New York Sun,* 'Prince of Wales submits to "cutting in" at dance'.[30] While Edward won approval for democratically insisting on being treated like a brother officer, his dancing skills were not highly rated: 'Prince of Wales bum dancer but Yanks teach him' commented the *Wichita Daily Eagle.*[31] Elinor Whittemore, a YMCA worker from Boston, reported that she had danced four dances with the Prince and that he was very gallant. '"You American girls" he said, "are the finest dancers in the world!"' Another partner complained that he had 'one-stepped all over her feet'.[32]

For his part Edward was impressed by his American hosts. 'They are a big power in the world now,' he wrote to the King, 'I am just crammed full of American ideas...'[33] In February he visited the HQ of the American Expeditionary Force at Chaumont near Verdun, where he was entertained by General Pershing. On 17 February 1919 the Prince accompanied Pershing to a review of the entire US 35th Infantry Division, a National Guard formation from Kansas and Missouri. Thirty thousand men trudged ten or twenty miles through the pouring rain to attend. The doughboys were in awe of 'Black Jack' Pershing, leading the inspection with a group of senior officers on horseback, but were disappointed by the Prince of Wales. 'I expected to see a great big man with lots of braid and medals on his uniform,' wrote Earl Conley from Kansas, 'Instead I saw a little slim kid of about seventeen years old.'[34] Edward was actually 24, but Conley was right: the Prince went out of his way *not* to look like a 'prince', for example refusing to wear the *Croix de Guerre* that the French had awarded him, on the grounds that he had done nothing to deserve it.[35] More informally, Edward had his first lesson in crap-shooting on the floor of Pershing's mess; his enthusiasm for all things American continued to grow.[36]

Meanwhile a chance encounter appeared briefly to dash hopes of an American queen. In February 1919 Edward was staying at the Hotel Meurice in Paris, when the Queen of Italy arrived at the same hotel.[37] Queen Elena was accompanied by her eldest daughter, Princess Yolanda, whom the Prince had met previously while serving on the Italian front in 1916. According to the gossip columns they had 'wandered together over the hillsides of northern Italy and unburdened their young hearts in a frank exchange of youthful confidences'. Yolanda's beauty was much praised: 'She has a beautiful face of the finest Italian type... a wealth of superb black hair and deep, dark eyes that are filled with feeling and expression.'[38] The French press immediately jumped to the conclusion that a royal engagement was about to be announced. The Prince was furious and demanded that the Embassy issue an immediate denial.[39] Queen Elena was also indignant about the false reports, and Edward found it necessary to apologize to her in person.

A few days afterwards the Prince returned to England. His war was over at last. In many ways it had been a bitter and frustrating experience. Denied an active combat role by his royal status, Edward was unable to share fully in the defining experience of his generation, in all its horror and intensity. Throughout the war he had been a 'red tab', a staff officer confined to a desk job. It reinforced his sense of inferiority and thwarted his burning desire 'to be found worthy and to share in the risks and struggles of men'.[40] On the other hand, military service had given him a degree of freedom and privacy such as he was never to enjoy again. Amongst the millions of soldiers on the Western Front, Captain Wales could move around inconspicuously, his presence largely unremarked. He even enjoyed a private life of sorts, mixing with his fellow Guards officers and pursuing sexual liaisons. In a speech to the City of London in 1919 Edward reflected on his war service:

> The part I played was, I fear, a very insignificant one, but from one point of view I shall never regret my periods of service overseas. In those four years I mixed with men. In those four years I found my manhood. When I think of the future, and the heavy responsibilities which may fall to my lot, I feel that the experience gained since 1914 will stand me in good stead.

The speech was probably written for the Prince rather than by him, but it has the ring of sincerity about it, and it was widely quoted in the press and in contemporary biographies.[41] The double meaning of the phrase 'I found my manhood' would have been lost on his audience, but it encapsulated an obvious irony for Edward himself. He had found his manhood not in the killing fields of France but in the boudoirs of Paris and London. In any event, by the end of 1919 the comparative anonymity of his wartime life was gone for ever. Edward, Prince of Wales, had become a global celebrity, with photographers and newsreel cameramen following his every move.

The Prince faced a heavy workload on his return to Britain. Unlike most European monarchies, the House of Windsor had survived the war, but there was still a real fear of serious disorder, even revolution. Early in 1919 there was a wave of strikes across the country, and in Glasgow striking workers raised the red flag over the town hall.[42] Across the British Empire troubles were multiplying. The weary King George, prematurely aged by the terrible responsibility of leading the nation through the war, looked increasingly to his eldest son to share the burdens of monarchy. In particular, Edward was to undertake a series of tours round the British Empire to thank the dominions and colonies for their contribution towards the war effort: first Canada, then Australia and New Zealand, then India.[43]

The immediate occasion for Edward's recall to England at the end of February 1919 was the wedding of his cousin Princess Patricia, daughter of the Duke of Connaught and granddaughter of Queen Victoria. She was popular in Canada, where her father had been Governor-General during the war. She even had a regiment named after her—Princess Patricia's Canadian Light Infantry. Before the war she had resisted attempts to marry her off to the sons of European royalty. Instead she fell in love with one of her father's aides-de-camp, Alexander Ramsay, a distinguished naval officer. The marriage marked a decisive break with the tradition of the British royal family marrying members of foreign royal houses. Although aristocratic by birth as the son of an earl, Ramsay was a commoner. On his marriage he was not even raised to the peerage, although he was later knighted. On her wedding day the bride renounced her royal status and chose in future to be styled Lady Patricia Ramsay. The wedding attracted favourable comment in America. The *Richmond Times-Despatch* carried a full-page article headlined, 'When H.R.H Princess Patricia becomes plain Mrs Alex Ramsay'. Noting that before the war British peers of the realm had been considered of insufficient rank to be suitable matches for the Princess, *The Times-Despatch* commented approvingly: 'The war taught humanity truer values. It taught the British royal family that "reasons of state" and royal rank should not be able to overcome the desires of the heart.'[44] As the first major royal event after the war, the wedding was an opportunity for popular celebration. Cheering crowds lined the route to Westminster Abbey, where 'Princess Pat's' regiment provided the guard of honour.[45] Sitting in the Abbey as he watched the ceremony, Edward must have felt a little envious of his cousin, marrying for love and happily retiring into private life.

Edward's entry into public life had been delayed by the war. His twenty-first birthday in 1915 had passed without celebration, and his continuing military service meant that he had not had the opportunity fully to take on the conventional role of a senior adult member of the royal family. He had no establishment of his own, nor any dedicated staff, and he was not widely known in the country. He had little experience of public speaking or following the treadmill of royal engagements. All this had to be rectified before he departed for North America in August 1919. First it was necessary to select the key members of his staff. He chose as his Private Secretary a young Foreign Office official called Godfrey Thomas, an old Harrovian and the son of a baronet. With his calm competence and diplomatic skills, Thomas was the ideal foil for the mercurial Prince. The relationship proved an enduring one, and Thomas was to remain in Edward's service until the Abdication. The Prince also appointed two equerries, or personal assistants: Lord Claud Hamilton, seventh son of the Duke of Abercorn, a Grenadier officer and war hero, with a reputation as a ladykiller; and Piers 'Joey' Legh, the son of Lord Newton, another Grenadier, who had been aide-de-camp to the Duke of Connaught as Governor-General of Canada.[46] In 1920 Legh married an American war widow, Sarah Polk. This was to be the core team who over the next few years accompanied the Prince on his overseas tours. At the same time Edward needed a home he could call his own. He chose York House in St James's Palace, and made it into a modest and rather ramshackle set of bachelor rooms.[47] On 1 July 1919 the Prince moved out of Buckingham Palace and formally took up residence in St James's. From that date the London *Times* issued a separate Court Circular for the Prince, marking the establishment of his own independent household. At the age of 25 he had finally escaped from the parental home.[48]

In order to accelerate the Prince's overdue entry into public life, numerous engagements were crammed into a few weeks in the spring of 1919, representing what Edward later described as the 'nursery slopes' of royal ceremonial. In quick succession he was made an honorary Bencher of the Middle Temple, an Elder Brother of Trinity House, and a Freeman of the City of London. He paid visits to his duchy of Cornwall estates in London and the West Country, and received an enthusiastic welcome in Cardiff on his return to Wales for the first time since his Investiture in 1911.[49] He became Chancellor of the University of Wales, a Trustee of the British

Museum, and Grand Master of the Order of St Michael and St George. Societies and associations all over Britain clamoured for his patronage, from the Royal Cornwall Agricultural Society to the Windsor and Eton Chrysanthemum Society.[50] In the midst of all this activity preparations were under way for his North American tour.

As the Prince prepared for his visit to the New World, and as Britain and America celebrated the signing of the Treaty of Versailles and the formal end of hostilities, the two nations suddenly began to feel much closer together. It was not merely the continuing presence of American troops in Britain, or the experience of fighting together in the last months of the war. The change was a technological as well as cultural one—the age of transatlantic flight was about to begin. For many years the London *Daily Mail* had offered prizes for feats of aviation: in 1909 Louis Blériot had won £1,000 for the first cross-Channel flight. In 1913 the *Mail* offered £10,000 (equivalent to approximately £650,000 in today's currency) for the first transatlantic flight. The prize was suspended during the war but reinstated soon after the Armistice. The challenge required that the aviator fly a single aeroplane across the Atlantic within seventy-two hours.[51] The rapid advances in aviation during the war made the crossing a real possibility, and in the spring of 1919 a race developed between the British and the Americans to make the first transatlantic flight.

The Americans made the early running. Between 8 and 27 May a US Navy squadron of Curtiss seaplanes ventured cautiously across the ocean via the Azores to Portugal. They were supported by no fewer than fifty-three naval vessels strung out across the Atlantic. One of the planes, the NC-4, captained by Commander Albert C. Read, managed to make the entire crossing and then flew onto England where it landed off Plymouth on 31 May. There the crew were greeted by the city's mayor on the very spot from which the Pilgrim Fathers had set sail in the *Mayflower* almost three hundred years before.[52] Later, after a tumultuous welcome in London, Read and his officers were entertained to lunch at the House of Commons by the Prince of Wales and Winston Churchill. The Prince congratulated the Americans on being the first to fly the Atlantic, and Commander Read thanked the British for their sportsmanship, saying, 'The British people are good winners, but they are wonderful losers.'[53]

The British took a more swashbuckling, if less systematic, approach to the challenge. Because the stately progress of the NC-4 flight across the ocean had greatly exceeded seventy-two hours, the *Daily Mail* prize still remained to be won. In the middle of May the Sopwith pilot Harry Hawker set off from Newfoundland in a last-minute attempt to beat the NC-4 to Europe. He was dismissive of the American safety-first approach: 'If they placed a ship every 50 miles', he argued, 'it merely showed they had no faith in their machine.'[54] However, his machine did fail him; engine trouble forced him to ditch half-way across the Atlantic, where he was picked up by a passing steamer. Then on 15–16 June, John Alcock and Arthur Whitten Brown made their celebrated non-stop flight, departing from Newfoundland and landing in an Irish bog sixteen hours later. They had won the *Daily Mail* prize, which they promptly invested in government Victory Bonds. Amidst national rejoicing they were summoned to Windsor Castle where they met Prince Edward and were knighted by the King. On the way back to Windsor station Sir John Alcock was carried shoulder-high by Eton schoolboys, who deposited him on the wrong platform so that he had to race across the tracks to catch his train.[55]

Commentators on both sides of the Atlantic were quick to stress the symbolic importance of these achievements. 'Now that America and this country have been brought within 16 hours of one another,' said Lord Reading, the former British ambassador in Washington, 'let us hope and trust that our hearts would also be drawn closer together... On these two peoples the future of the world must, more than anything else, depend.' In reply the American ambassador, John Davis, noted that, while Alcock was British, Whitten Brown was American-born. 'From that I draw the confident assurance that in any cause and in any enterprise, America and Great Britain united are truly invincible.'[56] In July 1919 a British airship, the R34 (with a US Navy observer on board) made the first transatlantic return crossing, from Britain to America and back again. The entire round trip took eleven days, considerably less than the NC4's single crossing a few weeks earlier. On the return journey, as a publicity stunt, the R34 carried copies of the Philadelphia *Public Ledger* for 9 July. Four days later they were delivered as the first transatlantic airmail service by the newspaper's editor, Cyrus Curtis, to the King, the Prince of Wales, and Lord Northcliffe. The Prince replied with a personal letter of thanks to Curtis.[57]

With his love of modern technology Prince Edward took a keen interest in aviation. He was an enthusiastic flyer, although as a passenger rather than pilot; his father would not permit him to take flying lessons. After the Armistice the Prince paid several visits to aircraft factories, and there were plenty of flying aces with time on their hands who were happy to take him up for a 'flip'. In January 1919 a young British ace, Bobbie Cunningham-Reid, flew the prince over Cologne: 'we stunted over the Cathedral and again over the Rhine so that we could spit in it,' boasted Edward to his mistress.[58] According to Cunningham-Reid's account the Prince did rather more than spit in the Rhine, as the stunting made him violently airsick. Nonetheless he declared it a 'ripping' experience.[59] A few weeks later he accompanied the Canadian hero and VC, Billy Barker, on a test flight of a prototype Sopwith Dove. Barker had suffered terrible injuries in the action for which he was awarded his VC. He could only walk with sticks and still had his left arm in a sling. 'Prince of Wales stunts with one-armed VC' ran the headline in the London *Daily Mirror* next day.[60] When King George heard of the incident he immediately banned the prince from any further flying. Edward was not allowed in the air again until 1929, when he bought his own Gipsy Moth.[61]

The 'drying-up' of the Atlantic Ocean provided the perfect backdrop to the victory celebrations in London in July 1919, in which the Americans played a prominent role. General Pershing led a composite regiment of over 3,000 men representing all the units of the American Expeditionary Force. During the celebrations Prince Edward spent much of his time with the Americans as a prelude to his forthcoming North American tour. On 18 July the Prince welcomed the troops to Britain at a review in Hyde Park, where he was accompanied by Winston Churchill, now Secretary of State for War. The Prince's speech of welcome was drafted for him by Churchill, and echoed the familiar themes of the English-speaking nations fighting shoulder to shoulder as kith and kin.[62] At the same ceremony Pershing presented the Distinguished Service Medal, awarded by President Wilson, to several members of the British High Command.

On the following day the American regiment took part in the 'Peace Pageant', the victory parade through London which marked the end of hostilities following the signing of the Treaty of Versailles on 28 June.[63] The *New York Tribune* noted approvingly that the Americans had the place of honour at the head of the procession.[64] The Prince took the salute at the parade alongside King George, and afterwards the royal family entertained Marshal Foch, Pershing, and other Allied commanders to lunch at Buckingham Palace. During the afternoon Edward managed to escape the festivities briefly for a game of squash with his brothers, and in the evening they watched a spectacular firework display from the roof of the Palace.[65]

Figure 2.1. The Prince, General Pershing, and Winston Churchill review American troops in London, 1 July 1919

The Prince's most important 'stunt' during the celebrations, and the one he was most nervous about, was to host a dinner for more than four hundred Allied generals and senior officers at the Carlton Hotel. The purpose was no doubt to give the inexperienced Prince some practice at formal set-piece speeches in preparation for his North American tour. His nervousness stemmed from the fact that he was hosting the event on his own, entertaining commanders like Foch and Pershing with little support from the government, though he did manage to bully Lloyd George into attending at the last minute. Again he took advice on speech-making from Churchill, although the advice on this occasion was rather eccentric: 'take a tumbler and put a finger bowl on top of it, then put a plate on top of the finger bowl and put the notes on top of the plate;... one has to be very careful not to knock the whole thing over as once happened to me.'

Edward worked hard on his speech all weekend, writing it out longhand before memorizing it. In the end it appears to have gone well.[66]

Despite his busy official schedule Edward still found time to pursue his affair with Freda Dudley Ward, and their relationship reached a new level of intensity during the summer of 1919. Freda's husband William was the Vice-Chamberlain of the Royal Household, and the couple had a house at Kilbees Farm near Windsor Great Park, within cycling distance of the Castle. There Edward visited Freda and her two young daughters, and when in London they would often meet at the house of a mutual friend, Gwendolyn 'Poots' Francis, in Duke Street near Grosvenor Square.[67] During March and April 1919, before the Prince's diary began to fill up with official engagements, the couple appear to have seen each other almost every day. Edward's feelings deepened from infatuation to all-consuming love. On 2 May he crossed an important psychological barrier in signing a letter to Freda as 'David', his personal family name, rather than 'Edward', his official 'royal' name.[68] Soon afterwards they exchanged signet rings with spider motifs, which they called 'Mr and Mrs Thpider', and Edward used his ring to seal letters to Freda. Over the summer the couple frequently made a foursome with Edward's brother Bertie and his lover Sheila, Lady Loughborough, a young Australian beauty who had married Lord Loughborough, the son and heir of the Earl of Rosslyn. Sheila was a great friend of Freda's. They called themselves 'the 4 Do's', and spent summer weekends together in the country. Revelling in his love for Freda, Edward encouraged Bertie's affair with a married woman. As he wrote to Freda in late May 1919, 'What fun we 4 have, don't we angel, and f—the rest of the world.'[69]

We do not know what Freda's true feelings towards the Prince were at this time because her side of their correspondence does not survive. We do know that she had other admirers, and that as a respectable married woman in society it was vital to her that the affair be conducted discreetly. However, Edward's ardour and impetuosity made this virtually impossible. By July gossip about the couple was circulating so widely in London society that Freda was talking of ending the relationship. In order to prevent further scandal she cancelled a proposed trip to Canada which was scheduled to take place at the same time as the Prince's tour.[70]

Edward's romantic summer idyll was soon over. Ahead of him loomed a daunting programme of Empire tours. As soon as the war ended, plans were put in train for the Prince's visits to the Dominions, beginning with Canada. Prime Minister Lloyd George was eager to capitalize on the wartime comradeship amongst the Commonwealth troops, and the King was determined that the Prince should gain experience of the countries and peoples he would one day rule. Once the plans for the Canadian tour were revealed, the American press campaigned for Edward to visit the USA, and in July, at the height of the victory celebrations in London, it was announced that he would visit Washington and New York as the guest of the American government.[71] To emphasize the importance of the Prince's mission, HMS *Renown*, one of the Royal Navy's fastest and most powerful warships with a crew of more than one thousand men, was assigned for the Atlantic crossing. The date of departure was set for 5 August 1919.

On the eve of the tour Edward was in a state of emotional turmoil at the prospect of his separation from Freda. The night before he set sail for Canada, rather than studying the itinerary or dining quietly with his family, Edward was in bed with his mistress. In fact, it appears that he got no sleep at all that night, returning to St James's Palace at 6 a.m.[72] On the day of his departure he wrote to Freda three times, his letters full of misery and heartache at their parting. He visited her yet again early in the morning before catching the royal train to Portsmouth, even though she had specifically asked him not to. That afternoon *Renown*'s log recorded that the Prince briefly disembarked before the ship sailed at 6 p.m., in all probability to dispatch one last letter to his love.[73] It was in this fragile emotional state that Edward sailed to Canada to face the greatest test he had yet experienced as Prince of Wales.

3

A New World

Edward's Tour of North America, 1919

Prince Edward's tour of North America was the first of a series which would take him all the way round the British Empire. In 1919 the empire was as large as it had ever been. Over four hundred million people nominally owed allegiance to the British Crown. Within it there were in fact three empires: the Dominions—Canada, Australia, South Africa, and New Zealand—self-governing nations which had been extensively settled by emigrants from the British Isles; the colonial empire, comprising the British colonies in Africa, Asia, and the Caribbean; and India, an empire in itself, where the British Raj had supplanted the Mughal Emperors. There was also a fourth, informal empire in Latin America, where British capital and investment dominated the continent's economy. The government had decided that Edward should visit all these empires as soon as possible. In six years between 1919 and 1925 he visited forty-five countries and travelled 150,000 miles, a distance equivalent to six circumnavigations of the globe.[1]

What was the purpose of this prodigious effort? The idea of introducing the heir to the throne to the peoples of the empire was nothing new. Edward VII had visited Canada and India as a young man, and George V toured Australia and Canada in 1901 and India in 1905–6. However, in the aftermath of the First World War the circumstances were entirely different. The empire was in crisis: British imperial authority was being challenged at every turn. India saw a surge of nationalist discontent following the Amritsar Massacre, Egypt was in open insurrection, while in Ireland the War of Independence had already broken out. In order to rebuild British influence, Prime Minister David Lloyd George proposed a series of tours by the young and attractive Prince.[2] Loyalty to the British monarchy, and specifically the royal family, was one of the few common ties that united the

disparate parts of the empire. In the words of the Canadian general Sir Arthur
Currie, speaking in London during the victory celebrations in June 1919,
'it was marvellous when one considered the extent of the British Empire
and the number of people within its borders, how much of the bond
which held it together was the sentiment which centred around the
Royal Family'.[3]

Planning for the tours was carried out by the Colonial Office, and in
particular by Leo Amery, the arch-imperialist who was Acting Secretary of
State.[4] Initially he proposed an unrealistically arduous schedule for the Prince:
following four months in Canada and the US, he was to tour Australia and
New Zealand in 1920, and then with barely a break he would visit India for
the opening of the new Legislative Assembly in 1921.[5] In the event the tour
to India was postponed, but the programme was still punishing enough to
test the Prince's powers of endurance to the limit.[6] Although the tours were
not overtly political, they obviously had significant political overtones.
Amery's specific objective in promoting them was to strengthen the bonds
of empire and to reassert Britain's standing as a world power. For example,
he inserted into the voyage to Australia a stop-off in the West Indies, where
American influence had grown during the war. There had even been suggestions that Britain should sell its Caribbean colonies to the USA in payment of its war debts, a proposal which Amery was determined to squash.[7]
He appointed as political officer on the Prince's staff Edward Grigg, a colonel
in the Grenadier Guards and another committed imperialist. Grigg's role
was to write the Prince's speeches and to ensure that he remained properly
'on message' during the tour. The notion that the Prince might wish to
express opinions of his own was of course not considered.

Nevertheless, Edward had very definite ideas as to how the tour should
be conducted. From his experiences during the Great War and his long stays
with imperial and American troops after the Armistice, he had a much better
understanding of what his public expected than the officials organizing the
schedule in Canada. His first act on arriving on Canadian soil was to sack
Sir Joseph Pope, the elderly civil servant who had supervised his father's
tour of Canada in 1901 and who had prepared the itinerary for the Prince.[8]
Edward's 'ragtime jazz party', as he called his staff, reorganized substantial
sections of the tour and reduced formal pageantry in favour of motorcades
and mass receptions.[9] These events were to become a hallmark of the Prince's
tours. Wherever he stopped, in great cities or tiny railway halts, he would
hold open receptions to meet the general public.[10] The newsreels show him

standing on windy platforms, shaking hands with people as they file past in a never-ending stream. Half-way through the Canadian tour his right hand became so bruised and painful that he had to use his left.[11]

The Prince's approach was vindicated from the day he set foot on the Canadian mainland at St John, New Brunswick. 'People wildly enthusiastic over Prince of Wales,' proclaimed the *St John Evening Times-Star*, 'tremendous welcoming ovation,'[12] Grigg immediately wrote to Prime Minister Lloyd George recounting the Prince's success and enclosing the press cuttings. 'The popular reception was extraordinary,' he wrote, 'it rained a good deal but nothing dampened the enthusiasm of the crowds who came out to welcome him.'[13] The Prince himself was delighted, and in his letter to Freda that night allowed himself a rare note of self-congratulation: 'I am really rather bucked and satisfied tonight, as today . . . at St John went off extraordinarily well; I really received a marvellous welcome.'[14] Edward's reception at St John foreshadowed even more tumultuous scenes in Quebec, Toronto, and Montreal. The newsreel cameras captured the action, and cinema audiences across the world were able to follow his progress. Excitement at

Figure 3.1. Edward addresses a crowd of 40,000 veterans in Toronto, August 1919

Edward's arrival rippled across Canada and the United States. Sometimes the crowds were so vast and excitable that the Prince's staff feared for his safety. In Montreal the police almost lost control of the crowds: 'If the Police had not been lusty, the Prince might have been suffocated or clawed to death...Scratches on the Prince's neck showed where people had caught him with their fingernails in their eagerness to touch him.'[15] In Toronto he was manhandled from his horse by a huge crowd of veterans who passed him from hand to hand over their heads until he reached the platform from which he was to address them.[16]

The Prince's success was immediate and it was lasting. It was repeated in the USA, and subsequently in Australia and New Zealand, and also across India and Africa. Why did the Prince's appearance have such an impact? In part it was a simple matter of timing, but the magic of royalty and Edward's fragile charisma proved an irresistible mix. Victory in the Great War and the signing of the Versailles Treaty heralded a brief moment of optimism for a more peaceful and prosperous world. The young Prince symbolized that optimism. In Ottawa the Canadian Prime Minister Mackenzie King hailed the Prince as 'the Sir Galahad of the Royal household, the young knight and our future King'.[17] Years later Leo Amery recalled the bright confident morning of the Prince's early triumphs:

> The Prince's winning smile, his beautiful speaking voice, his natural gift of saying the right thing, his genuine human interest in all kinds and conditions of men and women and, not least, his very youthfulness, made an irresistible appeal. Here was the living embodiment of the bright hopes of unity and happiness...throughout the world.[18]

It was surely no coincidence that when the Prince met the tribe of Stoney Indians at Banff in western Canada, they named him Chief Morning Star.[19]

The key to the Prince's appeal was his informal, 'democratic' style. He was impatient with pompous ceremonial and determined to make himself available to ordinary people. The King, although pleased with his son's success, thought the mob scenes and endless handshakes undignified. Edward responded, tactfully setting his father right: 'one thing above all others that won't go down and which one has to be careful not to put on is "side" and pompousness!!'[20] The North American newspapers were quick to take up the theme: 'Democratic Prince meets all comers in handshaking handicap' was the headline in the *Winnipeg Tribune*, above a photograph of Edward working a crowd in Toronto. 'Prince charms eight thousand hearts at ball, grand military dance truly democratic', reported the *Vancouver Daily World* in September 1919. In particular the newspaper noted that the Prince made no use of the royal box throughout the entire evening.[21] Even the sternly republican editor of the *San Bernardino Sun* in California softened at the Prince's efforts: 'we are not disposed to gush over the Prince of Wales...yet one must give [him] credit for showing a more democratic spirit than was to be expected'.[22]

Not the least of Edward's appeal was that he was the world's most eligible bachelor. As the *New York Evening World* put it: 'So dear young ladies there is no telling. Who knows? Stranger things have happened than that Edward Albert Christian Andrew Patrick David should fall desperately in love with Mazie Moofletums, the daughter of a rich but honest Harlem profiteer.'[23] Nor did his devotion to his mistress in England prevent him from enjoying female company. While he wrote letters to her virtually every night, they often include mention of the balls he has attended and the girls he has met. He dutifully emphasized how dull and ugly they all were, but reading between the lines it is clear that the Prince was partying very hard.[24] Competition was fierce for tickets to the public balls in honour of the Prince, and of course it was the dream of every girl to secure at least one dance with the royal guest. Photographs of the lucky few would appear in the newspaper reports; some proud parents even published press notices that their daughter had danced with the Prince of Wales.[25] Any ball at which Edward danced more than twice with the same partner provoked a flurry of press comment. 'Danced six times with the Prince', ran the headline the morning after a ball in Hamilton, Ontario. 'She was the least plain of a very plain bunch,' explained Edward sheepishly, enclosing the offending press cuttings in a letter to Freda.[26] Girls who got close enough to the Prince would seek souvenirs of the occasion: 'they not only ask me for autographs but shove my cigarette ends down (well you know where...!!)'.[27] The impact of the Prince's tour was greatly amplified by newsreels and press photography. In the previous decade thousands of picture houses had sprung up across North America and Europe. In the UK alone there were around 4,000 cinemas attracting twenty million attendances a week.[28] There were sixteen journalists, photographers, and cameramen in the Prince's party, and their output filled the newspapers and newsreel bulletins across the world.[29] At the end of the tour the London *Times* estimated that twenty million people across North America had seen the newsreel bulletins of the Prince's visit.[30]

One photograph in particular captures the essence of Edward's appeal. It was taken early in the Canadian tour at Halifax, Nova Scotia, by Ernest

Figure 3.2. The Smiling Prince: Edward signing the visitors' book at Halifax, Nova Scotia, August 1919

Brooks, the official royal photographer. The Prince, in the uniform of a Royal Navy captain, is signing the visitors' book. He is smiling because, as he signed the book, a bystander in the crowd shouted, 'Be careful, Sir, you're signing the [teetotal] pledge!'[31] The photograph is unusual in a number of ways. There are very few photographs of Edward in which he is smiling so broadly. His normal expression was somewhat wistful and hangdog. In addition, the picture is taken showing the Prince's less favoured right profile, emphasizing the prominent Hanoverian eyes. Edward much preferred his left profile; when he became King he insisted that British postage stamps display it. The cigarette provides the final touch, clamped jauntily between the Prince's teeth and extending the upward curve of the lips. There are echoes of Franklin Roosevelt, whose dauntless cheerfulness was emphasized by the ever-present cigarette in its holder. The photograph has long been superseded in popular memory by pictures of the Abdication, but in the 1920s and 1930s this image of 'Our Smiling Prince' was endlessly reproduced on postcards, china, ashtrays, and chocolate boxes. Here indeed was a modern prince for a democratic age.[32]

In order for Edward to impress the Canadian public it was not enough for him simply to smile and look winsome; he had to convey the right messages as well. In this he was directed by Prime Minister Lloyd George via his speech-writer Edward Grigg. The central message which Lloyd George urged upon the Prince was that he was coming not as a visitor, but as a fellow Canadian. This was not a tactic of which the King approved, but the Prime Minister prevailed, and Edward duly repeated that line in speeches across the country.[33] Whether through luck or good judgement on Lloyd George's part this was precisely the sentiment that Edward himself wished to express, and his obvious sincerity made a deep impression. If the intention was to encourage Canadians to claim the Prince as their own, then the strategy was a brilliant success. Welcoming him to Ottawa, the Canadian Prime Minister Sir Robert Borden said, 'The Prince has come among us for the first time but not as a stranger. He comes as a Canadian in the higher sense.' Edward was hailed as 'the Democratic Prince', 'the People's Prince', or simply 'Our Prince'.[34] The possessive adjective was significant: to some extent the persona of Edward, Prince of Wales, was a blank canvas on which the public could project their hopes and dreams. The Prince could be whatever his audience wanted him to be.[35] It was no accident that Edward's mentors were Lloyd George and Winston Churchill, the two greatest popular politicians of the age. He proved an apt pupil.[36]

Having toured the great cities of eastern Canada, Edward set off on a six-week trip out West, courtesy of the Canadian Pacific Railway. 'A democratic train for a democratic Prince', commented the US press reports, noting the lack of luxury on the royal train.[37] There were, of course, numerous functions, receptions, and balls en route, but the pace was slower, and leisure time was built in to allow the Prince some much-needed rest and recreation. The Prince had his first taste of western life when he attended a 'stampede' at Saskatoon in Saskatchewan—an exhibition of cowboy skills such as bronco riding, lassoing, and steer-roping. At the end of the afternoon the Prince went down into the arena to talk to the competitors. They offered him a mount, and to the cheers of the crowd he rode at the head of a posse of cowboys, down the track and past the stand.[38] At Calgary in Alberta the Prince was entertained at a huge party given by returned war veterans. The dancing went on until 3 a.m., and it was generally acknowledged by

Edward's staff to have been one of the highlights of the tour.[39] On the following day a group of girls from the party joined the royal train as far as Banff in the Rockies, where they dined with the Prince and then insisted that the entire party go for a midnight swim in the hot springs.[40]

Edward was entranced by the remoteness and magnificence of the prairie, and while out West he took the opportunity to try his hand at cattle ranching. After visiting Calgary he was invited to stay at the Bar U ranch near High River in the foothills of the Rocky Mountains. His host was the cattle king George Lane, one of the leading ranchers in the country and a founder of the Calgary Stampede, the great annual rodeo festival.[41] There he met the cowboys, took part in a cattle round-up, and went hiking in the hills above the ranch. The Prince was so taken with his experience of ranching that he decided to become a rancher himself.[42] On hearing that the Bedingfeld ranch adjacent to the Bar U was up for sale, he immediately put in train arrangements to purchase it, with Lane acting as his agent. The deal was done within a month, so that Edward was able to announce it publicly at Winnipeg on his way back east. 'The atmosphere of western Canada appeals to me intensely; the free, vigorous, hopeful spirit of westerners makes me feel happy and at home.'[43]

After trying his hand as a cowboy, at the next stop on his tour Edward was made an Indian chief. At Banff he was welcomed to a powwow of Stoney Cree Indians. Their chief, Young Thunder, affirmed his tribe's loyalty to the Prince and his father, and presented Edward with a feathered head-dress and a decorated buckskin suit. 'In memory of the happy days that are gone', said Young Thunder, 'I declare you chief of this band of Stoneys and bestow on you the name Chief Morning Star.'[44] The Times remarked on the striking contrast between the two chiefs as they faced each other, one with straight black hair, a green silk scarf, and white wool leggings, and the other fair-haired, wearing a grey suit and Guards tie.[45] The Prince at once put on the headdress, thanked the Indians for the honour they had paid him, and called them his friends and brothers.[46]

The easy-going western mood continued into British Columbia. By the time they reached the west coast the royal entourage was so relaxed that all formalities were dispensed with. At Kamloops in British Columbia even the punctilious Grigg turned out in casual clothes. Edward called it 'a proper ragtime stunt... I was chewing gum and nearly crashed when reading my reply to their address!! We are all rather ashamed of ourselves.'[47]

Figure 3.3. Chief Morning Star, Banff, Alberta, September 1919

Back in London *Punch* magazine neatly captured the atmosphere of Edward's western tour in a cartoon titled 'Mutual Attraction'. Somewhere in the Canadian wilderness the Prince is paddling a canoe. He leans forward eagerly. In front of him a beautiful cowgirl reclines languorously, blouse open to the bust. The Prince: 'You don't mind my falling in love with you?' Canada: 'Well, I rather hoped you might.'[48]

There was little time for serious romance in the Prince's congested timetable, but while in Vancouver he enjoyed a flirtation with an American war widow, Sarah Polk Shaughnessy. Sarah was distantly related to James Polk, the eleventh President of the United States, and had been married to Alfred Shaughnessy, son of the Canadian railway magnate Lord Shaughnessy. Her friend Joan Mulholland described the Prince as 'very épris with Sarah' at this time, and Edward's equerry Lord Claud Hamilton was keen to encourage the potential match. 'If only it would happen it would be the most wonderful thing in the world and save the British Empire.'[49] In fact Edward seems to

Figure 3.4. 'Mutual Attraction', *Punch*, 1 October 1919

have spent most of his time with Sarah talking about Freda Dudley Ward, and within a year Sarah had married the Prince's second equerry, Joey Legh.[50] Nevertheless, the fact that in 1919 a member of Edward's staff seriously entertained the possibility of his marrying an American bride illustrates how radically expectations of royalty had been changed by the Great War.

Edward's overseas tours were far longer than their modern equivalents. By the time he returned back East to Ottawa early in November he had been in Canada for three months and had visited all of the country's ten provinces.[51] Weeks of extensive press coverage and regular newsreel reports whetted the appetite of the American public for the Prince's US visit, scheduled for mid-November. 'Enthusiastic Canadians lionize Prince of Wales' was a typical headline.[52] The American press noted Edward's democratic tendencies approvingly, attributing them to the good influence of the US troops with whom he mingled at the end of the war.[53] In New York the Prince's arrival evoked memories of Edward VII's visit to the city in 1860. 'Will British Heir dance with American girls like Grandfather?' asked the Brooklyn Eagle before the Prince's arrival in Canada.[54] It was assumed that Edward would visit Newport, Rhode Island, the playground of the super-rich, where he could be entertained by families such as the Vanderbilts.[55]

In reality the Prince's trip to the USA was in doubt until the very last minute. In the autumn of 1919 the political and diplomatic situation was extremely delicate. The invitation had originally been a personal one to the King from President Wilson in return for his hospitality at Buckingham Palace in December 1918. Returning to the States in June 1919, Wilson faced an uphill struggle to secure the ratification of the Versailles Treaty in the Senate, where he encountered determined opposition from the Republicans led by Henry Cabot Lodge. Despite poor health, Wilson embarked on a barnstorming railway tour during the summer to sell the Treaty to the country. Exhausted by an itinerary even more rigorous than the Prince's, Wilson suffered a series of strokes, and on 26 September he was forced to cut short his tour.[56] In addition, the deteriorating situation in Ireland raised questions over the advisability of the Prince visiting New York, with its large Irish American population. Groups sympathetic to Sinn Fein, the Irish Republican Party, were hostile to the royal tour. The Mayor himself, John Hylan, was a Tammany Hall machine politician reliant on the Irish vote. When he appointed William Randolph Hearst, the anti-British press baron, to the reception committee for the Prince's visit, the Ottawa Journal ironically suggested that he should appoint Eamon de Valera, the Irish republican leader, as well.[57]

On the British side there was prolonged debate as to whether the visit to the US should go ahead. When he heard of Wilson's illness in mid-October the King sent a cable ordering the Prince to cancel the visit.[58] The US government was lukewarm about the trip, fearing that it might provoke anti-British sentiment and make ratification of the Versailles Treaty even harder.[59] Edward himself was still keen to go, even for an unofficial visit, and he was strongly supported by his political adviser, Edward Grigg. Significantly the Prince was concerned not so much with the US government as with the American people: 'the American public don't care a d—n for the President or the Government, and... abandoning my visit... might undo all the hard work and trouble that I have taken to make good with the Yanks!!'[60] He was angry at his father's interference, attributing it to the King's hostility to the United States.[61] King George was proud of the fact that he had never been to the USA and saw no reason why his son would want to go.[62]

This was a seminal moment in the Prince's career, and one which was to have far-reaching consequences. He could easily have obeyed the King's command, particularly as he was exhausted after his gruelling trip and eager to be reunited with Freda. That he chose to challenge the decision is a mark of his new-found confidence in the wake of his success in Canada. Eventually King George relented and allowed Lord Grey, the Ambassador in Washington, to make the decision. The deciding factor proved to be the official visit to the USA of the King and Queen of the Belgians, which was taking place while Edward was in Canada. They were entertained in Washington by Vice-President Thomas Marshall, and Edward wired Lord Grey to suggest that he should be received in the same way. After consultation with the US government, the trip went ahead.[63] The decision to proceed with the American leg of the tour was a notable victory for the Prince, especially in challenging a direct instruction from his father. Despite the risks of taking on 'the Big Apple', Edward understood intuitively that he had generated sufficient momentum to repeat the success south of the border. It was an exhilarating moment.

Prince Edward crossed the US border and changed trains at Rouses Point, New York, at 8.20 p.m. on 10 November 1919. The entire population of the little town turned out to greet him. At the station there was an honour guard of doughboys, and a band of girls holding a large cloth canopy made up of the Union Jack and the Stars and Stripes sewn together to symbolize the meeting of the two Anglo-Saxon peoples. The reception committee on the platform was led by Secretary of State Robert Lansing.[64] After the formal greetings were over, the onlookers crowded round the Prince as he boarded the American train, thrusting autograph books and photographs at him for signature. In the crowd he recognized a Canadian veteran who had been gassed at Vimy, and warmly shook his hand.[65] 'Formality lacking at Prince's arrival', reported the *Washington Times*, praising the 'utter democracy and dearth of formality' of the occasion.[66] The Prince's itinerary in America was confined to Washington, DC, and New York, with visits to West Point and the US Naval Academy at Annapolis. On the advice of the British Embassy Edward avoided the temptations of Newport, where he had been expected to meet America's wealthiest heiresses. While in New York his base was to be HMS *Renown*, moored in New York harbour.

In the United States Edward was welcomed not so much as the heir of the King-Emperor, but rather as an international celebrity familiar from newsreels and the press. In this respect he had more in common with that other English star of the silver screen, Charlie Chaplin, than with President Wilson. As Will Rogers, the American comedian, once quipped, people knew Charlie by his baggy pants and the Prince because his were not.[67] This was at the same time a liberating and daunting experience for the Prince: liberating because he was not 'on duty' in America in quite the same way as elsewhere; and daunting because Americans, and the American press in particular, were less deferential and potentially more critical. His position as Prince of Wales did not automatically gain him respect. With its republican traditions and egalitarian culture, America was instinctively anti-monarchist. If they liked the Prince it was in spite of his royal status, not because of it.[68] This was something that Edward relished because the mantle of Prince of Wales weighed heavily on him and he longed to be respected for himself rather than his position.[69]

The royal visit to the US capital was a comparatively muted one after the euphoria of Canada. Official Washington was in the throes of a major political crisis. As President Wilson lay ill in the White House, incapacitated by a series of strokes, his battle to secure ratification of the Versailles Treaty and to establish the League of Nations was foundering in the Senate. Among politicians and the press there were many who were suspicious that the League was an Anglo-French plot to maintain their global empires using American resources. As for entertaining European royalty, Edward was not the only show in town. Admittedly there was greater interest in the Prince's visit: flats available for rent at $150 a week during the visit of the King and Queen of the Belgians were marked up to $250 for the arrival of the

Prince.[70] While in the capital the Prince paid a duty visit to the President's sickbed and took tea with Mrs Wilson. He did not stay at the White House as originally planned but was entertained in Washington by Perry Belmont, a wealthy ex-Congressman, who had a French Renaissance style mansion on New Hampshire Avenue.

The warmth of the capital's welcome was dampened, not merely by rain and freezing weather, but also by the recent introduction of Prohibition. The Volstead Act banning the production and sale of intoxicating liquor had been passed on 28 October 1919. This made official functions even harder going than usual for the Prince, especially after the alcohol-fuelled parties of western Canada. At one dinner in Washington he gratefully accepted the offer of 'White Rock', believing it was a brand of American whisky. It turned out to be iced water. Prohibition could have unintended consequences, however. On an excursion to the US Naval Academy, the Prince's motorcycle escort became hopelessly drunk after falling in with a group of federal agents in possession of a large cache of bootleg liquor. Edward had to intervene personally to prevent their immediate dismissal.[71]

Whilst in Washington Edward worked hard to impress his American hosts. He visited a military hospital, awarded decorations to American veterans, and laid a wreath at Washington's tomb at Mount Vernon. The symbolism of King George's son paying homage to King George's nemesis was a powerful one for Americans: it was barely a century since the Royal Navy had sailed up the Potomac River and set fire to the White House during the war of 1812. He attended dinners and receptions and gave major speeches three nights in succession. It was estimated that in four days the Prince shook hands with ten thousand people.[72] He met every member of Wilson's cabinet and held a reception for members of Congress and their families in the Library of Congress. There he stood in the receiving line for over two hours, greeting guests individually.[73] The message that Edward delivered in the USA varied only slightly from his 'stump speech' in Canada. He was coming to the States as much as a Canadian as a Britisher; he did not feel a stranger because he had already made many American friends during the war; he was grateful for the magnificent effort of American soldiers and sailors; and, despite the differences in their political systems, America and Britain shared a common set of values based on democracy and freedom.[74]

The most critical audience that Edward faced was the Washington press corps, which had an intimidating reputation.[75] An initial encounter on his arrival did not go well. He was nervous and tongue-tied and was reduced to making small talk about the weather.[76] However, he accepted an invitation to visit the National Press Club that evening, where he met two hundred journalists and insisted on shaking hands with all of them. The chairman greeted the Prince as a soldier and a veteran, and Edward's unaffected charm and affability worked its magic. 'Prince wins capital' was the headline in the *Washington Post* the following day, 'democratic air impresses all who greet him'. Commentators remarked upon the Prince's diplomatic skills in balancing warm comments about the Democratic President Wilson with praise of Republican Theodore Roosevelt, who had died earlier in the year.[77] No doubt Edward had been well briefed by the British Ambassador, Lord Grey. King Albert of Belgium had garnered similar headlines while in Washington, but independent confirmation that the Prince's charm offensive had paid off came from the doyen of the diplomatic corps, the French Ambassador Jean Jules Jusserand. He reported back to Paris that '[the Prince] has enjoyed complete success among all different kinds of people. The English have never done anything which so effectively serves to erase old animosities.'[78]

The Prince's staff managed to squeeze a few private social functions into the packed schedule of official engagements. 'He holds very strongly that he can influence American feeling even better by dancing with Senators' daughters than by talking to Senators,' wrote Grigg to the King.[79] To the bemusement of the press correspondents Edward would periodically disappear from the programmed route to attend a private dance or party. On his second day in Washington, after visiting the widow of Admiral Dewey, the conqueror of the Philippines, he slipped away to a tea dance at the house of Joseph Leiter on Dupont Circle, where he met the most popular debutantes of the Washington season.[80] The dance was such a success that the party reconvened the following night at the house of Speaker Frederick Gillett after a dinner at the British Embassy. There the Prince danced with senators' daughters until four o'clock in the morning. After three fourteen-hour days in Washington and a hundred days on tour, there could be no doubt of Edward's devotion to duty.

On leaving Washington the Prince and his staff enjoyed a short weekend break at White Sulphur Springs, a mountain spa resort in West Virginia, where Edward relaxed by playing golf and hiking in the pine forests. He impressed the locals by his ability to turn a somersault off a diving board.[81] On Tuesday, 18 November, the royal party set off for New York City, for the last leg of the tour.

In 1919, at the beginning of the American Century, New York was the future. Now that the heart of every great metropolis seeks to rival Manhattan, it is difficult to recapture the sense of wonder and strangeness that European visitors to the city experienced in the early twentieth century. The most well-known imaginative response to New York in this era is Fritz Lang's movie *Metropolis*. The film was directly inspired by Lang's first visit to New York in 1924. 'I looked into the streets—the glaring lights and the tall buildings—and there I conceived *Metropolis*.'[82] But whereas for European audiences the built environment of *Metropolis* was science fiction, for New Yorkers it was daily living. The Manhattan skyline expressed in concrete form the shock of American modernity and economic power.

Both sides awaited the encounter with eager anticipation. Prince Edward was keen to see New York, and New York was ready to party. This was the final stop on the Prince's North American odyssey and New Yorkers were determined to show that the best had been saved till last. HMS *Renown,* which had spent three months on a goodwill cruise to the West Indies and South America, was anchored on the Hudson River off the Columbia Yacht Club on West 86th Street, awaiting Edward's return.

It was universally acknowledged that, for maximum impact, New York should be approached from the sea. The fact that the Prince was arriving from Washington by train troubled the reception committee not at all. He must have a harbour welcome. His train was therefore shunted off to Jersey City, where Edward was met by the welcoming party and ushered onto an admiral's barge to cross the harbour to Lower Manhattan. Among those who greeted the Prince was the chairman of the reception committee, Rodman Wanamaker, the retail department millionaire and philanthropist. Wanamaker already knew the Prince, having ingratiated himself with the royal family by donating a silver altarpiece to Sandringham church in memory of Edward VII. He was accompanied by 'Mr New York', Grover Whalen, the architect of the proceedings and the impresario of New York's distinctive form of public ceremonial.[83] As the barge crossed the harbour it was met by a chorus of horns and whistles from the scores of vessels which had come out to welcome the Prince. The royal party landed at Battery Park shortly after 11 a.m. on 18 November, and was greeted by a marine band and a choir singing 'God Bless the Prince of Wales'. The park was crowded with onlookers, and office workers hung out of neighbouring buildings. The Prince posed for the cameras for several minutes, intermittently looking up at the skyline as if to assure himself that it was real. Thus far the welcome was enthusiastic but familiar. Then Edward, Wanamaker, and Whalen climbed into an open limousine at Bowling Green for the drive up to City Hall. 'All set Prince?' asked Whalen, 'OK, let's go.' The Prince was about to be treated to a New York ticker-tape welcome.[84]

Ticker-tape parades were normally reserved for returning heroes and heads of state. There had been two already in New York that autumn: for the victorious commander General John Pershing; and for King Albert of the Belgians, whose brave but futile gesture in defying the Kaiser's armies in 1914 had won him worldwide admiration. Edward had no such credentials, indeed he embodied an institution which many New Yorkers despised.[85] Yet so powerful had been the impact of his tour, for the American and Canadian public alike, that the reception committee felt bound to rise to the challenge. New York's welcome would be bigger than Montreal's, more tumultuous than Toronto's, more vibrant than Washington's.

As the limousine drove up Broadway's 'Canyon of Heroes' through the business district, a blizzard of ticker tape descended upon the Prince. Stunned by the spectacle, the noise, and the stench of petrol fumes, he gaped up in wonder at the fifty-five-storey Woolworth Building, then the tallest building in the world. The cacophony was indescribable. The masses of spectators lining the route fought with police to get a better view of the passing parade. After a few moments the Prince collected himself. He stood up in the back of the car, smiling, bowing, and waving to the crowds. It was an acclamation 'thrilling beyond description'. At City Hall he was met by Mayor Hylan and made a freeman of the city. In reply he made a gushing speech in praise of America in general and New York in particular: 'the most vivid imagination can never see to what bounds the wealth and the power of this great continent, and the power of this great city will one day attain'. The crowd basked in the flattery. 'The boy's there,' said an onlooker, 'he'll do.'[86]

One of the distinctive features of the royal visit to New York was the presence of HMS *Renown* moored on the Hudson in the heart of the city. Built in 1916, it was the largest battleship ever seen in New York. It was 800 ft long, and carried a crew of over a thousand men. *Renown* had not been sent to New York for diplomatic purposes, but merely to provide the Prince with accommodation during his stay. It had been given no special entertainment allowance, but in the event it became one of the main centres of the celebrations. The *Renown* had arrived in New York several days before the Prince on its return from South America, and for a week the ship's company enjoyed an endless round of lavish hospitality. The officers were made honorary members of the principal clubs, a suite of rooms was set aside for their use at the Waldorf–Astoria Hotel, and six limousines were made continuously available to them. Several theatres on Broadway offered free tickets, and a special Sunday performance of the musical *Magic Melody* was laid on for the crew. There were numerous parties, dances, and receptions, both official and private, but the hub of the entertainment was the Crystal Room of the Ritz. 'We seemed to live there,' recorded the ship's magazine *Aren't We Lucky,* 'dancing on the most perfect floor ever laid.'[87] The crew of the *Renown* was keen to return this hospitality, and there were constant lunch, tea, and dinner parties on board. Invitations to the ship became the hottest tickets in town, and not merely because of the charms of British naval officers. The *Renown*, being British territory, was 'wet' and Prohibition did not apply there. For a few days the ship became an enormous floating speakeasy. New Yorkers almost drank the *Renown* dry. On one day the wardroom mess was charged for 500 cocktails, and on another for 104 bottles of whisky.[88] After a particularly good party one of the officers received a thank-you note from a guest, who signed herself 'Brat': 'would you please be so nice as to pay my very dutiful respects to Mr Liquid Chocolate Eyes and to tell him that I have found one person at least who appreciates them'.[89] The *Renown* was doing its bit for Anglo-American relations.

While the ship's company partied, Prince Edward continued on his duty rounds. He faced a schedule of fourteen-hour days in which every minute was organized. For example, on 21 November he had seven engagements, beginning with a visit to the grave of Theodore Roosevelt at Oyster Bay, and ending with a dance which continued until after midnight.[90] The endless treadmill of official functions drew some sympathy for the Prince. 'There should be formed a Society for the Prevention of Cruelty to Princes,' wrote one columnist. 'Show him a girl show instead of Grant's Tomb. Take him to Coney [Island] instead of City Hall. Let him go to the Polo Grounds instead of the Public Library!'[91]

The most glittering social event of the visit was a gala concert at the Metropolitan Opera House on 18 November. Although it was headlined by the legendary Italian tenor Enrico Caruso, there was no doubt who was the real star that night. It was nearly 10.30 p.m. by the time Edward and his party arrived, having been delayed by the crowds in the streets outside jostling to get a glimpse of him. As the Prince stepped to the front of his box there was a roll of drums and the orchestra struck up 'God Bless the Prince of Wales'. At once the music was completely drowned out by a storm of clapping and cheering. In the stalls the audience crowded into the aisles to get a better view of the Prince. Visibly embarrassed by his reception, Edward stood blushing and looking down, uncertain as to how to react to the ovation. There were two huge gilt chairs in the royal box, reminiscent of royal thrones, which occupied the entire front row. For a few moments there was a pantomime as Edward tried to persuade members of his staff to sit in them. Then they were removed and several ordinary chairs set in their place. The audience was transported by this democratic gesture. 'Three cheers for the Prince of Wales,' cried a voice from below. Edward's triumph was complete: royalty had entered the age of celebrity.[92]

There were gala performances on board HMS *Renown* as well as at the Met. The crew invited the cast of *Magic Melody* onto the ship for 'tea' in return for their show the previous Sunday. Pearl White, the star of the silent movie series 'The Perils of Pauline', led the entertainment for the crew on the mess deck. That afternoon the mess ran out of whisky.[93] On 21 November, the Prince's last full day in New York, the *Renown* threw a party for a thousand of the city's children. The capstans had been turned into roundabouts, and slides and other fairground rides set up. In the event the playground was little used, for more adults than children were brought from shore. The prospect of one last drink was too good to waste on a group of infants.[94]

That evening the Prince was entertained by the Pilgrims of New York, the sister organization of the Pilgrims of Great Britain, at a banquet for a thousand guests at the Plaza Hotel. The function was so large that it spread across four of the Plaza's banqueting rooms. In order to hear the after-dinner speakers, the guests in the outer rooms carried their chairs above their heads and crowded into the main hall.[95] There Edward was elected a life member of the Pilgrims by acclamation. The octogenarian president of the Pilgrims, Chauncey Depew, reminisced about the visit to the States of the Prince's grandfather, Edward VII, almost sixty years earlier. He recalled that King Edward, then Prince of Wales and only 18 years old, had enjoyed a night off with the cadets at West Point. Having delivered a brief formal reply, the Prince responded with an impromptu aside, 'Well I must say that grandfather did better than I have done. I have not had a night off, at West Point or anywhere else!' After the Pilgrims dinner Edward went on to a variety performance at the Hippodrome, where he was greeted by a five-minute standing ovation, before attending a reception given in his honour by Rodman Wanamaker at the Seventh Regiment Armory.[96]

The final day of the visit, Saturday 22 November, was full of theatre and symbolism. In the morning Edward held an investiture on board the *Renown*,

decorating US servicemen and nurses, after which he held a reception to
thank his hosts, shaking hands with them all individually. Then he went
ashore for the last time to review a parade of five thousand boy scouts. In
his farewell message Edward wrote: 'I refuse to say goodbye. I am going to
pay you another visit. I can never forget this trip and I am proud to be a
New Yorker in my own right.' Finally, HMS *Renown* headed out of
New York harbour escorted by seven US destroyers and a battleship.
Thousands of well-wishers crowded into Riverside Park between 79th Street
and 86th Street to see the Prince off. Edward climbed the rope ladder to the
ship's fighting top and waved his white naval cap in farewell. Before departure, one of Edward's motorcycle escorts, Patrolman Howard Smith of the
New York Police, sang 'Dear Old Pal of Mine' on the forward deck while
the Prince held the sheet music. As the sun set behind the Manhattan skyline, *Renown* slipped through the Ambrose Channel and out to sea. In the gathering darkness, and in defiance of naval regulations, USS *Delaware* fired a
twenty-one-gun salute. Five hundred miles out to sea five carrier pigeons
were released from the *Renown* bearing messages of thanks from the Prince
to New York.[97] The mood on the *Renown* after departure was summed up
in a doggerel rhyme which appeared in the ship's magazine:

> You honoured our Prince–you did more than that
> You'd have kept him if you'd been let
> And that from a great Republican State
> Is a thing we shall never forget
> New nations may come, old states may go
> But from now till Doomsday's dawn
> Edward of Wales the *Renown* and New York
> Are in threefold friendship sworn.[98]

In deference to Canadian sentiment, *Renown* did not sail directly home but
made her last port of call in North America at Halifax, Nova Scotia, before
crossing the Atlantic. The Prince arrived back in Portsmouth on 1 December
1919 after sixteen weeks on tour. The King and Queen welcomed him at
Victoria Station, and in an unusually demonstrative gesture King George
embraced his son, kissing him on the cheek. In London he was welcomed not
by ticker tape but by torrential rain. Nevertheless he rode in an open carriage
to Buckingham Palace, where a large crowd chanted 'We want our Prince'
until he appeared on the balcony to acknowledge their cheers. That night the
King held a private dinner in honour of Edward's return. He congratulated
the Prince warmly on the success of his tour: 'You have played up from the

beginning to the end.' This was high praise, invoking Sir Henry Newbolt's celebrated anthem of the British ruling class, 'Play up, play up and play the game' (to 'play up' meant to rise to the occasion and show selfless commitment to duty). The King also read out a telegram he had received from the Canadian Prime Minister, Sir Robert Borden: '[the Prince's] labours have been indefatigable and untiring; his tact and courtesy have been unfailing and his natural charm of manner has made an irresistible appeal to all our people.'[99] On the public stage the Prince of Wales had exceeded all expectations.

On a personal level the relentless programme of touring had taken its toll on Edward. By the time he returned to England he was physically and mentally exhausted. There were two main reasons for this. The first was Edward's intensive style of public engagement, more akin to political campaigning than a conventional royal progress. He did not spare himself at all, often shaking hands with thousands of people in a single day. The second reason was that Edward found it very difficult to relax while on tour. At the end of a day full of official functions, which would frequently include a dinner or ball continuing late into the evening, Edward was so keyed up that he could not sleep. He would chat to his staff, write letters, and continue drinking and smoking into the small hours. Letters to Freda were rarely written before 1 a.m., and often at 3 or 4 a.m. Writing to him after the end of the tour, his private secretary, Godfrey Thomas, was blunt: 'How you survived Canada I cannot imagine... You never allowed yourself a moment's rest the whole time. You sat up every night, often quite unnecessarily, till godless hours...'[100]

It is generally assumed that King George was responsible for the brutal pace of the Prince's tours, but in fact the King was sympathetic to his son's plight, having experienced it himself to a lesser degree. It was actually Lloyd George's government which set the timetable.[101] What made matters worse was that the detailed itinerary was arranged by the Dominion governments. This meant that prime ministers and governors competed to get as much of the Prince's time as possible and to fit as many engagements as they could into his schedule. By a peculiar coincidence of circumstances—the sheer size of the British Empire, the post-war democratization of royal ceremonial, the rise of the mass media, and the discovery of his own charisma—Edward found himself on a vicious treadmill of public demand.

Fundamentally Edward was the victim of his own success. In Canada and the USA he had played the leading role in fashioning a new, more informal, and intimate style of monarchy for the post-war world. He played the role

of democratic prince to perfection. Some American commentators wryly
thought he must be running for office and in a sense they were right.
He was campaigning for the survival of the British Empire, and indeed the
British monarchy. The Prince's 'ragtime jazz party' was in tune with the
public mood in a way that the courtiers of the King's generation, who had
come of age in the reign of Queen Victoria, were not. Edward was bringing
royalty down from the pedestal to the man in the street.[102]

The contrast between the old and the new is exemplified in the difference
between the public events at the beginning of the Prince's tour and the end of
it. Whereas in eastern Canada the hapless Sir James Pope attempted to organize
ceremonial on the Victorian model, in New York Wanamaker and Whalen
choreographed a breathtaking display of public theatre, using the city's futur-
istic architecture as a backdrop. America fell in love with Edward because he
confounded its expectations of what a prince should be: Edward fell in love
with America because, like the immigrants to the New World arriving in
sight of the Statue of Liberty, he was weary of the 'storied pomp' of the Old
World and was 'yearning to breathe free'.[103]

4

Jazzin' Around

Panama, San Diego, and Hawaii, 1920

The Prince's progress across North America had been closely followed in Britain through the newspapers and above all in the weekly newsreel reports. He returned home not merely as heir to the throne but as an instantly recognizable film celebrity. On 17 December 1919 the Canadian Pacific Railway arranged a special showing in the Royal Albert Hall of the complete film of the Prince's tour. By contemporary standards this was a blockbuster movie: whereas the typical newsreel was 300 feet long and lasted five minutes, the tour movie was 8,000 feet long and lasted for over two hours.[1] It brought home to the domestic audience the scale of Edward's triumph, as well as giving an unprecedented close-up portrait of the Prince. As the London *Times* commented, 'the film was full of the intimate touches that the descriptive writer, however good, cannot altogether convey'.[2] Edward himself was enthused by his experiences in North America. He had shown his commitment to Canada by the purchase of the EP ranch, and he was eager to make a return visit to the USA. When he stepped ashore at Portsmouth, virtually his first words were: 'I hope often to be in Canada and I shall pay another visit to the United States at the first opportunity.'[3]

Unfortunately Lloyd George's government had other plans. Within days of Edward's return from North America the Colonial Office was preparing for the next phase of his imperial tours. On 15 December Leo Amery, the acting Secretary of State, wrote to Prime Minister Lloyd George outlining the Prince's provisional itinerary for the next two years. Amery proposed that Edward should tour Australia and New Zealand in the spring and summer of 1920, before visiting India late in 1920 for the inauguration of the newly reformed Imperial Legislative Council.[4] The programme would involve almost twelve months of continuous touring for the Prince.

Before that there was a family Christmas at Sandringham to be endured. Edward had not spent the festive season at home since 1913, and after so long away he found the rigidity of palace life particularly oppressive. 'York Cottage (F–ck it!!!!) Sandringham', wrote Edward to Freda on 23 December, '10 weeks remain before my next f–cking world trip'.[5] Between the festivities he spent his time shooting, playing golf, and sparring with his father. As the euphoria of the tour subsided, Edward succumbed to exhaustion and depression.[6] After Christmas he tried to postpone the start of the Australasian tour, scheduled for early March 1920. However, Amery was determined that there should be no delay; 'the Colonial Office are being foul to me in fact vewy vewy ruf wiv us re. the date of my sailing in March', Edward complained in January 1920.[7] Edward Grigg was reappointed to the Prince's staff as political adviser. After the North American tour he had briefly resigned following a dispute with Edward's chief of staff, Admiral Halsey, over control of the political aspects of the tour. He was only persuaded to return after Lloyd George intervened personally to insist that he should have complete control over the arrangements for the Prince's programme in Australasia, including press relations.[8] Grigg was the Colonial Office's man and he was there to ensure that the tours ran smoothly and on schedule. There was to be no let-up for the Prince.

There was one new recruit to the Prince's staff for the Australasian tour. Lord Louis 'Dickie' Mountbatten, Edward's second cousin, was then a bumptious 19-year-old naval officer. He riled the other members of the staff by his familiarity with the Prince, calling him by his family name, David. Although he had served in the war, they despised him as a 'Hun' on account of his German ancestry.[9] Nevertheless, Edward liked him, partly because he knew Freda, and also because he provided welcome companionship for the Prince on the long tour.

From the middle of the nineteenth century the established sea route from Britain to Australia was eastwards via the Suez Canal, the 'Clapham Junction of the Empire'. From Gibraltar to Ceylon there was a continuous chain of British bases and colonies across the Mediterranean, the Red Sea, and the Indian Ocean. On this route the Prince would have remained on British territory throughout the entire voyage, but there were fears at the Admiralty that HMS *Renown* was too big to pass safely through the Suez Canal.[10] One alternative would have been the longer and more arduous passage via South Africa and the Cape of Good Hope. However, within the previous decade an entirely new, westward route had opened up through the

Panama Canal. Built and controlled by the USA, the canal had opened in August 1914, just as Europe was sliding into war.[11] It was large enough to accommodate the *Renown*, although the overall voyage to Australasia via the Pacific was considerably longer than via Suez.

Travelling through the Panama Canal meant that the *Renown* would be reliant on the hospitality of the US Navy in the eastern Pacific. Strategically insignificant during the Great War, the Pacific was the one ocean where Britannia did not entirely rule the waves. The two rising Pacific powers, internationally recognized in the Washington Naval Treaty of 1922, were the USA and Japan. *Renown*'s voyage involved three stops for refuelling on American-controlled territory, at the Panama Canal Zone, San Diego California, and Hawaii.[12] From the Colonial Office point of view there was, however, one compensating factor in having the Prince travel via the Americas. During the war the USA had expanded aggressively in the Caribbean, occupying Haiti and the Dominican Republic in order to pro-tect the eastern approaches to the Panama Canal.[13] A proposal had been floated in Washington that the British West Indies should be transferred to the US in liquidation of Britain's war debt, an idea taken up in Britain by the press baron Lord Rothermere.[14] A visit from the Prince of Wales would demonstrate Britain's commitment to its Caribbean colonies.[15] The Panama Canal route was settled on by the Colonial Office late in January 1920, and the departure date was set for 16 March.[16] Fortuitously, only a few months after his trip to Washington and New York, Edward was to make a return visit to American territory.

The prospect of back-to-back tours of Australasia and India, entailing long separation from Freda, plunged Edward further into depression. Again he spent the last night before his departure with his mistress, and when Mountbatten came to collect him the following morning, he was in tears.[17] To the Foreign Secretary, Lord Curzon, he cut a sorry figure on his departure from Victoria Station. 'In a tight naval uniform which clung close to his figure he did not look above fifteen, quite a pathetic little person.'[18]

The passage out to Barbados took nine days. Edward passed the time pursuing his passion for fitness by running and playing squash and deck hockey.[19] He even found time to read a book, a rare pastime for the Prince. This was *Susan Lenox: Her Fall and Rise* written by the American 'muckraker' journalist D. G. Phillips, which was later made into a Hollywood film starring Greta Garbo and Clark Gable. It was the mildly salacious story of a girl who 'learnt to live, but paid the price', and found herself in a succession of compromising situations. The book, which had probably been brought on board by Dickie Mountbatten, became a talking point among the Prince's staff.[20]

HMS *Renown* stopped for two nights in Barbados, long enough for the usual formalities to be performed. There was an official dinner on board ship, a parade of veterans, a tour of the island through cheering crowds, and a ball at the House of Assembly. As the Colonial Office intended, Edward took the opportunity to reassure the islanders that Barbados was not about to be sold to the USA.[21] There was dancing on both evenings and Edward appointed Mountbatten to procure suitable partners for him. On the first night the company was so bad that he stopped the proceedings at midnight. The second night was a little better: Mountbatten managed to find the Prince 'a little American bit who wasn't a bad mover'.[22] It was to be a recurring theme of the Prince's tours that American girls were good dancers who knew the latest steps.

On 27 March 1920 the *Renown* left Barbados and headed for Panama, arriving three days later. Built with American capital and expertise between 1904 and 1914, the Panama Canal was an engineering marvel and the greatest construction project of the age. At its opening the canal was hailed as the 'Thirteenth Labour of Hercules', a remarkable tribute to American ingenuity, determination, and organization. Much of the labour force was drawn from the British West Indies, attracted by far higher wages than the agrarian island economies could offer.[23] Panama itself was an American protectorate, and the Canal Zone, extending five miles either side of the waterway, was US territory.

HMS *Renown* arrived at Colon, at the Atlantic end of the canal, early in the morning of 30 March, escorted by six US naval planes performing aerial stunts. American officers joined the ship to act as pilots, and President Lefevre of Panama was formally welcomed aboard at the Gatun Locks, together with the US Governor of the Canal Zone, Chester Harding. The Prince was given a tour of the control house and the spillway and watched as the massive lock gates opened and closed automatically.[24] Shortly before the *Renown*'s arrival there had been a landslide in the canal. Half a hillside had collapsed at a bend in the Culebra Cut, which slices through the continental watershed. Twenty ships were backed up outside the canal, waiting for the blockage to be cleared. Despite its size, the *Renown* should normally have passed through the canal safely enough; its draught was only 8.2 metres, whereas the depth of the canal was 12 metres. However, with the channel narrowed by debris there was a risk of the ship suffering damage or even running aground. Blasting operations were necessary to clear the obstruction, at the risk of dislodging further landslides, and the *Renown* was then towed carefully through.[25] The ship's propellers did suffer minor damage, but not enough to require immediate repair.[26]

After twelve hours in stifling tropical heat *Renown* finally berthed at Balboa on the Pacific Ocean. The Prince immediately landed and drove to Panama City, where a dinner and reception were given in his honour at the Tivoli Hotel by the British Minister, Percy Bennett. There was dancing after dinner, and once more Mountbatten was detailed to pick out the nimblest and prettiest partners for the Prince. On this occasion he spotted a superb dancer, the 18-year-old Carolyn Granberry from Balboa. She was the daughter of an American electrician based in the Canal Zone, and worked as a salesgirl in the local commissary store. Mountbatten introduced her to the Prince, who proceeded to monopolize her for the rest of the evening, much to the disgust of the local society families and their daughters.[27] On returning to the ship Edward cooled off with a midnight swim, only to be accosted in the darkness by three American girls on a raft.[28] 'I've been jazzing around some,' he wrote to Freda later that night. 'Sorry for breaking into real Yank...but it's being in the Canal Zone and amongst the Yanks ashore.'[29]

Edward of course played down his meeting with Carolyn Granberry in his letters to Freda, but it appears that next day members of the Prince's staff visited her home and invited her to lunch on board. Certainly the Prince danced with her again at the state banquet given by President Lefevre on the following evening, which suggests she must have been invited at his specific request. Edward told Freda that she had offered to come back to the *Renown* with him, although she was already booked up with a man for the night.[30]

Prince Charming's brief flirtation with Cinderella in Panama was hardly the stuff of great romance, but coming so soon after Edward's US visit it caused a sensation in the American press. 'Humble Shopgirl Takes Prince Captive' ran the headline in the *Washington Times*, 'Calls Him "Boy" in the Moonlight'.[31] Carolyn's photograph appeared in the *New York Times* and in newspapers across the country.[32] A few weeks after the Prince's visit a journalist tracked Carolyn down and she gave him an interview which was widely syndicated across America. In the authentic style of fairy-tale romance she described how she had sold cosmetics at her counter to ugly

Figure 4.1. Carolyn Granberry

old matrons, never dreaming that she herself would attend the ball and see the Prince. Invited unexpectedly, she watched the 'grotesque procession of "very select" girls and women' who were presented to the Prince. Then a 'handsome man of twice her age' approached (the 19-year-old Mountbatten). He introduced her to the Prince, who invited her to dance. 'A ripple of astonishment went around the grand ballroom when the Prince, ignoring ever so many "select women", led Carolyn Granberry, counter clerk and daughter of an electrician, in a dreamy waltz.' When the *Renown* left for Australia, Carolyn was at the quayside to wave her Prince off. He stood on the quarterdeck 'until he could no longer see the white dress of the little girl who waved her handkerchief at him. "I'm sorry he's a Prince, she said".'[33] Sadly Carolyn's story did not have a fairy-tale ending. Eleven years later Edward visited Panama again, on his way to South America. He visited the Governor's offices, where Carolyn was working as a personnel clerk. Although she stood within a few feet of him, the Prince walked straight past without recognizing her.[34]

HMS *Renown*'s next destination was San Diego, California. It was intended as a brief refuelling stop before the long voyage across the Pacific Ocean. It had not been arranged as another official visit to the United States, and both Edward and Grigg were keen to avoid public engagements. California's politicians had other ideas. The mayor of San Diego, Louis J. Wilde, was mired in a corruption scandal—Edward described him as 'an absolute wrong'un who may be "jugged" at any time'—and the arrival of the Prince of Wales in his city was a heaven-sent distraction.[35] Still more importantly, Wilde's daughter Lucille was 17 and about to 'come out' into society. The Prince would be the ultimate celebrity guest for her coming-out ball. Wilde immediately appointed a political crony, Duncan MacKinnon, to chair the Reception Committee, and plans were soon in place for the Prince to address the people of San Diego at the city's stadium, and for an official ball at the Coronado Hotel. When he heard of Mayor Wilde's plans, Governor William Stephens of California insisted on being invited to the proceedings. Washington sent special agent J. M. 'Bill' Nye to handle security and the British Embassy dispatched the air attaché, Lionel Charlton, to act as diplomatic liaison. Before long the Reception Committee was one hundred strong, with sub-committees for finance, entertainment, sight-seeing, luncheon, stadium events, and the ball.[36] San Diego was clearly attempting to match New York in the magnificence of its reception for the royal visitor. The city did not have the towering architecture suitable for a ticker-tape parade, but it had a 55,000-seat stadium ideal for a ceremonial procession.

Because of poor communications the proposed programme for the visit did not reach the *Renown* until 5 April, two days before its arrival in the city. When he saw it, the Prince was horrified; in particular he was unhappy that he was scheduled to give a public address at the city stadium. Grigg immediately cabled Charlton, the diplomatic liaison, ordering him to cancel the stadium engagement. The Reception Committee begged the Prince to reconsider, arguing that to cancel at such a late stage would cause great public disappointment. Grudgingly Edward relented on condition that all the speeches be kept as short as possible.

In scenes reminiscent of New York the previous autumn, half the population of San Diego turned out to greet the Prince when he landed at the Municipal Pier in the heart of the city. 'Led by Mayor L. J. Wilde, who never fails to shine as an entertainer, San Diegans gave Prince Edward the time of his young life,' proclaimed the *San Diego Union*.[37] The crowd broke through the barriers and swarmed round the official motorcade, delaying the start of the procession to the stadium. When it finally arrived, the Prince's car drove a ceremonial lap round the stadium with Edward standing and waving to the cheering spectators. On the platform the Prince encountered a loudspeaker system for the first time, courtesy of the Californian Magnavox company. He was so impressed with the 'magnaphones' that he asked the company to send him some equipment to experiment with.[38]

When he arrived in San Diego, the Prince received an invitation from a Los Angeles film company offering to send eight aeroplanes to fly his staff to see the making of a movie. Edward had reluctantly to refuse the offer, as following his stunt with the one-armed Canadian ace Billy Barker the previous summer, the King had banned him from flying.[39] However, if the Prince could not come to see Hollywood, Hollywood was eager to see the Prince, and indeed to gatecrash the royal visit. At San Diego Edward was caught up in a spectacular publicity stunt involving Charlie Chaplin and his first wife, Mildred Harris. Mildred had been one of Hollywood's first child stars, and had appeared as 'the favourite of the harem' in D. W. Griffith's silent epic *Intolerance*. In 1920 she was at the peak of her career, but her short-lived marriage to Chaplin was failing and they were going through an acrimonious divorce.

At the San Diego stadium Dickie Mountbatten, the Prince's diarist on the tour, noted laconically that there were four ladies in the royal box: the Governor's wife, the Mayor's wife and daughter, and Mrs Charlie Chaplin. Edward politely shook her hand, and she was photographed beside him. No one quite knew why she was there, until it emerged that she had paid Mayor Wilde $5,000 to be allowed to join the party. She had also bribed the Prince's photographer. Meanwhile, on the same day, Charlie Chaplin engaged in a very public fistfight with Mildred's manager, Louis B. Mayer, in the lobby of the Alexandria Hotel in downtown Los Angeles. According to witnesses Chaplin walked up to Mayer and told him to take off his glasses. In true slapstick style, Chaplin took a swing at him, and missed. Mayer then punched Chaplin, knocking him over. Chaplin was carried away bleeding to a washroom.[40] Needless to say, the incident attracted saturation newspaper coverage, providing perfect publicity for Mildred's latest movie, *The Inferior Sex,* 'a startling exposé of married life and domestic problems', which was then playing in cinemas across the States.[41] In San Diego her efforts were not quite so successful. Although she managed to get into the ball, and even danced with Mountbatten, special agent Bill Nye

ensured that she was cut out of the official photographs. There was speculation as to whether she would appear at the reception on board the *Renown*
the following day, but according to Mountbatten, Nye persuaded her that
she had a pressing engagement in Los Angeles.[42]

As in New York, lavish entertainments were laid on for the crew of the
Renown. When they landed at the Municipal Pier the ship's officers were
met by a fleet of cars, each containing two San Diego girls ready to whisk
them off on a city tour. The official dinner and ball took place at the
Coronado Hotel. The ball doubled as the coming-out party for Mayor
Wilde's daughter Lucille, and at dinner she presented Edward with
the keys to the city gates. To the British, the hotel seemed like a film set.
In the words of the ship's magazine, 'one expected Charlie Chaplin to
appear at any moment'.[43] At the dinner the talk was all of Hollywood and
movie stars.

There is a persistent legend that Wallis, then the wife of Winfield Spencer,
met Edward at the ball at the Coronado Hotel, although the Duchess herself denied the encounter in her memoirs.[44] Wallis was then a young navy
wife, and Spencer was commanding officer of the North Island Naval Air
Station in San Diego. Interviewed many years later, Spencer claimed that he
had attended the ball with his ex-wife, and that they had met the Prince in
the receiving line. Detailed research has shown, however, that Wallis was in
San Francisco at the time. Her marriage to Spencer was already in difficulties,
and she had gone alone to stay with a friend, Jane Selby Hayne, to watch the
winter season polo matches.[45]

Although he danced dutifully with Lucille Wilde, the Governor's daughter, Edward was not in party mood that evening and left the ball early. The
reason is that the first mail from England had arrived on the *Renown* that
morning, and there were no letters for him from Freda. He was plunged
into deep gloom. A mail train was due to arrive in San Diego the following
day (8 April) and the *Renown* delayed its departure in the hope of receiving
another delivery. None came: Edward would have to wait another six
weeks before Freda's first letters caught up with him in New Zealand.[46]
He shut himself in his cabin and poured out his heart to Freda in a series
of tearful letters.[47]

Edward's brief stopovers in Panama and San Diego were fully covered
in the American press. His flirtation with Carolyn Granberry did him no
harm at all. 'Panama girl wins Prince's favor; heir democratic: Yankees
pleased' was the succinct headline in the *Oregon Daily Journal*.[48] The general

verdict of San Diegans was that he was 'a regular guy'.[49] The reporters who came aboard the *Renown* noted the Prince's manly handshake. 'There was nothing limp or soft about those handshakes. They were typically American.'[50]

From San Diego the next stop on *Renown's* voyage to New Zealand was Hawaii, where the large naval base at Pearl Harbor provided facilities for berthing and refuelling. Honolulu in 1920 was an exotic place for the British, a legendary spot known only from geography lessons, like Timbuktu or Trincomalee.[51] Nevertheless Edward was not the first royal visitor to the islands. His great-uncle, Alfred, Duke of Edinburgh, had stopped there in 1869 while serving in the Royal Navy. There was residual affection for the British amongst the islanders; the Hawaiian flag still includes the Union Jack. In the nineteenth century the last kings of the islands had tried to maintain their independence from the United States by allying with the British Empire. However, American strategic and economic interests proved too strong, and in 1898 Hawaii was annexed by the US with British acquiescence. The *Renown's* officers detected discontent in Hawaii and nostalgia for happier days under the British flag. They lamented the mess that the Americans had made of the tropical paradise, and regarded it as axiomatic that the islands would have been better off under the British. In particular, they saw the attempt to impose Prohibition as a disaster. The absence of 'clear whisky, gin or wine' simply encouraged the production of poisonous illicit liquor.[52]

Hawaii was merely a refuelling stop en route to Australasia, and the *Renown* was only scheduled to dock there for twenty-four hours. But it was not every day that a royal prince appeared in Honolulu, and the authorities literally pushed the boat out to welcome him. The ship was escorted into port by twelve American destroyers, while a squadron of seaplanes buzzed overhead and dropped *leis*, or garlands, on the deck. The highlight of the visit for the Prince was the opportunity to have a surfing lesson on Waikiki beach. After the welcoming ceremonies were over Edward and Mountbatten went down to the beach, where a large crowd had turned out to watch. They were met by the Olympic swimmer Duke Kahanamoku, the father of modern surfing, who introduced the sport to both southern California and Australia. Mountbatten provided a thrilling description of their first experience of surfing.

> [Edward and Mountbatten] embarked in a large surf canoe and paddled out to where the surf was breaking. Duke Kanahamaku [*sic*], the world's champion

swimmer, was the coxswain, and when the canoe reached the turning-point another Hawaiian entered the craft. The canoe was then turned shorewards and when Duke saw a big wave approaching he ordered 'Paddle' and everyone paddled for all they were worth. The stern of the canoe was lifted up by the wave as it caught up with her, and the canoe with its great outrigger appeared to be racing downhill into a non-existent valley in the water, which it never reached, at a speed which must have been over 20 knots. HRH, who was sitting right in the stern sheets, had the crest of the wave all round him nearly as high as his head. The canoe was then turned and this performance repeated three times. After the third ride HRH dived overboard and tried a surf board. He had hardly mounted when he slipped off again. However, he was soon on and had one or two successful rides. The others then all dived overboard and swam about, most of them trying surf boards also. . . . All this while, two cinema men kept abreast of the party in a canoe making a film of them.[53]

Edward enjoyed surfing so much that he arranged to extend the *Renown*'s stopover at Hawaii on the return trip by an extra two days. If he had no other place in history, he would be remembered as one of Britain's first recorded surfers.[54]

The real business of the tour began when the Prince and his party landed at Auckland on 24 April 1920. Edward spent a month in New Zealand, followed by three months in Australia. There he visited every state, and covered thousands of miles across country, mainly by train. The welcome in the Australian cities was even more raucous and enthusiastic than it had been in North America. In Melbourne it was estimated that a crowd of 750,000 turned out for Edward's arrival—more than the entire population of the city, since people had come from the surrounding areas to catch a glimpse of the Prince. At a public reception, 20,000 veterans filed past him in two

Figure 4.2. Edward surfing with Louis Mountbatten, Hawaii, April 1920

hours: a hundred people fainted and three were taken to hospital.[55] 'Blimey, the crowd!' wrote one Australian reporter. 'Thought I'd seen some in London and Glasgow, but a guy hasn't room to use a hanky here.'[56] Edward became a victim of the 'touching mania'. He was manhandled, clapped, and prodded until he was covered in bruises. Those who could not reach him threw confetti, gifts, and boxes of chocolate into his car.[57] Australian crowds were less deferential than those in Canada, and there was much good-natured banter. 'Oh, Percy, where did you get that hat?' they shouted, as the Prince drove by in full dress uniform. At Ballarat in Victoria, the six hundred girls of the Lucas factory presented Edward with a pair of embroidered satin pyjamas. After the ceremony, the presenter turned to the crowd and shouted, 'Is it for his honeymoon, girls?' To which the girls chorused, 'Yes!'[58] The crowds were also quick to register their disappointment if the Prince did not rise to the occasion. At Gilgandra in New South Wales, the royal train stopped briefly at 7 a.m. to take on water. A small crowd shouted, 'We want Teddy!' and began to hammer on the carriage windows. When the Prince, who was asleep, failed to appear, they 'counted him out', a traditional Australian method of expressing disapproval of unpopular speakers.[59] On the return journey Edward stopped the train at Gilgandra to make amends, and was duly 'counted back in' to the strains of 'For he's a jolly good fellow'.[60]

The mental and physical strain of touring began to take its toll on the Prince. After the novelty and excitement of America, it was in Australia that the sheer grind of his official duties set in. 'Lonely drives through tumultuous crowds, the almost daily inspection of serried ranks of veterans, the inexhaustible supply of cornerstones to be laid,...and always more hands to shake than a dozen princes could have coped with—such was the substance of my official days.'[61] Concerns began to be raised about his health soon after his arrival in Australia. On 2 June, the Governor-General, Sir Ronald Ferguson, cabled the King to say that Edward's doctor had ordered him to take a week of complete rest before proceeding with the remainder of the tour.[62] The Prince's staff were finding his behaviour increasingly difficult. 'I don't feel capable of undertaking another tour with the Boy [Edward] in his current state,' wrote Joey Legh, 'sometimes he becomes impossible, loses his temper and behaves like a naughty schoolboy.'[63]

Although the Australasian tour was undoubtedly a demanding one, the Prince may have been exaggerating the nervous strain he was suffering, in order to delay his trip to India, scheduled for the winter of 1920–1.[64] Edward continued to party as energetically as he had in North America, and often stayed up drinking and dancing into the small hours. One party on board the *Renown* ended at 3.30 a.m. with dancing on the tables; the Prince's staff performed a Maori *haka* and their female guests responded with a Polynesian *poi* dance. One of the girls left the ship struggling to extricate a fork which had been put down the back of her dress.[65]

As if the strain of touring were not enough, Edward also faced a crisis in his relationship with his mistress, Freda Dudley Ward. The King and Queen had been aware of Edward's love affair with Freda since at least the summer of 1919. They may have hoped that it would cool off as a result of Edward's long absences from Britain; if so, they failed to appreciate the intensity of the Prince's passion. Soon after his departure for Australasia King George and his advisers decided that the relationship must be terminated. The first step was to detach Edward's brother Prince Albert from his mistress, Sheila, Lady Loughborough. The couple had made a foursome with Edward and Freda the previous year as 'the 4 Do's', and Sheila was a close friend of Freda's. The King promised to make Albert duke of York on condition he give up his mistress, which the compliant Bertie duly did.[66] Albert was then dispatched to persuade Freda to break off the relationship with Edward by letter, presumably on the rather callous assumption that Edward would have time to recover during his long tour. Edward's suspicions were aroused when he received a letter from his brother early in June. 'Old Bertie has written me a mad one which I can't fathom at all. He mentions long yarns with you and Sheilie, and arrangements and suggestions and you wanting to make things easier for me!!'[67] This was the prelude to Freda's 'No. 8' letter, probably written in mid-April 1920, which the Prince received on 24 June shortly before sailing for Western Australia.

Freda's letter does not survive, but Edward's reply to it was so detailed that it is possible to reconstruct some of its contents, and to catch an echo of her voice. The gist is that Freda appeals to Edward to end the affair and give up their love. She asks him to help her be strong, saying that she will never love anyone else, and knowing that her suggestion will cause him pain. She can never be any good for him in his life, and she must think of her two young daughters. She subtly places the onus on Edward to make the break, implying that she lacks the strength to do it herself.[68]

Joey Legh described Edward's reaction to the letter. 'The Boy has had an appalling fit of depression since the arrival of the last mail and has been sending endless cables in code. He has rather given himself away by suddenly announcing that he doesn't care whether he stays on here an extra three months or goes to India etc. I have never seen him so upset before.'[69] Edward's misery was all the more acute because he was unable to confide in any of his staff, not even Mountbatten. He could only pour out his feelings late at night in anguished, stream-of-consciousness letters to Freda.[70]

The clumsy attempt to separate Edward from his lover had the opposite effect from the one intended. He regarded it as an intolerable intrusion into his private life; it drew him closer to Freda and opened up a damaging breach between him and the rest of the royal family. Writing of himself in the third person, he told Freda, 'how cruelly bitter he's become towards his bloody family and their still more infamous crowd of satellites known as "the Court". If they really have been surrounding our poor little molehill and making it vulgar and notorious, as Bertie seems to have told you they have, God's curses be upon them!'[71]

In Western Australia, where he arrived shortly after receiving the 'No. 8' letter from Freda, Edward's exhaustion and misery became obvious to the press reporters who were travelling with him. Probably with the encouragement of the Prince's staff, the correspondents of *The Times* and *Morning Post* cabled warning messages to the government in London. 'Renewed signs of nerve strain of Prince of Wales very disturbing' cabled *The Times* reporter, 'convinced pressure should be brought to bear in England to cancel Indian visit'.[72] These warnings finally persuaded the reluctant King to postpone the Prince's tour to India, scheduled for autumn 1920. The Duke of Connaught was sent in his place to open the new legislative assembly.[73] Ironically, by the time the postponement was announced, the Prince had ceased to care whether he went to India or not, because he thought his affair with Freda was over.

HMS *Renown* set sail from Sydney on 19 August 1920. The homeward voyage was leisurely and involved few formal engagements. On the return visit the ship's stopover in Hawaii was extended for forty-eight hours to allow Edward time for surfing, golf, and polo. In the evening, after dinner and dancing at the Moana Hotel in Honolulu, the Prince and his party bathed in the moonlight off Waikiki beach. On his departure he issued a statement warmly thanking his American hosts for their hospitality. 'I always feel happy amongst Americans and in American territory, because American life appeals to me greatly, and I have many American friends, especially since my short visit to the United States last year.'[74] He was less grateful for the over-enthusiastic attentions of one of his dance partners, who had been drinking aboard the ship: 'I got let in for a nightmare dance with a completely toxy woman...she called me "darling" and said I was stiff and formal when I refused to kiss her.'[75] After refuelling at Acapulco in Mexico, the *Renown* passed back through the Panama Canal and on to Trinidad and British Guiana (now Guyana). Steaming through the Caribbean, the Prince paid brief visits to half-a-dozen island colonies, in an attempt to raise the morale of the British administrators and counter the growing dominance of the USA in the region. Apart from Jamaica, where there was an epidemic, the only British dependency in the West Indies which Edward did not visit was the Bahamas. Despite a plea from the Governor, this remote corner of the Empire was considered too insignificant to merit even a one-day visit from the Prince. After the Abdication, Edward was to spend five years there as Governor during the Second World War.[76]

The *Renown* finally docked at Portsmouth on 11 October 1920. In a trip lasting 210 days, the Prince had travelled nearly 46,000 miles by land and sea, and visited over two hundred towns and cities en route.[77] Contemporaries judged the trip to have been a great success, reinvigorating the British monarchy and strengthening the ties of empire.[78] On the day of Edward's return, *The Times* commented: 'the triumph of his visits was a personal triumph, won by his natural humanity, his pluck, his energy and tact, his conscientiousness and his unfailing response to the demands upon his personality on great public occasions.'[79] Large crowds gathered in London to welcome him home, and at London's Victoria Station there were banners on the walls with 'Well Done' and 'Welcome Home' in letters three feet high.[80] The Governor-General of Australia wrote that '[his] charm and his very marked sense of duty have carried him triumphantly through the whole ordeal of a somewhat onerous programme'.[81] British writers were not alone in praising the Prince. The *New York Times* also offered him a warm tribute: 'He won personal liking wherever he went—a personal liking that will be a help not only to himself but also to his country when he comes into his kingdom.'[82]

Edward's return to Britain after a lengthy absence prompted a wave of speculation in the press about his future. On 14 October, only three days after he had landed, *The Times* carried a leading article titled 'The Marriage of the Prince'. The paper justified this intrusion into the Prince's privacy by invoking public interest: 'He is 26, and the marriage of the Prince of Wales is inevitably a matter of deep public concern.' The leader argued that the Prince should be free to choose his own wife, but expressed the hope that he would marry 'one of his own race'—presumably meaning an Anglo-Saxon bride rather than a European princess.[83] The article was reproduced throughout the British press and across the empire, and prompted widespread debate. One suggestion was that the time had come to repeal the Royal Marriages Act of 1772, passed in the reign of George III, which required the consent of the monarch to royal marriages.[84] It is unlikely that *The Times* would have published such an article without first consulting Buckingham Palace. Indeed, given the close links between *The Times* and the government—which were to be so important during the Abdication crisis—it is possible that the article was inspired by the King's advisers in an attempt to remind the Prince of public expectations.[85] In Canada, the *Toronto Star* came close to the mark when it speculated that there was a dispute going on 'in higher altitudes' in which *The Times* hope to exert pressure.[86]

The controversy over the Prince's marriage also attracted attention in the USA, and gave rise to further discussion as to whether Edward would marry an American bride.[87] The *Louisville Courier-Journal* pointed out the irony of the British press requiring the Prince to fall in love, preferably with an Anglo-Saxon girl: 'the Prince will no doubt be comforted in the thought that his royal wife may be left to his own choice. Yet the suggestion of *The Times* is clearly that the Prince must proceed to fall in love.'[88] Although the American public was interested in Edward's marriage prospects, at the same time there were more sensational stories of royal marriages filling the front pages in the USA. Zizi Lambrino, the morganatic wife of Prince Carol, the heir to the throne of Romania, had refused an offer of five million dollars to release her husband from the marriage; Prince George of Greece had travelled in secret, disguised as a peasant, to marry his sweetheart, Princess Elizabeth of Romania, against the wishes of her family; while a succession crisis in Greece raised the possibility that an American heiress, Nancy Stewart Leeds, the wife of Prince Christopher, might become queen.[89]

By coincidence, Edward's marriage prospects were the theme of a new play which opened on Broadway in New York a few days after the *Times* leader. Entitled *Just Suppose*, it was a saccharine romantic comedy inspired by the Prince's visit to the USA the previous year. 'George', a thinly disguised version of the Prince of Wales, escapes from a formal dinner in Washington and goes for a drive through Virginia, with his aide, Sir Calverton Shipley. They call in on some old friends of Shipley's, the Staffords of Fairview. Following Shipley into the house, the Prince meets a lovely young Southern belle, Linda Lee Stafford. It is love at first sight. 'Tired of handshaking the Western Hemisphere and making his firm solid with the United States', the

Prince offers to relinquish his royal job and marry Linda Lee, if only she will say the word. She knows, however, that he belongs to his people, and sends him back to marry the bride chosen for him by the state.[90] Although one critic commented that the play would have been more successful if it had been put on during Edward's visit, the stories of his flirtation in Panama with the shopgirl Carolyn Granberry provided an ideal backdrop to the production. After opening briefly in Washington, *Just Suppose* transferred to Broadway in November 1920, where it enjoyed a three-month run. It was not well received by the critics; the *Brooklyn Daily Eagle* called the play 'light as thistledown', while *Billboard* magazine described it as a 'teary paradise for matinee Niobes'.[91] Nevertheless, the production was sufficiently successful to go on tour for several months in 1921, and it was made into a silent movie in 1926. Most of the actors in the stage company were British; the part of Sir Calverton Shipley was played by the young Leslie Howard, later to achieve screen immortality as Ashley Wilkes in *Gone with the Wind*. One critic noted that Howard looked far more like the real Prince of Wales than the actor who played 'George'.[92]

The great irony of the worldwide press speculation over the Prince's marriage was that in his own mind Edward was already married. In a letter to Freda from Australia, he wrote, 'I used to love Paris when I was "jeune homme". I've never been there as a "married man" which despite all you are sweet enough to say, angel, I feel I am more than any man could feel.'[93] There are also hints in the letters that Edward hoped that Freda was pregnant with his child, although of course she was not.[94] As soon as he got home from Australia, he resumed their affair, and there was no slackening in its intensity. Freda's attempt in her 'No. 8' letter to break off the affair appears to have been forgotten: perhaps she was genuinely fond of the Prince and flattered by his attentions; perhaps he threatened suicide if she left him, as he was to do with Wallis many years later.[95] Also Freda may have been upset by the behaviour of other members of the royal family. After breaking with his mistress Sheila Loughborough in the summer, Prince Albert had snubbed Freda at parties and dances.[96] Writing on 30 December 1920, Edward urged Freda to look forward to their future married life together. 'We don't want anything to happen to old Duddie [Freda's estranged husband], but please concentrate *mon amour* and I've so often told you that I know that one day we'll be far happier than we are even now!!'[97]

At the same time, the opposition of his family to his relationship with Freda deepened Edward's estrangement from them. Back at Sandringham for Christmas in 1920, Edward felt isolated and alone: 'I feel quite a stranger here somehow... I've absolutely nothing in common with the rest of my family, and have drifted away from them altogether.'[98] Edward's alienation from his brother Albert was particularly significant. The two were close in age and had grown up together; the previous year Edward had encouraged Bertie in the pursuit of his affair with Sheila Loughborough. Now, Bertie had sided with his father against Edward and Freda, and had played an active part in the plot to break up their relationship.[99] The rift between the brothers was an important psychological turning-point, which foreshadowed Edward's growing isolation from his family in the ensuing years. The episode only served to widen the emerging divide between 'Edward' the Prince, and 'David' the private man.

5

The EP Ranch
A Fantasy of Escape

Prince Edward discovered the EP ('Edward Prince') ranch on his first visit to North America in 1919. He was looking forward to the western leg of his Canadian tour and, at his request, a few rest days had been included in the itinerary. In particular, Edward wanted to see a 'real ranch', so a brief visit was arranged to the Bar U cattle ranch in the foothills of the Rocky Mountains, south of Calgary in Alberta.

The Bar U ranch was an obvious choice, being one of the oldest and most successful ranches in the Canadian West. It had been established in 1881, with cattle herds driven north across the border from Montana, and in 1919 it was owned by the cattle king George Lane. Born in Iowa, Lane was an American cowboy who came to Alberta in the 1880s to help establish the fledgling Canadian ranching industry. Lane was a shrewd businessman, and became one of the leading ranchers in the country. He was one of the 'Big Four' cattle men who established the Calgary Stampede in 1912.[1] The Bar U retained close links with the USA and enjoyed associations with some of the legendary figures of the Wild West. Henry Longabaugh, better known as the Sundance Kid, worked there for a time while using Canada as a safe haven from arrest in the USA. Ebb Johnson, the foreman of the ranch in the 1890s, was the model for the hero of *The Virginian* by Owen Lister, the first great Western novel.[2]

As he travelled west across the continent, Edward began to spin a fantasy that he would escape from the trammels of his royal duties and move to Canada with his mistress, Freda Dudley Ward. 'If only WE could settle West (British Columbia or Alberta) darling, what heaven and we could be the happiest couple in the whole world,' he wrote to Freda on 19 August 1919, while he was still in eastern Canada. He returned to the theme several times in his letters over the next few days.[3] The seed of abdication had already germinated in Edward's mind, nurtured by the desire to share his life with the woman he loved.

After a month of intensive touring, the Prince and his party arrived at the Bar U on 15 September. The break came not a moment too soon. Despite the success of the first part of the tour, Edward was exhausted and depressed by the constant demands of his role as Prince of Wales. 'I am really down and out tonight,' he wrote to Freda the evening before setting out for the Bar U. 'I've never taken such a hopelessly miserable and despondent view of life as I do now... all on account of having had to do the P of W stunt and play to the gallery until I can do it no more!'[4]

Darkness was falling as the Prince arrived at the Bar U late in the afternoon of 15 September. The ranch-house was supplied with electricity from a generator, and eager to impress his guests, Lane ordered all the lights to be switched on. Predictably, the circuit became overloaded, and the ranch was plunged into darkness. This only increased the conviviality of the evening for the Prince, who enjoyed a home-cooked supper by candlelight round the ranch-house table.[5] Edward rose at dawn the next morning, climbed out of his bedroom window so as not to wake up the house, and went for an eight-mile run before breakfast. Later in the morning he joined the ranch hands for a round-up of cattle.[6] He impressed the locals by declining a ride back to the ranch in a car, returning instead on horseback in a heavy downpour. When he arrived at the house and saw that lunch was ready, he sat down with the cowboys in his wet clothes, the pockets of his jacket turned inside out. His down-to-earth demeanour impressed the ranch hands. 'That's the way he kept surprising us all that day,' one of them recalled, 'none of us thought princes were like that.'[7]

After lunch Edward greeted war veterans from the Bar U and neighbouring ranches, and then took a long walk with Professor William Carlyle, Lane's veterinary expert. The hills near the ranch offered commanding views of the surrounding countryside, and Edward was able to look down on a neighbouring ranch owned by an Englishman, Frank Bedingfeld.[8] Impressed by the beauty of the scene, the Prince remarked to Carlyle that he would love to own a place like that.[9] He departed reluctantly at 6 p.m. to catch the train back to Calgary in order to attend a gala ball for returned soldiers. 'Some ranch!' he wrote in the Bar U visitors' book, telling reporters that although he spent only twenty-four hours at the ranch he wished it had been twenty-four years. Before he left he presented George Lane with a silver cigar holder and Alexander Fleming, the ranch manager, with a silver match case bearing his coat of arms.[10]

Edward's brief visit to the Bar U ranch had a powerful impact upon him. Its situation was spectacularly beautiful, and the late summer weather was fresh and invigorating. As he tramped through the foothills of the Rockies, he briefly glimpsed a way to realize his dream of settling in the West with his beloved Freda by his side.[11] No doubt the myth of the Wild West was as appealing to him as it was to any other young man of his generation. As a boy he had been taken by his grandfather Edward VII to see Buffalo Bill's Wild West Show on its London tour in 1903. After the show he went backstage to meet the performers, including an Indian boy of his own age, Moses Red Star, who gave him one of the clay shooting targets used in the arena by Buffalo Bill.[12] More specifically, the ranch provided Edward with a brief moment of escape from the relentless pressure of being the Prince of Wales. There were no pressmen to bother him, and no royal duties to perform. Part of the attraction was the camaraderie and lack of deference which he found amongst the cowboys—similar, perhaps, to his experience of military service during the war. The American comedian Will Rogers later recounted a story that Edward had told him of his stay at the Bar U. The Prince was assisting at the cattle round-up when George Lane yelled at him, 'Hey Prince, get out of here; you are scaring these cattle and you are in the way of the cowboys!'[13]

As he travelled west from Alberta, Edward heard from Lane that Frank Bedingfeld was willing to sell his ranch, and with the encouragement of his staff he decided to buy it. While in Vancouver he telegraphed his father, the King, to tell him of his plans. On 2 October, on his way back East, he met Lane near Calgary to finalize the transaction. It was agreed that Lane would purchase the ranch on the Prince's behalf and that Carlyle, whom Edward had met at the Bar U, would manage it.[14] The sale was completed on 7 October. Edward acquired 1,440 acres freehold, with a half share in a lease of a further 41,000 acres, for 130,000 Canadian dollars. In honour of the event the citizens of High River, the nearest town to the ranch, presented their new neighbour with a painting by the American cowboy artist Charles Russell.[15] The ranch was renamed the EP ranch.

The deal took place so quickly that Edward was able to reveal it as he was travelling back across Canada on the return leg of his tour. He made the announcement at Winnipeg on 7 October 1919:

I shall not say goodbye to western Canada, but only au revoir. I think this western spirit must be very catching, at least I know I've caught it very badly. I feel so much at home here by this time that I want to have a permanent home among the people of the west, a place where I can come sometimes and live for a while. To this end I have purchased a small ranch in southern Alberta, and I shall look forward to developing it and making it my own.[16]

The EP ranch nestled in the foothills of the Rockies on one of the small creeks which ran down from the mountains. Tommy Lascelles, the Prince's aide, gave a vivid description of it when he visited in 1924:

The Ranch consists of the homestead—a large wooden bungalow in which we all live—and three or four barns and cattle-sheds, all thrown down by the side of the little Pekisko river, which winds through a narrow belt of trees and scrub from the Rockies, bounding the whole horizon some thirty miles to the west. There are two low ranges of hills on each side of the river, and between them lies a vast, undulating plain, broken only by occasional bluffs, set with stunted trees. It is not really beautiful country, save for the wonderful line of the mountains, but the space and cleanness of it make one love it.[17]

In his memoirs Edward returned to the longing that the EP ranch had inspired in him. 'In the midst of that majestic countryside I had suddenly been overwhelmed by an irresistible longing to immerse myself, if only momentarily, in the simple life of the western prairies. There, I was sure, I would find occasional escape from the sometimes too confining, too well ordered, island life of Britain.' This in itself was hardly surprising. Members of the royal family often sought remote locations where they could escape temporarily from the pressures of public life: Victoria and Albert built Balmoral in the Highlands and Osborne House on the Isle of Wight, while Edward VII acquired Sandringham in Norfolk. However, the sheer remoteness of the EP ranch, and the fact that it was more than 4,000 miles from home, suggest that Edward had a fantasy not of temporary but of permanent escape. In 1936, when he was considering the sale of the ranch, he said to Tommy Lascelles in a candid moment, 'You know Tommy, I always planned to keep it as a place that I could retire to.' 'You mean for a holiday, Sir?' replied Lascelles. 'No, I mean for good,' Edward answered.[18]

The dream of making a new life in the West was shared by many royal and aristocratic contemporaries of the Prince. Lord Minto, the son of a former Governor-General of Canada, owned a ranch north of Calgary, and the Dukes of Manchester and Sutherland also owned property in the western provinces. Some made their home permanently in Canada, like Lord Rodney, who ran a successful cattle and horse-breeding ranch in Saskatchewan. Edward's cousin Prince Erik of Denmark had settled on his ranch in Alberta. In 1924 he renounced his claim to the Danish throne in order to marry a Canadian heiress, Lois Booth.[19] The life-changing quality of the North American wilderness was a key theme of Sara Jeannette Duncan's 1914 novel *His Royal Happiness*. While Prince Alfred, Edward's fictional counterpart, is recovering from illness in America, he dreams of making a new life as a rancher in Colorado. 'He would not return. He would take up land out there and raise cattle...In Colorado he would be just a rancher earning his living—paying his way. His bosom swelled.'[20]

The significance of the Prince's acquisition was not lost on his contemporaries. As the *New York Times* commented, 'the EP Ranch is a polite hint to Britain that the Prince of Wales is no longer dependent on the vicissitudes of a throne. If labor becomes restive, he can say, "very well, I will retire happily to my ranch in Alberta".'[21] In the event, Edward never seriously considered moving permanently to Alberta: indeed, after his Abdication he made only two fleeting visits there. Nevertheless, the purchase of the ranch was more than a mere whim: it was a small gesture of defiance against his destiny as Prince of Wales, and an assertion that his future life might embrace other possibilities than the ones to which he had been born.

If the Prince had bought the ranch on impulse, a persuasive rationale for the acquisition soon emerged. Throughout his tour of Canada, with the encouragement of his political adviser, Edward Grigg, Edward had stressed that he came to the country as much as a Canadian as a Briton. His purchase of the EP ranch gave real substance to that claim. At a speech to the Canadian Club in London in 1922 he boasted of his western credentials: 'I always feel that I have a right to call myself Canadian, because I am, in a small way, a rancher. I always feel that my small ranch in Alberta is to me a great link with Canada, and that it is an assurance that I shall return there one day.'[22] It was a coup for the Canadian government to have established such a close personal tie with the royal family, and the Governor-General's staff were delighted. Edward had forged an important new link with the Dominions, and one which reinforced the relevance of royalty as a unifying force within the empire.

At home the King was bemused by his son's decision to buy property in Canada. He worried that the Prince would now be expected to acquire estates in other Dominions such as Australia and South Africa. As usual,

King George failed to sense the winds of change. The *New York Times* saw things more clearly: -

> the Prince has in him that rare and peculiar ability to do spontaneously and on the spur of the moment what afterwards looks like the result of deep design. The acquisition of the EP Ranch seemed at first like a mere whim. The shrewdness that prompted it is now apparent. The very word 'ranch' identifies the Prince with the Dominions. It is a word belonging exclusively to 'the oversea'.[23]

From the outset Edward was determined that the EP ranch should be a practical and economic business operation, and not merely a showplace. As Duke of Cornwall he owned large agricultural estates in England and Scotland, which included farms that specialized in breeding pedigree strains of cattle, sheep, and horses. The EP ranch was not large enough to sustain a a commercial cattle-rearing operation like its neighbour the Bar U. Instead Edward and his estate managers decided to run the EP as a centre for introducing premier British livestock breeds into Canada.

The ranch was administered as an overseas extension of the Duchy of Cornwall, and William Carlyle, the manager, became an employee of the Duchy. Late in 1919 he travelled to Britain to meet the Prince and to select suitable stock from the Duchy farms for shipping to Alberta. In the course of the next few years Carlyle built up pedigree herds of shorthorn cattle, Shropshire sheep, and Dartmoor ponies, which regularly won prizes at the major North American agricultural shows. The Prince's commitment to the success of the ranch is demonstrated by the high levels of investment which were maintained throughout the 1920s. The Duchy transferred several thousand dollars a year to the EP for upkeep and building improvements, while the value of the livestock exported has been estimated at $100,000.[24]

It was several years before Edward was able to inspect his new ranch in person. The constraints of the royal calendar meant that the only realistic time of year for a visit was between August and October, when the royal family took their traditional summer holiday at Balmoral. In 1920 the Prince hoped to travel back from his Australasian tour by way of Vancouver and the Canadian Pacific Railway, but the Colonial Office resolved instead on a return via the Panama Canal and the British West Indies. It was only after Edward's marathon tour of India and the Far East in 1921–2 that the opportunity finally presented itself.

The specific timing of the Prince's first visit to the EP ranch may have been prompted by a scandal which erupted suddenly in the summer of 1923, and threatened to embroil the Prince. The historian Andrew Rose has reconstructed the remarkable story of the French courtesan Marguerite Alibert, who achieved worldwide notoriety when she shot and killed her husband, the Egyptian Prince Ali Fahmy, in the Savoy Hotel in London in July 1923. Charged with murder, she was defended by the famous advocate Marshall Hall, and acquitted at a sensational trial at the Old Bailey, London's central criminal court.

Marguerite had been Edward's mistress in Paris for several months during the war. In the course of their relationship Edward had written her several letters, which she had retained after the end of their affair in 1918. Rose argues persuasively that, following the shooting, Marguerite threatened to make the letters public unless the prosecuting authorities procured her acquittal. Perhaps it was a coincidence that the announcement of the Prince's trip to Canada was published on 12 July, only two days after the shooting, but it was certainly convenient for Edward to be out of the country during the trial. Writing to his wife early in September 1923, Lord Curzon, the Foreign Secretary, passed on the choice morsel of gossip. 'The French girl who shot her so-called Egyptian Prince in London and is going to be tried for murder, is the fancy woman who was the Prince's "keep" [mistress] in Paris during the war . . . and they were terribly worried he might be dragged in. It is fortunate that he is off to Canada and his name is to be kept out.'[25]

Edward left England on 5 September 1923, less than a week before the opening of Marguerite's trial on 10 September. Since the visit was a private one, without any official duties, he travelled incognito as 'Lord Renfrew'. This meant that the Canadian government did not have to acknowledge his royal status while he was in the country. The Prince was accompanied by less than half his usual entourage: apart from his valet and detective, only Godfrey Thomas and his companions 'G' Trotter and Fruity Metcalfe were in attendance. The party crossed the Atlantic on the Canadian Pacific liner *Empress of France*. Many of those on board were emigrating to western Canada, and Edward won the admiration of passengers by making a visit to the steerage deck to encourage the immigrants in their new lives. After a journey of eleven days, the Prince and his party finally arrived at the EP ranch on 16 September. Although there were no official welcomes at High River, the railway halt at which Edward disembarked from the royal train, press photographers and newsreel cameramen were out in force, and the road to the ranch was lined with hundreds of sightseers. At the ranch itself,

Figure 5.1. The EP ranch, September 1923

however, the press was kept at a distance, and Edward was at last allowed a brief opportunity to realize his fantasy of escape.[26]

The ranch-house had been extended and redecorated in preparation for the Prince and his staff. A three-bedroom annex had been added, and the plumbing modernized. 'Even York House, the London residence of the Prince, can boast nothing more attractive than the white tiled baths and shower,' claimed the *Calgary Herald*. The accommodation was comfortable but unpretentious. In the living room there were wicker armchairs, oriental rugs on the wooden floor, and equine prints on the walls. The most striking feature was the pair of large brass floor lamps made from wartime German shell cases decorated with maple-leaf motifs.[27]

Satisfying his craving for strenuous physical exercise, Edward immediately set to work in the fields. It was harvest time, and for the first three days he lived the life of a ranch hand, cutting sunflowers, stooking oats, and filling the silos with winter feed. 'I've even helped muck out the cow house', he wrote to his father, 'and I chop and saw up wood, and I can assure you that it's very hard work indeed.'[28] Other days were spent riding, hunting, and visiting his ranching neighbours. After about a week, Edward had exhausted the activities which the ranch had to offer, and he interrupted his stay for a long weekend playing golf at the Rocky Mountain resort of Banff. Much of the second week was spent preparing for a livestock show and picnic which Edward gave for members of the Alberta Shorthorn Breeders Association on the eve of his departure. About five hundred people attended, and the highlight of the day was a rodeo display organized by the American cowboy impresario Guy Weadick, the manager of the Calgary Stampede. Afterwards Weadick taught the Prince how to perform tricks with a lasso, a skill which he was later to put to use in the unlikely setting of a hotel bar in Cannes.[29] Although he had been unable to attend the Stampede, Edward had commissioned a magnificent silver trophy for the champion bronco rider, and during the rodeo he presented it to the winner, Peter Vandermeer.[30]

The cattle men's picnic was the highlight of Edward's holiday. Chatting to his neighbours, listening to the yarns of the old-timers, and learning cowboy rope tricks from the rodeo entertainers, he enjoyed a rare moment of connection and belonging. 'This has been the happiest day of my life,' he said to Carlyle after the party. 'This is the first time in my life I've felt like a real man. I've met all my neighbours and I like them. What's more I think they like me, not because I'm a Prince but because I'm one of the gang.' The Canadian air seemed to act like a tonic on the Prince. On his return to Britain the newspapers remarked how fit and tanned he looked: on the homeward crossing on the *Empress of France* he even took a turn in the engine room, stoking the ship's boilers. The holiday had been such a success that, in the absence of an overseas tour, Edward decided to visit his ranch again the following year.[31]

In 1924 the original plan was for Edward to spend a month at the ranch after a week's stopover on Long Island to watch the international polo matches. In the event his stay in the States stretched out to three weeks, and the visit to the EP ranch proved an anti-climax after the excitements of Long Island and New York. He spent much of the train journey across Canada planning further trips to the United States, and decided to cut short his stay at the ranch in favour of a trip to the Pacific coast and a visit to Chicago and Detroit. 'So after all you are only spending a week on your ranch,' commented Queen Mary drily. 'What a pity when I thought that was the raison d'etre for your going out.'[32]

The Prince's party arrived at the ranch on 26 September in the middle of a sleet storm. Edward was suffering from a streaming cold and felt thoroughly depressed. However, the sun soon came out, and the Prince was able to spend a few days riding the range, shooting, fishing, and entertaining guests. On the final afternoon Carlyle had arranged a livestock auction. An estimated three thousand visitors turned out and the Prince mingled with the crowd, chatting with neighbours such as George Lane. That evening the Prince and his party set off for Vancouver, and despite spending three more weeks in Canada, they did not return to the ranch. There were too many other distractions in North America to divert Edward's attention: his restless energy made it hard for him to stay in one place for any length of time, and his constant need for amusement—for golf, dancing, and parties—could not be satisfied by the arduous monotony of ranching life.[33]

Although the Prince may have begun to lose interest in the ranch, by the mid-1920s it had attracted international attention as a flourishing commercial operation. With support and investment from the Duchy of Cornwall estate, the EP rapidly established itself as one of the leading stockbreeding ranches in North America. In 1925 the ranch's prize shorthorn bull, 'King of the Fairies', was Grand Champion at the International Livestock Exposition in Chicago. As well as cattle and sheep the ranch also bred racehorses: King George leased his champion stallion 'Will Somers' to the ranch for the development of pedigree bloodstock in Canada. Under Carlyle's management the ranch acquired a reputation as a centre for the application of the most advanced stockbreeding techniques. Delegations of scientists and journalists visited the EP in order to learn more about the ranch and to study the latest developments. In the summer of 1925 Carlyle entertained a group of sixty-five journalists from agricultural journals in the USA.[34]

The ranch also had a steady stream of British visitors, often at the invitation of the Prince. The Duke of Devonshire, then Governor-General of Canada, paid a visit in 1921, and thereafter it became obligatory for his successors to make the pilgrimage to the ranch. Winston Churchill came with his son Randolph on one of his North American tours, as did the Fleet Street press baron Lord Rothermere, and Edward's friends Duff and Diana Cooper.[35] In 1927 the editors of more than forty British provincial newspapers were given a tour of the ranch.[36] The ranch became familiar to a wider public through newsreel footage and through international exhibitions. At the British Empire Exhibition in 1924 the highlight of the Canadian pavilion was a sculpture of the Prince at his ranch, carved out of butter. In 1928 a diorama of the entire ranch was built by the Imperial Institute and exhibited at the British Industries Fair, while another large-scale model was the main attraction at the summer exhibition at Crystal Palace in 1931.[37] On one occasion the ranch was even used as a movie set. Some of the scenes of the Western *The Calgary Stampede,* starring the cowboy film star Hoot Gibson, were filmed at the EP in 1925.[38]

After 1924 it continued to be the expectation that the Prince would make regular summer visits to the EP ranch whenever his official schedule permitted. The year 1925 was taken up with a lengthy tour to Africa and Latin America, but in 1926 the British and American press confidently reported that Edward would again spend his holiday in Alberta after a projected tour of the industrial cities of the Midwestern USA which he had announced before leaving New York in 1924.[39] It was not until late August 1926 that the Prince's staff announced that he would not be travelling to America after all, ostensibly because of a heavy schedule of engagements in Britain in October.

In the event, Edward did not return to his ranch until August 1927, and then only for the briefest of visits. The occasion was the diamond jubilee of Canadian confederation, which the Prince attended with Prime Minister Stanley Baldwin. Edward behaved badly throughout the tour, making no attempt to conceal his boredom, even during public functions. He kept officials waiting, refused to acknowledge welcoming crowds, and, during one major speech, deliberately omitted a crucial passage about the relationship between King and Empire.[40] After the celebrations in Ottawa were over, he travelled out to Alberta with Tommy Lascelles and other members of staff, ostensibly for a week's rest at the ranch. An expectant crowd gathered to meet him at the railway station at High River, but Edward missed the train in order to play a round of golf in Calgary, and drove directly to the ranch later in the day.[41] After a stay of less than twenty-four hours, Edward decided to visit Edmonton, over two hundred miles away, at the invitation of the lieutenant governor. He was apparently so bored at the ranch that he seized any opportunity to get away.[42] On 15 August Edward left his ranch, having spent barely two days there. He was not to return until 1941.

Why had the ranch lost its appeal? One of the original spurs behind his purchase—his fantasy of escaping to the prairie with Freda Dudley Ward—had long since faded. Moreover, in practical terms it was simply too far away for Edward to visit with any frequency. It was nearly a fortnight's journey from London and, having got there, Edward found very little to occupy his butterfly mind. The jaded prince of 1927 was seeking a different sort of refuge from the war-weary youth of 1919; the nightclubs of London and Paris were more attractive than the wide open spaces of the western prairie. In addition, the EP did not prove to be quite the remote refuge he had expected. Under the Prince's ownership it became the most famous ranch in Canada, and a popular tourist destination. During the 1920s there might be as many as two hundred visitors a day in summer, many of them from the USA, a hundred miles to the south. Special arrangements had to be made for the tourists: a picnic ground was prepared, and a pictorial souvenir of the ranch printed.[43] In any event, King George's illness in 1928 forced Edward to curtail his foreign travel. His discovery of Fort Belvedere near Windsor soon afterwards provided Edward with a secluded weekend retreat which could be used all year round, making the EP still more redundant. At the time of the Abdication, Edward came close to selling the ranch, but the discovery of oil in the nearby Turner Valley persuaded him to hold onto it in the hope of becoming an oil baron. Despite extensive drilling, however, the EP never yielded hydrocarbons in commercial quantities. Edward's managers drastically scaled back the ranching activities, and he finally sold out to a neighbour in 1962.[44]

If the reality was that Edward's enthusiasm for his ranch soon faded, the image of the cowboy Prince proved far more enduring. The myth of the cowboy—manly, self-reliant, and individualistic, the embodiment of American values—has been one of the most powerful in modern culture, nurtured by the

Figure 5.2. Edward on the EP ranch, September 1923

popularity of the Western as a movie genre.[45] Successive American presidents, from Theodore Roosevelt to George W. Bush, have identified themselves as cowboys as a means of enhancing their political appeal. By acquiring the EP ranch, Edward associated himself with the myth, forming another bond with the American public. Frequent press articles, illustrated by the Prince in cowboy garb, recounted his love of the ranching life and described activities on the EP ranch.

They ran under headlines such as 'The Prince of Wales is a Happy Rancher', and 'It's Too Bad He's in the King Business; He's a Good Cowboy'.[46] American tourists visited the EP, and the ranch's prize livestock were regularly exhibited at agricultural shows south of the border.[47] Edward's unexpected incarnation as an American cowboy added another side to his reputation, and reinforced his image as a modern democratic prince breaking free from the conventions of traditional monarchy.

6

An Englishman in New York, 1924

After three years of imperial tours culminating in an eight-month visit to India and the Far East, Edward spent most of 1923 and 1924 back home in Britain. His schedule of official engagements nevertheless continued to be very heavy. In April 1923 he paid a visit to the battlefields and cemeteries of Belgium, in May he made regional tours of Yorkshire, in June the North-East, in August Nottinghamshire, and in October North Wales. He was in constant demand as a patron and speaker for all manner of organizations, from the Royal Academy and the London Society of Medicine to the Child Emigration Society and the Gardeners' Royal Benevolent Society.[1] Inevitably the Prince had to make choices as to where he would concentrate his energies. During these years his activities came to focus on four main roles: the leader of the war veterans, the ambassador of empire, the champion of British commerce and industry, and the promoter of Anglo-American relations. Of those roles the first three were virtually self-selecting. Edward's experience of the trenches made him the obvious choice as President of the Imperial War Graves Commission, and the figurehead of veterans' organizations such as Toc H. His imperial tours gave him the knowledge and authority to act as spokesman for the British Empire, while the urgent need for post-war reconstruction led him to pursue an interest in industrial development and innovation.

The final role which the Prince adopted, as promoter of Anglo-American relations, was more a matter of personal choice, and reflected his own particular enthusiasm for the cause. For some years Edward had been cultivating a network of American contacts from all walks of life: not only politicians and diplomats but also businessmen, financiers, and industrialists. One particularly important medium of communication was the Pilgrims Society, an influential Anglo-American fellowship association which had a sister organization in the USA. The Pilgrims were extremely well connected, and welcomed leading American figures to their meetings. It became a tradition in the 1920s and 1930s that an incoming US Ambassador made his first speech on British soil to the Pilgrims. Edward attended his first Pilgrims dinner in New York in 1919, and regularly appeared at the London dinners thereafter. In February 1921, for example, he spoke at the dinner in honour of the departing US Ambassador, John W. Davis.[2]

Early in 1923, after returning from his Asian tour, the Prince picked up these connections. His return coincided with a crucial period in Anglo-American relations. Since the end of the war, Europe had lurched from crisis to crisis. France, its wealthiest regions devastated by the fighting, sought full payment of the reparations agreed by Germany in the Treaty of Versailles. Germany dragged its feet on reparations as its economy, dislocated by war and defeat, collapsed into hyperinflation. Britain, suffering a post-war slump and burdened by its American war debt, was desperate for the revival of international trade and finance. America, having rejected the Versailles Treaty, stood aloof from Europe, determined to avoid any linkage between the repayment of its war debts and German reparations. In January 1923 the French government lost patience and sent troops into the Ruhr, Germany's main industrial region, in order to enforce reparations.

It was against the backdrop of this crisis that Stanley Baldwin, then Chancellor of the Exchequer, went to Washington early in 1923 to secure an agreement on the repayment of the UK's $4.3 billion war debt as the prelude to a more general economic settlement. Although the deal was later much criticized, at the time it represented a crucial step in the re-engagement of the USA in European affairs, and paved the way for the Dawes Plan for post-war reconstruction in 1924.[3]

On 28 February 1924, Prince Edward attended a dinner of the Pilgrims Society held in Baldwin's honour following his return from the USA. Most unusually, the Prince was not required to give a speech: indeed, he accepted the invitation on the strict understanding that he would not have to speak.[4] It was a private engagement which he attended out of personal interest. At the Pilgrims Dinner the Prince heard George Harvey, the American Ambassador, lavish praise on the deal which Baldwin had struck. 'It involved far more than the greatest financial transaction recorded in history,' said Harvey. 'It bore with it the ... everlasting friendship of the two great nations to which the entire world looked for the preservation of solvency and stability which were essential to the prosperity and happiness of all mankind.'[5] The following evening the Prince was guest of honour at a dinner of the American Universities Union, and his speech there echoed the theme of Anglo-American cooperation and emphasized the underlying unity of the English-speaking peoples. 'When we get together like this we bring out each other's many good points, and we come out better Anglo-Saxons than we went in.'[6]

American connections aside, the Prince's primary responsibility in 1924 was promoting the success of the British Empire Exhibition. The aim of the exhibition was to present the modern, progressive face of the British Empire as a commonwealth of nations, working together for mutual benefit. It enabled the Prince to combine two of his main roles, as ambassador of empire and as champion of industry. He had been president of the organizing committee since 1919 and helped to shape the character of the project, which involved the construction of a purpose-built exhibition park on a 200-acre site at Wembley in north London.[7] Designed as a showpiece for the industry and natural wealth of the empire, the exhibition was opened by the Prince and King George on St George's Day, 23 April 1924. The newly founded BBC broadcast the opening speeches round the empire.[8] The exhibition proved a great success, attracting 18 million visitors. One of the most popular attractions in the Canadian pavilion, illustrating the latest refrigeration technology, was a life-size statue of the Prince, carved out of two-and-a-half tons of butter. It showed the Prince at his ranch in Alberta, standing beside a handsome prairie horse. The highlight of the exhibition was intended to be the Pageant of Empire, a huge spectacular with a cast of thousands and music by Elgar, re-enacting famous scenes from British history. In the event the British public preferred C. B. Cochran's Wild West rodeo show, which played to capacity crowds in Wembley Stadium despite an attempted prosecution by the RSPCA for cruelty to the animals.[9]

Edward was also prominent in a number of the international congresses that were held at the Wembley Exhibition Centre in 1924 with the aim of fostering trade and development as a means of relieving the world's economic problems. In June Wembley played host to the first World Power Conference. Prince Edward gave the opening speech, in which he compared the role of the conference in the industrial sphere to that of the League of Nations in politics.[10] This was followed a few weeks later by the Annual Convention of the Advertising Clubs of the World. Despite its name the convention was a largely American organization: 2,300 of its 2,500 delegates

Figure 6.1. Prince Edward at the EP ranch, sculpted in butter, at the Canadian Pavilion, British Empire Exhibition, 1924

came from the USA. Its motto was 'the furtherance of Truth in Advertising'. The importance of the event to Anglo–American relations was underlined by the high-level speakers who addressed the convention. Edward gave the opening speech of welcome and was followed by government ministers and senior politicians such as Winston Churchill and Stanley Baldwin. The Prince's arrival in the conference hall at Wembley was greeted by prolonged cheering. In his address he praised the advertising industry for its role in increasing global trade and prosperity. Replying, the convention's president emphasized the Prince's popularity in America. 'We love him as our own', he added, to renewed cheers from the delegates.[11] Before he left, Edward accepted an invitation to visit the New York Advertising Club later in the year.[12] In an editorial leader the following day, the *Daily Express* pointed out how appropriate it was that the Prince had opened the Advertising Convention. 'He is a human commodity of such compelling qualities that the world simply had to be told about him...when there is anyone so worth talking about as the Prince of Wales the power of advertising is seen at the heights of its efficiency and usefulness.'[13]

The most important congress to be held in London in the summer of 1924 was the Reparations Conference, which opened shortly after the end of the Advertising Convention. Its objective was nothing less than the stabilization of the European economy. Earlier in the year, the Reparations Commission established under the Treaty of Versailles had set up an expert committee to advise on the overhaul of the German financial system and prepare a new reparations plan. It was chaired by the American banker Charles Dawes, and its members included Owen D. Young, the chairman of General Electric and the Radio Corporation of America. Edward's friend, the American Frederick Bate, was an assistant to the committee, and was able to introduce Dawes and Young to the Prince. The 'Dawes Plan' prepared by the commission recommended the rescheduling and reduction of German reparations and the advance of a large international loan to Germany. Its main purpose was to revive the German economy in order to enable it to resume reparations payments to France and Britain. The London Conference was convened to implement the Dawes Plan and make the necessary amendments to the Versailles Treaty.

The conference was officially a meeting between representatives of the governments of Britain, France, and Germany, and the US government did not send delegates. Behind the scenes, however, it was the Americans who called the shots. The J. P. Morgan banker Thomas Lamont was a key figure in the negotiations, and Owen Young, from the Dawes Committee, was there as an 'observer'. Secretary of State Charles Hughes was also in London, ostensibly as chairman of the American Bar Association, which held a large conference in Westminster in late July.[14]

Edward used this opportunity to get to know the leading American negotiators. On 21 July the Pilgrims held a dinner in Hughes's honour, which was attended by Prince Edward and several British government ministers, as well as Owen Young, Thomas Lamont, and the US Treasury Secretary, Andrew Mellon. The Prince gave the address of welcome, referring to his previous meeting with Hughes in New York, and his own wish to make another official visit to the States. In reply, Hughes, while stressing that he was not in England in his capacity as Secretary of State, set out a detailed statement of American government policy on Europe. He warmly endorsed the Dawes Plan but emphasized the US policy of 'neutrality', rejecting any notion of US government intervention, such as the advance of loans to Germany.[15]

Figure 6.2. The Pilgrims Dinner, 21 July 1924: seated, l to r, US Treasury Secretary Andrew Mellon, the Prince, US Secretary of State Charles Hughes, the Duke of Connaught

A few days later Edward invited Owen Young and his wife to lunch before a royal garden party at Buckingham Palace given for the American Bar Association visitors, and also had a lengthy discussion with Young at the garden party itself.[16] He sought Young's advice about improving Britain's image in the US; Young suggested a meeting with the press mogul William Randolph Hearst, whose newspapers had maintained a stridently anti-British stance since the war.[17]

In the midst of this activity Edward found time to visit Paris for the summer Olympic Games. The Prince attended the opening ceremony in early July, and was the speaker at a banquet given by the British Olympic Committee in honour of Pierre de Coubertin, the French founder of the Olympic movement. Speaking in French, Edward congratulated Coubertin for his long record of fostering the spirit of good sportsmanship in international competition. He concluded: 'if in time of peace we can teach the youth of the world to play the game, to become true sportsmen, we shall then see realized the great object of this movement'.[18] As to the Games themselves,

Edward was reputedly 'bored to extinction' by the athletic events. He escaped from the stadium at the earliest opportunity to watch the Olympic polo matches, where Britain and America were in contention for medals.[19]

Today the Paris Olympics are best remembered as the 'Chariots of Fire' Games. David Puttnam's 1981 film concentrated on the triumph of two British athletes, Harold Abrahams and Eric Liddell, over American competitors.[20] The reality was that the USA was by far the most successful nation in Paris, winning forty-five gold medals—more than three times the number won by its closest rival, Finland. The dominance of the Americans made them extremely unpopular in Paris at a time when France, like Britain, was struggling with the repayment of war debt. The French christened the large US team 'the army of occupation', and when they defeated France in the final of the rugby competition the American players had to be escorted off the field by police for their own safety. Both the British and American teams felt that France had besmirched the Olympic ideal and failed to come up to Anglo-Saxon standards of sportsmanship.[21] The hostility of the French press and public to the Americans was in marked contrast to the warm welcome received in London at the same time by US delegates to the Advertising Convention and the American Bar Association Conference.[22]

While he was in Paris, Edward received an invitation from the US Polo Association to attend the match series between America and Britain on Long Island later in the year. The Prince, who had already announced that he would be returning to Canada for a holiday, quickly accepted the offer. It was arranged that he would spend a fortnight in America in September, before an extended visit to the EP ranch.[23] Unlike the 1919 tour, the Prince's trip was intended to be a private one, without any official engagements. As a result, it was decided that Edward should take only a small staff with him. Admiral Halsey and Godfrey Thomas, who had accompanied him throughout his three imperial tours, remained at home.[24] In their place were Alan 'Tommy' Lascelles, the Prince's assistant private secretary, a comparatively junior member of staff; General 'G' Trotter, an old Grenadier and war hero whose enthusiasm for dancing was in no way dampened by having lost his right arm in the Boer War; and Edward 'Fruity' Metcalfe, an Irish cavalry officer who had joined Edward's staff in India, and who managed the Prince's equestrian activities.[25] Whereas Lascelles was a bookish and rather austere administrator, both Trotter and Metcalfe were party animals, who saw it as their duty to enable the Prince to enjoy life as much as possible.[26] If Buckingham Palace had been able to foresee the extraordinary press interest which the Prince's visit would generate in America, his staff would almost certainly have been reinforced with more senior advisers, and in particular an experienced press officer.

On a holiday trip it was inappropriate for the Prince to make use of a Royal Navy battleship, as he did on his official tours. Instead Fruity Metcalfe was sent ahead with the polo ponies while Edward and the rest of the entourage booked a scheduled passage on a Cunard liner, the SS *Berengaria*. One of the thrills of transatlantic travel in the 1920s was the possibility of rubbing shoulders with the rich and famous, and as soon as the Prince's reservations were announced there was a frantic scramble for tickets on the same crossing. Cunard's office in London was besieged by American tourists with marriageable daughters trying to secure tickets for the homeward trip aboard the *Berengaria*. By the time the ship sailed there was a passenger waiting list of over 500.[27]

The *Berengaria* sailed on 23 August, 'filled with women and marriageable daughters', and with a sizeable contingent of American reporters.[28] Cunard provided the Prince and his staff with a large suite of rooms, and it would have been easy for Edward to stay in seclusion for the whole of the six-day voyage to New York. But he was in holiday mood, and eager for diversion. He threw himself into life on board, taking walks on deck and appearing frequently in the public rooms. He took his meals in the first-class dining room, and characteristically rejected the high table in favour of an inconspicuous side table.[29] There were other friends on board, including Lord Louis Mountbatten and the politician Duff Cooper and his wife, Lady Diana Cooper. They became his main companions on the voyage, walking, chatting, and listening to jazz records on his portable gramophone.[30] Mountbatten organized a tug-o'-war team from amongst the Prince's staff, but it was soundly beaten by a beefy squad of American college boys. Duff Cooper, who took part, recorded in his diary that the Americans pulled them over so easily that they thought the rope must have broken.[31] Edward was no more successful in the individual sports, losing to another American in the pillow fight and suffering disqualification in the potato race. His run of bad form continued when he was awarded the booby prize in the fancy-dress contest for his Apache dancer costume.[32]

The press reporters on board gave the Prince and his staff a foretaste of what they were to experience in America. One evening, to Edward's intense annoyance, a drunken reporter tried to stalk him round the deck. In order to stop them bothering the Prince, Tommy Lascelles agreed to a twice-daily

Figure 6.3. Crossing the Atlantic on SS *Berengaria*, August 1924: l to r, 'G' Trotter, the Prince, Tommy Lascelles, David Boyle

press briefing. 'Mine is no light job,' he complained, 'one must think about every word one says to the brutes, and to say nothing that could be twisted or perverted.'[33]

Every evening during the voyage there was a ripple of excitement as the Prince entered the ballroom. 'Solomon in all his glory did not equal the majority of the women between 14 and 84, resplendent with fine raiment and sparkling jewels,' reported the *New York Times*. True to form, Edward singled out a young American as his regular dance partner for the voyage. Leonore Cahill from St Louis, Missouri, was returning from Europe with her aunt. She was small in stature, with soft brown hair and hazel eyes. The Prince danced with her on several occasions, and on the last evening 'G' Trotter entertained her to dinner at his table.[34] Commenting on the news reports, the comedian Will Rogers joked that there would now be hundreds of disappointed debutantes demanding their money back from Cunard.[35] Like Carolyn Granberry in Panama, Leonore enjoyed her brief moment of national fame, giving much-needed copy to the numerous reporters on board. She described the Prince as democratic and easy to talk to, 'exactly

Figure 6.4. Leonore Cahill aboard the SS *Berengaria*, August 1924

like an attractive young American'.[36] By the time her photograph appeared in the papers Edward had already begun an affair with a wealthy New York socialite he met on Long Island.[37]

If Edward had hoped to slip into America unobtrusively he was to be disappointed. The *Berengaria* arrived to the largest gathering of reporters and photographers ever seen in New York. Since he was making a private visit, he had not planned to speak to the press, but at the last minute the British Ambassador, Sir Esme Howard, sent a radio message advising that he should give a brief press conference after all, as a boatload of seventy-five correspondents was waiting to meet the ship after it cleared quarantine.[38] Lascelles naively assumed that this would encourage reporters to leave Edward alone while he was on Long Island. It was an uncomfortable interview. In one-hundred-degree heat the pressmen surrounded the Prince 'like a pack of hounds' and fired questions at him simultaneously. Flustered and visibly embarrassed, Edward felt in his pockets for a prepared statement. Suddenly a young woman journalist pushed through the throng and asked the inevitable question: 'would you marry an American girl if you fell in love with one?' According to the contemporary newspaper reports the Prince smiled but did not reply. Recounting the incident in his memoirs, however, Edward claimed that his affirmative answer had been drowned out by the gale of laughter from the other reporters which followed the question.[39] Edward's recollection was remarkably good, as he quoted the reporter's question verbatim as recorded in the papers the following day. If he really had said 'yes' it would have caused an international sensation, and the King would probably have summoned him straight home. Perhaps the sheer directness of the question prompted him to come to that conclusion, unsaid, within his own mind.

A private yacht was waiting off Staten Island to pick up the Prince and his staff and ferry them on to Long Island. The yacht took them through the heart of New York, under Brooklyn Bridge, and up the East River. Like Edward in 1919, Tommy Lascelles was dazzled by his first sight of Manhattan; he compared it with the Taj Mahal in terms of its architectural impact.[40] Their final destination was the Woodside mansion in Syosset, near Cold Spring Harbor on Long Island, which the industrialist James Burden had lent to the Prince for the duration of his stay.[41]

Before the Prince could start his holiday proper, however, he had to pay a courtesy call on President Calvin Coolidge, who had invited him to a private family lunch in the White House on 30 August. Determined to keep the visit as brief as possible, Edward made a day trip to Washington by rail, entailing a round trip of ten hours on the train and only three in the capital.[42] In order to make an early start the Prince spent the night in the Pullman car of the royal train in a siding near the Burden mansion. Reporters camped out all night nearby to track his movements. Edward was expected at the Pullman at about 11 p.m. but did not arrive until 2 a.m., when a fleet of Rolls-Royces drove up from the house. Everything then went quiet, but at about 4 a.m. the Prince was seen smoking a cigarette on the observation platform of the carriage, still fully dressed. One reporter suggested, with unwitting irony, that the only time the Prince could get any privacy was when everyone else was asleep.[43]

The train set off in the early morning and arrived in Washington about noon. Large crowds awaited the Prince's arrival at Union Station, where he was met by Secretary of State Hughes, now returned from Europe.

There was no formal welcoming ceremony, and he was driven straight to the White House. The lunch itself was brief; the Coolidges were mourning the loss of their teenage son, Calvin junior, who had died suddenly of blood poisoning a few weeks earlier. The Coolidges' surviving son, John, was at the lunch—he was to meet Edward again at the White House nearly fifty years later.[44] After the meal, Coolidge showed Edward round the White House and introduced him to members of the cabinet before Edward caught the train back to Long Island in mid-afternoon. On the return journey he enthusiastically accepted the opportunity to stand in the driver's cab as it passed through the tunnel under the East River.[45]

For the first two weeks of his vacation Edward devoted himself exclusively to his favourite pastimes: polo, parties, jazz, and dancing. There was no shortage of entertainment—the elite of Long Island's 'Gold Coast' fought for the honour of inviting him to their houses. He regularly attended several functions in one night, arriving back at the Burden mansion at five or six in the morning, and rising again at noon for polo practice. Whenever he appeared in public, for example at the Belmont racecourse, the Prince was mobbed by large crowds seeking to catch a glimpse of him.

Relations between the Prince and the press were strained from the outset. Having no official schedule, Edward had expected that reporters would show the same restraint as the British press, and leave him in peace to enjoy his holiday. In an attempt to protect the Prince's privacy, the police threw a cordon round the Burden mansion so that reporters could not get within five hundred yards of the estate. The pressmen, on the other hand, scenting a promising human-interest story, wanted to know every detail of Edward's day. With no public engagements to report, the press made the Prince's taste for all-night parties the main story. 'Wales and milkman arrive about the same wee morning hour' was a typical headline; 'Prince spends third consecutive night dancing until sun up'. At the end of the first week one newspaper calculated that Edward's average time of return was 5.17 ¾ a.m.[46]

Kept in the dark about the Prince's whereabouts, the pressmen took to chasing him round Long Island in a long motorcade, while Edward's chauffeur drove at breakneck speed to elude them. One afternoon a woman reporter from the *Daily News* managed to engage the Prince in conversation as he was going out to practise at the Grace Polo Field. When the Prince complained to her about the press harassing him, the reporter explained that because there were no briefings, the press was forced to trail him in order to cover his activities. She asked that a member of the Prince's staff give twice-daily press conferences, to which Edward readily agreed. The reporter then asked an incredulous Prince what he had eaten for breakfast.[47] From then on, Lascelles was required to hold regular press briefings, and tried to deal with them as if he were in London, issuing short statements along the lines of the traditional Court Circular.

The international polo series, which Edward had come to Long Island to watch, was something of an anticlimax. The matches were postponed several times because of torrential rain, and when they were finally played the US team won with embarrassing ease. The dominance of the Americans on the polo field was as complete as it had been at the Olympic Games. On 13 September a crowd of 35,000 at the Meadowbrook Club saw America beat Britain 16–3. According to The Times, the British polo team sustained the most overwhelming defeat in the history of the international matches,[48] and the American press christened the US team 'the Four Horsemen of the Polo Eclipse'. The second match was little better, with the USA winning 14–5. By the second period of the match most of the crowd had lost interest and were on their feet trying to catch a glimpse of the Prince. Edward upheld Britain's growing reputation as sporting losers by enthusiastically applauding the Americans' play and by drinking from the victors' cup at the end of the day.[49]

Early in September the American Polo Association gave a dinner in Edward's honour at the Piping Rock Club on Long Island. The after-dinner speaker was Will Rogers, the famous 'Cowboy Comedian', who was then performing in the Ziegfeld Follies in New York.[50] In the spring of 1924 Edward had suffered several riding accidents, and his frequent falls had become a standing joke in the US press. Will Rogers was one of his few defenders: as a professional horseman he knew that riding was dangerous and that, even for the most accomplished riders, falls were frequent. He asked, 'Are the Prince and I supposed to fall with the horse or are we supposed to stay up in the air until the horse gets up and comes back under us?'[51] Heartened by Rogers's support, Edward sent Metcalfe backstage at the Follies to invite him to speak at the Piping Rock dinner.

Tommy Lascelles described Rogers's stand-up routine at the dinner: 'His stunt is just to stand up and make a rambling, extempore speech about current topics...it was one of the funniest things I've ever listened to—mostly about HRH—who adored it.' Rogers's usual routine went on for fifteen minutes but on this occasion he continued for over half an hour, prompted by Edward, who whispered suggestions in his ear. Rogers joked that although he could not offer the Prince a Long Island mansion, he could give him a

Figure 6.5. Will Rogers

cot in his dressing room at the Ziegfeld Follies, where some of the most beautiful girls in the world passed the door. 'You have made yourself right popular, Prince, in spite of your birth,' said Rogers. 'I admire a man that can rise above his surroundings.'[52]

The Prince and the comedian struck up an immediate rapport. They chatted about horses and ranching, and Edward invited Rogers to play polo with him the following day. A fortnight later, Rogers entertained the Prince again at a private dinner in Manhattan.[53] He wrote up their meeting in his weekly column, giving a favourable but very perceptive sketch of the Prince's character: 'Kidding aside, the Kid is there. He is a Regular Guy, and that is saying a whole lot in his case, for everyone around him...seems to try their best to keep him from being human.'[54] For Rogers the kudos of being 'Purveyor of American Gags to His Majesty the Prince' was obvious, and he recycled the material into his regular performances at the Ziegfeld Follies and in his newspaper columns. But there were benefits in their friendship for the Prince too. Rogers's endorsement of him as a 'Regular Guy' enhanced his reputation as a genuine and democratic personality, and he subsequently suffered less derision in America over his riding mishaps.[55] They kept up their acquaintance: Rogers later bought one of the Prince's polo ponies, and in 1926, when Rogers was on tour in London, Edward went to see his show and invited him to visit his London home at York House.[56]

Despite Will Rogers's encouragement, Edward did not, as far as we know, strike up a relationship with a showgirl from the Follies while he was in America. Nevertheless, he did find time for a brief holiday romance. 'We hadn't been in the house two hours', wrote Lascelles, 'before a new comet blazed across our sky and Honey's [i.e. the Prince's] wagon was firmly hitched to it... it is of course only a matter of time before the telescopes of Hearst pick it up.'[57] The 'comet' in question was Pinna Cruger, the wife of a New York haberdashery millionaire, Frederic Cruger. Before her marriage she had been a silent-movie actress. She was petite and brown-haired with large hazel eyes, and an excellent dancer. Scott Fitzgerald described her as a 'damned attractive woman'. Pinna became Edward's favourite dance partner, and probably his lover, during his stay on Long Island. As Lascelles had feared, the relationship did find its way into the press. The papers reported that in the small hours the couple would retreat to Rodman Wanamaker's houseboat at Cold Spring Harbor, where they would dance and Edward would play the drums with the orchestra. The Crugers were guests at a party given by the Prince in Manhattan on the eve of his departure.[58] Before he left he gave Pinna a gold and diamond Cartier cigarette case, inscribed in the Prince's hand, 'Pinna 1924 love—EP'. Rumours of the gift circulated in the press; in one report it was said to be a platinum vanity box encrusted with diamonds and emeralds.[59] Pinna's voyage to Europe in 1925 prompted speculation of a more lasting affair, but the following year, having divorced Cruger, she remarried.[60]

By coincidence, at the very time when Edward was holidaying on Long Island, 'that slender, riotous island which extends itself due east of New York',[61] Scott Fitzgerald was on the French Riviera finishing *The Great Gatsby*. The Prince could easily have appeared in the novel as a minor character, playing polo with Tom Buchanan, or slipping into one of Gatsby's parties after midnight for a late supper. Edward was feted at the fashionable mansions of the 'old-money' families which Nick Carraway gazed at across the bay from West Egg. The Prince's own account of a party given by Clarence Mackay at Harbor Hill would not have disgraced the pages of *Gatsby*.

> As darkness fell and the guests began to arrive, the trees lining the winding avenue leading to the house were illuminated with orange coloured lights. Towering above the roof was the Stars and Stripes in electric lights... The dance music was provided by two bands directed by the great Paul Whiteman, who at a later stage was inspired to lead his musicians in a march round the hall weaving in and out of the shadowy figures in armour.[62]

Edward does make an appearance in a short story by Zelda Fitzgerald, titled 'The Girl the Prince Liked', in which Helena, a Long Island heiress, has a brief affair with an English prince who is clearly modelled on Edward.[63] The story is little more than a sketch, one of five 'girl' stories written shortly before Zelda's breakdown in 1930. Helena is a brilliant and charismatic figure, who cuts a swathe through Jazz Age America, breaking hearts. The Prince picks her out at a party in Chicago, and 'sat talking with her through a heavy, silhouetting moon, on a balcony, both of them dangling their legs over the Renaissance balustrade'. They meet again in Paris and London, and at the end of the affair, perhaps in an echo of the rumours of Pinna Cruger's cigarette case, the Prince gives her a jewelled bracelet. The story closes on an ambivalent note: '[she] has so little of the romantic about her that, so the story goes, she took the bracelet (which she will always keep as proof that romance has not passed from the world) into a jeweler's to have it valued'.

The Prince was not the only one in search of a holiday affair. During the visit Fruity Metcalfe caused a brief panic when he left his wallet behind at the Manhattan apartment of Virginia de Lanty, a pretty, dark-haired dancer. 'The incident might do the Prince serious harm', Lascelles wrote to his wife, 'but we have all rocked with laughter over it.'[64] In one garbled account of the affair, Fruity was visiting a brothel, and finding he was unable to pay, was forced to flee without his trousers. The truth appears more prosaic. After leaving Virginia's apartment on 72nd Street, Metcalfe realized his wallet was missing. Thinking that she had stolen it, he called the police, who on investigation found the wallet behind a radiator in the apartment. The press caught wind of the affair and quickly tracked Virginia down. In a lively interview she claimed that the wallet in fact belonged to the Prince, and that she had taken Edward and Fruity in disguise on a late-night tour of the nightclubs of Greenwich Village. She was unimpressed by the Prince, describing him as a miserable waltzer, who talked of polo ponies as if they were human beings. The latter detail has the ring of authenticity, although it could have applied equally well to Metcalfe.[65]

The incident gave the Prince and his staff a few anxious days as they waited to see whether the press would pursue the story. Lascelles wrote the British Ambassador a panicky letter referring to 'a misadventure of Metcalfe's in which he lost his pocket-book in surroundings where he had much better not have been'. He stressed that the Prince had not been involved in any way. Although the story did leak out, it was not pushed hard in the American press, perhaps because of the 'gentlemen's agreement' by the big newspaper editors following their meeting with the Prince a few days earlier. Not surprisingly, Metcalfe was in disgrace, and Edward's relationship with him cooled perceptibly for a while.[66]

The Prince and his staff were totally unprepared for the tsunami of press coverage which they encountered in America. Conditioned by the deferential approach to the monarchy of the Fleet Street editors in the UK, they had expected that the American press would behave in the same manner. Frustrated by the adverse coverage, and worried about the likely reaction from the King and his advisers, Tommy Lascelles had to improvise a response while they were on Long Island. He drafted a statement giving details of the Prince's official work in the UK and overseas. It emphasized that the Prince's tours were motivated above all by a desire to meet ordinary people. 'It is this love for frank and active humanity that has inspired in the Prince a real affection for America and Americans.' The main news item in the statement was an announcement that the Prince intended to make a tour of the industrial regions of the USA at the earliest opportunity.[67] Released through the Associated Press Agency so that it would not be directly traceable to the Prince's staff, the statement was carried in newspapers across America, and helped deflect criticism of the 'indefatigable vacationist'.[68] What really made the difference, however, was a tea party which Lascelles organized for the Prince to meet the leading New York press editors. The group included Arthur Brisbane and Herbert Swope, whom Lascelles described as 'Hearst's ablest and most vitriolic editors, who have done us infinite harm since the War'.[69] It was a high-risk strategy, which Lascelles had not cleared with the British Embassy. The editors could have refused the invitation, and generated further negative headlines in the process. As it turned out, the Prince worked his charm successfully. 'It was a howling success,' wrote a relieved Lascelles to his wife. 'It was amusing to see how every one of them ... succumbed to him completely after five minutes talk.' The editors kept the meeting confidential, and afterwards the press coverage was noticeably friendlier towards the Prince.[70]

Lascelles was right to be concerned about the reaction from the Palace to the American press reports. News of Edward's strenuous holiday regime soon filtered back to Britain. The accounts in the British press of late-night parties and mob scenes at polo matches were restrained by comparison with those in America, but they were enough to alarm the King and his advisers. In October the King's Private Secretary, Lord Stamfordham, received a letter from a British expatriate in New York, complaining of the Prince's unseemly behaviour in America and enclosing press cuttings. Stamfordham sought the advice of the British Ambassador in Washington, Sir Esme Howard, who played down the whole affair: 'the press has become such a byword for exaggerated fiction over here that people are paying less and less attention to it'. Unfortunately the Ambassador's soothing words were soon undermined by reports of Metcalfe's misadventure in Manhattan, which apparently reached the desk of Queen Mary.[71]

The Prince had originally planned to spend only a fortnight in the US, but with the repeated postponement of the polo matches he decided to stay an extra week. Having danced Long Island to a standstill, Edward chose to fill the time with a series of informal visits to New York. The idea was to display the more serious side of his character, and to dispel the impression that he was only interested in frivolous pursuits. His host was Colonel Arthur Woods, the former New York City Police Commissioner, who acted as his unofficial guide round Manhattan. On 12 September he rode the subway, went to the top of the Woolworth Building—the tallest building in the world—and made an impromptu call at the Port Society, a hostel where British sailors stayed between Atlantic crossings.[72] On subsequent trips he went to Wall Street and the Stock Exchange, toured the Natural History Museum, and saw a ballgame between the Giants and the Cincinnati Reds at the Polo Grounds; he admired the facilities of the newly built Julia Richman public school, and was shown round the New York Times offices on 43rd Street. Edward's programme was not announced in advance and, hoping to escape attention, he travelled without a police escort. However, he was frequently recognized, and when he drove down Broadway to the financial district, the crowd of admirers pressed so tightly round his limousine that the doors could not be opened. The Prince did not confine himself to sightseeing. In the course of his visits to the city he had meetings with leading businessmen, including Harrison Williams, the founder of American Gas & Electric, Clarence Dillon of Dillon Read, and Charles A. Coffin of General Electric. He also followed up on his speech at the Advertising Convention in London in July by making a brief visit to the New York Advertising Club. On his final evening in Manhattan, on 18 September, the Prince went to the theatre, and afterwards threw a farewell party for his hosts at the Lido Venice restaurant. Will Rogers again provided the entertainment, along with the Dolly Sisters vaudeville dance act.[73]

The Prince finally left Long Island on 21 September. The following day he was already planning a return visit to the USA. He outlined his proposals in a letter to Esme Howard. After his successful discussions with the New York newspaper bosses, he was keen to meet William Randolph Hearst in person. Judge Ebert Gary, the Chairman of US Steel, had offered to set up a meeting for the Prince late in October, on his return from the EP ranch. Edward also wanted to visit Chicago to see the stockyards, and the Ford Motor works in Detroit. In reply, Howard was enthusiastic about a short tour of the Midwest, but opposed the idea of the Prince returning to New York. He was concerned that a meeting with Hearst could be interpreted as having a political motive, in view of the impending presidential election in early November. The trip to the Midwest went ahead, but Edward had only the briefest stopover in New York before the voyage home.[74]

After the long train journey across Canada, the Prince and his staff finally arrived at the EP ranch on 26 September. The original intention had been to spend several weeks there. In the event they stayed there for only five days before Edward's restlessness got the better of him, and they set off again through the Rockies for a visit to Vancouver. They were soon back in the USA, arriving at Duluth, Minnesota, on 12 October en route to Chicago and Detroit.[75]

The Prince's visit to the Midwest reflected his interest in industrial development, and was the result of personal invitations from Louis F. Swift, the Chicago meat-packing entrepreneur, and Henry Ford. Edward had met Swift on the *Berengaria* on the voyage from England, and Ford on his North American tour in 1919.[76] The main purpose of the visit to Chicago was for the Prince to see the Union Stockyards, the largest meat-packing district in the world. Swift took Edward around the animal pens on horseback, and showed him the various stages of meat processing, including the margarine factory. He was entertained to lunch at the University of Chicago, and later visited the Field Museum, where he met Canadian and US veterans. After tea and a game of squash at the Racquet Club, Edward went on to a dinner and dance at the Saddle and Cycle Club. He left shortly before 1 a.m. and travelled overnight by train to Detroit.[77]

Henry Ford had prepared an elaborate reception for the Prince's visit on 14 October. It was reported that $50,000 had been spent removing machinery and widening the aisles at the Highland Park factory so that Edward could be driven through the plant in a Lincoln limousine. On the way round the plant the Prince watched a crack team, dressed in white overalls and wielding nickel-plated spanners, assemble a 'Prince of Wales Special', in which Henry and Edsel Ford then drove him round the site. The team had hoped to beat the company record of 11 minutes 40 seconds for the assembly of the car, but the Prince asked them so many questions about the process that they took a full 16 minutes. Ford was impressed with the level of the Prince's knowledge of industrial processes. Edward surprised him with his understanding of electrical engineering, apparently learned during his naval training. The two men spent several hours together, and Edward promised to return to Detroit in the near future. In an interview with the *Detroit Free Press* a few days later, Ford concluded, 'England is to be congratulated on him. I'll be glad to see him when he comes again.'[78]

Edward's brief tour of the Midwest showed that there was a more serious side to his American vacation. Tommy Lascelles was in no doubt: 'All the surface chat in the papers gives a totally wrong impression of the visit. Underneath he has in his own little way done as much good to the British Empire as the Baldwin debt settlement.'[79] Lascelles admired the Prince's extraordinary ability to charm even the most hostile audiences, from Irish republican factory workers to hard-bitten press barons. The *New York Times*, which had followed the Prince's trip closely, took a similar view: 'His coming was welcome, his presence a pleasure, and his departure is regretted. He could claim that he had served both his country and this one too, by increasing the amity which is so essential to the prosperity of both.'[80] In the USA he was 'off duty' in a way that he never could be within the vast shadow of the British Empire. He could pursue his own interests and inclinations, and briefly shrug off the straitjacket of royal protocol. He used the opportunity to extend his impressive network of American contacts. All doors were open to him; he had met President Coolidge and renewed his acquaintance with Secretary of State Charles Hughes. He was on good terms with industrial giants like Henry Ford and Louis Swift. He knew the leading financiers, Charles Dawes, Owen Young, and Andrew Mellon. They all responded to his infectious enthusiasm to learn about the American way of doing business. The Prince was keen to build on these links by returning to the USA as often as he could. When he left New York on the SS *Olympic* on 25 October, he issued a press statement saying that he had enjoyed his stay and that he looked forward to returning soon, a reference to his planned visit to industrial centres in 1926.[81]

The King and his advisers drew the opposite conclusion from the Prince's American holiday. Edward faced an extremely cool reception from his father on his return. When they met, King George had a large pile of cuttings on his desk. Near the top was one which read, 'Here he is girls, the most eligible bachelor yet uncaught. Oh, who'll ask him what he wears asleep?' The King, accustomed to the exaggerated deference which the British press showed towards the royal family, was horrified. He told his son, 'If this vulgarity represents the American attitude towards people in your position, little purpose would be served in exposing yourself to this kind of treatment.'[82] It was an ominous warning, dashing Edward's hopes of returning to the States for further visits.

A few weeks after his return from North America, Edward was the guest of honour at the Thanksgiving Dinner held by the American Society in

Figure 6.6. Miguel Covarrubias, *The Prince of Wales and Other Famous Americans*, frontispiece

London. There he gave a remarkable speech. Written in the style of a Will Rogers monologue—presumably by Tommy Lascelles—it was witty, informal, and full of Americanisms, testifying to the impact upon him of his trip to the USA. Acknowledging the warm reception he received from the mainly American audience, he said that he felt transported back across the Atlantic, and that, 'if I look out of the window, I shall see the Woolworth Building and the Wrigley Twins'.[83] Referring to the blanket press coverage which accompanied his trip, he said that he hesitated to tell the audience about his experiences: 'if any of you read your American newspapers during the time I was there, you would know a great deal more about my stay than I do myself'. He alluded briefly to his visits to Chicago and Detroit: 'one turns live pig into little bits as fast as the other turns little bits into live automobiles'. He referred to the friendship he struck up with Will Rogers, despite the jokes which Rogers had made at his expense. Finally, he once more expressed the hope that he would be able to return to the USA very soon.

Edward's North American trip of 1924 established his popular reputation in the USA as the 'Jazz Age Prince', a party loving playboy who danced until dawn and rose at noon to play polo. Writing a decade later, an American biographer of the Prince observed: 'He belonged very definitely to the period—the dance-mad, jazz crazy, war-marked five years, that were . . . to end in the tragic crash of October 1929.'[84] Because Edward did not return to the US until after his Abdication, the visit long remained the strongest impression which most Americans had of the Prince. Over the years the hectic summer days and nights on Long Island were often recycled into feature articles about the Prince.[85] The year 1924 also consolidated Edward's position as an authentic American celebrity. In 1925, the Mexican-American artist Miguel Covarrubias published a collection of cartoons titled *The Prince of Wales and Other Famous Americans*.[86] The title reflected the extent to which the Prince (or more accurately the image of the Prince created by the US media) had been absorbed into American popular culture. Formally dressed as if for a race meeting, a cigarette in one hand and a cane in the other, Covarrubias's Prince is part bachelor-about-town and part vaudeville song-and-dance act. The caricature captures the essence of Edward's appeal to the American public.

Whereas in Britain he was a revered, almost sacred figure, in America he was more like a Hollywood star. Glamorous and stylish, familiar yet unattainable, he was above all a media celebrity.

7

'The Prince of Wales and Other Famous Americans'

Edward and the American Media

'The Press creates; the Press destroys', wrote the Prince ruefully in his account of the Abdication crisis in 1936. 'All my life I had been the passive clay which it had enthusiastically worked into the hackneyed image of a Prince Charming. Now it was bent upon demolishing the natural man who had been there all along.'[1] For twenty years Edward was the most famous man on earth, his travels, speeches, tastes, lifestyle, and dress reported in the most trivial detail in the media throughout the world.[2] In Britain and the empire his position as Prince of Wales conferred an automatic fame upon him. It is less immediately obvious why Edward came to attract such an extraordinary level of public attention in America, with its strongly republican traditions and history of anti-British feeling. Between 1919 and 1935, Edward transcended his role as a British prince to emerge as one of the greatest American celebrities of the inter-war era: a figure as famous as Babe Ruth, Charles Lindbergh, and Clark Gable, and a media phenomenon in his own right.

'These Yank pressmen are b____ds': Facing the Media

The rise of the mass media in the USA was the product of the rapid industrialization and urbanization of the country which took place in the two generations after the American Civil War. Central to its development was the creation of a national communications and information network, initially in the form of print journalism. Press barons such as William Randolph Hearst and E. W. Scripps, the founder of the news agency UPI, built up national chains of newspapers, centralizing management and standardizing content through the establishment of wire services and syndicated feature articles. Technological advances made possible the transmission and reproduction of photographic images, facilitating the development of tabloid photo-journalism and mass-circulation magazines. Newspapers extended their appeal to a much broader cross-section of society, especially women and working-class readers. From the 1890s a national mass culture developed in the USA, displacing older regional cultures. This reflected wider trends in American society, with the consolidation of industries into national groupings, improvements in transport, and the expansion of the role of the federal government.[3]

The development of a national print culture was soon followed by the growth of the movie and radio industries in the first three decades of the twentieth century. Both these new media spread across America with astonishing speed. The first 'nickelodeons' began to appear in around 1905, and by 1930 there were over 20,000 movie theatres across the country, catering to weekly audiences of 90 million. The radio networks developed even more quickly. In 1920 only one in five hundred households in America had a radio; by 1930 there was one in virtually every home.[4]

Prince Edward was the first member of the British royal family directly to encounter the modern American media and, with the possible exception of Princess Diana, he filled more column inches than any other member of the House of Windsor in the twentieth century. At the end of his three-week holiday on Long Island in 1924, the Hemstreet Clipping Bureau presented Edward with a complete set of press cuttings for the visit. Twenty-four clerks had worked continuously for fourteen days to compile the cuttings. There were 61,120 items in all, contained in an album weighing 325 pounds. The Bureau confirmed that it was more than any President had received in so short a time.[5] Such a huge weight of press coverage was all the more remarkable in that nothing of importance had happened during the Prince's stay. The only contemporary event in America which was to surpass it as a media phenomenon was Charles Lindbergh's historic solo flight across the Atlantic in 1927.[6]

Why did Prince Edward appeal so strongly to the American press and public? It was a heady mix of royalty and personal charisma. Undoubtedly Edward's status as the heir to the British Empire made him the subject of great public interest in the USA. Britain was still a world power in the 1920s, and the historical and cultural links between the two nations made the British royal family an obvious focus of media attention. American public life lacked the traditional ritual and pageantry at which the British monarchy excelled.[7] Events such as the coronation of King George V and the investiture of Edward as Prince of Wales in 1911 were widely covered in the press and in newsreel across the States.

Combined with the mystique of monarchy, and yet subtly contrasting with it, was Edward's own personality. He was young, handsome, and unmarried, with an unmistakable air of diffidence and vulnerability. His behaviour was democratic and his tastes modern: he hated pomp and formality, and enjoyed jazz, dancing, and competitive sports. On a personal level he could charm even the most obdurate: hard-bitten journalists, Irish republicans, and socialist trade unionists all fell under his spell. Pondering the question of the Prince's appeal, one American commentator came to the following conclusion:

> He is a romantic figure, who declares he will marry the girl he loves; he is game; he is a boy—like a son coming home; he is the Peter Pan of the European nobility; Americans love romance, adventure, gameness and good looks, coupled with personality.[8]

What the American public experienced, of course, was an image of the Prince refracted through the media of the press, film, and radio. That image was an artificial construct, a compromise between the royal personage that the Prince's advisers sought to project and the portrait which newspaper editors and newsreel producers decided to present to the public. As a result, Edward's media image in America evolved differently from his image at home. In Britain the monarchy was an important symbol of national unity and identity, and in the inter-war period it was virtually above criticism. Media coverage of the royal family was extremely deferential and operated within tight parameters. Fleet Street, where the British national newspapers were based, was still a small and close-knit world, dominated by influential editors such as Geoffrey Dawson of *The Times*, and press barons like Lord Rothermere of the *Daily Mail* and Lord Beaverbrook of the *Daily Express* who maintained close links with the political establishment. The press was generally prepared to portray the monarchy as it sought to present itself, and to restrict reporting largely to the royal family's public role. Their private lives were strictly taboo, except to the extent that they reflected an idealized model of the happy British family.[9] As a result, the British public between the wars had an idealized view of the prince, untainted by any knowledge of his flirtations and love affairs.

The American media were under no such constraints, and while coverage of the Prince was for the most part positive, it focused far more on his private life and personal tastes than on his official duties. American journalists had no tradition of deference to royalty, and were far less restrained in pursuing royal stories. 'These Yank pressmen are b——ds', wrote Edward from the SS *Berengaria* on his way to New York in 1924. 'One does resent their d——d spying so, and they get so tight!'[10] When Edward and his staff came to America they brought with them expectations of media behaviour that they derived from their experience in Britain—broadly that the media would report the stories presented to them by the Prince's press officers, and keep a respectful distance when Edward was off duty. On the official tour of 1919 this mismatch of expectations did not matter: the Prince's programme was so full that there were more than enough stories to report, and Edward, eager to impress his American hosts, charmed the media and public alike.[11] In 1924 relations with the press were much more strained. Edward and his staff were unprepared for the extent of coverage which they encountered, and attempted at first to keep the media away from the Prince. Since Edward was not carrying out any official engagements apart from his flying visit to Washington, the newspapers gave exaggerated publicity to his 'amusements, expensive tastes, uselessness etc', as Tommy Lascelles described it.[12] The Prince felt harried by the press, and the press found the Prince's staff arrogant and unprofessional.

Prince Edward's encounter with the American press in 1924 revealed the ambivalence which underlay royal attitudes towards the media. Like most public figures, members of the House of Windsor were happy to use the media on their own terms, to project the image which they wished to present to the world. However, at the same time they sought to impose strict controls on media access, and the content of stories which newspapers should publish. In Britain this was possible, but in America the press could not be held on such a short leash. Shortly after Edward's departure a critical but well-reasoned account of the visit appeared in an article syndicated across America. The writer, the *New York World* columnist Oliver Garrett, blamed the tensions on poor press briefing by the Prince's staff. Journalists were given inadequate information and were forced to pursue Edward round Long Island because it was the only way they could find out about his activities.[13] The Prince had expected to be left alone because he was not in

America in an official capacity. What he failed to appreciate, according to Garrett, was that 'to men and women whose imagination was fired by him as by a fascinating tale, his private excursions became far more important and interesting than his formal appearances'.[14] The Prince's vacation was the human-interest story par excellence.

Perhaps the most intrusive element of the media's pursuit of the Prince, both in Britain and America, was the press photographer. To the men who had fought in the Great War, the ranks of cameramen that Edward faced wherever he went reminded them vividly of trench warfare. A journalist reporting the Prince's arrival in Canada wrote of the 'massed battalions of [mainly American] cameramen', carrying their heavy equipment 'with all the energy of Lewis gunners'. In 1927 Tommy Lascelles described Edward reading the lesson at an open-air service for veterans 'in the teeth of a heavy barrage of photographers and movie-men'. For Edward himself, to be shot by the cameramen was a form of assassination: as he wrote many years later, 'photography, killing the private lives of princes, made me familiar to all'.[15] In the 1920s and 1930s Edward's picture was as ubiquitous in newspapers and magazines across the world as was Princess Diana's sixty years later. In 1928 the *New York Times* included the Prince in its list of the ten most photographed persons on earth, alongside Lindbergh, Babe Ruth, and Mussolini.

Figure 7.1. The Prince faces the cameras, Canada, 1919

'Flying in an aeroplane or over a horse's head,' concluded the *Times*, 'he is the perpetual game of the camera hunter; there is no closed season for him.'[16]

The royal family themselves were partly to blame for this state of affairs. In the nineteenth century Queen Victoria and Prince Albert had embraced the new technology of photography as a means of promoting an image of the monarchy as the nation's model family.[17] Photographs of Prince Edward were published from his earliest infancy, beginning with the famous 'Four Generations' shots of his christening in 1894.[18] During the Boer War pictures were widely circulated of the 5-year-old Edward saluting with a wooden rifle. Buckingham Palace was happy for royal photographs to be published provided that they were authorized and reflected the traditionally dignified image of the monarchy.

Throughout Edward's childhood and youth, and while he was in the army, the royal household had no difficulty in controlling the images of the Prince. From 1919, however, as he set out on his tours of the empire, Edward became one of the most photographed men in the world. With portable cameras becoming standard equipment for press photographers, it was harder to ensure that unseemly pictures of the Prince did not become publicly available. Consequently Buckingham Palace sought both to restrict the type of photograph which could be taken, and to control the flow of images to the press by giving privileged access to an official royal photographer. Within the British Empire this policy was quite successful: cameramen were expected to adhere to a strict set of rules: the Prince should not be photographed in close-up; he should not be photographed playing golf or other informal sports; he should not be photographed with ladies; and finally, he should not be photographed 'whenever he royally does not want to be'.[19] An official royal photographer accompanied the Prince on all his tours; in America and Australia it was Ernest Brooks, who had grown up on the Windsor estate, and had been the royal photographer since 1910. He produced some of the most famous photographs of the Prince, including the 'Smiling Prince' portrait taken at the start of the North American tour of 1919.[20]

The Palace's restrictive policy on photography worked surprisingly well in Britain, largely owing to the compliant approach which the Fleet Street editors adopted on reporting the royal family. Although the American press was less constrained, in an age before the paparazzi few informal shots found their way to newspapers in the USA. Paradoxically, the ones that did usually emanated from the Prince's own staff. During the Australian tour, for example, a picture emerged of the Prince bathing with Louis Mountbatten

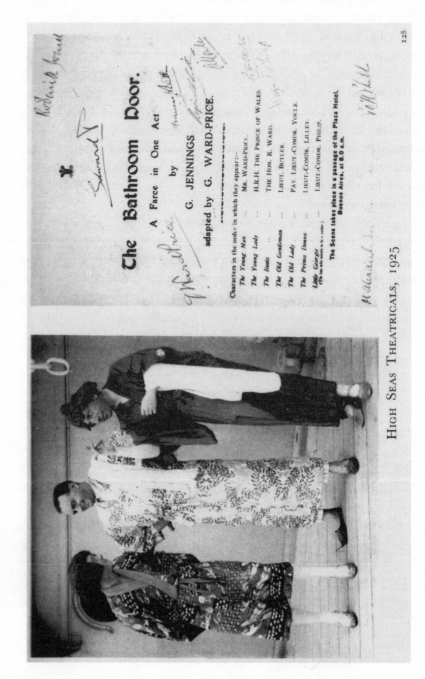

Figure 7.2. The Prince in women's clothes

on board HMS *Renown*. When the King saw it he was outraged: 'You might as well be photographed *naked*, no doubt it would please the public,' he complained to his son.[21] The shot had been taken by Brooks, the royal photographer, who had released it without authorization, and he received a reprimand from the Prince.[22] Still less dignified was a photograph printed in the *Washington Times* and elsewhere in 1925, showing the Prince dressed in drag. The British Ambassador in Washington assumed that it was a fake, and asked the Foreign Secretary if he should issue a rebuttal. In fact it was a picture taken of some amateur theatricals which Edward's equerry Joey Legh had written as a diversion aboard HMS *Repulse* on the long sea voyage during the Prince's tour of South America.[23]

Occasionally the Prince managed to subvert his own image in public, in front of the press cameras. His falls while hunting or steeple-chasing became so frequent that photographers would gather at the fences to catch his mishaps. He had a particularly bad fall at an army point-to-point near Windsor in March 1924, when he broke his collarbone. One cameraman captured a dazed

Figure 7.3. The Prince falls from his horse again, April 1924

and dishevelled Prince being helped to his feet, and this was the picture which was published in many American newspapers.[24]

In Britain the tabloid *Daily Mirror* published the shot, but most newspapers printed a less graphic photograph of Edward being carried off on a stretcher.[25] On another occasion, when the Prince fell at the first fence of a steeple-chase, he stood up and shouted at the photographers, 'Can't you b——s go to the second jump for a change?'[26]

Up-to-date pictures were an essential part of any story on the Prince, but for sheer immediacy still photography could not compete with the news-reels. The British newsreel companies were intensely patriotic in the inter-war period, and royalty was their favourite subject. After initial uncertainty the royal family had accepted the new medium during the Great War, recognizing it as an effective way of projecting a positive public image of the monarchy.[27] The official newsreel cameraman who accompanied the Prince throughout his North American tour of 1919 was Tracy Mathewson, a pioneering cinematographer from Atlanta, Georgia. Edward found 'Fatty' Mathewson highly entertaining, and the two men got on well with each other. Almost by chance, Mathewson played an important part in shaping the Prince's screen persona. When he began shooting in Canada, Mathewson was unaware of the rule that royalty should not be filmed in close-up, and got as close as he could to the Prince to take footage. Edward, for whom newsreel cameras were still a novelty, was not disconcerted, but looked dir-ectly into the camera and smiled broadly. The result was a dazzling series of images of the handsome and photogenic young Prince introducing himself to the American public.[28] Mathewson's films were shown in the USA as well as Britain, and by the end of the tour it was estimated that 20 million Americans had seen the newsreels of the Prince.[29]

Throughout the 1920s and 1930s Edward made regular appearances in the newsreels in America. There was no shortage of material, as the major US distributors had exchange contracts with British companies, which pro-duced footage specifically for the American market.[30] The official newsreels of Edward's later overseas tours were distributed in the USA, and American audiences also saw him in more routine domestic events such as the Armistice Day commemorations.[31] In 1933 a full-length feature film was made of the Prince's life, which was released in America following its British premiere.[32] When the opportunity arose, the Prince also performed for the American cameras. On their way to South America on the SS *Oropesa* in 1931, Edward and his brother Prince George made a special sound newsreel recording with US photographers. Fashionably dressed in double-breasted suits, bow ties, and two-tone shoes, they discussed the purpose of the visit to the British Empire Exhibition at Buenos Aires.[33]

Prince Edward was not only a familiar figure on America's theatre screens; he became a radio personality as well. In 1926 the National Broadcasting Company was established, and in 1927 a second network, the Columbia Broadcasting System.[34] With schedules to fill, the new networks looked for high-profile events to cover. The Prince was already an experienced broadcaster, having spoken many times on the BBC; he appeared so often on the radio in the 1920s that a baby's crying became known as 'another broadcast from the Prince of Wails'. He was a keen radio fan himself and had a radio system installed in the EP ranch to enable him to listen to the latest dance tunes.[35] The opening of the Peace Bridge over the Niagara River between Canada and the USA in August 1927 provided the opportunity for Edward to make his first American radio broadcast. The entire two-hour ceremony was carried live, culminating in speeches by the Prince and Vice-President Charles Dawes as they stood in the middle of the bridge. According to the news reports Edward's voice was high-pitched, clear, and easy to understand, although he spoke hesitantly.[36] The broadcast went out on stations throughout America, and it was heard by an estimated 50 million people. Thereafter Edward made frequent broadcasts on US radio. In July 1930 NBC relayed a speech from London which the Prince was giving to launch a fund-raising appeal for the international activities of the National Union of Students. In the course of his speech, ever mindful of his American audience, he praised John D. Rockefeller as a model philanthropist.[37] Edward's visit to South America in 1931 to promote British trade was closely followed in the US, on the radio as well as in the press. His opening speech at the British Empire Trade Exhibition in Buenos Aires was broadcast live on the American networks, and a few weeks later they also carried his speech from London reporting on his visit to a group of businessmen.[38]

'That Marriageable Enigma': Portraits of Prince Charming

The narrative which the American media constructed of Edward's life between 1919 and 1935 was woven out of three main themes: his marriage prospects and romances, real or imagined;[39] his lifestyle and personal tastes;

and his work as a modern, democratic member of the royal family and 'Prince of Sales' for the British Empire. The question of the Prince's marriage was one of the great media stories of the age. Ironically, the constraints under which the British press operated in reporting on the monarchy severely limited the scope of what they could print on the subject. The issue could be raised in general terms, as one of genuine public interest, but the discussion of potential brides was muted, and Edward's affairs with his mistresses were off limits. Before 1936 so little was known in Britain about Edward's private life that there was an assumption in some quarters that he remained a bachelor because he was gay.[40]

By contrast the American press speculated freely and at great length throughout the 1920s and early 1930s as to whom and when the Prince might marry. Reports of possible marriage partners had appeared even before the Great War, but the end of the war gave the topic new impetus. In particular, the *Daily Express* article in 1919 suggesting that Edward should marry an American bride brought home the realization that it was no longer his destiny to marry a German Protestant princess.[41] The field was open to all comers.

In the immediate aftermath of the war it was generally accepted that the Prince would be quickly married off. He was 25 in 1919, and England had not had an unmarried monarch since Queen Elizabeth I. The American press assumed that his most likely choice lay between a princess from the remaining royal houses of Europe and the daughter of a British aristocrat. 'Unusual Tug-o'-War for the Prince of Wales' Heart' ran the headline in the *Richmond Times-Despatch,* as it weighed the charms of Princess Yolanda of Italy against those of Lady Rachel Cavendish, the daughter of the Duke of Devonshire.[42] Nevertheless, the possibility of an American bride was not entirely discounted, especially as several of the wealthiest American families were already related by marriage to the British nobility. Edward's tour of the USA in 1919 prompted lively discussion of potential candidates among eligible heiresses. The *Washington Times* suggested the popular debutante Flora Payne Whitney, whose mother was a Vanderbilt, while on his visit to Washington the Prince was reported to have been very attentive to a Southern belle, Marguerite Calhoun Simonds from Charleston, South Carolina. Marguerite's visit to London in 1920 gave rise to speculation that she was to be presented at Court as the Prince's fiancée, despite the fact that Edward was in Australia at the time.[43]

None of the rumours about Edward's impending marriage which were reported in the early 1920s had any basis in fact. The reality was that during this period Edward regarded himself as 'married' to his mistress, Freda Dudley Ward, and in any event the long series of imperial tours which he undertook left him little time to find a wife even if he had been seeking one.[44] The absence of facts did nothing, however, to deter American journalists from keeping the story alive. Any news item about the Prince or the royal family was viewed through the lens of his marriage. Thus his trip to India in 1921 inspired stories that he was to marry the daughter of a Maharajah. In 1923 the marriage of his younger brother Prince Albert was accompanied by reports of growing anxiety in Britain that Edward was still a bachelor.[45] If the Prince visited Belgium it was because he was wooing the King of Belgium's daughter; the arrival of the King and Queen of Romania in London was a sign that Edward would soon be engaged to their daughter Princess Ileana.[46] Throughout the 1920s American newspapers regularly carried confident reports that the Prince would marry yet another European princess: in 1920 Princess Yolanda of Italy, in 1926 Princess Astrid of Sweden, in 1927 Princess Beatrice of Spain, and in 1928 Princess Märtha of Sweden, Astrid's older sister.

After Edward had passed his thirtieth birthday in 1924 with no sign of marriage in prospect, his failure to find a bride became a story in its own right. 'Bachelor king to sit on throne of Britain: London abandons hope that Prince of Wales may wed' was a typical headline. There was no shortage of speculation as to why the Prince remained single, and occasionally the American press came close to the truth that love and duty were in conflict. 'It is a good wager', commented one New York newspaper, 'that he will in time be compelled to marry someone he doesn't care for half so much as someone the state would never permit him to marry.'[47]

By the 1930s the Prince's marriage prospects had become a journalistic cliché, and were the subject of frequent jokes in the American press. On his fortieth birthday on 23 June 1934 the *Anniston Star* in Alabama published an almanac entry for the day: '1894—Prince of Wales born; 1934—Prince of Wales reported engaged for 387th time'. On April Fools' Day 1935 the *Miami Daily News* carried a fake photograph on its front page showing the Prince's 'marriage' to Princess X. The bride is wearing a mask to conceal her identity from several thousand members of the 'Girls Who Have Danced With the Prince of Wales Association' who were rioting outside the Palace.[48] Yet even at this time, after twenty years of fruitless speculation, the Prince's love life continued to be a compelling human-interest story for the American public. In May 1935 the *Des Moines Register* devoted an entire page to 'Twenty-Eight Women in the Life of the Prince of Wales', providing a comprehensive résumé of all the princesses and 'dancing partners' whose names had been associated with Edward over the years. Most of those on the list were long since married, but the article was remarkably well informed about Edward's mistresses. Freda Dudley Ward and Thelma Furness were featured as close friends of the Prince, while Wallis Simpson figured prominently as Edward's frequent companion on recent vacations in Cannes and Biarritz.[49] By the time of his accession to the throne in January 1936, the American public were infinitely better informed about Edward's relationships with women than his British subjects. Whereas in England Edward's love affair with Wallis came as a bolt from the blue, in America it was the sensational dénouement of the longest running romantic saga in the history of journalism.

While they waited for the Prince of Wales to find a wife, the American newspapers pursued a lively interest in his bachelor lifestyle. Unlike the British press they reported little of Edward's ceaseless round of official duties—giving speeches, planting trees, and inspecting parades of veterans. Instead they focused on his passion for riding and polo, his love of nightclubs and jazz, and his tastes in fashion. The Prince was a reckless and accident-prone rider, and while participating in steeple-chases during the mid-1920s he fell off his horse eleven times in three years.[50] Despite the best efforts of the comedian Will Rogers to defend him, Edward's mishaps became a standing joke in the American press.[51] Soon every American who picked up a newspaper knew that the Prince was constantly falling off his horse. One writer suggested that republican conspirators must be using an 'Anti-Prince of Wales Steeplechase Radio Beam' to stun the horse as it approached a fence.[52] The image became so familiar that it was used as an advertising device: 'We're Off Again—With the Prince of Sales', proclaimed Butler's grocery store of Pittsburgh, under the picture of a cartoon Prince being thrown from his horse.[53]

If the Prince spent his days steeple-chasing and playing polo, by night, according to the American press, he was to be found in the nightclubs of London and Paris, dancing to jazz music. Journalists tracked him down to his favourite clubs, the Embassy or Ciro's in London, or Bricktop's in Paris, where he was often surrounded by American friends. They saw him chatting to the bandleader Paul Whiteman, learning to dance the Black Bottom, or taking over the drum kit himself and playing with the band.[54] The Prince's love of American jazz was a particularly favourite theme: according to one report he liked 'red-hot syncopation' and had the latest Cab Calloway and Duke Ellington records shipped over to him from Hill's music store on Madison Avenue.[55]

The interest which the American public showed in the Prince's lifestyle naturally extended to the fashion styles he adopted. In Britain the Prince of Wales had always been the undisputed leader of fashionable society, and after 1919 Edward stepped into the shoes of his grandfather Edward VII in this regard. Between the wars Europe still led the world in fashion, and even in America trend-setters continued to look to Paris for couture and to London for the latest men's fashions. The Prince's visits to the USA in 1919 and 1924 reinforced his role as a fashion-plate for American men, and increasingly for American women as well. 'Wait till the Prince of Wales comes before you buy that new fall suit,' advised the *Bismarck Tribune* in August 1919.[56] The Prince's taste in formal wear was closely followed in America as much as in Britain,[57] but, in an increasingly democratic world, he had a more significant effect on fashion for the mass market. Edward's arrival in New York in August 1924, wearing a grey, snap-brim fedora, transformed fashions in men's headgear overnight. His purpose in wearing it was apparently to avoid recognition; when he went out in public he sported the hat 'brim-down', in a half-hearted effort at concealment. This strategy was quite successful, but for an unexpected reason—the Prince had started a new fashion. Within days the traditional summer straw boater had been abandoned,[58] and when Edward attended the Belmont races on Long Island in early September, the spectators could not pick him out in the stand because so many men were wearing grey fedoras. 'It was like trying to pick out a private in the Confederate Army,' quipped the *New York Times.*[59] One hatter in Detroit wittily advertised two versions of the fedora: with the brim up it was called 'the Prince'; brim-down it was styled 'the Renfrew', Edward's incognito name when travelling abroad unofficially.[60]

Edward's taste for brightly coloured golfing outfits, such as checked plus-fours and patterned sweaters, was widely copied in the USA. Perhaps his most enduring contribution to fashion was the Fair Isle sweater. In 1921 an enterprising Shetland Island hosiery dealer called Joseph Smith presented the Prince with a long-sleeved sweater in the classic multi-coloured Fair Isle pattern. Edward found it ideal for golf, and wore it when he played himself in as Captain at the Royal and Ancient Golf Club at St Andrews in Scotland the following year. The style caught on immediately on both sides of the Atlantic, helped by the growing demand for informal leisurewear.[61] Edward's

Figure 7.4. The Prince incognito in his grey fedora, 'brim-down': Long Island, 1924

holiday visit in 1924 gave a strong stimulus to American demand for Fair Isle sweaters just in time for the autumn season, and the fashion became popular for women as well as men. 'Sponsored by the Prince of Wales—worn by well-dressed girls everywhere,' ran one advertisement.[62] The Prince's name became permanently associated with the style, and in the 1920s and 1930s the Shetland Islands enjoyed an extraordinary boom in the knitwear industry which helped lift them out of a post-war economic crisis.[63]

As the last word in style and elegance, the Prince's name might be invoked as part of a marketing strategy to promote American luxury brands. The Hupp Motor Car Company enjoyed a major success when Edward used one of their Hupmobile limousines in a motor procession on his South African tour of 1925. Reportedly he commented on the quietness and power of the car, and asked to examine the engine.[64] Hupmobile capitalized on the association by incorporating the Prince into their publicity campaigns. An advertisement for the company's Century range in 1929 shows the bottom half of the Prince on horseback, with an elegantly dressed woman

Figure 7.5. The Prince of Wales, by John St Helier Lander, 1925

waving to him in front of a Hupmobile: 'when the Prince appears in new style riding clothes, the world hears about it instantly. Because they are smart and right and there's authority back of them. It was that way with the new Century cars...'[65]

After the Wall Street Crash of 1929 Edward's image as the fashionable Jazz Age Prince faded, as a more sober and serious side of his personality came to be emphasized. The Prince's work to address Britain's social and economic problems during the Great Depression attracted attention in the USA, and in particular his attempts to use his prestige to win back Britain's export markets lost to the USA since the end of the war. The American newspapers christened him the 'Prince of Sales', and his trip to Latin America in 1931 to open the British Empire Trade Exhibition in Buenos Aires, and drum up business for British companies, was regarded as a real threat to US interests. 'Wales, Royal Salesman, Boosts British Goods' was one headline after the Prince's inaugural address in Buenos Aires.[66] 'If England fails to take back from the United States the bulk of its South American export trade,' wrote

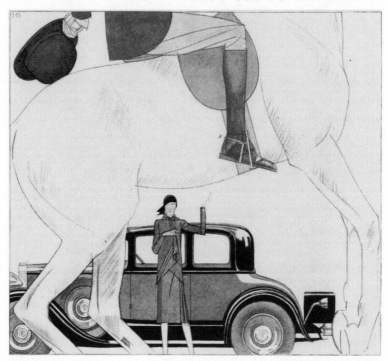

The Literary Digest for May 11, 1929

CREATORJ OF THE MODE

HER FROCK BY WORTH....HER CAR BY HUPMOBILE

When the Prince of Wales appears in new style riding clothes, the world hears about it instantly. Because they are smart and right and there's authority back of them · · · · It was that way with the new Century cars. Smart and right, and backed with twenty years of HUPMOBILE engineering authority · · · · Other cars complimented the new Century style by fashioning after it · · · · But HUPMOBILE remains a step ahead and an idea ahead. Surface details may be duplicated, but not the distinguished ensemble created by twenty years of creative designing in the automotive field. That remains wholly HUPMOBILE'S · · · · and at this very tick of your watch, it is still dated twenty months ahead! · · · · The CENTURY SIX $1345 to $1645 · · · · The CENTURY EIGHT $1825 to $2625 · · · · Custom and standard, all prices, f. o. b. factory · · · · Equipment, other than standard, extra.

THE NEW HUPMOBILE
CENTURY JIX & EIGHT

Figure 7.6. Advertisement for Hupmobile, May 1929

the editor of the *Kentucky Post*, 'it will not be the fault of the Prince of Wales... the tour is pure, cold, hard English business.'[67]

The intense media interest in the Prince generated a steady stream of royal biographies on both sides of the Atlantic. Between 1919 and 1935 there were at least a dozen biographical studies of Edward, some of which were serialized in American newspapers and magazines. Whereas British authors stressed the Prince's devotion to duty and his commitment to the British Empire, American biographers were more concerned with providing intimate insights into his personality and private life. Some of the works were merely cut-and-paste compilations from newspaper clippings, but others were based on interviews with those who knew the Prince. The first American biography of Edward, by the journalist and feminist writer Genevieve Parkhurst, was published in 1925.[68] In researching the book Parkhurst had travelled to Britain and interviewed Edward's private secretary, Godfrey Thomas, as well as his old tutor, Henry Hansell, and Sir Herbert Warren, the President of Magdalen College, Oxford. Parkhurst focused mainly on Edward's early years, with a wealth of anecdote about his childhood and youth. The book was copiously illustrated with photographs from the Prince's private collection, although these had apparently been supplied by Ernest Brooks, the royal photographer, without proper authorization, and Brooks was dismissed soon afterwards.[69] A later, semi-official biography by Leonard and Walter Townsend was published in Britain and America in 1929. It had been vetted by Godfrey Thomas, who deleted several thousand words of the manuscript. The result was a predictably bland account of the main public events of the Prince's life, but nevertheless it was widely serialized in the American press. Reflecting the high levels of public interest in the Prince, the *Pittsburgh Post-Gazette* printed daily extracts from the Townsend biography for an entire month in November 1929.

One biographer went to great lengths to win the Prince's confidence. The American journalist Frazier Hunt, who worked for Hearst Newspapers, met Edward for the first time in London in the early 1920s at a party given by the socialite Nancy Astor. In 1926 he bought the Eden Valley ranch, next to the EP ranch in Alberta, and so became the Prince's Canadian neighbour. On his visit to Canada in 1927, Edward invited Hunt to stay overnight at his ranch, and the two men chatted late into the evening. 'The Prince and I talked about American roads and how to write a novel, and about that time he had been socked in the eye in a polo game in Manila, and the strange feeling you have when twilight drops down on the Khyber Pass...'[70]

After midnight, when most of the Prince's staff had gone to bed, they continued chatting over cold ham and beer in the ranch-house kitchen. As events turned out, Hunt's man-to-man conversations with the Prince gave him little insight into his character and intentions. In 1935 he published an obsequious biography in the USA titled *The Bachelor Prince*, in which he portrayed Edward as a 'Serious Prince' ready for kingship, and firmly predicted that he would never marry.[71]

'Heartbreaker of the world': the Prince as an American Celebrity

At the heart of the new mass media which emerged in the inter-war period was an important paradox, which the moguls of the newspaper and film industries were quick to exploit. As new technologies created audiences of unprecedented size, the most effective strategy of communication was found to be personal and subjective. The mass media created the illusion of intimacy between the communicator, the celebrity, and the public. For newspapers, this meant an insatiable demand for human-interest stories about the rich and famous. How did they live, who did they love, what were they really like? In the movie industry it led to the development of the star system which promoted and magnified the celebrity of leading screen actors. It was the rise of Hollywood above all which gave birth to the distinctive culture of celebrity that emerged in America between the wars.

In many respects Edward's status as an American celebrity was very similar to that of a Hollywood movie star. He was young, glamorous, and stylish, with matinee idol good looks. His public saw him frequently in the newsreels at the movies, and sometimes even in the movies themselves. He acted out the fairy-tale role of Prince Charming in a wardrobe of elaborate costumes. Like a film star he enjoyed a lavish and exotic lifestyle beyond the imagination of ordinary people. Contemporaries were quick to make the comparison. 'Have you ever seen nicer screen features?' asked *Photoplay* magazine in 1920. 'If that smile were given a chance in matinees alone it would go a long way to clearing up the war debt.'[72] The verdict was just as enthusiastic after the advent of the 'talkies'. In 1931 the *New York Times* ran a feature entitled 'Headliners Who Meet the Screen's Rigid Test', selecting ten public figures whose presence and speaking qualities made them the most effective screen performers. The list included Thomas Edison, General Pershing, Mussolini, and the Prince of Wales. 'The Prince...seems to have a corner upon American popularity so far as royalty goes,' said *The Times*.'[He] is the beau ideal of screen personality.'[73]

At the same time, style magazines such as *Vanity Fair* bracketed the Prince together with Hollywood stars as icons of celebrity. The September 1932 issue of *Vanity Fair* carried a satirical article, 'The Hollywood Express', which imagined a train leaving New York for California carrying an all-star cast to play in the forthcoming 'extra-super-mastodon production *Sex of 1932*'. The Prince was billed to play the role of Giovanni, a champagne salesman, in a cast including Charlie Chaplin, Douglas Fairbanks, Mary Pickford, and Tallulah Bankhead.[74] In November 1932 the magazine featured the Prince of Wales and Clark Gable in one of its series of spoof 'Impossible Interviews'. In a striking double caricature by the Mexican artist Miguel Covarrubias, the pale, drooping Prince was depicted shaking hands with a brutally Cubist Gable. In the interview Edward accepted that his reign as 'heartbreaker of the world' had come to an end, and conceded his title to the new King of Hollywood.[75]

In the 1920s characters deliberately resembling the Prince frequently appeared in Hollywood films, particularly in the era of silent movies. The lost silent comedy, *A Regular Fellow,* starring Raymond Griffith, was a gentle parody of Edward's life. Described in the *New York Times* as a skit on the Prince of Wales, it tells the story of Alexis, the prince of a European monarchy. Alexis is burdened by an endless round of trivial official duties. He falls in love with a commoner, but every time they try to steal a moment together he is recognized, and surrounded by adoring crowds. The Prime Minister refuses to allow him to marry, and when the old king dies, the Prince resolves his dilemma by helping a revolutionary overthrow the regime. The monarchy is abolished, but Alexis is so popular that he is elected President. Fortunately he is now a commoner and is able to marry the woman he loves.[76] In 1926 a film was made of the 1920 Broadway play *Just Suppose*, the fantasy romance in which the Prince falls in love with a girl from Virginia, but renounces her for a life of duty.[77] In the starring role Richard Barthelmess imitated Edward's characteristic mannerisms—straightening his tie, fidgeting with his collar, and toying with his pipe. The film also included a scene in which the Prince fell off his horse, in an obvious reference to Edward's frequent riding accidents.[78] In one silent movie Edward was even impersonated by an actress. In *Beverly of Graustark* Marion Davies played the heroine, an American cousin of the Crown Prince, who stands in for him when he is

Figure 7.7. The Prince of Wales and Clark Gable by Miguel Covarrubias, *Vanity Fair*, November 1932

injured, in order to foil the plot of a pretender to the throne. 'Dressed in uniform,' wrote one reviewer, 'Davies is almost a double for the Prince of Wales.'[79] Occasionally Edward actually appeared in the movies themselves. Film footage showing the Prince watching the Horse Show at Madison Square Garden in 1919 was inserted into the romantic drama *Devotion* (1920), starring Hazel Dawn. The Prince also made a fleeting appearance, with other European celebrities like Mussolini, in *Chasing Through Europe* (1929), a Continental travelogue disguised as a romantic comedy.[80] As noted earlier, in 1925 scenes for the Western *The Calgary Stampede*, starring the cowboy Hoot Gibson, were filmed at the EP ranch. Although Edward himself did not appear, his name was used in the publicity for the film.[81]

Like a movie star Edward received substantial fan mail from his American followers. Shortly after his return from the USA in 1919, he told the Pilgrims dinner in London that he was still receiving the most charming letters from America, 'not all of them from the fair sex'. His mailbag at that time included an average of forty-five letters a day from American women, some of them love letters enclosing photographs and locks of hair.[82] A letter in the Royal Archives from the time of the Abdication gives a flavour of their likely content:

> I am taking the liberty of writing to you, knowing you will take it in the spirit in which it is written. I know you are human, like the rest of us...I am enclosing a picture of you I cut out of a magazine when I was about fourteen, and I think you were about the same age. I fell in love with the picture then and have kept it ever since...You know and remember perhaps what one goes through at that age. I was always somewhat romantic and so have kept my first love all these years.[83]

Hollywood actors themselves appreciated that the Prince had true star quality, and more than one tried to engineer a photo opportunity with him. While Edward was relaxing at White Sulphur Springs before his visit to New York in November 1919, a starlet called Kay Laurell checked into the same hotel and offered Ernest Brooks, the royal photographer, $2,000 for a picture with the Prince. Laurell managed to accost Edward as he was returning from a game of golf, but Brooks's nerve failed him at the last moment.[84] We have already seen how, when the Prince was in California in 1920, Mildred Harris, then the wife of Charlie Chaplin, bribed her way into the Mayor of San Diego's official party to meet the Prince.[85]

By the late 1920s Edward had become one of a handful of figures whose names were bywords for celebrity in America, transcending the specific walk of life from which they came. Along with Charlie Chaplin, Babe Ruth, and Charles Lindbergh, the Prince was famous simply for being famous. He appeared frequently in the 'top ten' lists of celebrities periodically published in the press.[86] In 1931, for example, *Vanity Fair* put a challenging dilemma to its readers. If they were lost in a trackless desert with a dozen celebrities, including Al Capone, Mussolini, Lindbergh, and the Prince, which four would they choose to leave behind?[87] In 1933 Margery Wilson, the head of a New York charm school, published a list of the ten most charming people in the world. It was headed by President Roosevelt, and included Einstein and Mussolini. The Prince was included in the list because 'he will still be the Prince of every woman's dream long after he is king'.[88]

The American celebrity who had most in common with the Prince was the aviator Charles Lindbergh. In May 1927 Lindbergh became famous overnight after his pioneering solo flight across the Atlantic from New York to Paris, and the two men met soon afterwards when Lindbergh came to London. Both men were young, handsome, and romantic figures, and both were reluctant celebrities. For the comedian and columnist Will Rogers, their public image was similar: 'they both got a quiet reserve and dignity that is exactly alike. There is some inborn intuition in both these fellows that tells them the right thing to do.' Like Edward, Lindbergh fought doggedly but unsuccessfully to protect his private life from press intrusion, and the level of media interest in both men was out of all proportion to their real-life activities and achievements.

Edward was one of the superstars of America's first age of media celebrity. His status was all the more remarkable in that he was a European prince who only made two brief visits to the USA. He was, of course, an immensely popular figure in Britain, and received extensive coverage in the British media. However, his fame in America was of a completely different order. In Britain he was royalty: in America he was a celebrity. In Britain he was just one representative of the enduring institution of monarchy, which had been at the centre of the nation's life for a thousand years. In America his personality overshadowed the monarchy of which he was part. It existed in the realm of celebrity, like a movie star's, detached from reality.

8

Luckiest of Females
The Prince and American Women

Edna Deane was one of Britain's greatest ballroom dancers. Seeing her in London in 1929, Fred Astaire described her as 'authentic poetry in motion'. At a ball in the mid-1920s she so captivated the Prince of Wales that he danced with her nine times. The incident inspired a popular song, the chorus of which ran: 'Glory, Glory, Alleluia, I'm the luckiest of females / For I've danced with a man, who danced with a girl, who danced with the Prince of Wales.'[1] The song neatly captures the breathless admiration which the Prince commanded in Britain and America throughout the 1920s. As Diana Vreeland, the fashion editor, recalled, 'he was the Golden Prince... to be a woman of my generation in London—any woman—was to be in love with the Prince of Wales'.[2] It was a truth universally acknowledged that the Prince of Wales must be in want of a wife, and after the war the field of prospective brides was much wider than before. Dancing, 'the perpendicular expression of a horizontal desire', was the primary opportunity for social and physical contact between young men and women, so it was inevitable that Edward should be the most sought-after partner in the world.[3] In the American press the term 'dancing partner' became a euphemism for the Prince's mistresses. Girls who danced with the Prince, like Carolyn Granberry and Leonore Cahill, became famous overnight. Proud parents placed notices in newspapers that the Prince had honoured their daughter with a dance. In America a parody guide to etiquette, *Perfect Behavior*, advised that no wedding party was complete without a bridesmaid who had danced twice with the Prince of Wales.[4]

In contrast with his public image as an unattached bachelor looking for a wife, by 1919 Edward was already deeply in love with a young married Englishwoman, Freda Dudley Ward. Freda was the daughter of one of the many Anglo-American marriages of the late nineteenth century. Her father, Charles Birkin, was the son of a wealthy Nottingham lace manufacturer, and her mother was Clare Howe, from a prominent East Coast political family. Freda was the wife of William Dudley Ward, a politician and courtier, and had two young children. Edward met her at a party in London in 1918, and for the next five years they carried on a passionate love affair.[5] As Wallis Windsor herself acknowledged, Freda was Edward's first true love.[6]

Freda was born in July 1894, a month after the Prince. When they met they were both 23 years old, although she played the role of mother to Edward's spoilt child. She had a petite figure and a pale, fragile beauty, with large wide-spaced eyes and soft brown hair cut in a bob. Winston Churchill described her as 'a delightful little porcelain shepherdess', but she also inherited some of her family's business acumen, and ran a successful interior decorating business. Married in 1913, by 1918 she and her husband were living separate lives, and Freda was pursued by a 'barrage' of admirers.[7]

The Prince's love for Freda showed the same passionate, obsessive quality which was later evident in his relationship with Wallis.[8] Hundreds of love letters from Edward to Freda survive, many written while he was abroad on official tours.[9] They are endlessly repetitive, expressing the Prince's undying devotion, his unworthiness as a lover, his childish apologies for inconsiderate behaviour, and his misery at separation. In the early years of the correspondence, Edward cherished a fantasy that he would be able to marry Freda, even though this would necessitate her divorce from William Dudley Ward. At one time he even appeared to be hoping that Freda might be pregnant with his child.[10] He regarded himself as married to her emotionally, and in consequence brushed aside any attempts from his family to make him consider matrimony.[11] Freda knew that Edward's dreams were unrealistic, and that any attempt to fulfil them would irreparably damage his position. Under pressure from Buckingham Palace she sought to cool down their relationship, first in 1920 and more successfully in 1922. By the end of that year the tone of their correspondence began to change. In the spring of 1923 Edward reluctantly accepted that Freda was no longer in love with him and was pursuing affairs with other men.[12] However, he continued to pine after her for many years afterwards. Freda remained Edward's ideal woman, and it is noticeable how much his later lovers resembled her facially or in physical type.

The issue of divorce meant that there was never any realistic prospect of Freda marrying Edward. Although divorce rates in Britain had doubled after the Great War, they were nevertheless extremely low at less than 2 per cent.

Figure 8.1. Freda Dudley Ward

This contrasted with the USA, where more than 16 per cent of marriages ended in divorce by the later 1920s. Until 1937 the principal ground for divorce in Britain remained adultery, and the associated costs and legal complications meant that in practice only the wealthiest could afford the process. Divorce also carried with it considerable social stigma in Britain. It was not recognized by the Church of England and could be a significant barrier to professional advancement or a career in public life. It was not until 1924 that a divorced politician was appointed to the Cabinet, and the Conservative Party upheld the ban on divorcees in government until after the Second World War. An army officer who was the 'guilty party' in a divorce might be expected to resign from his regiment, and of course no person who was divorced, or even separated, could ever be received at the royal Court.[13] As a result, couples in the British upper classes often remained married in order to preserve appearances, while carrying on affairs and living separate lives.

Paradoxically the intensity of his relationship with Freda did not prevent Edward from having affairs while he was away from her, particularly when he was overseas. He admitted being unfaithful in his letters to her, at the same time tearfully begging forgiveness. In 1918 he had a brief liaison with an Englishwoman in Rome, while serving with British forces in Italy. At first he lied about the affair, but later confessed, abjectly apologizing in letter after letter.[14] Freda took a tolerant view of such infidelities, perhaps recognizing that, being subject to so much temptation in his position, Edward was bound to commit them: 'you are marvellously wise, sweetheart, when you say that "les petits amusements ne content [sic] pas" and I now only call it medicine'.[15]

Edward's earliest sexual liaisons were with English and French women, but as the 1920s wore on, he increasingly found himself attracted to American dance partners and lovers. He had his first encounter with American women just after the end of the Great War, at a dance at the American Officers' Club in Koblenz, Germany.[16] Although by all accounts an unremarkable occasion, it was widely reported in the American press, and was immortalized in a painting by the American artist James Gardner Soper. Titled 'May I Have This Dance', it depicts an incident at the dance when a US army lieutenant tried to 'cut in' on the Prince and take his partner. A Red Cross nurse in full uniform is shown with the smiling Prince, looking over her shoulder at a predatory American officer. Draped flags swirl above them as, incongruously, a kilted Scotsman looks on. The painting was reproduced in the popular American monthly *The Ladies Home Journal* in June 1919, illustrating the romantic and democratic portrayal of the Prince which was to emerge so strongly during his North American tour later in the year.

The Prince's early tours gave him ample opportunity to get better acquainted with American women. At every stop there were balls and parties at which all the female guests were eager to dance with him. 'The kid has a Ziegfeld eye,' commented one American observer, referring to the beautiful dancing girls of the Ziegfeld Follies. He noted that whereas Edward would dance with his aged hostess in stony silence, he would be all smiles and conversation with a 'beautiful young thing'. Many of his partners flirted openly with him. 'These women out here are as hot as hell,' he wrote to Freda, 'one has to be on more than one's best behaviour.'[17] Carolyn Granberry, the girl who made front-page news by dancing with the Prince in Panama in 1920, offered to sleep with him. 'She said I could take her home if I wanted, although she was already booked up with a man for that pleasure...I got first prize when we got back to the ship and were all telling what women had said to us during dances!!'[18]

Edward's zest for dancing and love of jazz gave him a weakness for American showgirls. He loved to attend the latest productions and to meet the entertainers after the show. In the early 1920s his name was linked with two American 'sister acts', the Duncan Sisters and the Dolly Sisters.

Figure 8.2. 'May I Have This Dance?'

Rosetta and Vivian Duncan were a comedy duo whose most famous roles were as Topsy and Eva in a musical travesty of *Uncle Tom's Cabin*. They met the Prince in London in June 1921, when Edward went to see them performing in a review called *Pins and Needles*. He invited them to a party afterwards, where they taught him the latest dance, the 'Chicago'. For the next few weeks he added their names to the guest-lists of the parties he was attending during the social season, including a dinner given in the Prince's honour by Mrs Cornelius Vanderbilt, the American *grande dame* who had taken a house on Carlton House Terrace off Pall Mall for the summer. There Edward retreated to the conservatory with the Duncan Sisters and his cousin King Alfonso XIII of Spain, and they proceeded to dance the night away, keeping Mrs Vanderbilt and her guests waiting two hours for dinner.[19]

Rather more glamorous were the Dolly Sisters, Rosie and Jenny, a pair of Hungarian-American twins who began their careers in the Ziegfeld Follies, and went on to top the bill at the Moulin Rouge in Paris. They became rich through the devotion of admirers such as King Carol of Romania and the retail millionaire Gordon Selfridge. They met Edward in London in March 1921 when they were starring in a review called *League of Notions,* and in 1924 there were rumours the Prince was carrying on an affair with Jenny Dolly during his numerous trips to France that year.[20] When Edward was in New York in September 1924, the Dollies entertained him alongside Will Rogers, and as with the Duncan Sisters, the Prince ensured that they were invited to the parties he attended.[21] In an interview for the New York papers, the Dollies were full of praise for the Prince. 'He is a very wonderful dancer, and wonderfully popular... He throws Paris into a riot. He dances like an American and does all the dances well, but loves jazz the best. He plays the drums exquisitely. Oh, he is terribly smart. He's the cutest trick.'[22]

Before his arrival in America in 1919, the US press speculated as to the kind of American girl the Prince would find most attractive. The New York columnist Marguerite Mooers Marshall, a popular romantic novelist, reviewed the possibilities for him. 'This is the real land of opportunity, for we have brains and beauty in both blonde and brunette styles, demure debutantes and athletic amazons, girls who are dolls and girls who have dollars—his problem will be not to find but to choose.' The accompanying cartoon showed a smiling prince surrounded by eight American 'types', including the Blonde Girl, the Baby Doll, the Southern Belle, and the Gibson Girl.[23]

By 1924, the American press had taken the measure of the qualities that the Prince found attractive in a woman. Shortly after his holiday on Long

Figure 8.3. Pinna Nesbit Cruger

Island, when Edward had made headlines by dancing with American beauties like Leonore Cahill and Pinna Nesbit Cruger, an article appeared in
newspapers across America which gave an uncannily accurate prediction of
his future bride. Reviewing the evidence of Edward's favourite 'dancing
partners', the article concluded: 'the next Queen of England will be a petite
brunette with large dark eyes, who is a good dancer'. The feature concentrated on the former movie star Pinna Cruger as an example of Edward's
'type'. Described as a dancer of exquisite taste, Pinna was of medium height
and brown-haired, with an oval face, a slender figure, and large hazel eyes.
The Prince's taste was to prove remarkably consistent: the photographs of
Pinna bear a striking resemblance to the young Wallis Simpson.[24]

Why was the Prince so strongly attracted to American women? There
can be no doubt that, from the Dolly Sisters and Pinna Cruger to Thelma
Furness and Wallis Simpson, he found them profoundly exciting. For Edward,
the sophistication and modernity of American women represented the sexual equivalent of the Manhattan skyline. The Prince had grown up in the

age of the New Woman, and he admired the qualities of independence and strength which she embodied.[25] Although the New Woman was to be found on both sides of the Atlantic, the looser and more egalitarian structure of American society meant that her values were more widespread in the USA than in Britain, where class and social hierarchy still prevailed. It was not simply that American women were more forthright and assertive than their British sisters; they also looked different. The global dominance of the American movie industry in the inter-war period meant that the USA led the world in popular trends in women's fashion. American women were the first to model their looks and style of dress on Hollywood stars. They bobbed their hair, wore lipstick and eye shadow, and plucked their eyebrows. In America Max Factor created the first mass market for cosmetics, and a new generation of working women could buy the latest fashions at affordable prices in department stores. They were personified by the Brinkley Girl, the creation of newspaper illustrator Nell Brinkley, a modern, independent working girl who was also fun-loving and sexually adventurous. Carolyn Granberry, the American shopgirl who charmed the Prince in Panama in 1920, was a typical Brinkley Girl.[26]

Of course it was not long before American fashions followed American movies to Britain. British women too tried to look like Hollywood film stars, but the result was generally a pale imitation of the original.[27] American women were more vivacious, they dressed more stylishly, and they were better groomed. The novelist Evelyn Waugh caught the nuances of difference in describing Celia, the English wife of Charles Ryder, the narrator of *Brideshead Revisited:* 'In Europe my wife was sometimes taken for an American because of her dapper and jaunty way of dressing and the curiously hygienic quality of her prettiness; in America she assumed an English softness and reticence.'[28]

One of the characteristics which Edward found particularly attractive in American women was that, unlike British women, they were not overawed in his presence. Rather, they had a healthy republican disrespect for royalty. When the Duncan Sisters met the Prince and King Alfonso, the King asked them if they had not been a little afraid at the prospect of meeting them. 'Now don't put on airs, Alfonso,' said Vivian Duncan. 'We're from Los Angeles where the movie people do their stunts and we see kings every day riding in the streetcar. We are just plain American actresses and it takes more than a king to scare us.' 'Good!' replied Edward. Similarly, when the aviator Amelia Earhart was presented to the Prince after her pioneering flight across the Atlantic in 1932, she gave him a slight nod while others subsided into a deep curtsy. Edward was delighted to meet Amelia, and immediately gave up his chair for her. They chatted about flying and Edward monopolized her on the dance floor for the rest of the evening.[29]

The years 1923 and 1924 marked a watershed in Prince Edward's emotional life. His love affair with Freda Dudley Ward had petered out, and he had found no new lover to take her place. Although his main programme of imperial tours was complete, he continued to spend as much time as he could overseas. In 1924 he made several trips to France, as well as visiting Canada and the USA. In 1925 he toured Africa and South America, in 1927 he returned to Canada, and in 1928 he went on safari to East Africa. His lifestyle became more promiscuous, with a constant stream of casual affairs, conducted mainly while he was abroad. Tommy Lascelles, who was constantly in the Prince's company during the 1920s, confirmed that 'there was always a *grande affaire*, and coincidentally, as I know to my cost, an unbroken series of *petites affaires*, contracted and consummated in whatever highways and byways of the Empire he was traversing at the time'.[30] Whether or not Edward was carrying on a serious affair, he also conducted an unbroken series of lesser liaisons wherever he happened to be in the British Empire. When he was at home he filled his leisure time with frantic activity, pursuing his passions for riding, hunting, and steeple-chasing. In 1923 he suffered a series of riding accidents, perhaps the result of greater recklessness arising from his unrequited love for Freda.[31] However, there is little evidence from these years that Edward carried on affairs in England: this may have simply been lack of opportunity—that he was too busy, and the constraints of his position made them too difficult to manage. It seems more likely, however, that it was a way of demonstrating his enduring devotion to Freda. He continued to visit her regularly, and became an informal godfather to her two daughters, Penelope and Angela, who called him 'the little Prince'.[32] In 1927 Winston Churchill, seeing them together, observed that Edward's love for Freda remained 'obvious and undisguisable'.[33] The following year, when Edward discovered that Freda was having an affair with Rodman Wanamaker, the American retail millionaire who had welcomed him to New York in 1919, he wrote: 'it's so damned silly that you and I aren't married, my angel. I absolutely know that you'd be far happier with me now than any bloody Pappapacker.'[34]

Following his father's serious illness in 1928, Edward adopted a more settled lifestyle. He acquired Fort Belvedere as a weekend residence in 1930, where he was able to invite his own circle of friends. By contrast with his bachelor apartments in St James's Palace, the Fort needed a hostess to help him entertain guests. Although he was still devoted to Freda, she had long since ceased to be his mistress. Instead his choice fell on a beautiful young American socialite, Thelma Morgan Furness.

Thelma was the daughter of Harry Hays Morgan, a wealthy American diplomat, and his Chilean-American wife, Laura Kilpatrick. Thelma's mother's family claimed descent from the royal house of Castile, which would have made her a very distant relative of Prince Edward.[35] She and her twin sister, Gloria Morgan Vanderbilt, were leading society beauties of their day, featuring in the gossip columns of the American press.[36] Already married and divorced by the age of 22, Thelma briefly pursued a career in Hollywood before taking as her second husband Marmaduke, Viscount Furness, an English shipping magnate twice her age. By the time she met the Prince in 1929, that marriage too was failing, and the couple were living apart.[37]

Edward's affair with Thelma began in the summer of 1929, and blossomed when they met on safari in East Africa early in 1930. If Thelma's gushing account is to be believed, they succumbed to the romantic atmosphere of starlit nights deep in the African bush. 'This was our Eden, and we were alone in it. His arms about me were the only reality; his words of love my only bridge to life. Borne along on the mounting tide of his ardour, I felt myself being inexorably swept from the accustomed moorings of caution...'[38]

Figure 8.4. Thelma Morgan Furness with the Prince, 1932

Thelma fitted easily into the Anglo-American circle of friends that Edward had made for himself. Edward already knew her elder sister Consuelo Morgan Thaw, whose husband, the American diplomat Benjamin Thaw, had entertained him in Buenos Aires on his South American tour in 1925. Other mutual acquaintances included Edward's old friend Fred Bate, and the Bovril heir Orman Lawson-Johnston and his wife Betty.[39] The society diarist Chips Channon later blamed Thelma for 'Americanizing' the Prince, but in reality she was the symptom, rather than the cause, of Edward's Americanization.[40]

One notable feature of the Prince's social set in the 1930s was that many of its members had been through at least one divorce. In this respect the experience of Edward's wealthy and cosmopolitan friends was more representative of America's East Coast social elite than it was of British society. Having divorced her first husband, Thelma went on to divorce 'Duke' Furness in 1933 while still Edward's mistress. Her sister Consuelo was also divorced and remarried, while Fred Bate had divorced for the second time in 1929. Among Edward's English friends, Freda Dudley Ward finally obtained a divorce from her husband in 1931, after many years of separation. Wallis and Ernest Simpson had of course both been divorced, but this proved to be no barrier to their entry into the Prince's circle. In view of their more relaxed attitude to divorce, Edward's friends found some English social customs hypocritical: because estranged couples often remained married, it was accepted practice for husbands and wives to accept invitations separately. In America it was rare to see a woman dining alone with a man who was not her husband; in England it was commonplace. At Prince Edward's favourite London restaurant, the Embassy Club, the maître d'hôtel was famous for his ability never to seat husband and wife at adjacent tables when they were accompanied by their lovers.[41]

Edward's relationship with Thelma lacked the intensity which is so evident in his love for Freda Dudley Ward, and later for Wallis Simpson. It appears to have been an affectionate, placid affair—the couple exchanged love tokens in the form of teddy bears—but not a passionate one.[42] In particular, there is no evidence that Edward ever wished to marry her, although it became hypothetically possible when she divorced 'Duke' Furness in 1933. Moreover, Edward never stopped seeing Freda Dudley Ward throughout the time when Thelma was his mistress. When in London he would call on Freda regularly during the week, while spending weekends at Fort Belvedere with Thelma and their friends. Thelma helped to create a congenial and

relaxing environment at the Fort away from the pressures of his life as Prince
of Wales. Her memoirs suggest that she had little interest in the Prince's
public life, and that he did not encourage it. 'I was pleased that we were spared
the *Sturm und Drang* that is the traditional background to a love such as ours.
Politics were never discussed; political figures never intruded into our private
world.'[43] The American press did run stories linking Thelma to Edward as
the Prince's 'dancing partner', but she attracted more publicity for her
divorce from 'Duke' Furness and her involvement in the famous Vanderbilt
child custody lawsuit, in which her twin sister Gloria lost the custody of her
daughter Gloria to her dead husband's sister, Gertrude Whitney.[44]

Between 1930 and 1934 Thelma was accepted in London society as
Edward's mistress, or 'the Princess of Wales' as Wallis Simpson called her.
The role was extremely demanding: Thelma found that Edward's outward
shyness masked a 'whim of iron'. In his private life, just as in his official life,
Edward expected everything to be done for him. Thelma managed his
household at the Fort and organized his social life. She hired the staff,
bought and wrapped his Christmas presents, and arranged his holidays in
Biarritz.[45] If her memoirs are to be believed, weekends at the Fort were
domestic to the point of tedium. The Prince gardened, played his bagpipes,
and practised embroidery. In the evening they played games and danced to
the latest jazz records. Edward invited his closest friends, and Thelma
picked guests who could entertain the Prince with lively conversation.
One such guest, whom Thelma had met through her sister Consuelo, was
Wallis Simpson.

9

David against Edward

In November 1931 a little girl called Daphne Digby-Jones took part in the Hallowe'en Ice Carnival, a charity event at Grosvenor House in London. The star guests were the Prince of Wales and Charlie Chaplin. Daphne asked the Prince to autograph her programme, which he duly did, using his normal signature, 'Edward P'. In response she wagged her finger at him. 'You know that is not your name,' she said, referring to the fact that Edward was known within the royal family as David.[1]

It was not unusual for a member of royalty to have a family name different from his official name. Edward's grandfather Edward VII was always known as Bertie, although his official style was Edward, Prince of Wales, before he became king. In the case of Edward/David, however, the duality came to symbolize a psychological divide which deepened as the Prince grew older. Between 1914 and 1936 a personality split developed between the quintessentially British 'Edward', the Prince (and later King), and David, the increasingly Americanized private man. This chapter explores the Prince's peculiar psychological make-up, which is vital to an understanding of his life as Prince of Wales, his relationship with Wallis, and the course of the Abdication crisis in 1936.

Edward was a man of many names and titles. His full style was 'His Royal Highness Edward Albert Christian George Andrew Patrick David, Prince of Wales and Earl of Chester, Duke of Cornwall, Duke of Rothesay, Earl of Carrick, Lord of Renfrew, Lord of the Isles, Prince and Great Steward of Scotland'. Outside the royal family a few favoured friends were allowed to call him 'Eddie'; otherwise he was addressed as 'Your Royal Highness' or 'Sir', while Americans simply called him 'Prince'. Only two people outside the extended royal family were ever permitted to call him David: Freda Dudley Ward and Wallis Simpson.[2]

Edward's personality presents a puzzling contradiction. On the one hand he was a royal prince, with all the sense of entitlement and superiority which that implied. On the other, he was beset from his early youth by the feeling he was not worthy of the role into which he had been born. It was an unstable combination, and accounts for much of the moodiness and depression which were a feature of his life. At the end of his memoirs Edward wrote that, as prince, he was 'obsessed with the desire to be found worthy, and to share in the risks and struggles of men'.[3] However, his royal status, which helped to foster that obsession, isolated him from other people, and made it impossible for him to establish normal, sharing human relationships. In the words of the author Compton Mackenzie, one of Edward's stoutest defenders after the Abdication:

> The Prince might have desired wildly to be taken for granted, but his position was eternally forbidding it. The struggle in his mind between these two compulsions was persistent... steeple-chasing, squash-racquets, violent exercise, dancing, even flying, all represent the efforts of a mind wrestling with the irreconcilable dualism of character and status.[4]

All his relationships were asymmetrical, in the sense that they were determined by his status rather than the content of his character. The unease and restlessness that is so evident in his career as Prince of Wales resulted from the unresolved tension between his royal status and his desire, as he saw it, to be treated like an ordinary human being.

The starting-point for any analysis of Edward's personality is the fact that he was born royal. His forebears had been kings and queens of England for more than a thousand years. He was descended from Alfred the Great, William the Conqueror, and Edward III: royalty was literally in his DNA. To be born royal was to be different. 'You must always remember your position and who you are,' warned his father.[5] There was of course little danger of Edward forgetting who he was: the manner in which he was addressed, the deference he was invariably shown, the exaggerated praise he received, and the honours that were showered upon him, all were a constant reminder of his royal status. Those who were born royal were members of the world's smallest and most exclusive club; even husbands and wives who married into the royal family did not fully belong unless they were themselves of royal blood. Queen Mary, despite being a great-granddaughter of George III, was at first mocked by her in-laws because her father, the Duke of Teck, was the product of a morganatic marriage.[6] Edward himself had similar prejudices, deriding the royal pretensions of Henry Lascelles, Earl of Harewood, the husband of his sister Princess Mary. 'Every day I get commoner, and every day Lascelles gets royaller and royaller,' he is reported as saying in 1927.[7]

A defining characteristic of the royal charisma was that it was innate and effortless, requiring no exercise of will. Its effects, nevertheless, could be dramatic. Wallis Simpson experienced it first-hand on her travels with the Prince.

> For all his natural simplicity, there was nevertheless about him...an unmistakable aura of power and authority. His slightest wish seemed always to be translated instantly into the most impressive kind of reality. Trains were held; yachts materialized; the best suites in the finest hotels were flung open; aeroplanes stood waiting. What impressed me most of all was how all this could be brought to pass without apparent effort: the calm assumption that this was the natural order of things, that nothing could ever possibly go awry.[8]

The aura of royalty was so powerful that it could survive even under the most extreme circumstances. The psychiatrist Bruno Bettelheim, who spent a year in the Nazi concentration camp of Dachau in 1938–9, noticed that the handful of members of former royal families in the camp coped much better than ordinary prisoners.

> They looked down on most other prisoners nearly as much as they despised the SS. In order to endure life in the camp they seemed to develop such a feeling of superiority that nothing touched them. Thus, from the outset, they acquired a feeling of detachment, a denial of the 'reality' of the situation in which they found themselves, that came to most prisoners only after the most excruciating experiences.[9]

Those who were royal therefore possessed an unshakable sense of superiority over the rest of humanity. For a monarch or a prince, a duke was just as inferior as a coal miner. Although the aristocracy regarded themselves as the natural companions of royalty, the royals for their part saw no need to be constrained by such class distinctions. They felt free to associate with whomever they pleased. Queen Victoria, for example, enjoyed an intense relationship with her Scottish manservant John Brown, and later with her Indian tutor Abdul Karim, 'the Munshi'.[10] Seen in this light, Edward's 'democratic' instincts may be interpreted more as the expression of traditional royal condescension than of a sense of equality with his fellow men. He was quite capable of suddenly 'turning royal' if he chose. When his official duties took him to Oxford, he would visit his old college, Magdalen. On one of these visits, all the undergraduates stood up when he entered the Junior Common Room, and he asked them to be seated, saying that he wanted to be treated without ceremony as a member of the college. The next time he came, no one stood up, at which the Prince asked curtly if that was the way to treat the heir to the throne.[11]

The paradox of Edward's personality, however, was that his inherent sense of royal superiority was counterbalanced by deep-seated feelings of unworthiness and inferiority, which he poured out endlessly in diaries and letters. In part his inferiority complex may have been the result of his upbringing, with its unrelenting emphasis on duty and service, and his early awareness of the burdens that were in store for him.[12] It probably also derived from his puny physique. At 20 he was five feet six inches tall, and weighed barely eight stone. His features were soft and feminine, with a pink complexion and no perceptible facial hair; he could not have grown a fine beard like his father and grandfather.[13] Those who met him thought he looked much younger than his years. A fellow Grenadier officer who met him in 1916 (when he was 22) described him as looking like a rather immature 15-year-old.[14] Four years later, seeing the Prince depart on his Australian tour, the Foreign Secretary, Lord Curzon, thought the same.[15] Moreover, the Prince's acute shyness as a young man had the effect of reducing his physical presence still further. One observer noted that he could not get in or out of a room except sideways. A caricature by the satirist Max Beerbohm depicted the young Edward at an imaginary banquet as a tiny, insignificant figure, eyes lowered, dwarfed by the diners around him.[16] The nicknames he was given reflected his slight stature, but also managed to convey a sense of his immaturity: to Fruity Metcalfe he was always 'the Little Man', a tag adopted by Thelma Furness and Wallis Simpson; Joey Legh, the Prince's equerry, called him 'the Boy' in correspondence to his wife; while he was on safari in East Africa, the locals named him, 'Georgie's toto' (George's little boy);[17] even Freda Dudley Ward's infant daughters called him 'the little Prince'.[18]

Edward's boyishness and immaturity even as a middle-aged man reminded contemporaries of Peter Pan, the boy who would not grow up. When Wallis Simpson returned from her holiday with the Prince in the summer of 1934, she told her husband, Ernest, that it was like being 'Wallis in Wonderland'. Ernest replied, with a touch of sourness, that it sounded more like a trip to Peter Pan's Never-Never Land. From then on he always referred to the Prince as Peter Pan. Wallis herself used the nickname for Edward in correspondence with Ernest after their divorce, and she evidently shared his views on the Prince's immaturity. After one particularly difficult evening in May 1935, when Edward had bombarded Wallis with telephone calls at home, causing a row with her husband, she wrote him a devastating note of reprimand. 'Sometimes I think you haven't grown up where love is concerned, and perhaps it's only a boyish passion, for surely it lacks the thought of me that a man's love is capable of... be kind to me in the years to come, for I have lost something noble for a boy who may always remain Peter Pan.'[19] Reflecting after the Abdication on the peculiarities of Edward's personality, Tommy Lascelles concluded that he suffered from a form of arrested development. 'For some hereditary or physiological reason his normal mental development stopped dead when he reached adolescence... his only yardstick in measuring the advisability or non-advisability of any particular action was, "Can I get away with it?"—an attitude typical of boyhood.'[20]

When George V ascended the throne in 1910, Edward, as his eldest son, became heir to the throne. He inherited the title of Duke of Cornwall, with extensive landed estates across the country, but he did not automatically become Prince of Wales. That title, which is a personal honour in the gift of the sovereign, was conferred upon him by the King on his sixteenth birthday in June 1910.[21] A year later Edward underwent a formal investiture as prince in the ruins of Caernarvon castle in north Wales. It was a classic example of invented tradition; no investiture had taken place for three hundred years, and the ceremony was based on the legend that King Edward I, the conqueror of Wales, had presented his baby son, Edward of Caernarvon, to the Welsh people as their new prince. It was also a spectacular piece of political theatre, devised by the radical politician David Lloyd George as a celebration of Welsh national culture. Dressed in a mock medieval costume of white satin breeches and purple velvet surcoat, Edward went through a form of coronation. King George placed a crown on his head and handed him a sceptre of office; a purple mantle trimmed with ermine was placed round his shoulders. The King and the Prince then climbed to the castle battlements, where Edward was 'presented' to thousands of spectators below, stammering out a few words of Welsh which Lloyd George had taught him.

For the 17-year-old Edward, shy and self-conscious as he was, the investiture was an excruciating experience. He protested at the 'preposterous rig' he was expected to wear, worrying that he would be the laughing stock of his Navy friends. It was the first time that he had been fully exposed to the public side of his role as Prince of Wales, and he discovered that he was deeply uncomfortable with the attention and adulation that it brought. All he wanted, in his own words, 'was to be treated exactly like any other boy of my age'. The accident of his birth meant that it was a wish he was always to be denied.[22]

The Prince of Wales has no constitutional duties under English law, and no formal job description. Like the Vice-President of the United States, his role is to stand and wait, and the only specific requirement for the post is to possess a heartbeat. Edward himself felt he was 'being kept on ice' until the day his father died.[23] In practice Edward's job was to assist and represent the monarch in carrying out the ceremonial duties of kingship, such as opening buildings, planting trees, and laying foundation stones.[24] When he travelled abroad as prince, the government of the host country would treat his visit as a state occasion and accord him an official welcome.[25]

In normal circumstances Edward would have had plenty of time to adjust to his new role as prince; his father was only 45, and it was unlikely that he would succeed to the throne for many years. However, the outbreak of war in 1914, shortly after his twentieth birthday, provided a forceful reminder of the ornamental nature of his position. Although he volunteered for military service and was eager to fight in France, he soon discovered that his trophy value outweighed his military usefulness. The death or capture of the Prince of Wales would have been a great propaganda victory for the enemy, and so he was not permitted to serve in the trenches, but was assigned instead to staff duties well behind the lines.[26]

Edward's letters and diaries during the war reveal his intense frustration at being prevented from going on active service. In December 1914 he managed to visit a Grenadier battalion about a mile behind the front, but was spotted by an officer and sent back to his base. 'Bloody having to say goodbye to them all,' he wrote in his diary, 'it did bring it home to one how wretched it is to be the bloody P. of Wales.' During the Battle of Neuve Chapelle in 1915 he wrote to Lord Stamfordham, his father's Private Secretary, lamenting that he was confined to the role of spectator. Later in the war he was reprimanded by his commanding officer, Lord Cavan, for not reading the papers and taking no interest in world politics. 'Of course he is right really,' Edward admitted to his diary, 'and I don't attempt to be P of W or prepare for being so, but how I hate all that sort of thing, and how unsuited I am for the job.'[27] Ironically it turned out that Edward's time on the Western Front was an excellent preparation for his future work as Prince of Wales. His presence alongside the troops, and his eagerness to get to the front line, gave him credibility with ordinary servicemen and contributed significantly to his popularity after the war.[28]

Edward's enforced inactivity during the war was humiliating for him, and reinforced his sense of inferiority. He was acutely embarrassed to be awarded the Military Cross in 1916, when he had done no actual fighting. 'All I can say about my MC', he wrote to a brother officer, Captain Wilfrid Bailey, 'is that I wish it had been given to you and not to me, who has no more earned it than a pol [prostitute] in London.'[29] In an attempt to compensate for his inability to fight, Edward pursued a number of overtly masculine and risk-taking behaviours. He punished himself physically, abandoning his staff car to walk or cycle for miles through the mud of the Western Front. He frequently sought to slip his leash at Army Headquarters in order to visit troops on the front line; he became known to the staff as 'Dynamite' Wales because he was always 'going off'. He adopted the expletive-laden language of ordinary soldiers, and exchanged obscene jokes and risqué stories with his fellow officers. Under the anonymity of khaki he visited 'pols' and shared accounts of his sexual exploits with friends.[30] As the war went on, the Grenadier Guards became a substitute family. Alienated emotionally from his parents, he developed close bonds with a small group of officers who befriended him in France. In 1919 his callous reaction to the death of his disabled younger brother, Prince John, which deeply upset his mother, revealed the coarsening effect of the war on his sensibilities, and revealed how distanced he had become from his family.[31]

Edward's wartime experiences convinced him that the 'job' of Prince of Wales deprived him of the freedom to lead the kind of life which he would otherwise have chosen. It was not a role which he identified with and embraced as part of his royal destiny, but one which he assumed with reluctance, and which he felt was alien to his true self. He was like an actor in a never-ending soap opera, unwillingly forced to play a character with whom he was out of sympathy. David, the shy, insecure private man, was trapped in the glare of the spotlight as Edward, Prince of Wales, the Smiling Prince, the symbol of the nation's hopes, the Ambassador of Empire.

Edward's love affair with Freda Dudley Ward, which began in 1918, opened up an entirely new dimension to the conflict between his public and personal lives. It completed the process of his emotional alienation from his parents which had begun during the war, and later led to a rift with his brother Albert when Edward discovered that he had tried to persuade Freda to end the relationship.[32] For Edward, as Louis Mountbatten perceptively pointed out in 1920, Freda was a substitute mother: 'she's absolutely been a mother to him, and he has brought all his troubles to her and she has comforted and advised him'.[33] Edward fell deeply and obsessively in love with Freda, to the point where he fantasized about marrying her, even though she was already married with two young daughters. However, as an upperclass Englishwoman, Freda knew the rules of the game. She could be the mistress of the Prince of Wales, but never his wife. Nevertheless, in reaction to the society gossip swirling round their affair, and the disapproval of Palace officials, it was Freda who put the idea into Edward's head that, as long as he discharged his public duties conscientiously, he was entitled to pursue his private life without hindrance or criticism. 'How right you are darling, in defining the difference between official capacity and private life,' Edward wrote to her in July 1919. 'It's that difference which none of these —— old courtiers realise, it's so so vast that their pompous minds can never grasp it.'[34]

For Edward this was a turning-point, which was to have dramatic long-term consequences for his future. Freda's insight crystallized his own ambivalence about his role as Prince of Wales, and gave him the justification for placing his public and private lives into separate compartments. Why should he not seek his own personal happiness and fulfilment, even if he was a prince? In Freda, Edward found not only a lover and confidante, but a counsellor, who for the first time provided him with advice independent of the royal family and Palace officials. From that time onwards Edward regarded his private life as entirely his own concern, and rejected any advice from his staff and the King's advisers which contradicted that belief. In fact, the 'old courtiers' whom Edward derided knew better than he did that the gap opening up between his private life and his public role had to be bridged. It was Edward's refusal to accept this that ultimately led to the Abdication.[35]

As soon as the war was over, Edward was sent on his lengthy tours of the British Empire, which required him constantly to remain 'in character' as Prince of Wales. He found the demands of touring immensely stressful, and in his letters to Freda Dudley Ward from Canada and Australia he complained frequently about the 'thankless and rotten job of P. of W.' He would refer to 'the Prince of Wales' as if he were a separate person: early in his Canadian tour he wrote, 'I always loathe the first drive through a city before they get to know one and that the cheering is merely for the P of W and not for me. I get my look in on the second day sometimes!!'[36] There were many things 'David' wanted to do which Edward, Prince of Wales, prevented

him from doing. In particular, being Prince took 'David' away from Freda
and made it impossible for him to start a new life with her in Canada after
the war.[37] Mid-way through his North American tour in 1919 he confided
to Freda that he was already beginning to have thoughts of abdication. 'I do
get so terribly fed up with it and despondent about it sometimes, and begin
to feel like "resigning"!! And then I should be free to live or die according
to how hard I worked though I should have you all to myself sweetheart and
should only then be really happy.'[38] Even in trivial matters the Prince of
Wales thwarted 'David's' natural impulses. At Christmas 1919 he wanted to
lend Freda some horses from his stables so that she would have a safe mount
for the hunting season:'if only—but then it's the usual reason why I shouldn't
lend you horses, merely because I'm the bloody f-cking P. of W!!!!'[39]

Sometimes, when overwhelmed by the pressures of being Prince of
Wales, Edward would fall into bouts of depression. Louis Mountbatten
described how, while on tour, black moods would suddenly descend on
him; he would shut himself away in his cabin and refuse to see his staff.[40] At
such times he had thoughts of suicide. In the middle of the war, after a day
on which he had again been refused a visit to the front line, he confided to his
diary:'I wanted to be alone in my misery. I feel quite ready to commit suicide
if I didn't think it unfair to Papa.'[41] This may have been self-dramatizing, but
royal suicides were by no means uncommon. A few years before Edward's
birth, Crown Prince Rudolf, the son and heir of the Emperor Franz Josef of
Austria, and his lover Baroness Mary Vetsera, committed suicide together at
the royal hunting lodge at Mayerling. In the thirty years following his death
three of Edward's relatives killed themselves: Alfred, Prince of Saxe Coburg
and Gotha, in 1899; Adolphus Frederick VI, Duke of Mecklenburg, in 1918;
and Prince Joachim of Prussia, the youngest son of Kaiser Wilhelm, in 1920.
The precedent of Mayerling may have inspired Edward to form a suicide
pact with Freda Dudley Ward: while on tour in Canada he wrote, 'how marvellously divine if WE could die together; there's absolutely nothing I could
wish for more . . . I am just dippy to die with YOU'.[42] A few months later,
on the way out to Australia, he succumbed once again to depression. 'I honestly don't think I can face another [tour] like this one without going quite
mad; I honestly want to die as soon as we are together again though you
know I've promised you not to use that little 6 shooter till we meet again,
though Christ I long to tonight.'[43]

There were moments of reprieve. From time to time it was possible for
Edward to set aside his persona as Prince of Wales and assume an incognito

identity under one of his lesser titles, such as the Earl of Chester or Lord
Renfrew. This allowed him to travel overseas without the formalities of a
state visit, for example on his regular visits to France and his vacation at the
EP ranch in Canada in 1923. The custom was for the British press to respect
his privacy, and they did not report his activities while he was incognito. His
trip to the USA in 1924 caused a degree of difficulty because, although he
was coming to Long Island for a holiday, President Coolidge had also invited
him to lunch at the White House. The British government felt it would be
discourteous for Edward to meet the President as Lord Renfrew, so for
the duration of his twenty-four-hour visit to Washington he resumed his
status as Prince of Wales, reverting to plain Lord Renfrew on his return to
New York.[44] The American press regarded the contortions of British Court
protocol with wry amusement: 'It does seem a bit foolish to be changing
your royal status as a man changes from his business suit to dinner dress,'
commented the *Philadelphia Inquirer*, 'but it will mean comfort and a measure of freedom for the prince while he is here.'[45] As an attempt to ensure
Edward's privacy in America, it was of course a total failure. The distinction
was lost on American journalists and the crowds of sightseers who strained
to catch a glimpse of 'Lord Renfrew' at the Meadowbrook Polo Club or in
downtown New York. In a witty comment on Edward's incognito status,
one department store in Detroit advertised two versions of his trademark
grey snap-brim fedora: with the brim up it was called 'the Prince'; brim
down it was styled 'the Renfrew'.

But in spite of any snatched moments of reprieve, and in spite of his
extraordinary global success as Prince of Wales in the 1920s, Edward was
never fully reconciled to his princely role. As he entered his thirties, and the
prospect of succeeding to the throne came closer, he continued to bemoan
his lot. 'It's just the *chronic state* of being the P of W—of which I am so heart-
ily and genuinely fed up,' he wrote to Godfrey Thomas in 1927. 'It's just so
nerve racking and distracting sometimes that I really could go mad.' When
Tommy Lascelles resigned from his service in January 1929, the Prince sent
for him to ask why he wanted to leave. Free at last to tell Edward what he
really thought, Lascelles harangued him for almost an hour like an errant
younger brother, criticizing his lifestyle and warning that if he did not mend
his ways he could lose his throne. Edward listened in silence, and when
Lascelles had finished his lecture he said, 'Well goodnight, Tommy, and thank
you for the talk. I suppose the fact of the matter is that I am quite the wrong
sort of person to be Prince of Wales.'[46]

Having established a line of demarcation between his public and private lives, between the official world of the Prince of Wales and the jealously guarded private space where he spent his leisure time and carried on his personal relationships, how did Edward manage the friction between the two worlds, and prevent them from colliding? Over the years he developed a number of coping mechanisms, which fell into three main categories: escape, inner emigration, and adaptation. Behind those three lurked a fourth category, the 'nuclear' option which Edward occasionally considered, of abdication.

The simplest strategy was a straightforward flight response. Whenever the opportunity arose he would escape from Britain and flee to a foreign country or to a distant corner of the British Empire. This was his favourite strategy in the years immediately after the Great War. In 1919 he bought the EP ranch in western Canada, with a view to making regular summer visits there, taking in the USA on the way. Unfortunately it was so remote that, before the age of air travel, it took Edward ten days to get there, which made it impractical as a regular place of refuge.[47] A more convenient escape-hatch lay just across the English Channel, and Edward frequently visited Paris, Biarritz, and Cannes on holiday using his incognito.

Physical escape could provide only a temporary respite, however. In order to cope with his life as Prince of Wales while at home in Britain, he adopted the habit of 'inner emigration'. This involved outward compliance with the demands of his 'job' while retreating as often as he could into his private world, one which reflected his own Americanized tastes and interests. Fort Belvedere, the weekend retreat near Windsor which he acquired in 1929, embodied Edward's 'inner emigration' in physical form. In a highly symbolic gesture, the flag which Edward flew over the Fort carried the crest of the Duke of Cornwall, not the Prince of Wales.[48]

The most constructive and proactive approach, which Edward pursued with fitful energy, was to adapt and modernize the role of Prince of Wales to suit his own personality. The conditions for the modernization of the British monarchy were very favourable after the Great War, when the House of Windsor feared for its very survival following the demise of so many European royal houses. King George V had inherited from his father and grandmother a symbolic, ceremonial model of monarchy: politically impartial, stripped of all authority to govern, but providing the focus of unity and identity for the nation and the empire.[49] As its political power had diminished, so the splendour of its rituals increased. The twenty years before 1914 saw the great age of royal pageantry, from Queen Victoria's Diamond Jubilee in 1897, through the coronations of Edward VII and George V, to the Delhi Durbar of 1911 and Prince Edward's investiture at Caernarvon.[50] The traditional view of royal advisers was that such a model required the Crown to retain a certain mystique: the monarchy should remain on a pedestal, remote and mysterious to the people.[51]

Edward disagreed. His experiences in the war had convinced him that the traditional model of monarchy was out of date, and that one of his main tasks was to bring it closer to ordinary people. His belief was vindicated by the success of his overseas tours. As he grew more confident in his role, he developed a new and distinctive approach to royal duties. He combined considerable personal charm with an excellent memory for names and an instinctive ability to handle large crowds. Impatient with ceremonial, he tried increasingly to step out of the stifling constraints of royal protocol, in order to engage with the real world. His 'democratic' and informal style was well suited to the post-war era. It went down particularly well in the English-speaking Dominions which had contributed so much to the war effort and were on the verge of independent statehood.[52]

As Edward's views on monarchy diverged from the orthodox doctrine of Buckingham Palace officials, his relations with his own staff became increasingly strained. 'One is like a jockey', wrote Tommy Lascelles in a revealing letter to his wife, 'trying to induce a racehorse to race, whose only idea is to stop in the middle of the course and perform circus tricks; or an actor-manager, whose Hamlet persists in interrupting the play by balancing the furniture on the end of his nose.'[53] Beneath the comical analogies it is striking that Lascelles should compare his relationship with the Prince to that between rider and horse or manager and actor. The Prince's staff expected him to remain 'on message', to deliver lines that others had written for him. The idea that he might shape the message, and present a different, more up-to-date image of monarchy, was regarded as dangerous and disruptive.

Occasionally it is possible to see how these tensions played out in practice. In August 1927 Edward attended the Diamond Jubilee celebrations of Canada's Confederation in Ottawa. It was an important moment in the history of the British Commonwealth. The Imperial Conference of 1926 had declared that the Dominions—Canada, Australia, South Africa, and New Zealand—were autonomous countries, equal in status with the United Kingdom, but united by common allegiance to the Crown. The Colonial Office and Lascelles had prepared a carefully worded speech for the Prince to deliver at the Jubilee ceremony, emphasizing his own role as heir to the throne. The key section ran:

> To me in particular, as the King's eldest son, the conception [of the Commonwealth] has a special importance which in whatever part of the Empire I may be, I try always to keep in my mind. The Crown stands above all distinctions of country, race and party, and serves to mark the unity in which all such differences are transcended. If some day it should fall to my lot to assume that high responsibility, I trust I may be found worthy of it.[54]

Edward, however, thought that the passage was too pompous, and at the last minute he decided to leave it out, against Lascelles's protests, substituting a joke instead.[55] Given the ambivalence which Edward felt about his future role as king, it is not surprising that he objected to such a personal reference to his position. In any event, the Prince's attempt to depart from his script went unnoticed. Lascelles had circulated advance copies of the speech to the press, which printed the official version, ignoring Edward's omissions. Having outmanoeuvred his master, Lascelles noted with grim satisfaction that the one passage selected for praise and comment by both the Canadian and home newspapers was the passage the Prince had never spoken.[56]

The Prince's tours through Britain and the wider world opened his eyes to the extraordinary changes that were taking place across the globe, particularly in America, and fostered a lasting interest in social and economic issues. The experience shaped the approach he took to his duties as a prince and future king. Rejecting the notion that monarchy should remain on a pedestal, he sought out direct, personal contact with the people in order to understand the challenges that Britain faced. Whenever possible he preferred to make private, unofficial visits to inspect industrial developments and social conditions for himself. In response to the social and economic crises which the war brought in its wake, he reached across the class divide to discuss the problems of unemployment and poor housing with those who were suffering most acutely. These were issues with which he was passionately concerned, and where the personal interests of David the private man at last coincided with the duties of Edward, Prince of Wales. In the words of his cousin Prince Christopher of Greece, a frequent visitor to Britain between the wars, he 'was not only a prince concerning himself for the people he would one day rule, but a man who faced realities trying to find a solution to the problem he felt as keenly as though it were one of his own'.[57] Between 1929 and 1934, through his work campaigning against unemployment and social deprivation, Edward at last appeared to have attained a degree of psychological equilibrium. The conflict between his public and private lives was in remission. He was carrying out duties as Prince of Wales which he regarded as worthwhile and important; in his personal life he was in a stable, if tepid, relationship with his current mistress, Thelma Furness; and in Fort Belvedere he had found the private refuge he had long been seeking. If King George had died during this period, there would have been no question of Edward's abdication. He would have succeeded his father, undergone his coronation, and reigned over the empire as a bachelor king.

10

Inner Emigration

The Americanization of a Prince

Edward had enjoyed his American vacation in 1924 so much that he was eager to return as soon as possible.[1] The following year was out of the question because he was scheduled to make a tour of Africa and South America. His initial plan was therefore to return to the USA in 1926 to visit the industrial regions of the Midwest. However, Edward reckoned without the opposition of the King and his advisers, who had been appalled by the press coverage the Prince received in America in 1924. The projected 1926 tour did not take place, and although he was permitted to return for his fourth visit to Canada in 1927, it was only under the watchful eye of the Prime Minister, Stanley Baldwin. It is clear that King George had decided to prevent the Prince from travelling back to America. While the King did not issue a formal ban on visits, Edward found that obstacles always arose to block any plans for a possible trip. For the remainder of his life, the King succeeded in keeping Edward away from America. Despite repeated efforts, he was not to see the USA again until 1941, five years after his Abdication.[2]

Coping Mechanisms

For Edward this was to be a bitter disappointment. He was fascinated by American culture, he enjoyed the company of Americans, and he believed that Britain had a great deal to learn from the vigour and creativity of American industry. He responded to his father's ban with a form of 'inner emigration': he observed an outward compliance with the King's wishes, coupled with passive private resistance. The concept of 'inner emigration' has been used to describe the psychological coping mechanisms adopted by citizens of totalitarian regimes: while conforming to the external demands of the regime, an individual would retreat whenever possible into his private world—whether of family, the arts, or sport—in order to preserve something of his inner life from the authorities.[3] Britain in the 1920s was not a totalitarian state, and George V was not a dictator; nevertheless, Edward's position placed a similar burden of psychological pressure upon him. In public he had to play the role of Prince of Wales, the personification of British traditional values and the ambassador of the British Empire; in private he was strongly attracted to American society and culture, which many in his own country regarded as the antithesis of Englishness.

Edward was not alone in taking refuge in an 'inner emigration' to America; his experience was one shared with millions of his subjects. During the 1920s and 1930s well over half of the adult British population went to the cinema at least once a week, immersing themselves in the American cultural dreamworld of Hollywood movies. As the *Daily Express* complained in 1927, British picture-goers 'talk America, think America and dream America. We have several million people who to all intents and purposes are temporary American citizens.'[4] Edward's father could stop him from going to America, but he could not prevent America from coming to him. The Shakespearean example of Prince Hal sanctified the tradition that the Prince of Wales enjoyed the freedom to select his own circle of friends. If Edward chose to associate with Americans, there was little that the King could do to stop him. In the years that followed, the Prince's passion for jazz, his preference for American products, and his taste for American women became increasingly evident. He lionized visiting Americans, like the aviator Charles Lindbergh, the bandleader Paul Whiteman, and the golfer Walter Hagen. He paid frequent visits to Paris, where there was a large American expatriate community, to hear the latest 'hot jazz' rhythms in the nightclubs of Montmartre. He even picked up the typically American habit of chewing gum. While waiting for the royal train at a small country town near Winnipeg in Canada, Edward bought a packet of mint-flavoured gum at the general store.[5] Finding it to his taste, he stocked up with an additional supply before boarding the train. He became a regular user when he found that it helped his concentration while riding and playing polo. In 1924 a group of journalists watching him at a polo practice game on Long Island were surprised to see him chewing vigorously, and apparently throwing away a wad of gum. After the game was over they hurried to the spot and found the Prince's discarded gum in the grass. Will Rogers, himself an inveterate gum chewer, confirmed in his newspaper column that the Prince had adopted the habit. A few years later, when it was reported that Edward had given up cigarettes in favour of gum, the *New York Sun* concluded: 'the Americanization of England may be regarded as complete'.[6] When Edward acquired his weekend retreat at Fort Belvedere in 1929, he gathered round him a small coterie of intimate friends, many of whom were American, a group which Alistair Cooke later christened 'the Prince's private Anglo-American cafe society'.[7]

Edward's use of language reflected the degree to which he had absorbed American influences. From his first encounters with US troops in 1918, he was fascinated by American idioms and slang, and readily adopted them himself. In addressing an American audience in London in 1924, he showed off his expertise, peppering the speech with Americanisms.[8] Basil Woon, the journalist, who met the Prince in a Paris nightclub in 1926, remarked how Americanized his speech was, especially when talking to Americans. He pronounced words in the American way, for example saying 'eether' for 'either', and 'aLOOminum' instead of the British 'alyoominium'. In Canada in 1927 he deliberately used the American pronunciation of 'ranch', with a short 'a', to emphasize that the EP ranch was a business operation, not a hobby 'rawnch' for English amateurs.[9] Americanisms slipped into Edward's everyday conversation as he went about his public engagements in Britain. When visiting a Scottish regiment in the Highlands he arrived in driving sleet and commented, 'You have swell weather here!' Meeting the Prince for the first time in 1932, Alistair Cooke was struck by his American usage of the word 'field' for an academic discipline; a few years later an old colleague of Cooke's was outraged when Edward used the word 'radio' in his first BBC broadcast as King, in preference to the English term 'wireless': 'It's those Americans he goes with,' he shouted.[10]

To some extent Edward's Americanization reflected wider trends in British high society. During the 1920s and 1930s London society was dominated by American hostesses. As an example, the highlight of the London 'season' in June 1921 was the Lansdowne House Ball, a charity fundraiser for the Queen Victoria Institute for Nurses. It was organized by Countess Curzon, born Grace Hinds of Alabama, and attended by King Alfonso of Spain, the Prince of Wales, and his brother the Duke of York. Among the leading hostesses who gave dinner parties before the ball were Lady Cunard (born Maud Burke of San Francisco), Lady Ribblesdale (Ava Lowle Willing, the first wife of John Jacob Astor IV), and Mrs Cornelius Vanderbilt, the wealthy American socialite. Lansdowne House itself, one of the great London aristocratic town houses, was made available by its owner, Gordon Selfridge, the American retail millionaire.[11]

The Prince was, of course, the most sought-after guest at the salons of the leading Anglo-American hostesses, and he frequently accepted their hospitality. Nevertheless, he did not count them amongst his closest friends. They were pillars of London 'society' and also British citizens by marriage. Edward was more at ease with American expatriates—diplomats, businessmen, and entertainers—who were not subjects of the British Crown. He could meet them on more equal terms, setting aside the protocol and deference which crippled his social life as a royal prince. One of his oldest American friends was Frederick Bate, a Chicagoan by birth, who had come to Paris before the Great War to try his hand at painting. During the war he joined the American Ambulance Field Service, and after the Armistice he remained in France. Edward probably first met Fred Bate through his second wife, Vera Arkwright Bate, who was the stepdaughter of a cousin of Queen Mary. Alistair Cooke described Bate as 'courtly, modest, good natured, the apotheosis of savoir faire and New World courtesy'.[12] During the 1920s he worked in the secretariat of the Reparations Commission in Paris, and in 1924 he was seconded to the Dawes Committee, assisting Charles Dawes and Owen Young in their work on proposals for the reconstruction of the German financial system. Prince Edward visited Bate in Paris several times during the 1920s; they played golf together and Fred and Vera would take Edward to the latest nightclubs.[13] Bate moved to London in 1933 when he became the European representative for the NBC radio network, and with his third wife, Genevieve, he became a regular weekend visitor at Fort Belvedere. It was at a dinner given for the Bates by the Prince at the Dorchester Hotel in February 1934 that Edward and Wallis had their 'breakthrough' evening.[14]

Another close friend of the Prince was the diplomat Benjamin Thaw, through whom Edward was later to meet Wallis Simpson. Descended from a prominent Pittsburgh banking family, Benny Thaw met Edward in Buenos Aires in 1925, when he was First Secretary at the US Embassy. In the Ambassador's absence the responsibility for entertaining the Prince had fallen to Thaw.[15] The two men got on well with each other, and renewed their acquaintance when Thaw was posted to London and later to Paris. Benny's wife, Consuelo, was the sister of Thelma Furness, the Prince's mistress between 1929 and 1934, and during those years the couple became part of Edward's inner circle.[16] Thaw was the original point of contact between

Edward and Wallis Simpson. He had met Wallis while they were both in Washington in the 1920s, and introduced her to Thelma when Wallis and Ernest arrived in London.

One of the prerogatives of royalty was the opportunity to meet famous men and women, and Edward went out of his way to greet the American celebrities of the day when they visited Britain—entertainers like Charlie Chaplin, sportsmen such as the boxer Gene Tunney, and, most famous of all, the aviator Charles Lindbergh, the first man to fly solo across the Atlantic. Lindbergh's arrival in England shortly after his transatlantic flight caused the same degree of excitement as Edward's visits to the USA.[17] The Prince met him when he went to Buckingham Palace to meet King George, and they had a second encounter that evening at the Derby Eve Ball at the Royal Albert Hall. When the Prince arrived, Lindbergh climbed into the royal box to be photographed alongside him, amidst the cheers of the crowd.[18] Although their backgrounds were utterly different, their common love of aviation and a shared experience of the pressures of celebrity formed a powerful bond between them. Lindbergh later said that the Prince was the only man in the world who could truly understand his situation; the only differences were that Lindbergh faced celebrity alone, whereas the Prince had a team of staff to protect him; and Lindbergh did not care what the press said about him, whereas Edward did.[19]

The celebrities whom Edward was keenest to meet were his great sporting heroes, the golfers Walter Hagen and Bobby Jones. Golf was one of the many sports in which Britain succumbed to American dominance during the inter-war period. In the thirteen years from 1921 to 1933, American golfers won the British Open twelve times. Hagen won four Open titles and Jones three. The Prince was a passionate, if mediocre, golfer, and after he gave up riding in 1929 it was his main sporting pastime.[20] He presented the claret jug to Hagen after his third Open victory at Sandwich in 1928, and persuaded the American to stay in Britain for a few days to help him with his game. Hagen was a flamboyant, party-loving extrovert, the first professional golfer to make a living from playing the game rather than teaching it. He got on very well with the Prince and gave him several golf lessons. According to golfing legend their friendship was instrumental in breaking down the barriers against professionals in Britain. On one occasion they played a round at the Royal St George's Club in Sandwich, and went into the clubhouse for lunch. At that time professional golfers were still not allowed to enter a British clubhouse. In embarrassment, the club secretary reminded the Prince

Figure 10.1. The Prince presents the claret jug to Walter Hagen as winner of the British Open, 1928

that Hagen could not be served in the dining room. Edward replied, 'You must stop this, here and elsewhere. If this man is not welcome here, I shall see that the name "Royal" is removed from your club.'[21]

Edward also played golf with the great amateur champion, Bobby Jones. In 1930, when Jones was preparing for the British Open, the Prince went to the Sunningdale course near Fort Belvedere to watch him practise with other American golfers. An impromptu foursome was arranged, in which Jones partnered the Prince. At the end of the match Jones commented diplomatically that the Prince was a good golfer; all he needed to do was practise.[22] This was the year in which Jones achieved his unique 'Grand Slam' of victories in all four major golf tournaments.[23] Speaking at a Thanksgiving Day Dinner to the American Society in London later in the year, Edward hailed Jones's achievement as equal to Lindbergh's crossing of the Atlantic three years earlier: 'the whole of the sporting community admires to the utmost his unique achievement, which I predict will never be beaten'.[24]

All That Jazz

One of Edward's favourite forms of 'inner emigration' was jazz music. Introduced with the arrival of American troops in 1917, jazz soon became popular in Britain along with the dances associated with it, such as the Foxtrot, the Charleston, and the Black Bottom. Innovative, energetic, and quintessentially American, jazz epitomized the challenge which cultural exports from the USA posed to British identity and values after the Great War. One British critic described jazz as low and degrading, 'the symptom of a very grave disease which was infesting the country'.[25] For some members of the establishment, jazz threatened the very fabric of British society. A tongue-in-cheek editorial in *The Times* in 1923, entitled 'A Tithe Barn: Jazz in the Cotswolds', condemned the use of a medieval barn for jazz dancing. 'Oh, profanation! Oh, sacrilege!...jazzing in the Cotswolds! And worse, jazzing in a venerable edifice that must have been standing when they fought at Hastings. Have these jazzing villagers no historical sense, no respect for the *genius loci*?'[26]

In spite of its subversive, un-English qualities, or perhaps because of them, Prince Edward quickly fell in love with jazz. He first encountered it through the sanitized jazz styles of white American musicians, notably the bandleader Paul Whiteman. With a conventional classical training, Whiteman made his name by 'jazzing' the classics. Edward's cousin Lord Louis Mountbatten had heard Whiteman's orchestra play while on honeymoon in New York in 1922, and urged him to come to Britain. Whiteman duly organized a tour the following year, appearing in a revue called 'Brighter London' at the Hippodrome from April 1923. The Prince met Whiteman when he was playing at a private party thrown by the Mountbattens, and Edward became an avid fan, regularly attending late-night performances of the Whiteman orchestra at the Grafton Galleries, a West End nightclub.[27] Soon after his arrival in Britain, Whiteman experienced difficulties with the Ministry of Labour in obtaining work permits for his orchestra. Fearing for the livelihood of its members, the British Musicians' Union was strongly opposed to the employment of American players, and at first it seemed that the tour might not go ahead. However, the Prince intervened personally with the Minister to ensure that Paul Whiteman's orchestra would be allowed to play. A compromise was reached, whereby Whiteman was required to hire one British musician for each American member of his ensemble.[28]

The visit to Britain of the Paul Whiteman Orchestra attracted considerable press coverage in the US, particularly once the Prince's interest became known. Towards the end of the tour, in July 1923, the American show-business journalist Karl Kitchen interviewed Whiteman one evening at the Grafton Galleries. By this time the Prince and the bandleader were on the friendliest terms, and Whiteman had played for Edward several times at private parties. It was the height of the social season, the night of the Eton versus Harrow cricket match; the club was filled with fashionable London society in formal evening dress. As Kitchen chatted with Whiteman between sets, Edward was sitting at a nearby table with Freda Dudley Ward and the Mountbattens, smoking a huge cigar. Whiteman recounted several anecdotes about the Prince. At one private party he had personally served champagne to every member of the band; the drummer was so excited that he immediately ran off to cable his family back in the States. The interview was interrupted when a waiter came over to Whiteman with a request from the Prince: 'Paul, will you play the Nutcracker Suite,' Edward asked, 'I'm mad about it.' The orchestra played until 2 a.m.; Edward danced every dance with Freda, and when the club closed, Whiteman's musicians accompanied the Prince's entourage to the nearby Blue Lagoon Club, where the party continued until daybreak behind closed doors.[29] Thanks to the Prince's patronage Whiteman's British tour was a great success. It made Whiteman's reputation as the 'King of Jazz', and on his return to the USA he was greeted as a conquering hero. In 1924 he entertained Edward again at one of the most opulent parties the Prince attended on Long Island, and he returned to Britain in 1926 for a second tour.[30]

Paul Whiteman's classically influenced 'symphonic jazz' was very different from the authentic 'hot jazz' that was emerging from the clubs of New Orleans, Harlem, and Chicago in the mid-1920s. However, black jazz musicians and singers like Duke Ellington, Louis Armstrong, and Florence Mills were gaining recognition as stars in their own right, and found receptive audiences in Europe. In the early 1930s Armstrong and Ellington both made successful tours of the UK. Edward and his brother Prince George were fans of Duke Ellington: in June 1933 Edward attended one of his concerts in Liverpool, after watching his friend Walter Hagen playing in the Ryder Cup at nearby Southport. A few days later the two princes met Ellington at a party in London thrown by the newspaper magnate Lord Beaverbrook. While Prince George played piano duets with Ellington, Edward sat down on the floor next to the drummer Sonny Greer.

Figure 10.2. Paul Whiteman

'I noticed this skinny little guy squatting near the drums,' Greer later recalled.

> Pretty soon he asks can we play the Charleston. We did and he danced like crazy. Then he asked me could he sit in the drums and I said 'Of course, my man'. People kept on coming up and calling him 'Your Highness' or 'Wales', but he wouldn't move. We both began to get high on whatever it is we were drinking. He was calling me 'Sonny' and I was calling him 'The Whale'.[31]

Late-night jazz offered Edward a brief escape from the pressures of his official life in Britain. For a longer respite the Prince took refuge across the English Channel, at his favourite holiday destinations of Paris and Biarritz. In the mid-1920s, once his imperial tours were over, Edward visited France several times a year. One of the attractions was that Paris was the largest American city in continental Europe. The American colony was more than 30,000 strong; it had its own clubs, stores, schools, and newspapers. Many of the expatriates were financiers and businessmen—France was experiencing the same influx of American goods and services as Britain. However, with a favourable dollar/franc exchange rate, Paris also attracted a more bohemian sort, would-be artists like Edward's friend Fred Bate, and writers like Ernest Hemingway, Scott and Zelda Fitzgerald, and Ezra Pound.[32]

Where there were Americans, there was jazz. Edward would return from his trips to Paris with a collection of the latest jazz recordings obtained from the performers he had heard in Montmartre.[33] One of the best-known expatriates in Paris was the Chicago-born adventurer and nightclub entrepreneur Gerald 'Jed' Kiley. A journalist by profession, Kiley had volunteered alongside Fred Bate and Ernest Hemingway for the American Ambulance Field Service in France in 1917, and joined the US army when America entered the war. After the Armistice he organized dances for American servicemen in Paris, which were tolerated by the French authorities although public dancing was then forbidden under wartime regulations. He soon began operating a series of 'pop-up' nightclubs in Montmartre, keeping one step ahead of the police. His chief innovation was to feature a jazz band in his clubs, and Kiley acquired a reputation for hosting the latest 'hot jazz' from Harlem and Chicago. It was to 'Kiley's' that Fred Bate took the Prince while he was visiting Paris in April 1924. The party probably also included the dance duo the Dolly Sisters, who were performing in Paris at the same time.[34] The Prince enjoyed 'Kiley's' so much that he went back there on the following two nights. On one of the evenings, the staff staged a walk-out in protest at the sacking of the club's cashier. At the time the club was packed with wealthy Americans eager to rub shoulders with the Prince. Facing disaster, Jed Kiley frantically rang round the nearby restaurants to borrow one of their cooks. Instead, the guests came to his rescue. A famous New York lawyer served champagne, while American society hostesses went down to the kitchens to cook ham and eggs. The Prince himself, who was always delighted when the smooth running of his daily routine was disrupted, helped to hand round glasses and clear the tables. 'Kiley's' reputation was made: before long it was the most popular society venue in Montmartre; in Jed Kiley's words, 'my dance floor looked like an illustrated copy of Burke's Peerage'.[35]

Having a reputation for racial tolerance, Paris was a particular magnet for black American musicians. By the mid-1920s 'Kiley's' was just one of the many nightclubs in Montmartre catering mainly for the American expatriate community, where jazz and alcohol could be consumed in equal measure. One of the best-known black American entertainers in Montmartre was Ada 'Bricktop' Smith, a jazz singer and dancer who owed her nickname to the bright red hair she inherited from her Irish–American father. Cole Porter hosted parties in Paris at which Bricktop taught the Charleston, and in October 1926 she opened her own nightclub called the Music Box, which later became 'Bricktop's'. Bricktop had met Prince Edward at a private party given by the Boston millionaire Amos Lawrence, where she taught him the latest dance craze, the Black Bottom. Pleased to have mastered the new steps, Edward asked her to host an impromptu party for him at her new club the following night. As with 'Kiley's', the Prince's patronage ensured the lasting success of 'Bricktop's'. The club became a permanent feature of Paris nightlife, with a clientele which included Hemingway and the Fitzgeralds, Man Ray, and Picasso.[36]

Finding Fort Belvedere

By the late 1920s the Prince was taking every opportunity to escape from what he called 'the tight little island of Britain' whenever his official duties permitted.[37] In 1928, having grown tired of his Canadian ranch, and with the USA out of bounds, he discovered a new and exciting vacation in the form of an African safari. Whilst still in the East African bush, he began to plan further overseas trips, and his staff worried that his ties with England were growing increasingly tenuous.[38] However, Edward's globetrotting was cut short when his father fell ill in November 1928. While hunting in a remote corner of Tanganyika, the Prince received a flurry of coded cables advising him that the King was dying, and summoning him home at once. He was furious that his holiday should be interrupted, and suspected a political stunt from Prime Minister Baldwin. He had a row with Tommy Lascelles about returning home, and in a final act of defiance he went out and seduced the wife of the local district officer, a Mrs Barnes. After a two-week journey back to Britain by rail and sea, including a special train through Italy laid on by Mussolini, Edward reached his father's bedside on 11 December. 'Damn you, what the devil are you doing here?' grunted the King, and from that moment he began to improve.[39]

The King's illness proved to be a major turning-point in Edward's life as Prince of Wales. Although George V eventually recovered, he remained seriously ill for several months. Edward's succession to the throne suddenly seemed much closer. It was evident that he would have to modify his lifestyle. He agreed to give up hunting and steeple-chasing, and in February 1929 he sold his entire stable of horses. He also curtailed his foreign travel; although there were still to be major trips, such as his 'Prince of Sales' tour of South America in 1931, the Prince did not maintain the hectic pace of travel which had characterized his schedule throughout the 1920s.

One of the great imponderables of Edward's career is what would have happened if King George had died in 1928. Edward would have come to the throne in circumstances completely different from those which he faced in January 1936: before the Depression, before the rise of Hitler, and of course before he had met Wallis Simpson. He would have become a bachelor king and, like Queen Elizabeth I, would probably have remained unmarried. At his accession he would not have faced the wrenching dilemma of choosing between public duty and private happiness. His love affair with Freda Dudley Ward was long over, and although her friendship might have provided him with a degree of emotional support, there would have been no question of marriage. The constraints of his role as King would have provided him with little time and opportunity to build the social network of Anglo-American friends, based on Fort Belvedere, which he developed between 1929 and 1936. The crisis of the Depression, coming early in his reign, would have presented him with a great national challenge well suited to his modernizing instincts and democratic appeal.

In fact, the old king lived on, a semi-invalid, for the next seven years. George V's brush with death did give rise to a temporary rapprochement between Edward and his parents, as the Prince assumed many of his father's duties. In the same year, 1929, Edward also won his parents' gratitude for taking responsibility for rescuing his younger brother Prince George from drug addiction. George had become addicted to cocaine while carrying on an affair with the American socialite and drug user Kiki Preston.[40] Edward managed to persuade Kiki to leave the country, and personally supervised Prince George's rehabilitation over a period of several months.[41]

The sudden change in Edward's lifestyle in 1929–30 marked the watershed between his restless, picaresque youth and a more settled middle age. Having retired from riding, he gave up his 'hunting box', the apartments in Melton Mowbray in Leicestershire where he had spent most of his weekends during the fox-hunting season. He looked round for a secluded retreat within easy reach of London where he might spend his leisure time. In the summer of 1929 he found Fort Belvedere.

The Fort was situated on a hill at the southernmost edge of Windsor Great Park, overlooking Virginia Water. Originally built as a royal summer house in the eighteenth century, it was extended by George IV as a miniature fort in mock-Gothic style, complete with towers, battlements, and cannon. In the nineteenth century it was occupied by retired bombardiers from the Royal Artillery, who would fire off the ordnance on the sovereign's birthday. It later became a 'grace and favour' residence, but when Edward acquired it in 1929, it was a romantic ruin. The floorboards were broken, the sanitation was primitive, and the garden overgrown. 'What could you possibly want that queer old place for?' asked the King. 'Those damn weekends I suppose.'[42] Edward set about restoring and modernizing the place, and incorporated the latest features he had seen in houses in the USA—central heating, en-suite bathrooms, a steam bath, and built-in cupboards. In the garden he built a tennis court and a swimming pool with underwater lighting. Weekend visitors were press-ganged into clearing away acres of overgrown laurel round the house, which Edward replaced with a rockery, lawns, and herbaceous borders.[43]

One of the greatest advantages of the Fort was its excellent communications. Although tucked away within Windsor Great Park, it was only twenty-five miles from the centre of London, just off the main road to Southampton. It was also close to two major golf courses, Sunningdale and Wentworth, where the Prince could pursue his passion for the game. Most

Figure 10.3. Fort Belvedere undergoing restoration, 1929

importantly, it was accessible from the air; in 1929 King George had finally lifted his ban on the Prince flying, and Edward took to the air with enthusiasm. He acquired his own flight of aeroplanes, which he kept at Hendon aerodrome in North London.[44] He had a site cleared at Smith's Lawn in the Park for use as an airfield, and a road was constructed linking it directly with the Fort.[45] This allowed the Prince to fly directly from Windsor to public engagements all over Britain, greatly reducing his travelling time and enabling him to extend his weekends at the Fort until Monday afternoons.

Edward moved into Fort Belvedere in April 1930, directly after returning from his East African safari. He arrived in style by aeroplane, landing at Smith's Field after flying from Marseilles. The King and Queen were there to greet him, and together they looked around the refurbished Fort. For the Prince it was to be more than just a weekend retreat. As he lavished time and attention upon the Fort, it became his true home. St James's Palace was as much an office as a residence, and it did not have the facilities to entertain guests; the EP ranch had proved too remote to provide the sanctuary he sought. The Fort was his private haven where he could relax and escape from his official life as Prince of Wales. After Edward became King in January 1936, Fort Belvedere temporarily acquired a special status as 'the King's independent home'.[46] When in residence, he flew the flag of the Duke of Cornwall, rather than the royal standard, as a way of emphasizing that he was 'off duty'. Formal ceremonial was set aside and official business banned.

The fullest account of the Fort in its heyday is provided by Wallis in her memoirs, when she described her first visit with Ernest Simpson in 1932. Their initial glimpse of the house in the winter twilight was the outline of the nineteenth-century tower, picked out of the shadows by concealed floodlights. A narrow corridor from the entrance gave onto the octagonal hallway, which doubled as a dance floor; beyond that was the drawing room, also octagonal. The rest of the ground floor comprised a dining room and small library, together with Edward's own bedroom; upstairs were six guest bedrooms. Outside there was a terrace and lawn, which ended in a semi-circular stone battlement, mounted with eighteenth-century cannon. Beyond were extensive gardens sloping down to Virginia Water with a fine cedar walk planted with azaleas and rhododendrons. The tone was one of unostentatious luxury: Canalettos hung on the natural pine-panelled walls, behind Chippendale furniture.[47]

The Fort was large enough to entertain a house party of about a dozen people. Until 1934 Thelma Furness acted as Edward's hostess; thereafter her position was taken by Wallis Simpson. Edward's youngest brother, Prince George, was a regular visitor until his marriage in 1935. In the early days, Albert and Elizabeth, the Duke and Duchess of York, would sometimes call in from their Windsor home at Royal Lodge, although their visits became less frequent with Wallis's ascendancy. In general, however, the regular guests at the Fort were drawn from a narrow circle: Edward's closest companions, such as Fruity Metcalfe and 'G' Trotter; long-standing American friends, such as Fred Bate and Benny Thaw; and members of Thelma's and later Wallis's social acquaintance.[48]

Fort Belvedere gave shape and structure to the Prince's domestic life from 1930 onwards. It was not physically removed from the rest of his family: Windsor Castle was only a few miles away, and he would sometimes give his guests tours of the Castle's treasures. Nevertheless, the Fort was very much his own territory, and through it he made a number of significant statements about his approach to his royal role. It was an expression in stone of his long-held view that, as long as he discharged his official duties adequately, his private life was his own affair. The Fort enabled him to draw a clear line, temporal and spatial, between his public and private life. Its modest size conveyed his dislike of formality and ostentation, but it also confirmed that, at the age of 35, there was no immediate prospect of his marrying. On the contrary, the Fort provided Edward with a private retreat where he could live discreetly with his mistresses at weekends, concealed from the prying eyes of London society. During his last years as Prince, as his passion for Wallis grew into an obsession and his alienation from the rest of the royal family deepened, Fort Belvedere became Edward's bunker, at once the symbol and vehicle of his isolation.

By 1935, although he had not visited the USA in more than a decade, the future king was as Americanized as any man in England. He chewed American gum, drove an American car, danced to American jazz, socialized with American friends, had an American lover, and used American expressions. He even wore his trousers in the American style with a belt rather than braces.[49] The gulf between Edward, Prince of Wales, the embodiment of Englishness, and David, the Americanized private man, had never been wider.

11

'The Great Catastrophe'
The Prince, the Depression, and the USA

During the 1920s and 1930s, public criticism of the Prince was naturally very muted in Britain. Between the wars the monarchy was an almost sacred institution, and the royal family was treated with the utmost deference. Press coverage was restrained, and Edward's private life was strictly off limits. Nevertheless, after he passed his thirtieth birthday concerns began to be expressed about the Prince's immaturity and lack of application to his role. There was a vociferous group of anti-monarchist MPs in the Labour Party, who were critical of what they perceived as the Prince's frivolous lifestyle. One of them, the Scottish socialist David Kirkwood, attacked the spending on Edward's overseas tours. 'The money that the working classes produce ought not to be wasted on a nincompoop like the Prince of Wales. The young fellow ought to do some work instead of spending his time attending race meetings and dance halls.'[1] In March 1925 he proposed a parliamentary motion to reduce the government grant for the Prince's tour of Africa and Latin America.[2] On Edward's return from the tour in October, John Strachey, the editor of *The Spectator* magazine, published a critical article drawing attention to an incident on the tour when the Prince had caused offence by cancelling a morning engagement at short notice after a late-night party.

> We think that the Prince of Wales would rightly interpret the wishes of the nation if he made it impossible for people to have any excuse in saying that he is unduly restless or that he exhausts himself in giving to amusements too many hours which might be spent in preparation for work that is always exacting...the difficulty may be overcome if he would attach himself to some public cause which is entirely beyond and above faction. Being associated with a great purpose he would be bound to some regular application of his energies

which once and for all would put an end to any false notion that it is his desire to live a butterfly existence.[3]

The criticism was perhaps badly timed, given that Edward had just completed a gruelling eight-month tour of Africa and Latin America. However, it is unlikely to have been printed without the tacit approval of Buckingham Palace, and it reflected the growing concern that the Prince's over-enthusiastic pursuit of his private life was starting to have an impact on the performance of his public duties. The following year the *Daily News* columnist Alfred Gardiner published a critique in a similar vein, suggesting that Edward's apprenticeship was over and that it was time for him to grow up and take life more seriously:

> there is a lack of seriousness which, excusable and even natural to healthy youth, is disquieting in the mature man...the public would be relieved to read a little less in the encomiums of the Press about the jazz drum and banjo side of the Prince's life. We are not amused when we see the newspapers splashed with photographs of the heir to the throne disporting himself as a girl in farcical situations.[4]

The American press picked up the signals of disquiet about the Prince, and was able to express it in more forthright terms. Basil Woon, a British-born writer and journalist who worked in the USA, met Edward in a Paris nightclub in 1926, and used the encounter as the basis for a critical article on the Prince's lifestyle:

> The man who is to be King of England should be pretty well aware of his responsibilities, and act like it. The Prince doesn't. The English don't like his private life and they don't like his passion for American jazz and American cocktails...Their attitude is that they are paying him a huge salary to learn to be a king, and they think he should be a little more serious about it.[5]

The newspaper criticism of the Prince would certainly have come to the attention of his staff, and he may even have read it himself. In the years that followed, Edward did emphasize the more serious side of his character, and was less visible at parties and nightclubs. Whether or not he consciously heeded *The Spectator*'s advice, he also found a great national cause which he could champion: the campaign against mass unemployment and social deprivation.

Even before the onset of the Great Depression, unemployment was high in many parts of Britain, notably south Wales and the north-east of England. The mining industry was particularly badly hit after the war, as prices had collapsed with the import of cheap foreign coal. By 1928 more than 250,000

coal miners were unemployed out of a total workforce of one million.
On Christmas Day 1928, only a few days after his dramatic return from East
Africa to his father's sickbed, Edward broadcast a national radio appeal on
behalf of the Fund for Distress in Mining Areas. The appeal had an enormous impact, helping to raise over £300,000 (the equivalent of £17 million
at current values) within a month.[6] The appeal was also broadcast on the US
radio networks, and an anonymous American friend of the Prince's made
the largest single donation, of £20,000. Characteristically, having become
involved in the fund-raising, Edward wanted to see the worst-hit areas for
himself, and arranged a three-day tour of the Durham and Northumberland
coalfields at the end of January 1929. The Prime Minister, Stanley Baldwin,
was unhappy about the proposed visit; he felt that Edward was straying into
the political arena, and feared that he would be made a dupe of socialist
agitators. Summoning the Prince to his office at the House of Commons,
Baldwin interrogated him about the arrangements, and was only reassured
when Edward told him they had been made by the local Conservative Party
chairman.[7]

The tour itself bore all the hallmarks of Edward's distinctive style. He
insisted that it should be private and unofficial, thus obviating the need for
time-consuming ceremonial. No itinerary was published in advance; Edward
wanted to maintain an element of surprise, so that he could see actual living
conditions rather than model housing. He arranged to meet individuals
who had written to him from the pit villages, describing the hardship in
their communities. At East Hartford in Northumberland, Edward asked a
miner to explain to him the wage-rates and working conditions in the coalfields, and took away a bundle of wage-slips which showed that pay levels
were so low that it was better for miners to go on the dole. The Prince was
appalled at the poverty and deprivation that he found, saying he had no idea
that conditions were so bad.[8] The visit attracted extensive coverage in the
press, both in Britain and America, and Edward's outspoken comments
on the conditions in which the mining communities were living were fully
reported. The mine owners were furious. Lord Londonderry, a government
minister, wrote to Prime Minister Baldwin complaining that the Prince's
intervention played into the hands of the militant miners' unions.[9]

Here undoubtedly was the 'hands-on' Prince of Wales that Edward, in his
positive moods, aspired to be. It is no coincidence that his Christmas radio
appeal, and the ensuing tour of the North-East, took place while King George
was incapacitated by serious illness. For several months Edward acted as a de

facto 'Prince Regent' in place of the King, and he enjoyed greater freedom to put into practice his own vision of monarchy. The experience matured him, and gave him a new sense of purpose. In February 1929 he announced that he was giving up hunting and steeple-chasing; in an important symbolic gesture which signalled the renunciation of youthful pleasures, he sold his entire stable of horses.[10] A few days later he used a speech at the British Industries Fair, which again was broadcast on the BBC, to deliver a stinging attack on the failures of British business. It challenged employers to make more effort to find work for the 1.5 million unemployed, and criticized the poor quality of British 'salesmanship' (by which he meant marketing and customer service). 'Is the salesmanship of this country entirely up to date? Is the salesmanship of this country up to the standard of the workmanship of the men?'[11] The clear implication was that high unemployment was caused, at least in part, by the inertia of British industry.

Frazier Hunt, the American journalist who was the Prince's neighbour in Alberta, found Edward a changed man when he interviewed him in the summer of 1929 at his apartments in St James's Palace. 'He is a new prince,' wrote Hunt in an article for the US magazine *Cosmopolitan*, 'a prince reborn that day in the back country in East Africa when the word came that the King was sick unto death. From that moment when he started his six-thousand mile race with possible death, duty became the god of his waking hours.' He had embraced his princely duty with a new commitment, while performing the role in his own way. 'Neither his grandfather nor even his father would have dreamed of tramping through the mud and poverty and heartaches of the coalfields of Durham, with their tens of thousands of unemployed... to hundreds of poor miners and their families he came as a fresh pledge of help and friendliness.'[12]

Of course Edward was not the only member of the royal family to concern himself with social issues; where he diverged from the conventional doctrine of the post-Victorian monarchy was in his vehement condemnation of social deprivation and his demands for action. Rather than confining himself to charitable works and pious platitudes, he sought practical solutions. Although the Prince exercised no political power, his prominent position and popularity enabled him to influence the debate on the great issues of the day. Like President Roosevelt with his 'fireside chats', Edward was quick to appreciate the potential of radio as a platform from which to promote his agenda. As Prince of Wales he made more than fifty radio broadcasts—far more than any other public figure.[13] Some were straightforward charity appeals, but others, like his speech on slum clearance in May 1933, were direct attempts to influence government policy. In doing so he caused controversy, breaking the royal code of political impartiality by implicitly criticizing the government of the day for its failure to act.[14]

In the early 1930s Edward threw himself into campaigns to alleviate the effects of unemployment and to improve social conditions, especially as regards housing. In the summer of 1931 the Great Depression struck Britain with full force. Unemployment levels exceeded 2.8 million; one in six families had lost their livelihood. In January 1932, the Prince, as patron of the National Council of Social Service (NCSS), confronted the crisis in a major speech at the Royal Albert Hall in London. The audience was drawn from schools, universities, and youth organizations, and the speech was broadcast to several hundred meetings which were being held simultaneously across the country.[15] It was a stirring call to the young people of Britain to volunteer for service in bringing relief and support to the unemployed. The response to the Prince's appeal was 'immediate and overwhelming'. Offers of assistance flooded into the offices of the NCSS; by the autumn of 1932 the Council was in touch with several hundred schemes for the support of the unemployed, and by the end of 1933 some 2,300 centres had been opened, catering for a quarter of a million people.[16] A recording of the Prince's speech was released, and *The Times* published the text in pamphlet form.[17] Edward followed up his speech with tours of the 'distressed areas' in Tyneside, Yorkshire, the Midlands, Wales, and Scotland, and made frequent visits to clubs and schemes for the unemployed. At the end of one tour of Wales, the Prince was so exhausted that he fell asleep on the shoulder of the NCSS officer accompanying him, and had to be nudged awake from time to time to acknowledge the cheers of children lining the roadside.[18]

One of the worst affected areas was Glasgow, where the Depression had brought shipbuilding to a standstill. Work on the Cunarder '534', the future *Queen Mary*, had been halted in 1931, throwing thousands of men out of work. Before making a visit there in the spring of 1933, Edward was keen to find out what conditions in the city were actually like. Through the American-born MP Nancy Astor, he invited David Kirkwood, the revolutionary socialist who represented the Clydeside constituency of Dumbarton, to a meeting. As noted at the start of this chapter, a few years before the anti-monarchist Kirkwood had called the Prince a 'nincompoop', and opposed government funding for his tours.[19] At first he refused the invitation, but changed his mind in the hope that Edward's visit might do some good.

They met at a farewell reception for Andrew Mellon, the departing American Ambassador. Edward took Kirkwood aside, and they had a long talk during which the latter made a passionate plea for a government loan to finance the completion of the *Queen Mary*. Kirkwood was impressed by the Prince's openness and sincerity. 'I have never talked to any man in my life who was more eager to know just what the workers were thinking,' Kirkwood later recalled. 'We were two British citizens talking about our land and our people. A man's a man for a' that. It was as if we were on a ship in a storm, when class and caste and creed are forgotten.' The meeting converted Kirkwood from being an outspoken republican to an enthusiastic monarchist.[20] He attributed the government's subsequent decision to subsidize the building of the *Queen Mary* to the Prince's intervention, and it is likely that Edward did exert pressure on government ministers.[21] Certainly he paid close attention to the progress of the project, inspecting the vessel four times in the next three years.[22]

Edward was profoundly affected by the shocking housing conditions which he found in Britain's industrial cities. He later recalled that there were times when he returned home to Fort Belvedere feeling almost ill.[23] Thousands of working-class families still lived in overcrowded Victorian slums without adequate sanitation. On one visit, an American magazine reported that he had said to accompanying journalists, 'this sort of thing is a fucking shame, and you can say that I said so'.[24] He had some knowledge of housing issues from his role as Duke of Cornwall; the Duchy included a large estate in Kennington in south London, where it operated, by the standards of the time, as a model landlord.[25] It was a policy area where he felt practical steps could be taken to alleviate the social effects of the Depression. He consulted planning experts and architects and became an outspoken campaigner for slum clearance and the construction of modern affordable housing, acquiring in the process a reputation for radical views.[26] In May 1933 he gave a well-researched speech on the subject to the Association of Municipal Corporations. There were 98,000 families of five or more persons living in three rooms or fewer; there were 23,000 dwellings of three rooms or fewer occupied by two or more families, and of four or five rooms occupied by three or more families. 'They are not, and must not be, considered fit homes for the coming generation. I have been appalled that such conditions can exist in a civilized country such as ours...all statistics show the prevalence of maternal and infant mortality and epidemic diseases.'[27] As usual, Edward turned to the United States for examples of innovation in housing policy. He consulted a young Scottish architect who had studied the mass production of low-rent housing in America, and came up with a proposal of what would now be called a 'public–private partnership' for the redevelopment of a site on the Duchy estate in Kennington. However, the scheme was blocked by the London County Council, whose socialist leadership had ideological objections to the Prince's plans and distrusted his intervention in 'political' matters.[28]

The great crisis of the Depression brought out the best in Edward's character. The appeal to service and duty in the midst of a national emergency struck a deep personal chord within him, perhaps recalling to his mind the heady idealism of August 1914. The level of his personal commitment is revealed in the speech he gave to the NCSS at the Albert Hall in 1932. Although most of the speech was written by others, there was a brief but highly personal section at the end which must have been drafted by the Prince or at least sketched out by him:

> The world has passed into a new age with the end of the Great War. Never was a new age born in greater agony . . . What we make of it as a democracy is of vital concern, not only to ourselves, but to the whole world. So far as my part is concerned, many paths are closed to me. Much that I would like to do I cannot. But I have tried to bring more closely together the people of the Empire, the English-speaking peoples, and to further our interests abroad. I have had my failures I know, but in these years with few precedents to guide us, to have no failure is to have attempted nothing.[29]

This remarkable apologia represents Edward's first public acknowledgement of his personal struggle to come to terms with his role as Prince of Wales. Its confessional tone, and the recognition of the constraints upon him, suggest that he had, for the time being at least, come to terms with his royal destiny.

Anglo–American Relations and the Depression

In the late 1920s the close cooperation between America and Britain, which had dominated the early years of the decade, began to falter. The Anglo-American debt settlement and the Dawes Plan for German reconstruction had provided a breathing space, but Britain and the rest of Europe were slow to recover from the social and economic devastation of the war. In 1926 Winston Churchill, then Chancellor of the Exchequer, bitterly criticized the US Treasury Department for exacting in debt repayments funds which were needed for the economic rebuilding of Europe. Treasury Secretary Andrew Mellon responded by accusing Britain of using American war loans for self-interested commercial purposes. While American goods flooded into Britain and the rest of Europe, high US import tariffs made it hard for debtor countries to sell their products in American markets in order to earn the dollars to repay their loans. In the USA isolationist sentiment reasserted itself following Woodrow Wilson's ill-starred foray into international diplomacy at Versailles. This fed on the widespread suspicion that the European powers, and Britain in particular, wanted to use American money and support to prop up their tottering empires.[30] An additional source of friction was the growing naval rivalry between the two countries: the USA now demanded parity with the Royal Navy, which the British, after a century of unchallenged supremacy over the world's oceans, fiercely resisted.

The prickly nature of Anglo-American relations at this time is illustrated by an incident recounted in Edward's memoirs. The farcical aspects of the affair obviously appealed to him, because he devoted a full five pages to the story. When former Vice-President Charles Dawes was appointed US Ambassador to Britain in 1929, controversy raged in the American press as to whether he should wear the traditional court costume of knee-breeches and silk stockings for his audience at Buckingham Palace. Asked by a reporter if he intended to take a pair of 'knickers' with him to London, Dawes retorted with his usual bluntness, 'You can go plumb to hell, that's my business.'[31] As a consequence, Dawes flatly refused to don knee-breeches for the ceremony, despite the pleas of Palace officials. The King was reported to be extremely upset, and an international incident threatened to overshadow Dawes's arrival. The Lord Chamberlain, the head of the Royal Household, sought a crisis meeting with the Prince, who knew Dawes personally. Edward suggested a compromise: the Ambassador should arrive at the Palace wearing knee-breeches concealed under a pair of evening trousers. Once inside, he could then remove the trousers and attend the audience appropriately dressed. Dawes ignored this ludicrous suggestion. He presented himself in American-style formal dress, and the King and Queen turned a blind eye to the breach of etiquette. Twenty years later, when Edward, Duke of Windsor, visited Dawes in retirement in Florida, 'the word "knickers" was never once mentioned'.[32]

Despite the strained relationship between Britain and America, each nation continued to acknowledge the other as its most important international partner. Throughout this period, US presidents sent their most experienced politicians as Ambassadors to the Court of St James. As well as Dawes, they included the future Secretary of State Frank Kellogg, and the former Treasury Secretary Andrew Mellon. The Prince, being unable to visit the USA, was doubly keen to maintain his US contacts, and worked hard to maintain harmonious Anglo-American relations. As a member of the Pilgrims Club he regularly attended the London dinners held to mark the arrival and departure of US Ambassadors. In November 1930 Edward was the guest of honour at the Thanksgiving Day Dinner of the American Society in London, where he was hailed by Ambassador Dawes as a 'prince among men' for his work on behalf of Britain's unemployed. In his speech the Prince regretted that six years had passed since his last visit to the USA, and he expressed the hope of returning in the near future. He touched on the grim economic picture during the year on both sides of the Atlantic, which gave little cause for thanksgiving. On a more positive theme, he noted that the Atlantic Ocean had continued to shrink over the past decade, with the advent of air travel, transatlantic telephone, and radio. 'The very fact that America and Great Britain are continually striving to make the formidable ocean less of an obstacle than nature intended it to be, surely proves the people of those two countries are growing ever more anxious to join hand hands across it...that is, at any rate, something for which we can give thanks.'[33]

The Prince was convinced that the tensions and disagreements between Britain and America at this time could be resolved through personal contact. Welcoming Andrew Mellon as US Ambassador to Britain in 1932, he said, 'I set the greatest possible store by this personal contact between individuals of our two countries, because it enables us to see each other's viewpoint and understand each other as old friends do in ordinary life.'[34] A few years earlier he had made the same point informally to the journalist Frazier Hunt. 'More friendly understanding is all we need to iron out any little differences of opinion...fewer experts and more human beings to settle our difficulties...If we all could only play golf together, as I did recently with my good friend Mr [Frank] Kellogg, and later with Walter Hagen, we'd realise how close and necessary we really are to one another.'[35]

In his official functions Edward took every opportunity to meet visiting Americans and to associate himself with American philanthropy. In May 1929 he laid the foundation stone of the Eastman Dental Clinic in London, which was funded by a £200,000 benefaction from the founder of Kodak, George Eastman. In his address at the ceremony, the Prince said that the gift exemplified 'a friendship which springs from kinship of ideals as well as blood'. This may have been a conventional sentiment, but for the Prince it was clearly heartfelt, as he repeated it almost word for word several months later in his interview with Frazier Hunt.[36] At the World Scout Jamboree later that summer, he visited the American camp, and was presented with a Silver Buffalo, the highest award of the US Scouting Movement. The troop from Rochester, New York, also gave the Prince a 'boondoggle' (a braided lanyard), which he wore in his hat throughout the day.[37] The opening of the new Shakespeare Memorial Theatre in Stratford in April 1932 was very much an Anglo-American affair. American benefactors had helped to fund the construction, and Edward's speech at the ceremony was broadcast in the USA as well as Britain. In the presence of Ambassador Mellon, Edward made a point of acknowledging the American contribution to the project, as well as stressing Shakespearean drama as part of the common heritage of Britain and the USA.[38]

With the Wall Street Crash of 1929 and the onset of the Great Depression, the tensions between Britain and America grew dramatically, as governments on both sides of the Atlantic retreated into protectionism and economic nationalism. As the worldwide slump deepened, the two nations came to see each other less as partners and more as competitors in the struggle for economic survival. British and American businesses competed with each other to find new overseas markets. One major area of competition was South America. During the 1920s British influence was rapidly waning as the USA captured the expanding Latin American markets in automobiles, telecommunications, and consumer goods. Before the Great War, both countries had held about a quarter of the continent's import markets. By 1930 America's share had risen to nearly 40 per cent, while Britain's collapsed to 16 per cent.[39]

In 1931, with British industry devastated by the Depression, the Prince volunteered to visit South America to open the British Empire Trade Exhibition in Buenos Aires. This became the centrepiece of a four-month tour, which took Edward, accompanied by his brother Prince George, to all the major South American countries, through Peru, Bolivia, and Chile in the west to Argentina, Uruguay, and Brazil in the east. His outward journey took him once more through the Panama Canal, where he stepped onto American territory for the first time since crossing the Niagara Peace Bridge in 1927. On this occasion he was taken on a flight over the canal, enjoying an aerial view of the spectacular Culebra Cut, where HMS *Renown* had almost run aground in 1920.[40] In what was now a time-honoured royal tradition, Edward made the front pages by dancing with a pretty, dark-haired, brown-eyed American girl. She was Eleanor Nichols, the daughter of the commander of the Balboa Naval Radio Station. She said the Prince was charming, but found Prince George a much better dancer.[41]

Edward's Latin American tour as 'Prince of Sales' was closely followed by the newspapers in the USA. It was essentially a trade mission, and the American press saw his visit as a serious threat to US interests. 'British Scheme to Recapture Trade Behind Princes' Journey' ran a typical headline. One report warned, 'the globetrotting Prince of Wales and his travelling companions bid fair to bring back to Great Britain some of the commercial prestige it lost to the United States after the world war'. Edward's speech at the opening of the exhibition was broadcast live on the American networks. He prepared for it carefully, and delivered the second half in Spanish, to the delight of the large audience.[42] He put a brave face on the event, comparing it to the Great Exhibition of 1851, which signalled the triumph of Britain's industrial might in the nineteenth century. Privately, however, he was dismayed at the complacency and inertia of British businessmen in the face of the American challenge. While he was there he gave an outspoken interview to the *South Pacific Mail*, the English-language newspaper in Chile, in which he criticized the organizers of the exhibition for failing to invite British businesses from west of the Andes to send representatives to Buenos Aires.[43]

Edward came back from South America with a harsh message for British industry. Shortly after his return he addressed large meetings of businessmen in Birmingham and Manchester, warning them that they had fallen far behind their American competitors. Some passages of his speech were so critical of British companies that he asked the newspapers not to publish them. His comments were, however, reported in the American press. The Prince was particularly critical of the failure of British businesses to adopt American methods of advertising: 'I have heard many Englishmen say that the American form of publicity is very vulgar...the fact remains that our friends in the United States get away with it...if we wish to push our goods better, we will have to take a leaf out of their book.' He then painted a grim picture of the stranglehold which American industry had gained in the South American market for business equipment, cars, and consumer goods.

[The South American businessman's] telephone was of North American manufacture; 99 times out of 100 his car came from the United States; his office furniture and equipment was something up to date and efficient from the same source;...when he finished his day's work, he would find his American radio and his American gramophone, or American films in the movie theatres waiting to entertain him...We may hope that he will be pleased, when he takes off his shirt at night, that that article at least comes from Manchester.[44]

Despite the challenges which the USA posed to British industry through its aggressive expansion into overseas markets, the Prince continued to look to America as Britain's best hope for economic salvation. In May 1933, at the end of President Roosevelt's 'Hundred Days', Edward welcomed the new American Ambassador, Robert Bingham, at a dinner at the Pilgrims Club. Bingham reported in glowing terms on the economic recovery that was taking shape under the New Deal; he even quoted Roosevelt's famous phrase from his Inaugural Address, 'the only thing we have to fear is fear itself'. Echoing the theme, Edward spoke optimistically of how America could lead the world out of Depression: 'The eyes of the world are watching anxiously, but at the same time hopefully, what is happening in America...and we believe that in the midst of the great catastrophe in which all of us in the world are involved, America is realizing with us that under the inter-woven economic system of modern times no country can prosper in isolation.'[45] A year later, Bingham invited the Prince to an informal meeting at the US Embassy. Edward confided his belief that Britain was heading for radical social change, and required the kind of bold leadership that Roosevelt was providing in the USA.[46]

Even as he toured South America as the 'Prince of Sales' and the spokesman of British industry, Edward displayed a marked preference for American-made products. Reporting on the Prince's tour, the US Ambassador to Argentina noted wryly that at the same time as promoting British business, the Prince smoked American cigarettes, used a Kodak camera, and travelled in a Lincoln limousine.[47] Edward was particularly fond of American motor cars. In 1924 Henry Ford put a fleet of Lincolns at his disposal during his Long Island holiday, and later showed him round the Ford plant in Detroit. The following year he was so complimentary about the American Hupmobile limousines that were used for the royal tour of South Africa that the company built an advertising campaign round his image.[48] When it came to choosing a car for his own personal use, the Prince went not to the British luxury car manufacturer Rolls-Royce, but to the American firm Buick. In the summer of 1935 he turned up unannounced at the showrooms of Lendrum and Hartman, the Cadillac and Buick dealership in Mayfair in London, and ordered a Buick 90 Eight limousine. The Prince confided to the manager, Captain Hartman, that he did not believe anyone in Britain could build a car the way he wanted it, but only as they thought he wanted it built. His requirements were for a Fort Belvedere on wheels. The car was 'designed to give two passengers luxury and privacy'. Detailed specifications included drinks cabinets, vanity mirrors, reading lights, correspondence facilities, radio, smoker's cabinet, jewellery cabinet, compartments for canteen and luncheon trays, and a drawer to accommodate London telephone directories. One notable variation in the design was that the car had no rear quarter-light windows, presumably in order to shield the occupants from photographers. Edward took delivery of the car in February 1936, shortly after he became King. It ferried him to and fro between London and the Fort during the Abdication crisis, and accompanied him into exile after his Abdication.[49]

12

Wallis

Bessiewallis Warfield was born in June 1896. Her father died a few months after her birth, and she was brought up in genteel poverty, dependent on the charity of her Warfield relatives. Her mother came from an old but impoverished Virginia family, the Montagues, whom Wallis described as a 'magnetic, Bohemian clan'. The Warfields, by contrast, were strait-laced Baltimore businessmen. Her grandfather, Henry Mactier Warfield, supported the Confederate cause during the American Civil War, and had been imprisoned for refusing to take the oath of allegiance to the Union. Wallis grew up in the shadow of the Civil War. As a child she lived with her Warfield grandmother, who had an implacable hatred of Yankees.[1]

Wallis's Southern heritage was a defining part of her identity. For Southern families at the turn of the twentieth century, the catastrophe of the Civil War lingered in their collective consciousness, engendering a sense of loss and instability. Margaret Mitchell recalled what her mother had told her about the Old South: 'She talked about the world those people had lived in, such a secure world, and how it exploded under their feet. And she told me that my world was going to explode under me someday, and God help me if I didn't have some weapon to meet the new world.'[2] Wallis's chief weapon was her vivacious charm, coupled with a lively wit and a flair for hospitality.

As a young woman Wallis had no ambition other than to find a husband. She came out as a debutante into Baltimore society in 1914, and within two years she was married to Lieutenant Earl Winfield Spencer, a naval aviator. At first sight Spencer was a romantic figure. Dark, brooding, and brutally handsome, he bore a passing resemblance to Clark Gable. However, he proved an unstable and abusive husband. Wallis soon discovered that he was an alcoholic; when drunk he was prone to jealous rages in which he would mistreat and humiliate Wallis. On several occasions he locked her up in their apartment while he went out. In 1921 Wallis left him, and after one unsuccessful attempt at reconciliation they were finally divorced in 1927.[3]

For several years Wallis lived a precarious existence as an independent woman. She spent much of her time in Washington, DC, but also travelled widely, with lengthy spells in Paris, Hong Kong, and Beijing. While visiting friends in New York she met an American-born Englishman, Ernest Simpson, and in 1928 she married for a second time.

If Winfield Spencer was Rhett Butler to Wallis's Scarlett, then Ernest Simpson was Frank Kennedy. Dull, solid, and reliable, Ernest offered her financial and emotional security. It is clear from Wallis's letters to her aunt, Bessie Merriman, that she was not in love with him, but she was tired of her rootless existence and keen to settle down. Ernest was kind and considerate, and by marrying him she regained the position in society that she lacked as the 'extra woman' at dinner parties and social functions.[4]

Ernest's shipping business took him to London, and it was there that the couple moved in 1928. Through Wallis's efforts as a hostess they gradually built up a network of friends among the diplomats and businessmen in the American expatriate community. Within that circle were a number of couples who mixed socially with the Prince of Wales. One of their acquaintances was Benjamin Thaw, Thelma Furness's brother-in-law and a friend of the Prince's, whom Wallis had previously met in Washington. The Simpsons first met the Prince at Thelma's country house in Leicestershire in January 1931, when they were replacements for weekend guests who had dropped out at the last minute. Thereafter Wallis carefully cultivated Thelma's friendship, and the Simpsons began to receive occasional invitations to Fort Belvedere, the Prince's weekend retreat.[5]

In her memoirs Thelma Furness provided a vivid if waspish portrait of Wallis at the time she first met the Prince:

> Wallis Simpson was 'fun' and I did like her. At that time she did not have the chic she has since cultivated. She was not beautiful; in fact she was not even pretty. But she had a distinct charm and a sharp sense of humour. Her dark hair was parted in the middle. Her eyes, alert and eloquent, were her best feature. She was not as thin as in later years—not that she could be called fat even then; she was merely less angular. Her hands were large; they did not move gracefully...[6]

Wallis's rapid social ascent illustrates the privileged status Americans enjoyed in English society in the inter-war period. Had she been English, a woman in her position would never have met the Prince of Wales. Standing outside the finely calibrated hierarchy of the English class system, Americans could be received on an equal footing even at the highest social levels. The 'free

Figure 12.1. Wallis Simpson, 1934

pass' which Americans held for entry into society was reinforced by two
further factors: several of the leading aristocratic hostesses in London, like
Emerald Cunard and Lady Sackville, were themselves American; and the
Prince of Wales had a well-known enthusiasm for all things American.[7]

By the end of 1932, Edward's affair with Thelma was beginning to cool.
To relieve the tedium of weekends at the Fort, Thelma invited Wallis more
frequently: she was lively and witty and kept the Prince amused. When Ernest
was away on business she would come alone, squired by one of the Prince's
household staff.[8] In a letter to her aunt, Wallis described a typical weekend
scene, which would not have been out of place in a Jane Austen novel. Fruity
Metcalfe had retired to bed with flu, and Thelma and the Prince were sitting
in the drawing room doing needlework, while Thelma's father read aloud
from Dickens. Wallis was content to play the role of comedy relief, and to
dance with the Prince when the opportunity arose.[9]

In the spring of 1933, before her affair with Edward began, Wallis returned
to the USA to visit her Aunt Bessie. She travelled by herself, as Ernest's
business was in financial difficulties and he was unable to spend the time
away. Her acquaintance with the Prince gave her a new social cachet in
Washington, and she enjoyed a brief flirtation with an American diplomat,
John Cooper Wiley. On the return voyage she was flattered by the attentions
of no fewer than four men, including the ship's captain, whom she avoided

after he pinched her bottom at a cocktail party. Writing to her aunt on board ship, she commented wistfully, 'I know it [the American trip] was really my swan-song unless I can hang on to my figure and take a trip before I'm 40, which is only three years off.'[10] Back in London she found it difficult to settle back into domestic life. At the age of 37 she began to feel that her charms were fading. She admitted to her aunt that in Britain men had begun to treat her like an older woman. When John Wiley came to Britain for the London Economic Conference in June 1933, she tried unsuccessfully to rekindle their Washington romance. 'I don't find it as much fun having Wiley here as in Washington', she complained to Aunt Bessie, 'as I never see him alone.'[11]

Fortunately, the Simpsons' friendship with the Prince was growing increasingly close. By the summer of 1933 they were well established within the inner circle of Edward's American friends, and became regular visitors to Fort Belvedere. Edward threw a dinner party for Wallis at Quaglino's restaurant to celebrate her birthday on 19 June, adjourning afterwards to the Prince's apartments in St James's Palace, where they danced until 4.30 a.m. The Simpsons returned the hospitality by giving Edward a Fourth of July dinner at their flat in Bryanston Court with a group of American friends, serving him grilled lobster and fried chicken.[12] Thelma nevertheless remained 'Princess of Wales', and the Simpsons' access to Fort Belvedere continued to depend on her friendship. As long as Edward was constantly in Thelma's company, there was no chance of Wallis embarking on an affair with him.

However, there were signs that Thelma was tiring of her role as royal mistress. After four years, the tedious routine of weekends at the Fort began to outweigh the glamour of being the Prince's favourite. In January 1934 she sailed to America for two months to see her sister Gloria and to take a vacation in California. 'Oh Thelma, the little man is going to be so lonely,' Wallis said to her before she left. She promised to look after the Prince until Thelma's return.[13]

Edward had grown so used to Thelma organizing his social life that he was at a loss without her. Wallis Simpson, eager for a final, triumphant 'swan-song' with the Prince, and well equipped by upbringing and experience to entertain men, made the most of her opportunity. She was also lucky in that Freda Dudley Ward, Edward's old flame, was preoccupied at the time by her daughter's illness and had little time for the Prince.[14] Both Edward and Wallis recalled in their memoirs the crucial evening, probably in February 1934, when Wallis's assiduous attentiveness finally broke through the Prince's reserve, and their relationship moved to a new level. The occasion was a dinner party at the Dorchester Hotel which the Prince was giving for his old American friend, Fred Bate, the newly arrived European representative of the National Broadcasting Company. Edward had just returned from a tour of northern cities, visiting work-creation schemes for the unemployed. While the other guests were away from the table dancing, he suddenly opened up to Wallis about his work as Prince, a subject he normally avoided when 'off duty'. Accustomed to entertaining Ernest's business colleagues, she affected a keen interest. 'Wallis,' said the Prince, 'you're the only woman who's ever been interested in my job.'[15] In the following weeks Edward's visits to the Simpsons' flat became more frequent. Often he stayed so long that Ernest began to excuse himself and retire to his study. They became weekly guests at the Fort, and Wallis took to staying on after the other guests had left on a Monday.

Meanwhile, Thelma was enjoying her American holiday too much for the Prince's liking. While she was away she began an affair with Prince Aly Khan, the son of the Aga Khan, whose interest was no doubt piqued by the chance to steal the Prince of Wales's mistress. They travelled back on the same Atlantic liner, and drove up from Southampton to London together.[16] On her return she noticed that the Prince's attitude towards her had changed. He was cool and distant, and appeared jealous at the attentions which Aly Khan had been paying her. When Thelma saw Edward and Wallis together at Fort Belvedere over the Easter weekend (30 March–2 April 1934), she immediately realized that Wallis had replaced her in the Prince's affections. Accepting defeat with little sign of regret, she left the Fort—and the Prince's life—the following day. Soon afterwards she went to Paris to continue her affair with Aly Khan.[17]

Thereafter Wallis and Edward's affair developed very quickly. On 15 April Wallis wrote to her aunt saying that Thelma's 'rule' was over, and that she was trying to avoid seeing Edward alone, as he was being 'very attentive'.[18] It seems more likely that the opposite was true, and that Wallis was actively seeking opportunities to be alone with him. One of Edward's first gifts of jewellery to her was a small gold bracelet charm decorated with a red enamel figure '3'. On the reverse were three dates: 12 March, 9 April, and 14 May 1934, presumably marking significant events at the beginning of their relationship.[19] All three dates fell on a Monday, when the couple were alone together at the Fort after the other guests had departed. We shall never know precisely what those dates signified: did they mark the first three occasions on which Edward and Wallis made love, or perhaps more likely, the first three times they kissed? What is certain is that their affair had finally begun.

By late April the Prince was dropping in regularly at Bryanston Court on weekday evenings, and Wallis was struggling to manage his demands without upsetting her husband. In May, barely two months after the start of the affair, Edward abruptly broke off all contact with Freda Dudley Ward, his first great love, whom he had known since 1918. It is impossible to say whether Edward did this spontaneously or at Wallis's insistence, but there can be no doubt that it marked a decisive turning-point in Edward's emotional life. From that time onwards he committed himself, exclusively and irrevocably, to Wallis Simpson.[20]

No whisper of the affair appeared in the British press, but the American newspapers were quick to notice that the Prince had a new 'dancing partner'. In August 1934, Edward invited Wallis to share his summer holiday in Biarritz and the French Riviera. Ernest was unable to join them owing to business commitments in the USA; instead, Wallis's Aunt Bessie accompanied her as chaperone. Carried away by his new love, Edward's behaviour was nothing short of reckless. Once in France he made little attempt to conceal the affair, and at times appeared to flaunt it. The couple travelled together, and were spotted as soon as they crossed the Channel. Edward was seen at Calais railway station loading Wallis's luggage onto the train, and at Biarritz they were photographed together in a beachside café, deep in conversation. In Cannes they frequented the casinos and nightclubs, and the press reported that the Prince had regained his old enthusiasm for dancing until dawn. They stayed so late at a St-Tropez café, dancing to American jazz, that the police closed it down and prosecuted the proprietor. Shortly before their departure for Genoa, Edward made a midnight trip to a jeweller's shop in Cannes, coming away with 'his pockets stuffed with jewellery'.[21] Edward's equerry John Aird, who accompanied him on the holiday, was concerned that he had become too dependent on Wallis. He recorded in his diary that Edward had lost all confidence in himself and was following Wallis round like a dog. The Prince himself had never been happier. He told Godfrey Thomas that it had been the best holiday of his life.[22]

The supplanting of Thelma Furness and the emergence of another American woman as the new royal favourite was a major news story in the USA. By the end of 1934, when she was still unknown in Britain, Wallis Simpson had already become a familiar name in the American press. The Hearst newspapers devoted particular attention to the Prince's latest love affair. In December 1934 they carried a full-page illustrated feature on the 'inside story' of the rivalry between Wallis and Thelma, headlined 'Walesie preferred the Baltimore Beauty—so another Prince prefers Lady Furness'.[23] Written in tabloid style, and full of factual inaccuracies, the article nevertheless captured the essence of Wallis and Edward's relationship. 'It was clear', ran one paragraph, 'that there was a deep mental bond between them. Wasn't it marvellous, the dowagers on the sidelines whispered, for dear David to have a friend to whom he could pour out all the pent-up thoughts of a sheltered and necessarily lonely heir to the throne?'

The American public was intrigued that the Prince of Wales should have fallen in love with an apparently ordinary housewife from Baltimore. Unlike Thelma Furness she was not young, beautiful, or well connected. Her family, though respectable, was not part of America's social elite. She had already been divorced once and her husband was a struggling shipping executive. How had Wallis Warfield Simpson won the heart of the world's most eligible bachelor?

The answer, according to the press, was Southern charm. Several papers reported that a privately printed pamphlet was circulating in Paris, entitled 'What Charmed the Prince'. It supposedly revealed the secrets of Wallis's success, based on 'charm precepts any girl can learn'. These included: listening carefully to men, profiting from the mistakes of other women, and lacing compliments with 'a slight touch of vinegar'. An elegant accent was important: the Prince had reportedly described Wallis's voice as 'the most beautiful in the world'.[24]

Since 1936 many more theories have been proposed as to why Edward was so strongly attracted to Wallis Simpson.[25] Some thought she had bewitched or hypnotized him. One popular theory was that Wallis had enslaved Edward through the exotic techniques she had learned in Chinese brothels, which enabled her to give the Prince intense sexual pleasure.[26] The reasons which Edward himself gave were more prosaic, but they were linked to her American background. In his memoirs he praised her as the most independent woman he had ever met, a character trait which he described as 'one of the happier outcomes of the events of 1776'. He also greatly admired her forthrightness, so different from the fawning obsequiousness he usually encountered.[27]

For her part Wallis was at a loss to understand what the Prince saw in her. 'Searching my mind, I could find no good reason why this most glamorous of men should be seriously attracted to me. I certainly was no beauty...I was certainly no longer young. In fact, in my country I would have been considered securely on the shelf.' Like Edward, she attributed her appeal in part to 'an American independence of spirit'.[28] More significant, however, was Wallis's intuition of the profound sense of separateness and isolation from which Edward had always suffered because of his royal status. 'I sensed in him something that few around him could have been aware of—a deep loneliness, and overtone of spiritual isolation.'[29]

The internal dynamics of any personal relationship are inevitably difficult for outsiders to understand. On the one hand it is clear that the relationship between Edward and Wallis was asymmetrical. Edward was the lover, Wallis the beloved; Edward was the submissive partner, Wallis the dominant one. Viewing them together in 1935, one of his staff observed that Edward suffered from 'the sexual perversion of self-abasement', and Wallis had certainly manoeuvred herself into a position of domination. However, this is not the whole story. In the early stages of their affair, Edward was the dominant partner, playing Prince Charming to Wallis's Cinderella.[30] Freda Dudley Ward and Thelma Furness were both wealthy women, and had no need for the Prince's largesse. Wallis was poor by comparison, and had struggled to keep up appearances as a member of the Prince's circle. After April 1934, Edward showered her with gifts of jewels and cash, finally putting an end to the financial insecurity which had dogged her all her life.[31] Edward's ability to help Wallis, and to fulfil her needs, was important in strengthening the bond between them, and enhanced his sense that he was engaged in a meaningful human relationship, perhaps for the first time since the end of his affair with Freda. With a combination of boldness, charm, and perseverance, Wallis had succeeded in breaking through the shell of royal reserve and the psychological defences which Edward had built for himself during his years of isolation. The result was more dramatic than she could possibly have imagined.

Edward's affair with Wallis had a devastating impact upon him. As Prince of Wales he had long struggled to contain the internal conflict between his public and private lives. However, in the years since his father's illness in 1928, he had attained a hard-won psychological equilibrium between the two sides of his personality, and an acceptance of the constraints of his royal position. He had found a great national cause to campaign for, in alleviating the effects of the Great Depression upon Britain's unemployed; and his emotional needs were satisfied by his friendship with his old flame, Freda Dudley Ward, and a tranquil relationship with his mistress, Thelma Furness.[32] Within months, perhaps even weeks, of falling in love with Wallis, Edward's psychological equilibrium collapsed. His new love became an all-consuming passion, and he could not think of anything else. He became completely obsessed with Wallis: every absence from her was an agony, every public function a tiresome distraction. He lost interest in his official duties, and his conduct, both in public and private, became increasingly erratic. There are numerous accounts from 1934 and 1935 of the Prince's distracted and eccentric behaviour. His equerry, John Aird, described a dinner at which Edward repeatedly sent back the courses, ordered special dishes which he then refused to eat, and changed his mind over what he would drink. At a party he was hosting in honour of King George's jubilee in 1935, he turned up late and apparently drunk. On a visit to a hospital he was irritable with the staff, and made no effort to conceal his boredom; when the Superintendent's dog jumped up at him, he kicked it away.[33] It was the same even when he was on holiday. In August 1935 he turned up at the casino in Monte Carlo in oil-stained sailor's garb, and was refused entry before being recognized. Alone in the bar of the Carlton Hotel in Cannes, waiting for Wallis to arrive, he found a piece of rope and performed lasso tricks which he had learned from the cowboys at the EP ranch. On the same holiday he refused Wallis's urging to put on a hat when embarking on the destroyer HMS *Wishart,* saluting the quarterdeck bare-headed in breach of Royal Navy regulations.[34]

The Prince's staff grew deeply worried about his infatuation with Wallis, and the consequent deterioration in his behaviour. Aird concluded that Edward was going mad; Lionel Halsey and Godfrey Thomas, Edward's most senior advisers, steeled themselves to present their concerns formally in writing.[35] At the same time, the ailing King George fretted over his son's unsuitability for the task ahead of him. He made his famous prediction, 'After I am dead, the boy will ruin himself within twelve months', when Edward's affair with Wallis was in full swing. The marriages of his brothers, George, Duke of Kent, in 1934, and Henry, Duke of Gloucester, in 1935, served to deepen Edward's emotional isolation from his family. He was now the last of his siblings left unmarried, and it seemed certain that he would succeed to the throne as a bachelor king.

By the time he returned to England from his summer holidays in 1935, Edward had resolved in his own mind to marry Wallis whatever the cost.[36] However, this would inevitably entail a bitter confrontation with the King, and Edward shrank from such a painful encounter. Events in the autumn of 1935 provided excuses for delay: Prince Henry's marriage, a general election, and then the death of King George's favourite sister, Victoria. At Christmas the extended royal family gathered at Sandringham. The King's health was obviously failing, and again Edward did not think it was the time or the place to raise the subject of his marriage.[37] In mid-January, the King was suddenly taken ill; Edward was summoned urgently from Fort Belvedere to his father's bedside. A few days later he was dead. Edward was spared the pain of a final estrangement from his father, but the King's death came at a fateful time for him. In one sense Edward had been preparing for this moment for his whole life; yet when it came, he was less fit to take on the mantle of kingship than he had been for many years.

13

'The Greatest Story since the Crucifixion'

America and the Abdication

In 1936, two Southern women shot to fame in America and across the world: one was fictional and the other real. Margaret Mitchell's romance of the American Civil War, *Gone With the Wind,* was published in June 1936 and became an immediate bestseller. The heroine, Scarlett O'Hara, was depicted as a powerful and independent-minded woman, who through beauty, charm, and sheer force of personality shaped her own destiny in a world dominated by men. A few months later, the news media introduced the American public to a contemporary Scarlett O'Hara in the person of Wallis Simpson, whose lover Edward VIII bore more than a passing resemblance to Scarlett's beloved, Ashley Wilkes.[1] Like Scarlett, Wallis was a Southern belle, hardened by adversity and determined by whatever means to make herself financially secure. During the second half of 1936 the story of her romance with King Edward dominated the front pages of the US newspapers. Early in 1937, *Time* magazine declared Wallis Simpson to be its Person of the Year, the first time the honour had been given to a woman.[2] According to the magazine, she deserved the award because she was single-handedly responsible for the only voluntary royal abdication in British history. In 1936 she had come from comparative obscurity to become 'the most talked-about, written-about, headlined and interest-compelling person in the world'.[3]

America's experience of the Abdication was completely different from that of Great Britain, where the story of the King's romance with Mrs Simpson was suppressed for as long as possible. When it eventually broke, at the beginning of December 1936, the drama was already in its final stages, and

Edward was only days away from resigning the throne. The constitutional crisis overshadowed the great love affair. In the USA, by contrast, the story had been building to a crescendo for months. Already familiar to the US press as Edward's favourite 'dancing partner' while he was still Prince of Wales, Wallis became front-page news as a result of the couple's Mediterranean cruise in August 1936. Her divorce from Ernest Simpson in October, raising the possibility of an American Queen of England, generated a media frenzy. The relentless coverage of the royal romance in America proved a decisive factor in precipitating the Abdication crisis in Britain in the last months of 1936. Despite the domestic news blackout, the pressure of constant revelations from the far side of the Atlantic drove British government and Court officials to confront the King and force his hand. Bitterly criticized in Britain for its shameless gossip-mongering, the American press was triumphantly vindicated when it was announced early in December that the King indeed wished to marry Mrs Simpson. In the days that followed, newspapers on both sides of the Atlantic reported little else but the unfolding drama of the Abdication. It was, said the Baltimore journalist H. L. Mencken, 'the greatest story since the Crucifixion'.[4]

King George V died just before midnight on 20 January 1936. The royal family was gathered at his bedside, and as soon as he was pronounced dead, Queen Mary took Edward's hand and kissed it, in the first act of homage to the new King. His brother Prince George did the same. Overcome with shock, Edward wept hysterically. A few minutes later, having recovered his composure, he telephoned Wallis in London to tell her the news.[5]

The passing of King George V and the accession of Edward VIII was a solemn moment in the history of the nation. In the British press there were outpourings of grief for the old king, and extravagant praise for King Edward. The newspapers stressed the values and traditions of monarchy and its symbolic role as a unifying factor for the country and the empire.[6] The emphasis was on continuity rather than change. In America there was much speculation as to what the new reign would bring. Edward was a popular figure in the US, well known for his American tastes and democratic ways, and the columnists and headline-writers assumed that he would act quickly to modernize the hidebound British monarchy. 'Flying Monarch Proclaimed King Edward VIII' was the headline in many US newspapers on the day after his accession.[7] Edward's first radio broadcast as King, on 1 March, was praised in the US for its democratic tenor: he used the pronoun 'I' rather than 'we', and spoke of 'my fellow men' rather than 'my people' or 'my subjects', as his father had done. Commentators also noted its American nuances: his use of 'radio' instead of the English 'wireless', and 'broadcast' with a short 'a'.[8] His determination to maintain the informality which had been the hallmark of his style as Prince of Wales also won the approval of the American press. Reporting on his trip to Glasgow to see the completed liner *Queen Mary*, the *St Louis Star* wrote: 'King Edward, who last Sunday shattered precedent by speaking to "my fellow-men" instead of "my subjects", was cheered by workmen today... "Good old Teddy, give us a speech", the workmen shouted to the young bachelor monarch. It was a scene unprecedented in the annals of British royalty, and marked one more step in the popular Edward's almost revolutionary conduct of his office.'[9]

As Prince of Wales, Edward had defined himself against his father. Whereas George V's kingship was conservative, formal, and predictable, Prince Edward was innovative, informal, mercurial, and modernizing. George hated change, waging what his son called 'his private war with the twentieth century', while Edward embraced it. George disapproved of the novelties of the post-war world, many of them American in origin: painted fingernails, jazz, cocktails, bobbed hair. For Edward they were simply part of the world which he inhabited.[10] Paradoxically, although the differences between King and Prince produced tensions within the royal family, their contrasting styles provided a highly effective combination for the monarchy as an institution. They allowed it to present both a traditional and a modern face: George V was the reassuring father figure of his people, and Edward carried with him the nation's hopes for the future.

King George's death therefore presented Edward with a dilemma. Should he assume his father's mantle, and adopt the traditional post-Victorian pattern of monarchy with its grand ceremonial and unchanging routine? Or should he build on his work as Prince of Wales to create a new, forward-looking style of kingship, better suited to lead and inspire the country as it faced the challenges of the modern age? Edward himself was in no doubt about how he would approach his new role. His starting-point was that he was not going to be a king in the mould of his father. He told his friend and adviser Walter Monckton at the beginning of his reign that they must take him as he was, a man different from his father and determined to be himself.[11] Edward publicly emphasized this approach in his first radio broadcast. Without consulting the government, he added a personal section at the end of the speech. 'I am better known to you as Prince of Wales—as a man who, during the War and since, has had the opportunity of getting to know the people of nearly every country of the world, under all conditions and circumstances. And although I now speak to you as King, I am still the same man who has had that experience.'[12]

Since Edward was so determined to be himself, it was unfortunate that his key advisers, the main protagonists in the Abdication drama, wanted him to be his father. For the Prime Minister Stanley Baldwin, the Archbishop of Canterbury Cosmo Lang, and Edward's private secretaries Clive Wigram and Alexander Hardinge, King George had been the ideal monarch. Significantly, all of them except Hardinge were of the same generation as the old king. Baldwin was 69, Lang 72, and Wigram 63.[13] In their eyes the function of the monarchy was symbolic and passive: to stand above the political hurly-burly; to embody the traditional values of family, nation, and empire; and to provide the focus for national identity and stability. Speaking shortly after the old king's death, Baldwin praised him for taking service as his guiding principle; throughout his life he had rigorously trained his will to place the public interest first and last. 'Through his example men led better lives in the accomplishment of their daily duties... at home and to their country.'[14] A fundamental aspect of this selfless devotion to duty was that the King exercised no political authority. Real power lay not with the Crown, but in Parliament; monarchy possessed the shadow of authority, not its substance.

This is not to say that the monarch no longer had any constitutional role to play. George V played an important part in resolving two major political crises during his reign, the confrontation between the Liberal government and the House of Lords in 1910–11, and in the formation of the national government in 1931. But on both occasions he acted within the existing constitutional norms. He accepted the advice of his ministers in all political matters, and did not express his private views in public. A revealing insight into the relationship between King George and his ministers is provided by Ivan Maisky, the Soviet Ambassador to Britain in the 1930s. Attending a diplomatic reception, he noticed the King talking to Stanley Baldwin. He was too far away to hear what they were saying, but was struck by the body language between them. While King George gazed ingratiatingly at the Prime Minister, Baldwin leant back arrogantly, his arms folded across his chest. 'Which of the two is the master?' Maisky asked himself. 'It certainly did not seem to be the King.'[15]

Edward was less inclined than his father to accept that the King should be confined to a purely passive role. His experience as Prince of Wales had been radically different from that of King George a generation before.

During the war, and in the course of his tours of the empire and at home, he had mixed with ordinary men and women and seen the conditions in which they lived. He felt that he understood their lives and concerns as well as, if not better than, some politicians. For example, he regarded many Conservative MPs as out of touch with their working-class constituents because they did not live amongst them.[16] While he did not wish to turn the clock back three hundred years, Edward believed that there were circumstances in which the King should intervene in political matters. In 1925, on the return journey from his Latin American tour, he had a conversation with the *Daily Mail* correspondent George Ward Price about the looming political crisis in Britain and the prospect of a General Strike.[17] 'If it were a political quarrel,' he mused, 'I should be told that the Royal Family must stay out of politics.' Then he went on, 'If the growing unrest were to develop into a real struggle, I should be keener to play a part than I have ever been.'[18] Here he seemed to be implying that if Britain was ever threatened by revolution, he would break the royal tradition of political neutrality. When the General Strike broke out the following year, the King, just as Edward predicted, instructed his family to abstain from any comment or involvement in the crisis. Edward later described this stance as 'asking a man in a burning building to retire to his room while firemen coped with the blaze'.[19] If he had been King at the time, it is unlikely that he would have been so reticent. In his time as Prince of Wales he made several political and diplomatic interventions. In 1923 he persuaded the Ministry of Labour to grant work-permits to the members of Paul Whiteman's jazz orchestra. A few years later contemporaries attributed the Housing Act of 1930, which led to large-scale slum clearances, partly to Edward's vigorous campaigning for improved housing conditions in the preceding years. In 1933, following his interview with the Glasgow MP David Kirkwood, he almost certainly interceded with government ministers to secure funding for the completion of the *Queen Mary*. More controversially, the Prince's speech to the British Legion in June 1935, suggesting a visit of reconciliation to Germany, had a direct impact on the Anglo-German Naval Agreement being negotiated at the same time.[20]

On his accession to the throne reports circulated that he did intend to take a more active role in politics than his father. Diplomats at the US State Department took the view that the new King would not blindly accept government decisions: 'He felt it was his duty to intervene if the Cabinet were to plan a policy which in his view was detrimental to British interests.'[21]

Building on his policy interventions as Prince of Wales, Edward appears to have envisaged an active, even 'presidential', style of kingship, affording him more political and diplomatic involvement than was traditionally allowed to the monarch under the British Constitution. With little understanding of the complexities of government or foreign affairs, Edward saw politics and diplomacy largely in terms of personal relationships, and thus as an area in which he could make a contribution.[22] His pro-German views were well known, and there were real concerns within the government that he would try to dabble in sensitive diplomatic matters. Some on the political right in Britain hoped that Edward would provide the kind of charismatic leadership for the country similar to the fascist dictators in continental Europe. When he attended the opening of Parliament in November, the news magazine *Cavalcade* commented: 'there were a number in both Houses angry that the King was not turning out to be what they expected—timid, anxious for sober and dusty advice. The more modern spirits see rapidly developing the most forthright, direct-acting and at the same time human, king ever known—the leader Britain needs in a world of vigorous and fast-moving dictators.'[23]

Edward's reign was too short to tell whether he would have been able to remould the monarchy in his own image, as he had successfully done with the role of Prince of Wales. There were powerful conservative forces ranged against him, intent upon defending his father's legacy, and upholding the convention of royal neutrality in politics. In any event Edward was too preoccupied with his plans to make Wallis Simpson his bride to give systematic thought to the business of monarchy. Such evidence as there is from the early months of the reign suggests that even the modest reforms which he introduced into the running of the royal household met resistance. His determination to cut costs in the management of the estates at Sandringham and Balmoral was resented as cheese-paring. His attempts to curtail the less important ceremonies, such as the presentation of debutantes at Court, were regarded as insensitive. Even his decision to walk the short distance along Whitehall for a meeting, rather than taking the royal Daimler, raised eyebrows.[24]

Despite his new status, Edward wanted his life to change as little as possible, and tried to maintain, as King, the strict separation between his public and private lives which he had established as Prince. As he told Walter Monckton, he would be available for public business and public occasions when he was wanted, but his private life was to be his own and was, as far as possible, to be lived in the same way as when he was Prince of Wales. The Fort was to remain a retreat for weekends and for rest.[25] This proved unrealistic, as it failed to take into account the much greater volume of official business with which he had to deal as King. It also created logistical problems for his staff in managing his duties, as he was often away at the Fort with Wallis from Friday until Tuesday. The 'red boxes' of official correspondence sometimes went astray, or were returned unread. On one occasion Mike Scanlon, one of Wallis's circle of American friends, was asked to drop off some official correspondence at Buckingham Palace after a visit to the Fort. Scanlon was the Air Attaché at the US Embassy, and at the Palace Alexander Hardinge was not impressed to receive secret British state papers from the hands of an American intelligence officer.[26]

There was one particular respect in which the balance between Edward's public and private lives was fundamentally altered by his accession. As Prince, he had required the King's consent to marry, by virtue of the Royal Marriages Act 1772.[27] Now he was himself King there were no statutory constraints on his choice of bride, apart from the prohibition on his marrying a Roman Catholic.[28] His accession opened up the possibility that he might at last realize his fantasy of marrying his mistress, despite the fact that she was twice married. With his exaggerated belief in the power of his position as King, Edward convinced himself that he could, in one of his favourite phrases, 'get away with it'.[29] Now that his father was dead, he gambled that no one would be able to stop him, given his immense popularity in the country, and the lack of any legal prohibition on the marriage. In the circles in which Edward moved, divorce was relatively commonplace, and carried little social stigma. Sexual attitudes had changed considerably since the war, and many of Edward's generation adopted the 'American' view that marriage was a social habit rather than a sacrament. If the parties had made a mistake, it could be rectified by divorce and remarriage.[30] Edward thought it would be hypocritical to keep Wallis as his mistress, rather than accepting the reality of divorce. In this sense his attitude to marriage reflected his modernizing approach to monarchy, making it more in tune with the changes which were taking place in British society. Soon after he became King he set in motion a plan to make Wallis his wife and, if possible, his Queen.[31]

It is clear that events were driven by Edward's single-minded desire to make Wallis his wife. Wallis herself was carried along by the momentum of his obsession, never quite believing that it would actually happen. She feared that when Edward's plan to marry her became public it would irreparably damage his position, and she shrank from that responsibility. Recalling life as a single woman between her first two marriages, she envisaged that the time would come when she would 'fold her tent' and 'steal away', cherishing the memory of her fairy-tale romance with the King of England.[32]

There were two obvious barriers which Edward faced before he could fulfil his dream: Wallis would have to obtain a divorce from Ernest; and the British government and people would have to accept her as his wife. Edward was realistic enough to know that he would face fierce opposition from the Church of England and what he called the 'ultra-conservative Court circles'.[33] He decided to play the long game. He planned to introduce Wallis gradually into Court society as his partner, while outwardly disclaiming any intention of marriage. Wallis would then quietly divorce Ernest on the grounds of his adultery, and some months later, having prepared public opinion through sympathetic press outlets, Edward would declare his intention to marry her. His aim was for the wedding ceremony to take place in April 1937, so that Wallis could be crowned alongside him in May. It was a high-risk strategy, not least because it breached Edward's own long-held insistence on a rigid separation between his private and public lives. For it to succeed, there could be no suspicion before the Simpsons' divorce that the King wished to marry Wallis. In order for Edward to maintain control over events, it was essential to proceed, if not in total secrecy, at least with the minimum of publicity, especially in relation to the Simpson divorce.

There were some factors in his favour. Ernest Simpson proved surprisingly amenable to the divorce. Recognizing that Wallis had moved into a different world, from which she could never happily return to him, he began an affair with her old school friend, Mary Raffray.[34] It was obviously out of the question for Ernest to divorce Wallis on the grounds of her adultery with Edward, as that would have made the King a co-respondent in the lawsuit. Ever the gentleman, Ernest therefore agreed to allow Wallis to divorce him for adultery with another woman. On the political scene, too, matters looked favourable. Baldwin's government was too preoccupied with international crises to give much thought to the King's marriage plans: Hitler reoccupied the Rhineland in March 1936, and throughout the year diplomatic tensions were high because of Italy's invasion of Abyssinia. The British press was docile, and accustomed to respecting the private lives of the royal family. With the assistance of powerful press barons such as Lord Beaverbrook, Edward was confident that he could keep his relationship with Wallis out of the newspapers for as long as necessary. In addition, the sheer implausibility of the King marrying an American divorcee gave cover to his plans. After all, in 1933 his previous mistress, Thelma Furness, had divorced her husband without arousing speculation about their possible marriage. Despite his obvious infatuation with Wallis, very few of those who knew of the affair thought that Edward could be seriously contemplating marriage. Even Walter Monckton, Edward's closest confidant after he became King, did not suspect that he intended to marry Wallis until as late as November 1936.[35]

On the other side of the equation, apart from opposition from within the establishment of the British Church and State, there was one additional factor which Edward overlooked until it was too late: the reaction of the American press. This was all the more surprising in that he had personal experience of its aggressive pursuit of news about him from his Long Island holiday in 1924. As one of the world's leading celebrities, speculation about Edward's marriage prospects and love affairs had been a staple of US newspapers for twenty years. They knew of his relationship with Wallis from their summer holidays together in 1934 and 1935, and would inevitably pounce on any hint, direct or indirect, of marriage. Edward had no means of muzzling the American press in the way that he could the British, but initially he dismissed its significance, assuming it would have no influence on events in Britain.[36] It was to prove a fatal miscalculation.

The opening stages of Edward's campaign went according to plan, as he took the first steps to introduce Wallis into Court society. Together with Ernest, Wallis made her first appearance in the Court Circular, the official record of the activities of the royal family, as a guest at a dinner party at St James's Palace given by the King on 27 May. It was Edward's first formal dinner since the end of full mourning for the old King. The evening had a distinctly American flavour. The guests of honour were the aviator Charles Lindbergh and his wife Anne, who had fled to Britain from the USA following the kidnap and murder of their baby son, and the subsequent trial of his killer. Apart from the Simpsons, other American guests included the society hostess Emerald Cunard, and Sarah Legh, the wife of Edward's equerry Joey Legh. The guest-list attracted favourable press coverage in the US, in which Wallis received no more than passing mention.[37] The real purpose of the evening, however, was to introduce Wallis to one of the other guests, Stanley Baldwin; a few weeks earlier the King had told her that it was time for the Prime Minister to meet his future wife. Baldwin himself was rather bemused to find himself in such company at a royal dinner; he had heard rumours that Edward wanted to marry Mrs Simpson, but simply discounted them as unbelievable.[38] In June, Wallis was in the King's party at Royal Ascot, and rode from Windsor in one of the royal carriages.[39] In early July, Wallis made her second appearance in the Court Circular at another royal dinner, this time without Ernest. The other guests included the Duke and Duchess of York, Edward's brother and sister-in-law.[40] At about the same time, discreet references to Mrs Simpson began to appear in the British newspapers. The London correspondent of *Time* magazine noted perceptively how Wallis was gradually edging across the line that separated Edward's private life from his public life. 'Queen Mary has not yet dined with the King and Mrs Simpson, but the Prime Minister and Mrs Stanley Baldwin have...Socialite Britons assumed and freely said in Mayfair that British public opinion is now in the course of a great change, and soon the comings and goings of Mrs Simpson will be a popular topic in the popular press.'[41] At the end of July, Ernest Simpson booked into the Hotel de Paris at Bray by the River Thames to go through the charade of adultery that English divorce law then required. His companion signed herself 'Buttercup Kennedy' and the couple took breakfast in their room and were seen in bed together by hotel waiters. On 23 July Wallis wrote Ernest the standard letter drafted by her lawyer, which informed him that she was aware of his adulterous behaviour, and was commencing divorce proceedings. Ernest then moved out of their flat at Bryanston Court, and took rooms at the Guards' Club.[42]

At the end of the first six months of the reign, Edward must have been well satisfied with the progress of his marriage plans. The Simpson divorce was under way. Wallis had succeeded in keeping a low public profile, despite the fact that Edward spent all his spare time in her company. An important factor was the seclusion of Fort Belvedere in Windsor Great Park, beyond the reach of press cameras. The British press had maintained its traditional silence on the King's private life, and the American newspapers had been making largely routine references to Wallis as one of Edward's favourite 'dancing partners', rehashing titbits from the summers of 1934 and 1935. As late as July 1936, some US papers were still reporting rumours that the King would marry a European princess.[43] If that media calm had continued until October, then Wallis's divorce might have gone unremarked and unreported, and Edward, in his own words, would have had 'ample time to work things out' by the time the divorce was finalized in April 1937.[44] However, in August the situation was transformed by the couple's holiday cruise on the motor-yacht *Nahlin* in the Eastern Mediterranean, which generated blanket press coverage in the United States. At this crucial juncture, a few weeks before the Simpson divorce hearing, the King lost control of events through his own indiscreet behaviour. While on holiday, Edward was unable to stop himself flaunting his relationship in public, and the intensity of their love affair was prematurely revealed to the world outside Britain.

In pursuing his intention to carry on the lifestyle he had enjoyed as Prince of Wales, Edward broke with decades of tradition in taking a Mediterranean summer vacation as King. The more prudent course would have been to follow the royal holiday routine of his predecessors and spend a week at the Cowes Regatta in early August before travelling to Balmoral for the start of the grouse-shooting season on 12 August. As it was, the *Nahlin* trip attracted considerable attention even from British newspapers, which sent reporters and photographers to the Balkans to cover the cruise.[45] At first it seemed that Edward was anxious to avoid the publicity which had attended his holidays with Wallis in previous summers. As King, he now travelled under a new incognito as 'Duke of Lancaster', signifying that he was not paying official visits to the countries through which he passed. The beginning of the trip was cloaked in secrecy; the royal party was expected to fly across the Channel from the royal aerodrome at Windsor, where a crowd gathered to wave them off. Instead they drove to nearby Heathrow, then a private airfield, and flew to Calais, boarding the Vienna Express en route to Yugoslavia. The names of the King's guests were not divulged to the press, although their suspicions were soon confirmed when Wallis's luggage was unloaded from the train, labelled 'MRS ERNEST SIMPSON' in letters six inches high.[46] At Salzburg, where they stopped for sightseeing, the police confiscated cameras from photographers at the station.[47]

However, as soon as he embarked on the *Nahlin,* which awaited them at the Adriatic port of Sibenik in Yugoslavia, Edward abandoned all discretion. As if reacting against the constraints of kingship which he had endured for several months, he was intent on making his holiday as informal as possible, abandoning all pretence of royal protocol.[48] The privacy of the yacht at sea appeared to give him a false sense of seclusion. In fact, it was not an inconspicuous party. For a month the *Nahlin,* one of the largest yachts in the world, steamed up and down the coasts of Yugoslavia, Greece, and Turkey, accompanied by two Royal Navy destroyers. The vessel put in frequently at ports along the way, which, unlike the French resorts that Edward usually frequented, were not used to welcoming celebrities. Wherever they went, the couple were mobbed by large crowds, cheering and chanting 'Viva l'Amore'. They made no attempt to avoid the cameras. On one occasion Edward even made the local police hand back the cameras which they had seized from press photographers.[49] From the middle of August a stream of photographs began to appear in American newspapers, showing the King casually dressed in holiday gear, invariably accompanied by Wallis Simpson. Some of the photographs were very intimate by the standards of the day. One depicted Edward and Wallis alone together in a rowing boat; another showed Wallis resting her fingers protectively on the King's naked forearm as he climbed down into the ship's launch, hinting unmistakably at a physical relationship. One of the most psychologically revealing shots was a photograph of King Edward being driven though crowd-lined streets in Athens in an open car, with Wallis sitting beside him like his queen.[50] The couple were on their way to see King George of Greece, who lived openly with his English mistress, Joyce Batten-Jones. The image suggests that Edward was briefly living out his fantasy of being married to Wallis, and being able to acknowledge her as his wife before the world.

Why did Edward flaunt his relationship with Wallis so blatantly during their summer holiday on the *Nahlin,* when during the previous six months he had methodically pursued a plan of introducing her unobtrusively into his public life in Britain? There can be no doubt that the *Nahlin* cruise revealed to the world the intensity of Edward's relationship with Wallis, and set the American press on the trail which led directly to the Simpson divorce and the couple's marriage plans. It may have been that Edward simply lacked the self-discipline to pursue his plan patiently over a period of many months. His wilful determination to carry on his life as if he were still Prince of Wales suggests that he had still not come to terms with his new status as King. But there is a sense also that, by August, Edward was tired of caution and concealment: he had decided to make Wallis his wife, regardless of the consequences, and wanted the world to know of it.

There was a stark contrast between the coverage of the cruise in the British and American press. British newspapers, confounded by the ubiquitous presence of Wallis at the King's side, decided to confine their reporting to the factual details of the King's movements, without reference to Wallis or photographs of her. The American papers on the other hand produced a daily flow of new revelations, abundantly illustrated by pictures of the couple. The immediate effect of the cruise was to establish Wallis as an American celebrity in her own right. The Sunday supplements published full-page profiles detailing every aspect of her life: her background and upbringing, her tastes and fashion sense, and of course her two husbands. Her life story was serialized, and her photographs appeared on a daily basis throughout August and September. Typical headlines ran, 'Mrs Simpson Still Ace High to Edward VIII', 'King's Playmate Big Problem to British', and 'All Europe Buzzing Over Mrs Simpson'. Some of the reports which seemed particularly far-fetched at the time, for example that Edward had lavished a million dollars' worth of jewels on Wallis, subsequently proved to be true.[51]

Although Edward was travelling incognito as Duke of Lancaster, there was some official business on the trip. He met the heads of state of several Balkan countries, and became the first British monarch to visit Turkey, where he was entertained by Kemal Atatürk, the Turkish dictator. Because it was not a state visit, Wallis was able to accompany Edward, temporarily enjoying the status of royal consort. A photograph taken on Atatürk's yacht at Istanbul shows Wallis sitting in the place of honour on the dictator's right, with the King on his left beside an interpreter. Atatürk was impressed by Edward's charm and candour, but noting his enslavement to Wallis, predicted that he would lose his throne because of her.[52]

It was not until her return from holiday in mid-September that Wallis realized the extent of the media storm in America surrounding the *Nahlin* cruise, and what it revealed about her relationship with the King. Awaiting her were letters from her aunt, Bessie Merriman, enclosing bundles of newspaper clippings. Although she was no stranger to American press intrusion, this coverage was of a different order, and dispelled any illusions she might still have harboured about keeping her impending divorce out of the press. Horrified by what she had read, Wallis immediately grasped the implications: if they continued their relationship, Edward's position as King was in danger. Suddenly confronted with that reality, she wrote to Edward, telling him that she wanted to end their relationship and go back to Ernest. The letter was remarkably candid and clear-sighted, and contradicts any suggestion that Wallis was actively scheming to marry Edward. 'I am sure you and I would only create disaster together ... I feel sure I can't make you happy, and I honestly don't think you can me ... you will realise that no human being could assume this responsibility and it would be most unfair to make things harder for me by seeing me.'[53] Edward's response to her letter was extreme: he threatened to commit suicide if she did not return to him. Trapped by his emotional blackmail, and facing the choice between the risk of her lover's suicide and the risk of his abdication, she had little option but to put her trust in him to manage events. A few days later Wallis joined the King at Balmoral, and their relationship apparently carried on as before.[54]

Towards the end of September rumours began to circulate in the American press about Wallis's divorce. They were triggered by the discovery that Ernest had moved out of the marital home in Bryanston Square and into bachelor quarters.[55] Friends and relatives of the Simpsons in America stoutly denied the rumours; Mary Raffray, Ernest's lover and future wife, defended the 'perfectly innocent' relationship between Edward and Wallis.[56] A fortnight later the case-lists for forthcoming divorce hearings were published, showing that the Simpsons' suit would be heard at the Ipswich Assizes on Tuesday, 27 October.[57] The scoop was carried in the morning edition of the *Chicago Daily News* on 14 October. Within twenty-four hours the news had spread across America and was broadcast on the radio networks.[58] Three days later the *Washington Post* printed a report speculating that Edward was planning to marry Wallis. 'King Edward VIII of Great Britain plans to marry the glamorous American, Mrs Ernest "Wally" Simpson' reported the *Post*. 'He may not be able to make the erstwhile Baltimore belle his queen,' the paper said, 'but he is said to be determined to make her his wife even if it costs him the throne.'[59] The report, based on 'cabled advices' to the *Post*, noted the significant timing of the divorce hearing. Allowing for the six-month interval between the decree nisi and the decree absolute which then applied under English law, Wallis would be free to marry in late April or early May 1937. That suggested that Edward planned to marry Wallis before his coronation in May. Although it may have been based only on educated guesswork, the *Post*'s report provided a remarkably accurate account of Edward's secret marriage plans.

While the American public was reading reports of the King's innermost thoughts, senior members of the British government and Royal Household were scrambling to discover the basic facts. Alexander Hardinge, the King's private secretary, did not find out about the divorce hearing until 15 October, that is the day *after* the first American reports, and Prime Minister Baldwin was not informed until 16 October.[60] At Hardinge's request Baldwin arranged an audience with the King at Fort Belvedere to ask him to stop the divorce proceedings. At the meeting Edward, with evasiveness verging on dishonesty, told Baldwin that it would be wrong for him to interfere in a private matter simply because Wallis was a friend of his; Baldwin could not bring himself to ask the King directly whether he intended to marry her after the divorce, and the interview ended inconclusively.[61]

As soon as reports of the divorce hearing broke in the USA, Ernest Simpson was deluged with enquiries from the American news agencies. He confirmed the accuracy of the reports to the Associated Press on 15 October.[62] He telephoned Wallis, who was then staying at Felixstowe in Suffolk to establish her residency requirement for the Ipswich Assizes, and told her of the latest developments. Separated from Edward, the news from America revived all her misgivings about the divorce. Again she wrote to the King, suggesting that she should withdraw. 'Do you feel you still want me to go ahead... if I hurt you to this extent, won't it be best for me to steal quietly away?' Once more Edward dismissed her fears, but he agreed to speak to the press baron Lord Beaverbrook to ensure that the Fleet Street press kept quiet about the divorce hearing.[63] Beaverbrook spoke to the chairman of the Newspaper Proprietors' Association, Lord Harmsworth, and between them they persuaded the national and local press to suppress news of the divorce before the hearing, and to keep publicity to a minimum afterwards.[64]

On 26 October, the day before the Simpsons' divorce hearing, the press coverage in America reached a new level of intensity. The *New York American*, the flagship of the Hearst press empire, carried a front-page story under the headline, 'King Edward to Wed Mrs Simpson in June 1937'. The news was reported in definitive terms, on the basis of authoritative sources: 'King Edward's most intimate friends state with the utmost positiveness that he is very deeply and sincerely enamoured of Mrs Simpson, that his love is a righteous affection, and that almost immediately after the Coronation he will take her as his consort.'[65] Hearst had recently visited Britain, and was rumoured to have visited Fort Belvedere. However, he could not have obtained the story from the King's staff because Edward had not at that date shared his plans with any of his advisers. It is more probable that Hearst's source was Ernest Simpson. The British security services routinely monitored transatlantic cable traffic, and passed on relevant information to the Prime Minister's office. The government knew that Ernest was in touch with Hearst: Baldwin told the Australian High Commissioner that Ernest had an agreement with Hearst to supply information on the understanding that his newspapers would write up the marriage positively as a means of cementing good relations between Britain and the USA.[66] That was precisely the basis upon which the story was presented in the *New York American;* Edward was depicted as consciously turning away from an outmoded connection with European royalty, and towards a forward-looking alliance with America: 'he believes that the most important thing for the peace and welfare of the world is an intimate understanding between England and America, and that his marriage with this very gifted lady may help to bring about the beneficial co-operation between English-speaking nations'.[67]

The revelations of the Hearst press placed the British newspapers in an increasingly difficult position. Their silence over the relationship between the King and Mrs Simpson was predicated on the assumption that Edward had no intention of marrying Wallis, and that it therefore remained a purely private matter. With the Simpson divorce, the affair took on much greater significance. If they followed the lead of the *New York American*, and broke the story, they faced the full weight of English libel law should it turn out to be a false rumour.[68] If they remained silent, they were potentially missing out on one of the great news stories of the age.

American editors could not resist commenting on the craven self-censorship of the British newspapers. *Time* magazine was particularly scathing: in late October, under the headline 'Innocents Abroad', it described Britons arriving in New York as the 'sincerely bewildered products of the most subtle and effective press censorship in the world, a censorship whose chief weapon is the constant official British re-iteration that "there is no British censorship"'.[69] A month later *Time* took aim at Geoffrey Dawson, the revered editor of the London *Times*:

> Mr Geoffrey Dawson screwed his courage up and up last week, not to the point of printing so much as a word about the King and Mrs Simpson, but to the point of making a verbal intimation...Meanwhile the few thousand Britons who own radio sets able to pick up US broadcasts bombarded Editor Dawson with letters demanding that the *Times* either present the facts, or if US journalism were in error, come to the defence of the King. With such letters piling up in every London editor's office this week, the entire British press continued unanimously to ostrich.[70]

In late October the world's press gathered in Ipswich to report the Simpson divorce. The weekend before the hearing, the *New York Times* reported that all hotel rooms in the Suffolk market town were booked for the week.[71] On the day of the hearing there was a heavy police presence round the court-house to keep the press away from Wallis. She arrived fifty minutes early in the King's Buick, which swept directly into an inner courtyard, allowing her to enter the courtroom un-photographed. The public gallery of the court was closed; more than twenty reporters, at least six of them American, squeezed into the tiny press gallery. As the suit was uncontested, the proceedings were brief, commencing at 2.15 p.m. and lasting only seventeen minutes. The judge duly granted Wallis a decree nisi. After the proceedings were over the doors of the courthouse were locked to stop the reporters from leaving until Wallis had made good her escape. Outside there were scuffles between police and pressmen. Mounted police charged the ranks of cameramen in an attempt to disperse them, and two photographers had their cameras smashed. Police cars blocked the main routes out of Ipswich to prevent the photographers' cars from pursuing Wallis back to London.[72] Correspondents from the US news agencies hurried to file their stories. Virgil Pinkley, the European representative of United Press, dashed to a nearby store where a colleague was holding an open line to New York. He dictated a detailed account of the hearing, including a full transcript of the proceedings, which duly appeared on the front pages of the American evening papers the same day. The police managed to ensure that there were no photographs of Mrs Simpson, but the reports were accompanied by dramatic shots of the scenes outside the courtroom.[73] In contrast, the British press adhered to the 'gentlemen's agreement' which Beaverbrook had negotiated on the King's behalf, and reported only the basic facts of the divorce hearing without linking Wallis's name to Edward. *The Times,* for example, tucked away its report on an inside page devoted to local news.[74] There were cracks in the facade, however. *Time* magazine reported the indignation of British journalists at the suppression of the Simpson story. In defiance of their bosses, some were actively assisting American correspondents covering the case.[75]

Throughout the autumn, rumours of the King's love affair gradually seeped out across British society. Travellers returning from America brought the latest stories home with them. City businessmen involved in transatlantic commerce hurried to buy insurance against the postponement of the coronation, raising rates from 4 per cent to 25 per cent. MPs asked questions as to why American journals arrived with articles clipped out. At the British Legion rally in the Royal Albert Hall on Armistice Day (11 November), the veterans serenaded the King with the song, 'Who's Your Lady Friend?'[76]

The Simpson divorce, and the American press reaction which accompanied it, triggered a full-blown constitutional crisis in Britain. King Edward, isolated from the men who should have been his closest advisers, still maintained the fiction that he had no intention of marrying Wallis. Despite pressure from the King's staff, the Archbishop of Canterbury, and his own civil servants, Baldwin was still reluctant to confront Edward. The British press was growing increasingly restive. At the end of October Geoffrey Dawson, the editor of *The Times*, received an anonymous letter from the

USA, one of many drawing attention to the comment in the American newspapers. It was signed 'Britannicus in partibus infidelium'—a Briton in the land of the unfaithful—and was written by a British citizen living in New Jersey. It set out, in the starkest terms, the damage which the writer felt was being done to Britain's standing in America by the publicity surrounding Edward's affair with Wallis.

> The doings of the King, as reported in the American press, have in the course of a few months transformed Britain from a sober and dignified realm into a dizzy musical comedy attuned to the rhythm of jazz...The prevailing American opinion is that the foundations of the British throne are undermined, its moral authority, its honour and its dignity cast into the dustbin. To put the matter bluntly, George V was an invaluable asset to British prestige abroad; Edward VIII has proved himself an incalculable liability.[77]

Dawson falsely believed that the letter accurately reflected public opinion in the United States. In fact it grossly exaggerated the damage to British prestige caused by the affair in America. US press coverage was broadly favourable: the prospect of King Edward making an American woman his Queen was hardly calculated to cause dismay in America itself. However, the letter happened to reflect Dawson's own views of the crisis so closely that subsequently there were rumours that it had been written in the *Times* offices.[78] He immediately had copies made and delivered them in person to Baldwin and Alexander Hardinge, urging them to discuss its contents with the King. He emphasized that the silence of the British press could not hold much longer. When Hardinge finally challenged the King about his relationship with Wallis Simpson, which he did in a letter of 13 November, he specifically alluded to the impact of letters from British subjects living in foreign countries.[79]

From mid-November events moved swiftly. Following receipt of Hardinge's letter, Edward summoned Baldwin to Fort Belvedere on 16 November, and finally told him of his intention to marry Mrs Simpson once her divorce came through.[80] Baldwin warned him of the government's opposition, and that if Edward persisted, then he would resign and force a general election. There was talk of the formation of a 'King's Party' led by Winston Churchill, but Edward did not have the stomach for a fight, and was unwilling to divide the country over the issue of his marriage. He preferred to abdicate in order to marry Wallis. The British press at last broke their silence on 2 December, and for the next ten days, until Edward's abdication on 11 December, newspapers in Britain and America carried every twist and turn of the unfolding drama on their front pages.

As the crisis finally became public in Britain, the American radio networks saw their first opportunity to compete with the print media on international news, foreshadowing the famous radio broadcasts from London to the USA during the Blitz of 1940. By 1936 both CBS and NBC had fledgling operations in London.[81] NBC's Fred Bate, the old friend of the King's and a frequent guest at Fort Belvedere, should have had the advantage. However, with disastrous timing, he had returned to America for a holiday, arriving on 1 December, just in time to hear that a radio station in Schenectady, New York, had announced that Edward was going to abdicate. He immediately put in a call on the transatlantic telephone line to Alistair Cooke, who was then a young journalist based in London. He instructed Cooke to go at once to the BBC studios, where he had booked a broadcasting circuit to the USA for 11.45 p.m., just before CBS. He assured Cooke that NBC would break into their regular programming to carry the report. Cooke improvised a short talk on the British reaction to the story, or rather the lack of it, because the newspapers did not break the story until the following day.[82] For the next ten days Cooke broadcast news reports to America round the clock to catch the news bulletins in the various different time zones.[83] Not surprisingly Cooke fell ill in the course of this marathon, but Bate had a telephone line and microphone installed in his flat, so that he could continue broadcasting from his sickbed. Fortunately Cooke found a good leg-man, an American Rhodes Scholar called Walt Rostow,[84] who scurried round London gathering intelligence as the drama unfolded. The rival CBS network did not rely on a single journalist, but supplemented its news reports with nightly talks by Fleet Street editors and well-known figures such as H. G. Wells and Harold Nicolson.[85] The climax of the radio coverage of the crisis was, of course, Edward's Abdication speech on 11 December. It was carried on both the main US networks, and went out live at 5 p.m. Eastern Standard Time from three hundred stations across the country.[86] The broadcast brought America to a standstill; streets emptied as people crowded into hotels, bars, and radio stores to hear the ex-King. In Washington, DC, Eleanor Roosevelt, returning from a function in a radio-equipped taxi, sat outside the White House with the meter running while she heard the end of the speech. At Duke University the young Richard Nixon and his classmates gathered round a radio set to listen. In Columbia, South Carolina, firemen found a woman listening to Edward's broadcast while her house went up in flames around her. 'If the top of the house burns,' she told them, 'providing it doesn't cave in, I'm still going to listen to the King.'[87]

The Abdication left a bitter aftertaste in Anglo-American relations. Many in Britain blamed the American press for precipitating the crisis. Under the headline 'These lies poisoned the World', the *Daily Mirror* launched a vituperative attack on 'the newspaper hooligans of the United States'. According to the paper, America's largest recent export was 'venomous gossip and twisted headlines based on rumour'.[88] In slightly more moderate tones, *The Times* made the same point, writing of 'scurrilities of a section of the American Press ... engaged in competitive scandal-mongering'.[89] Across the Atlantic, commentators noted how the royal romance had brought out the anti-American sentiment which lay close to the surface of British society. Shortly before the crisis broke, *Time* magazine reported,

> In Mayfair, there is a small, swift, hard-drinking clique who are the King's only real friends. Most of those people seem 'American' to the circles in which Queen Mary and Prime Minister Stanley Baldwin move—and to those worthies 'American' is a revolting adjective. The worst feature of an appalling situation in their eyes was not that Mrs Simpson has one divorce and is about to have another, but that Mrs Simpson was in fact born in the US.[90]

For *Time*, the Abdication represented the reassertion of traditional British values against the Americanizing tendencies of the King: 'In England, the news that the King wanted to marry Mrs Simpson was the culmination of a tide of events sweeping the United Kingdom out of its cosy past and into a more or less hectic and "American" future. Against that trend, the spirit of John Bull resolutely set himself, and the flesh was that of the Right Honourable Stanley Baldwin.'[91]

In his negotiations with Edward during the Abdication crisis, Baldwin was shocked by the fact that Edward showed no sign of moral or intellectual struggle over his choice between Wallis Simpson and the throne: 'The last days before the Abdication were thrilling and terrible. He would never listen to reason about Mrs Simpson. He had *no* spiritual conflict *at all*. There was no battle in his will.'[92] This insight, coming from the only man in Britain able to force the King to confront the reality of his situation, rings true, and is consistent with the trajectory of Edward's personal development since 1918. In reality Edward had struggled long and hard over many years to come to terms with his royal destiny, but the battle had been lost well before 1936. 'David', the Americanized private man, had become so estranged from King Edward VIII of Great Britain that no reconciliation was possible in his choice of marriage partner. If the Abdication was an act of renunciation, it was also a striking act of affirmation by 'David', a final assertion of his true self.[93] Psychologically the Abdication represented a form of suicide by 'Edward', cutting 'David' free from his alter ego. He was not simply choosing Wallis Simpson over the throne, but an Americanized version of himself over his British identity. The ultimate tragedy, of course, was that Wallis was in love with Edward, not David.

14

The Frog Prince

The Windsors in Exile, 1937–1945

In January 1937, during their months of separation following the Abdication, Edward, now Duke of Windsor, sent Wallis a bejewelled frog as a love token.[1] Whether or not either party appreciated the irony of the gift, it was peculiarly appropriate for the circumstances in which the ex-King and his future wife found themselves. In a cruel reversal of the fairy tale, Wallis had kissed a Prince, who then turned into a frog. In abdicating the throne, Edward laid aside the burdens of kingship. At the same time, however, he had also unwittingly surrendered the benefits of being a member of the royal family—benefits which he had always taken for granted as his birthright. After acrimonious negotiations, Edward's brother King George VI agreed a generous financial settlement, but otherwise he was ostracized by the new Court.[2] All the ties with his former life were cut. None of his family attended Edward and Wallis's wedding in June 1937; worse still, the new King denied Wallis the title of 'Her Royal Highness' following the marriage—an act of calculated malevolence which wounded the Duke where he was most vulnerable, and which barred any prospect of reconciliation. The message was clear: Wallis was not to be recognized as a member of the royal family. The 1938 edition of *Burke's Peerage*, the British bible of royal and aristocratic lineage, expressed the official position with brutal clarity: it simply disregarded the marriage, pointedly excluding Wallis from the Royal Pedigree. 'The drawbridges are going up behind me,' Edward told Wallis despairingly, 'I have taken you into a void.'[3]

Edward was completely unprepared for the consequences of the Abdication. Whereas Wallis had felt repeated premonitions of disaster during the autumn of 1936, Edward had been so caught up in his determination to marry Wallis that he gave no consideration as to what life would be like as an ex-King.[4] He appears to have assumed that, after a decent interval, he would be able

to return to Britain with Wallis as his Duchess, and carry on life very much
as he had done as Prince of Wales. What he failed to appreciate was that all
the privileges he had enjoyed derived from the position he held as heir to
the throne and later as King.[5] Having resigned the throne to his brother,
he was an embarrassing anomaly. Medieval kings of England who had invol-
untarily 'abdicated' (that is, had been deposed) were quickly murdered by
their successors, and British governments after 1936 must sometimes have
wished that they still had that option. There was simply no constitutional
role for a living ex-King.[6] Edward was unwelcome in Britain because it was
feared that his popularity would overshadow the new King, George VI; his
overseas travels were discouraged because, in the febrile years before the
Second World War, the Foreign Office was concerned that he might commit
diplomatic gaffes or make statements contrary to government policy. The
Court and the government hoped that he would retire quietly into private
life, like his cousin Alfonso XIII, the deposed King of Spain. Edward, however,
was determined to carve out a new role for himself, and to secure public
recognition for his wife as a royal duchess.

For Edward, one of the most serious consequences of the Abdication was
that he was suddenly deprived of his corps of household staff. Throughout his life he had been supported by a team of equerries and private
secretaries who managed his diary, dealt with his correspondence, planned
his engagements, and generally looked after his affairs. They were diligent
and competent administrators, who understood the functions of monarchy
and advised Edward on what he could do and say. For twenty years he had
relied on men like Godfrey Thomas, Tommy Lascelles, and Joey Legh as
counsellors and companions. Now they were gone.[7] Of his immediate circle,
only Fruity Metcalfe followed his master into exile, and although he was
Edward's truest friend, he was no administrator.[8] None of the others even
attended his wedding. Without them, Edward floundered; his tragicomic
misjudgements after the Abdication were partly the result of the lack of
advice and support which a senior member of the royal family would normally
enjoy. Early in 1937 the British Embassy in Vienna did provide Edward with
a junior diplomat, Dudley Forwood, to serve as his equerry. Forwood was
to remain with the Duke until 1939, and accompanied the couple on their
visit to Germany in October 1937. However, he was too young and inexperienced to act as more than a personal assistant.[9]

In retrospect it is surprising that the British government did not do more
to provide Edward and Wallis with administrative and logistical support.
It was understandable that career courtiers like Thomas and Legh did not

wish to follow the Duke into what for them would have been a professional cul-de-sac.[10] Nevertheless, a little more guidance, particularly on public relations, would have improved communication with London and helped the couple avoid the embarrassing entanglements with Nazi sympathizers which marred their early years of exile. As it was, the rift over the Duchess's status embittered relations from the start, and the British government was too concerned with protecting the new monarch to give much consideration as to how the old one would occupy himself in exile.

The consequences of the Abdication were as traumatic for Wallis as they had been for Edward. Sensing disaster ahead, she had done everything possible to stop the King abdicating, hoping that she would ultimately be able to escape from the relationship.[11] When the final crisis broke at the beginning of December 1936, she fled to France, pursued by packs of reporters. She found refuge with her old friends Herman and Katherine Rogers, who had a villa in Cannes. There she was to remain for several months, a virtual prisoner of the press camped outside. She received poison pen letters and even death threats, and had to be given police protection. She became a social pariah in Britain, as Osbert Sitwell described in his cruelly apposite poem, *Rat Week*, and felt that she had been subjected to a campaign of vilification on both sides of the Atlantic.[12] She also found that some of her American friends betrayed her confidence in order to cash in on their acquaintance with her. She accused her old school friend, Mary Raffray (who later married Ernest Simpson), of collaborating with the American romantic novelist Laura Lou Brookman to produce a gushing biography, *Her Name Was Wallis Warfield*.[13] She also suspected that Thelma Furness and Gloria Vanderbilt had been paid by Hearst Newspapers to supply stories about her.[14] Still more upsetting was betrayal by a family member. Newbold Noyes, the husband of Wallis's cousin Lelia Montague Barnett, was associate editor of the *Washington Star*. In October 1936 Noyes volunteered his services to help Wallis improve her public image in the USA in face of what she considered to be the adverse publicity surrounding her divorce. She had accepted on the understanding that he would write a favourable character sketch of her without disclosing his privileged access. In November Noyes visited Fort Belvedere, where he discussed the American news coverage with Wallis and the King. He promised to provide discreet public relations assistance through his media contacts. Instead he wrote a series of sensational tabloid-style articles, which were syndicated across the US, giving an account of his private conversations at the Fort, and implying that they had been authorized by the couple.[15] In January 1937 Wallis issued a press statement from Cannes angrily repudiating the articles and threatening to sue Noyes.[16] Noyes threatened to counter-sue, before writing a letter of apology to Wallis, pleading misunderstanding. Nevertheless, Wallis permanently severed relations with her cousin.[17]

Having lost any official status as a result of the Abdication, Edward became a highly equivocal figure in Britain. Some, like the author Compton Mackenzie, defended him fiercely, and argued that he had been the victim of a conspiracy to oust him.[18] However, the general consensus, promoted by the Court and the government and endorsed by the press, was that in abdicating Edward had deserted his post and shirked his sacred duty. The country rallied behind the new King, and as the threat of war grew with every international crisis of the late 1930s, the turbulence of the Abdication quickly subsided. Edward had passed his symbolic role to his brother, and as an individual he faded from public view.

In the United States, the situation could not have been more different. Apart from the more serious East Coast papers, the press treated the Abdication as a great human-interest story rather than a constitutional crisis. It raised Edward's celebrity to new levels, and the couple's love affair was acclaimed as the romance of the century. In December 1936, *Time* magazine reported the reaction of the audience at a Manhattan newsreel theatre when some of the leading actors in the drama appeared on screen. 'Prince Edward (cheers); Mrs Simpson (cheers)... new King George and Queen Elizabeth (boos); Prime Minister Baldwin (PROLONGED CATCALLS AND BOOS!); King Edward and Mrs Simpson bathing in the Mediterranean (CHEERS!)'[19]

The couple's romance caught the popular imagination in America, and was celebrated in song and popular culture. In Chicago, a couple named their new-born twins 'Edward Windsor' and 'Wally Warfield'[20]. One of the hit tunes of 1937 was 'Edward the Eighth' by the Trinidadian calypso singer Lord Caresser, who played at the Ruban Bleu nightclub in New York. With a repetitive, dirge-like refrain, 'It was love, love alone, which caused King Edward to leave his throne', the song told the story of the Abdication:

> King Edward was noble, King Edward was great
> But it's love that caused him to abdicate...
> And he got the money and he got the talk
> And the fancy walk just to suit New York...
> On the tenth of December 1936
> The Duke of Windsor went to get his kicks...[21]

Fashionable hotels and nightclubs decorated their walls with murals of the couple. At the Famous Door club on New York's 52nd Street, Edward was depicted as part of a celebrity swing band, his crown askew, playing alongside the likes of Roosevelt, Hitler, and Stalin.[22] The Hotel Senator in Sacramento, California, caused controversy with the decoration of its new 'Empire' cocktail bar. Titled 'Choice of an Empire', it depicted the Abdication story in two large friezes. In the first, King Edward and Baldwin were portrayed as playing-card characters; as Baldwin offered the crown to Edward on bended knee, the King looked distractedly through a palace archway at Wallis, demurely dressed in Puritan garb. The second frieze showed Edward and Wallis in modern dress, walking away from the palace, led by a triumphant Cupid.[23] There was speculation that Edward and Wallis might spend their honeymoon in America, or even settle there permanently. The humorist H. I. Phillips parodied the popular mood, anticipating a visit by the couple to the United States:

> We can picture the greatest newsreel picnic in the history of our country... Special harbor rules announced to avoid chaos among excursion boats bound to meet the happy pair. Tugs bearing offers to Edward to appear in movies must keep to right, and let steamers bearing offers from literary agents pass... The Duke and Wally are taken from the liner in a state of collapse due to attempts to obey all orders of the camera and newspaper men. Edward begins to wish he hadn't quit throne... Seven hundred women and children hurt in riot caused by a shout of 'Hooray for Stanley Baldwin'... Wally finds she has been named Miss America, Queen of the Mardi Gras and Lady Visitor No. 1.[24]

With Edward cut off from the sources of advice and support upon which he had always relied, he became entirely dependent on Wallis and their network of loyal American friends. Immediately after the Abdication, Wallis arranged for him to stay with Kitty de Rothschild, the American wife of Baron Eugene de Rothschild, at Schloss Enzesfeld in Austria.[25] The Duke's old friend Fred Bate, the European head of NBC, visited the couple shortly before their marriage, and left an open invitation for the Duke to broadcast on American radio. Oscar Solbert, who had been the American liaison officer on Edward's trip to New York in 1924, encouraged him to pursue his plans to campaign for the international peace movement which was attempting to prevent the outbreak of a European war.[26] Most significantly, Wallis's friends Herman and Katherine Rogers introduced them to Charles Bédaux, a Franco-American time and motion expert, who had emigrated to the USA before the First World War and made a fortune in management consultancy. In January 1937 Bédaux offered Edward his mansion near Tours, the Chateau de Candé, as a temporary residence. Although the Duke declined the offer as being too close to Wallis in Cannes, the couple later chose it as the location for their wedding in June 1937.[27] Bédaux and his American wife Fern, hosted Edward and Wallis at Chateau de Candé for several weeks before the wedding, at a cost, Bédaux later estimated, of $60,000.[28]

Bédaux's business efficiency methods were highly controversial. It was based on the 'B' unit, representing a standardized measurement of productivity for manual labour. Bédaux consultants would determine how many 'B' units the average worker produced for a given task, from which a basic wage rate for the job was established. Known in America as the 'speed-up' or 'stretch-out' system, Bédaux's approach was fiercely opposed by trade unions as a pseudo-scientific management technique for cutting wages. It provoked many strikes in the USA and Europe in the 1920s and 1930s.[29]

In September 1937, at the end of their extended honeymoon, the Windsors again took advantage of the Bédauxs' hospitality, this time at their hunting-lodge in Borsodivanka in Hungary. Impressed by Bédaux's great wealth, and his obvious success as a businessman, Edward sought his advice as to how he might rebuild his international standing. The two men had interests in common: Bédaux was an expert on labour issues, and the Duke was keen to develop his interest in housing and working conditions for the industrial classes.[30] Edward was willing to travel to any country where Wallis was sure to receive a warm welcome. With Britain and the Empire excluded, the two countries with which he had the greatest affinity were the USA and Germany. Bédaux had operations in both countries and, looking to obtain some return on his investment in the Windsors, foresaw significant business advantages from exploiting his association with them.

While at Borsodivanka, Edward and Bédaux put together the programme for a tour. Bédaux approached his contacts in Nazi Germany, who were delighted to exploit the opportunity offered by a visit from the ex-King. Robert Ley, the head of the German Labour Front, took charge of the arrangements, and organized a twelve-day itinerary across the Reich, taking in factories and model housing projects. Bédaux agreed that he would organize the US tour himself, and even undertook to meet the cost of it.[31] Perhaps encouraged by the enthusiastic response to his plans from Germany, Edward decided to proceed at very short notice. On 3 October 1937 Forwood, the Duke's equerry, announced that the Windsors would be visiting Germany and the USA for the purpose of studying housing and working conditions in the two countries.[32] The couple were to arrive in Germany on 11 October, and hoped to make the transatlantic voyage before Christmas.

The Duke's attempt to relaunch his career quickly turned into an ignominious failure, revealing his naivety and poor judgement, but also a lack of good advice. His overseas tours as Prince of Wales had been meticulously planned and managed for him by his staff, liaising with the British government and colonial authorities. Without that support, Edward's reputation was at the mercy of unscrupulous strangers. The British Foreign Office would have nothing to do with the Windsors' German tour, and the Ambassador found an excuse to be away from Berlin when they arrived.[33] Since the trip was officially a private one, he was not given the full honours of a state visit, although he had a meeting with Hitler and other Nazi bigwigs such as Goebbels, Goering, and Hess. The Duchess was, however, ostentatiously given the status of 'Her Royal Highness' which the Duke craved for her, and crowds of cheering well-wishers were organized to greet the couple along their itinerary.[34] The price the Nazis exacted was to use the tour as a propaganda exercise for the achievements of National Socialism, and the Windsors were criticized, both in Britain and the US, as apologists for the regime.

The best that could be said of the Windsors' tour of Germany was that it had been well organized, albeit for the benefit of the hosts. The couple's projected tour of the USA, by contrast, collapsed in a welter of confusion. The Duke's abrupt announcement of the visit at the beginning of October appears to have been made without prior planning or consultation with the US government. Only when the Windsors' party arrived in Berlin, on 11 October 1937, did Bédaux approach the American Embassy to solicit an official invitation from Washington. The Ambassador advised that any approach should be made through the British Embassy, which of course had no knowledge of the Duke's plans. As a result, uncertainty reigned in Washington. The First Lady, Eleanor Roosevelt, said that she would be happy to show the Windsors round model housing projects in the District of Columbia. The Secretary of Labor, Frances Perkins, stated that her department would provide facilities for the visit, but was forced to issue a clarification a few days later that this did not constitute a formal invitation. The Interior Secretary, Harold Ickes, announced that at Bédaux's request he had cabled a list of US housing projects to him, but that it was up to the Duke arrange his own programme.[35] At the end of October, Bédaux returned to the USA to take personal charge of the arrangements. Dudley Forwood announced from Paris that the couple would definitely be sailing for America on 6 November on the German liner *Bremen* (chosen because it made no stops in Britain), and would be making a five-week, coast-to-coast tour, although the precise itinerary had not been finalized.[36] Mindful of their experiences with the US press before the Abdication, the Windsors hired an advertising agency, Arthur Kudner, to handle the publicity for the tour.[37]

Bédaux faced an unexpectedly hostile reception upon his arrival in New York. Although the 'Bédaux System' had been widely adopted by American companies—and bitterly opposed by organized labour—Bédaux himself was not a well-known figure. He spent much of his time in Europe, and kept a low profile. As soon as his association with the Windsors became public, however, articles about him appeared in the US press, charting his rise from immigrant construction worker to millionaire management consultant.[38] Suddenly the leading labour unions, the AFL and the CIO, had their enemy in plain view: a profiteer from the pitiless exploitation of the working man, rather than an impersonal business system. They mounted a vociferous campaign against the tour, and made direct attacks on the Windsors as well as Bédaux. The Baltimore Federation of Labor passed a resolution condemning the visit, and personally criticizing the Duchess: 'the wife of the Duke of Windsor, while resident here, in no way showed the slightest concern nor sympathy for the problems of labor or the poor and needy'.[39] The US government, always lukewarm about the tour, backed away; the British Embassy in Washington, on instructions from Buckingham Palace, maintained a glacial hostility to the Windsors' plans. The final straw appears to have been the refusal of the State Department to acknowledge the Duchess as 'Her Royal Highness', as the Germans had done.[40] In what *Time* magazine called 'a crescendo of anti-climax', Bédaux resigned as the Duke's adviser and the Windsors abruptly cancelled their tour only hours before they were due to set sail.[41]

The fiasco of the Windsors' abortive American tour was a humiliating reminder of the Duke's loss of prestige and status. Although the visit to Nazi Germany had attracted criticism, it is clear from contemporary press accounts that this was not the principal reason for the collapse of the tour. Far more important was the lack of any official support from the British government, so that Edward was forced to rely on a self-interested maverick like Charles Bédaux to make the arrangements. Travelling with Edward when he was Prince of Wales, Wallis had marvelled at the aura of power and authority which he possessed.[42] No longer: in the eyes of the British establishment, the Abdication had stripped Edward of his royal charisma and reduced him to the level of an ordinary mortal.

If the association with Bédaux had been embarrassing for the Windsors, for Bédaux himself it was catastrophic. The hostile publicity he attracted in

America badly affected his business. Soon after the tour was cancelled, Bédaux was confronted by the directors of his American companies and forced to withdraw from the operation of all the group's activities in the United States. The board of his British company also insisted that he resign. Soon afterwards he suffered a nervous breakdown, and spent several months recovering in a German sanatorium.[43] Arguably he was the victim, not only of his own ambition, but also of the Duke's impulsiveness and self-absorption. Like Wallis before him, he overcommitted himself to Edward's cause, and suffered the consequences disproportionately.

By the spring of 1939, Europe appeared to be sliding ever closer to war. Nazi Germany had already annexed Austria and dismembered Czechoslovakia, and was beginning to threaten Poland. In Britain, with the horrors of the Somme and Passchendaele still fresh in the nation's memory, there was still strong anti-war sentiment. A London newspaper, the *Catholic Herald*, issued a worldwide appeal for peace. It called on a figure of world stature to plead with leading statesmen to halt the drift towards war. Edward wrote approvingly to the paper, commenting, 'the Catholic appeal cannot fail to commend itself to many millions, irrespective of creed, race or political doctrines'.[44] A few days later, Fred Bate of NBC contacted the Duke to suggest that he should deliver a worldwide radio appeal via the American network. They agreed that Edward should use a forthcoming visit to the American battlefield sites near Verdun as a platform for the occasion. The preparations went ahead in secrecy; NBC announced the speech only forty-eight hours before its broadcast on 8 May, presumably to give London as little time as possible to object. Bate personally supervised the arrangements, setting up a studio for Edward in a Verdun hotel, Le Coq Hardi.[45]

Announced as 'an appeal to reason in the light of world conditions', the Duke's address was significant, not only because it was his first broadcast since the Abdication, but because it was the first speech which Edward is known to have written entirely on his own.[46] Speaking in a private capacity, from his experience as a soldier of the Great War, Edward urged the political leaders of the world to set aside purely national interests, and work together for peace. Its solemn tone reflected the many speeches which the Duke had given at war memorials and Armistice Day parades in his years as Prince of Wales: 'as I talk to you from this historic place, I am deeply conscious of the presence of the great company of the dead'. There were Churchillian echoes, suggesting that Edward had benefited from the tuition he had received from his mentor in public speaking: 'the grave anxieties of the time in which we live compel me to raise my voice in expression of the universal longing to be delivered from the fears that beset us'. Overall, it was a polished rhetorical performance, and was enthusiastically received in the USA.[47] As an attempt to turn Europe from the path of war, however, the appeal missed its mark. The original plan had been for Edward to make the speech in three languages—English, French, and German— and for NBC to relay the broadcast worldwide. Unfortunately, the Duke's speech coincided with the departure of King George VI and Queen Elizabeth for a tour of Canada and the United States, and the BBC refused to carry the broadcast for fear of upstaging them. The Germans ignored NBC's offer, and France also refused to broadcast the speech, so that in the end it was only heard in the USA. In the grim international climate of 1939, the Duke's appeal appeared naive and redolent of the failed policy of appeasement.

Within a few months of Edward's 'appeal to reason', Britain was again at war with Germany. The Duke and Duchess, who had been living at La Croe, a rented villa in Cap d'Antibes, returned to Britain. Edward rejoined the army with the rank of major-general, and during the 'phoney war' between September 1939 and May 1940, he was attached to the Military Mission in France, acting as a liaison with French forces. When the Germans invaded France in May 1940, the mission was forced to abandon Paris, and Edward was given leave to return to La Croe, where he was reunited with Wallis. A few days later, in the face of the rapid German advance, they fled across the Spanish border, arriving in Madrid on 23 June.[48]

The six weeks that the Windsors spent in Spain and Portugal in 1940, until their departure for the Bahamas on 1 August, showed Edward at his petulant worst. At the most critical point in the war, with Britain facing the imminent threat of invasion, Edward spent several days arguing with Churchill about the conditions for his return home, and demanding reassurances that the Duchess would be granted recognition by the royal family. At the same time, he continued to make unguarded statements about the need to agree a peace with Germany and end the war, some of which were reported back to the US State Department in Washington.[49] Such defeatist talk was inexcusable in June 1940, as Churchill rallied the nation to hold out against Hitler at all costs. It also encouraged the Nazis to think that they might be able to use the Duke for propaganda purposes to undermine British resolve to carry on the war. Ribbentrop, the Foreign Minister, hatched a plot to detain the Windsors in Spain, by force if necessary, where they would be susceptible to German pressure.[50] With King George and

Prime Minister Churchill in despair at Edward's antics, the impasse was only broken by the offer of the Governorship of the Crown Colony of the Bahama Islands, which the Duke immediately accepted.[51]

From London's point of view, the Bahamas posting was the ideal location in which to anchor the Windsors for the duration of the war. It gave the Duke official responsibilities in a remote corner of the empire, and it had no political or strategic importance. Indeed the Bahamas were so insignificant that they were among the few colonies which Edward had never visited as Prince of Wales on his imperial tours.[52] For the Windsors it was an igno-minious exile; Wallis soon came to refer to the Bahamas as 'our St Helena'. Nevertheless, the Islands did enjoy one great advantage: they were close to America—the capital, Nassau, was only 180 miles from Miami. In addition the appointment conferred diplomatic status upon the Duke, which gave him standing to deal with the US government, and also gave the Duchess status as the Governor's wife.

The Windsors were also lucky in that President Franklin Roosevelt was favourably disposed towards the couple. According to his son Elliott, Roosevelt was 'fascinated by kings and queens, half-amused, half-impressed by the pomp and pageantry that enveloped royalty'.[53] Roosevelt was intrigued by the per-sonality of the Duke and was keen to meet him. As a man who had struggled against great odds to achieve high office, he could not understand why Edward had abdicated the throne. When Lord Beaverbrook returned to America early in 1937, Roosevelt summoned him to Washington and quizzed him at length about the Abdication.[54] He had invited the Windsors to the White House during their projected tour of the USA in November 1937, and when it was cancelled, he wrote warmly to the Duke, expressing the hope that they would soon be able to visit America.[55] Roosevelt's sons sought out the Windsors on their trips to Europe before the war. In the summer of 1937 John Roosevelt met them at a boxing tournament in Austria; in May 1939 James Roosevelt, then a movie executive, invited the Duke and Duchess to the film premiere of *Wuthering Heights* in Paris.[56]

The Duke's appointment as Governor of the Bahamas attracted great interest in America, and the couple gave their first press conference to American reporters within twenty-four hours of their arrival in Nassau on 17 August 1940.[57] In their new position the Windsors decided to take charge of their own public relations campaign. After their bitter experiences in 1936, and at the time of the abortive visit to America the following year, they were determined that their side of the story should finally be told.

They agreed to give an exclusive extended interview to Adela Rogers St. Johns, one of America's leading women journalists, who worked for Hearst Newspapers. Rogers spent ten days with the Windsors in Nassau in the autumn of 1940, interviewing them both, dining with them, and accompanying them to official functions. In return for the scoop, Rogers wrote up the Windsors and their romance in the most glowing terms. The result was a series of fourteen articles titled 'The Windsors' Own Love Story', syndicated in newspapers across the USA, and published on consecutive days between 17 and 30 November 1940.[58] She presented the Duke as a saintly figure, stoically performing his duty for an ungrateful nation. She portrayed Wallis as a frail, heroic beauty, with eyes 'the colour of bluebells under water', a woman of legend, yet also an authentically American character: 'I was poignantly aware that I was in the presence of that one American woman whose name history will add to that brief mysterious scroll upon which time has written the names of Helen of Troy and Cleopatra . . . the Duchess of Windsor is a southern lady, a Scarlett O'Hara in a more gentle way, and with an entirely different story of course. But she has all the inborn tradition where men are concerned.' Many of the themes explored in Rogers's articles were later to be expanded and developed in the couple's 1950s memoirs, *A King's Story* and *The Heart has its Reasons*.

Once settled in Nassau, the Duke applied himself conscientiously to the task of governing the islands, while the Duchess devoted herself to war work at the Red Cross. The local economy was heavily dependent on American tourism in the winter season, and unemployment was chronically high. Edward tried to introduce measures to attract investment and diversify economic activity, against the opposition of the clique of local businessmen known as the 'Bay Street Boys'. With the Bahamas so close to the mainland, the Duke naturally looked to the USA, where he had extensive business contacts. The couple were eager to visit America as soon as possible, for pleasure as well as business, but the British government was equally determined to stop them. Within days of their arrival in Nassau, the Duke cabled London requesting permission to escape the stifling summer heat in order to visit the EP ranch, which he had not seen since 1927. However, the Colonial Secretary ruled that it was inappropriate for the Duke to travel through the States in the lead-up to the presidential elections.[59]

In December 1940, the couple asked to make a short trip to Miami so that Wallis could receive treatment for an infected tooth. London granted permission for the Duke to accompany her, but for the perverse reason that the visit happened to coincide with a cruise by President Roosevelt to the Caribbean, and the Foreign Office did not want Edward to meet him.[60] The Duke announced in advance that the couple's visit was purely a private one, and that they would accept no invitations and make no public appearances. However, the Mayor of Miami, Alexander Orr, had other ideas. He announced that the city welcomed the opportunity to become acquainted with the Duke and Duchess. Travelling from Nassau by sea, they disembarked at Miami on 10 December 1940, the fourth anniversary of the Abdication. It was Edward's first visit to the USA since 1924, and Wallis's first since 1933. In scenes reminiscent of Edward's arrival in San Diego in 1920, a reception committee led by four local mayors gathered at the quayside, while the entire Miami police force provided an honour guard.[61] A crowd of 12,000 welcomed the Windsors at the dock and along the route to the hospital where Wallis was to have her operation.[62]

The Windsors' return to American soil proved unexpectedly eventful. Wallis's dental treatment passed off successfully, although she had to remain in hospital for three days. Then, on 12 December, Lord Lothian, the British Ambassador to the US, died suddenly. On the same day, Edward received an invitation from President Roosevelt to join him aboard the USS *Tuscaloosa*, which was anchored off the Bahamian island of Eleuthera. The coincidence of these events prompted speculation that Edward would be appointed as Lothian's successor in Washington, and revived memories of his success in his role as 'ambassador of empire' as Prince of Wales[63]. On 13 December Edward flew out in a US navy seaplane to meet Roosevelt. Having brought no uniforms with him, he cut a somewhat Ruritanian figure in his blazer as a commandant of the Royal Yacht Squadron at Cowes, together with a yachting cap. The meeting lasted three hours, including an hour of private conversation. It was not their first encounter; as Assistant Navy Secretary Roosevelt had hosted Edward's visit to Annapolis in 1919. They discussed naval bases, and the economic future of the West Indies.[64] Edward expressed an interest in the Civilian Conservation Corps, a New Deal unemployment relief programme, as a model for the Bahamas, and Roosevelt promised to arrange a camp visit for him.

The welcome which the Duke and Duchess received in Florida was in stark contrast to the hostile treatment from the British Court and government which they had endured since the Abdication. Spurned as outcasts and exiles from Great Britain, they were feted in Miami as important celebrities. Cheering crowds greeted their arrival, and the President himself made

special arrangements to meet the Duke. Shortly after their return to the
Bahamas, the Duke gave his reactions to the visit. America had lost none of
its magic for him. 'I had a wonderful time in Miami... Our visit did us the
world of good. There is something so stimulating no matter where you go
in America. American vitality is a tangible quality. You can feel it in the
air... To go to the United States is like going to the big city. Your blood
begins to tingle; you come back strengthened and invigorated.'[65]

As if to celebrate Edward's return to America, NBC, which had carried
his Verdun peace appeal in 1939, invited him to broadcast a Christmas Day
message across the United States. Speaking only a few hours after his brother
King George had made his radio address to Britain and the empire, Edward
offered a prayer for an early end to the war and a peace settlement based on
justice, sanity, and goodwill. In one passage, which carried striking echoes of
a speech he had given in New York in November 1919, he contrasted the
bitter enmities of the Old World with the peaceful harmony of the New:
'on the continent of America there are two peoples that for decades have
lived peacefully side by side with a frontier several thousand miles long,
unguarded by a single fort or a single soldier, because they have the same
comprehension of the scheme of life which has been evolved in perfect
harmony by the New World'.[66] He finished with a prophecy that the end
of hostilities would see a 'colossal readjustment' in international relations,
and prayed that political leaders would have the wisdom and vision to rise
to that challenge. In an address to a still neutral America, that was a coded
message that after the war the USA would have the responsibility of crafting
a new world order.

After their triumph in Miami, it was natural that Edward and Wallis
should wish to visit America, and escape their Bahamian exile, as often as
the Duke's official duties would permit. Unfortunately Edward continued
to make gloomy statements about the war which infuriated the British
government. Most damaging was an interview in the American magazine
Liberty in March 1941, in which the reporter led the Duke to make statements implying that Britain would not be able to defeat Germany, and
would have to come to a negotiated settlement with Hitler.[67] This drew a
furious rebuke from Churchill himself: 'the language will be interpreted as
defeatist and pro-Nazi, and approving of the isolationist aim to keep America
out of the War... I would wish indeed that Your Royal Highness would seek
advice before making public statements of this kind.' As a result, the British
government continued to block the Windsors' travel requests to the USA,

even for official business. Churchill only relented when Edward wrote him a contrite letter promising to stick firmly to the government's line in future, and in September the couple were finally allowed to take a holiday trip via the USA to the EP ranch.[68]

The Windsors' North American vacation in the autumn of 1941, although formally a private visit, soon turned into a triumphal progress, recalling the heady days of Edward's tours as Prince of Wales.[69] The couple's six-week, seven-thousand-mile itinerary was crowded. They flew to Miami from Nassau on 25 September, and travelled by rail to Washington, where they were entertained at the British Embassy and had a brief meeting with President Roosevelt. From there they took the train to Alberta across the Midwest, via Chicago and St Paul, Minnesota, and spent ten days at the Duke's ranch. Early in October they travelled back East to Baltimore, where Wallis had a tumultuous homecoming. Edward returned to Washington for a second meeting with Roosevelt, before the couple went on to spend the last fortnight of their holiday in New York.[70]

Throughout the trip London kept a close eye on the Windsors' activities. Before they left Nassau, the Duke had to clear all the details of the arrangements with the British Embassy. They were assigned a press officer, René MacColl, whose task was to ensure that the Duke and Duchess had as little contact as possible with the American press.[71] Nevertheless, Churchill did recognize that Edward's popularity in the States could be put to good use if properly managed. He was permitted to make one speech, substantially drafted by Churchill, at the National Press Club in Washington. It dealt mainly with the Duke's role as Governor of the Bahamas, and stressed the strategic importance of the British West Indies for the defence of the eastern seaboard of the US. The speech ended with a powerful appeal for Anglo-American unity which was unmistakably Churchillian, but also reflected the Duke's own strongly held beliefs.

> This time of struggle and sorrow may be long, but it will only last until the righteous cause has prevailed. Thereafter an opportunity would be presented to the English-speaking peoples to render further services to all mankind in guiding them by their example and by their aid out of the dark valley of death and destruction into an age more rich in culture and prosperity, more warm, more cheered by security and social justice and more lighted by hope than any which history has known.[72]

Taking its cue from the British, the US government gave the Duke and Duchess a muted welcome to Washington. Nevertheless, large, enthusiastic crowds greeted them at Union Station and along the route to the Embassy. 'He's Still Prince Charming To Them' was the caption to one photograph showing Edward walking through a crowd of female admirers.[73] As *Time* magazine reported, the couple 'were prepared to be met by official luke-warmth, unprepared for a tumultuous, sigh-heaving, welcome-shouting crowd that followed them hour by hour'.[74] It was the same on the Windsors' journey through the Midwest. Friendly crowds gathered at every stop, and the couple made a point of stepping out onto the viewing platform of the train to acknowledge the well-wishers. 'Windsors Get Huge Welcome During Stop-Over' was one headline; 'The Windsors! Veni, Vidi, Vici' ran another.[75] The couple enjoyed a warm welcome even in Chicago, the country's 'isolationist capital'. 'The metropolis of the Midwest took the Duke and Duchess of Windsor to their hearts today ... They were "Wally" and "Eddie" to the good-natured throngs, totalling more than 5,000, who cheered and "yea-ed" them during the stop-over.'[76] At St Paul, where they broke their journey for dinner, an estimated 20,000 crowd watched them drive to the State Capitol in an open-topped car.[77] Passing through North Dakota, they made more than thirty appearances to wave at the crowds along the route.[78]

Crossing the border into Canada, the Windsors again met a cool official reception. The Goveror-General, Edward's uncle the Earl of Athlone, had refused to receive the Duchess, and the Prime Minister, Mackenzie King, sent Edward a letter of greeting which was carefully worded to exclude Wallis from the official welcome but did not leave her out altogether.[79] However, the crowds were as large and exuberant as they had been in America. In Moose Jaw, Saskatchewan, their first stop in Canada, they were surrounded by a friendly crush of 4,000 people.[80]

The Duke and Duchess finally arrived at the EP ranch on 29 September 1941. It was fourteen years since Edward's last visit. He remained popular in the vicinity, and received an affectionate tribute from the local *High River Times*: 'In the past he came to his EP Ranch as a Prince, but he remains in the memory of all who saw him and spoke with him not as a link with royalty but as a man of charm, simplicity, and great friendliness.'[81] In the intervening period the west Canadian ranching industry had suffered a severe recession, and most of the EP's livestock had been sold off, and its operations curtailed. Edward had been considering a sale of the property, but the news that the Canadian government was drilling for oil in the area led him to reconsider. In the ten days that they spent at the ranch, the Duke spent much of his time closeted with his business advisers. The Duchess spent her time relaxing and taking walks across the nearby hills. She was no countrywoman, and declined the offer of a ride on one of the ranch's Dartmoor ponies. Soon after their arrival the couple gave a press conference at the ranch-house. Edward confined his comments to his work in the Bahamas, and matters concerning the ranch, while Wallis sidestepped questions about her wardrobe and instead told reporters about her work with the Red Cross.[82]

The Duke and Duchess left the EP ranch on 8 October and headed back East. Increasingly, the visit began to take on the characteristics of a royal tour. The highlight of the return journey was their visit to Wallis's home town of Baltimore. At the Windsors' insistence the Mayor's reception committee scaled down plans for a grand civic reception, but the Duchess's homecoming was a spectacular affair nonetheless. After spending the weekend at the home of Wallis's uncle Henry Warfield outside the city, the couple entered Baltimore on Monday 13 October. Crowds estimated at 200,000 people crammed the streets to watch their motorcade. The Windsors received a formal greeting from Mayor Jackson at City Hall before going on to a reception at the Baltimore Country Club. There they shook hands with 1,200 guests, including many of Wallis's old school friends, and heard the opera singer Rosa Ponselle perform *Home, Sweet Home*.[83] Later in the week they inspected British war relief projects, lunched with the Governor of Maryland, Herbert O'Conor, and visited two camps of the Civilian Conservation Corps.[84] Throughout the week the Windsors remained firmly 'on message' in support of the British war effort, and even the British Ambassador, Lord Halifax, was forced to admit that the visit to Baltimore had been a success.[85]

By the time the couple reached New York, on the final leg of the trip, Edward had recovered his old confidence, and was revelling in the revival of his former role as the ambassador prince. They maintained a hectic schedule of semi-official functions. On one day, the Duke and Duchess made nine visits in seven hours, inspecting relief agencies, housing projects, and armaments factories. Edward played darts at the British Merchant Seamen's Club, and chatted to First World War veterans at an aircraft factory in Connecticut. As the *New York Times* reported, everywhere they went they attracted large crowds, 'who interfered with traffic, tossed tickertape and shreds of phone books, and must inevitably have recalled to the Duke his wild reception here as Prince of Wales'.[86] When Edward visited the navy yard in Brooklyn, he was greeted with the strains of 'God Save the King'.[87]

While they were in New York, the Duke received an invitation from Walter Chrysler to visit arms manufacturing plants in Detroit. Without consulting the Embassy, he immediately accepted—much to the annoyance of Lord Halifax, who was scheduled to go to Detroit a fortnight later.[88] In a single day, Edward toured the factories of Ford, Chrysler, and General Motors. His energy and engagement impressed his hosts, and even drew grudging acknowledgement from the British press. The *Detroit Free Press* gave a vivid description of the invigorating effect the city had on the Duke.

> An oldish young man, or a youngish old man—depending on which side of forty you are on—got off a train here Thursday morning [30 October]. He was wearing a salt-and-pepper overcoat and a well-worn smile, a little ragged round the edges. He went through the gestures of shaking hands with the British consul with all the animation of a well-greased pump handle...Then half an hour later, something happened. The man who had been king, the semi-exile, came alive again. Maybe it was the sight of those toys of war starting to pour out of Detroit for his Empire. But David, Duke of Windsor, for a few hours became the glamour boy of the British Empire.[89]

At the end of his tour Edward again met Henry Ford, who invited him back to his Dearborn mansion for tea. A few days later, Ford, who held strongly isolationist views, announced that he was reversing his earlier decision not to supply arms to Britain.[90]

As the Windsors' American trip drew on, and the evidence for their popularity grew, the Duke chafed at the restrictions which the British Embassy had imposed upon their dealings with journalists. René MacColl did his best to ensure that they gave no interviews, although a reporter occasionally managed to slip through the net.[91] Inevitably the press scrutiny was at its fiercest in New York, and the Duke and MacColl clashed publicly at a press conference at the Waldorf-Astoria Hotel, when MacColl tried unsuccessfully to stop Edward from talking to reporters. Nevertheless, the Duke had learned from his dressing-down by Churchill, and avoided the defeatist comments about the war which had so damaged his position in Britain.

Throughout their stay, the American press coverage of the Duke and Duchess remained largely sympathetic, although it was not uncritical. The sheer quantity of their luggage became a standing joke, with estimates varying from thirty-five pieces to seventy-three,[92] while the Windsors' stay at the luxurious Waldorf Towers in New York drew adverse comment. Few writers could resist the poignant contrast between the dazzling

Prince Charming of American popular memory, and the ageing, diminished Duke and his brittle Duchess. *Time* magazine captured their nostalgic appeal.

> [T]he Windsors were still romantically interesting human beings, a champagne bubble couple, the slightly moth-eaten Prince Charming, the faded Juliet...[93]

Less than a month after the Windsors returned to the Bahamas, Japan attacked Pearl Harbor, and the USA joined the war alongside Britain and the Soviet Union.[94] Now that America was an ally, rather than a neutral power, the British government was less concerned about Edward visiting the mainland, since the perceived risk of the Duke reinforcing isolationist sentiment had disappeared. Edward himself became much more sanguine about the outcome of the war. Moreover, there were compelling reasons for the Duke to make the trip: the Bahamas were now in the front line of the submarine war in the Atlantic, and the islands' economy, heavily dependent on American tourism, was devastated by the outbreak of hostilities. US military investment was needed to redress the balance. In June 1942, the Windsors paid a ten-day visit to Washington and New York to discuss defence and trade matters. Not everyone welcomed them; William Hassett, one of President Roosevelt's private secretaries, noted in his diary that the Windsors were 'about as welcome as a couple of pickpockets'. Nevertheless, the President treated them with great courtesy, breaking off delicate negotiations with the Soviet Foreign Minister, Vyacheslav Molotov, to lunch with them in the White House.[95] The Duke was forced to interrupt this trip to deal with a sudden outbreak of rioting and labour unrest in Nassau, but on his return to Washington on 15 June, Roosevelt invited him to lunch a second time. After the meal was over, Edward made to depart, but the President pressed him to stay, and the two men chatted for three hours. The papers noted that it was the longest presidential lunch since Pearl Harbor.[96] 'He talked and talked,' wrote the Duke many years later. 'To this day I haven't a clue what he really wanted of me. But from his occasional light questions as to my life, my experiences as King, I rather suspect it was because he, a man who had achieved on his own the highest summit of political power, was curious about the nature and reasoning of a man who could give up an inherited position of comparable renown.'[97]

Between 1942 and 1945 the Windsors made several lengthy trips to the USA. By the end of the war, Edward estimated that in total he had spent one year in America out of the five he had served in the Bahamas. Partly as a result of his friendship with Roosevelt, he came to enjoy a reputation in America as a senior statesman of the alliance which belied his lowly status as Governor of a minor British colony.[98] His visit to Washington in 1943 coincided with that of Winston Churchill, who had come for talks with Roosevelt about the next stages of the war following Allied victories in North Africa. The three men met together in the White House, and on the following day, the Duke attended Churchill's address to a joint session of Congress. When he arrived in the President's box in the congressional gallery, Edward received an enthusiastic round of applause; Lord Moran, Churchill's physician, thought that his ovation was greater than the one the Prime Minister had received.[99]

While they were in Washington, Edward took the opportunity to lobby Churchill about his promotion to a more congenial job. He felt that he had served his time in the hardship posting of the Bahamas, and was keen to move on. His favoured option was a diplomatic commission in the USA, not as Ambassador, but as a roving promoter of Anglo-American relations.[100] That was not a likely prospect, given the dislike in Buckingham Palace for Edward's freelance activities; however, there was no appetite in London even for a sideways move for the Duke. The best that Churchill could offer was the Governorship of Bermuda, technically a promotion, but if anything a colony even more remote and insignificant than the Bahamas. Edward turned it down, and the couple served out the rest of the war in Nassau. The Duke resigned his post in March 1945, and finally ceased to be Governor on 30 April, the day that Hitler committed suicide; a few days later Edward and Wallis sailed for Miami en route to New York.[101]

In his Abdication speech, the former King Edward had stated categorically, 'I now quit altogether public affairs', and the British government had taken him at his word. However, as a royal prince who had enjoyed worldwide popularity for almost twenty years, he found it very difficult to withdraw altogether into private life. Although as Prince of Wales he had complained bitterly about the demands of his public duties, as Duke he missed the 'buzz' of touring, the adulation of the crowds, and the contact with a wider public. Furthermore, he was anxious to secure recognition for Wallis as his Duchess, despite her rejection by the British royal family. During the war the Bahamas had provided a role for them both, however humble in comparison to the throne Edward had relinquished. Now that the war was coming to an end, the couple faced an uncertain future. King Edward was long dead, but the Windsors could not lay to rest his ghost.

Epilogue
A Fly in Amber, 1945–1972

The Duke and Duchess of Windsor left the Bahamas in 1945 without any clear plans for their future, or even where they would live. Before their departure Edward had tried unsuccessfully to obtain the promise of a diplomatic post from Winston Churchill. The Prime Minister was sympathetic, but as always the proposal foundered on the intransigence of the royal family, and their refusal to grant Wallis any form of official recognition. The uncomfortable truth was that the couple remained an embarrassment in Britain and throughout the Commonwealth. King George VI, the Duke's brother, did not want them to return to England, and the Canadian Prime Minister, Mackenzie King, was strongly opposed to the idea of Edward becoming Governor-General of the Dominion. Even the Ambassador to France, Duff Cooper—who was an old friend of Edward's—was unenthusiastic about their living in Paris. The obvious alternative for the Windsors was the USA; the Duke continued to be well received in Washington, and he was hopeful that he would be able to play some kind of role as a 'goodwill ambassador' fostering Anglo-American relations.[1]

After leaving Nassau at the beginning of May 1945, the Windsors spent a few days in Palm Beach before travelling to New York. They arrived unnoticed by the crowds at Pennsylvania Station, and took up residence at the Waldorf-Astoria, where they stayed for four months, awaiting the end of the war. In contrast with their visit in 1941, they were largely untroubled by reporters—a clear indication that, in the face of the historic events unfolding in Europe and the Far East, they had ceased to be front-page news. In between frequent holiday breaks, Edward spent much of his time consulting American industrialists, and may even have considered a career in private business.[2] In July the couple were entertained in Newport, Rhode Island, by the railway magnate Robert R. Palmer, Chairman of the Alleghany Corporation, who arranged for Edward to visit the company's headquarters in Cleveland, Ohio, to study American business methods.[3] A few weeks later he attended a lunch briefing in Washington on American post-war economic planning. Other guests included senators and senior federal government officials, and the Duke's presence caused a stir in the capital because the press wrongly jumped to the conclusion that he must be on a diplomatic mission on behalf of the British government.[4] While visiting Washington, Edward also paid a courtesy call on the new President, Harry S. Truman. The two men had met before, during a troop inspection in France at the end of the First World War, when Edward was attached to General Pershing's staff and Truman was a captain of field artillery in the 35th Infantry Division.[5]

Any plans which Edward might have been considering for his future were of course dependent upon the support, or at least the acquiescence, of his brother the King. With the war finally at an end, the Duke and Duchess returned to Europe in September 1945. While Wallis reopened their house in Paris, Edward travelled to London on his own to see his family for the first time in nearly six years. The reunion was cordial enough in personal terms, but the Palace's official position was as uncompromising as ever. After meeting his brother, Edward had a long discussion with Tommy Lascelles, the King's private secretary, who had once been a member of Edward's staff, but was now regarded by the Windsors as one of their principal enemies at Court. He set out the royal position with brutal clarity: no member of the royal family would receive Wallis; there was no question of any official work for Edward in peacetime, and the Windsors should not take up residence in Britain. Lascelles suggested that they should instead settle in America, perhaps somewhere in the South, where Edward could live the life of a country gentleman and promote the cause of Anglo-American cooperation.[6]

Why then did the Duke and Duchess not take up residence in the USA after 1945, when all factors seemed to point in that direction? Britain was clearly out of the question; France, still recovering from the effects of the Allied invasion after four years of occupation, was drab and impoverished, and racked by economic dislocation. On the other side of the Atlantic, the USA was booming and prosperous, untouched by the ravages of war. The Windsors loved the American lifestyle, and Edward could foresee useful work for himself there. Even Buckingham Palace was encouraging the move. There was, however, one fundamental stumbling block: taxation. Edward was a very wealthy man. When he abdicated, Edward had been permitted to take a substantial fortune out of the country tax-free, equivalent to over £50 million in modern terms. He had transferred part of that capital into Wallis's name. He also enjoyed a tax-free pension of £21,000 per annum (approximately £1.2 million today). While they lived in France before the war, the French government had likewise granted them tax-free status.[7] No such exemption was likely to be forthcoming in the USA, particularly as Wallis was an American citizen and therefore subject to tax on her world-wide income. The Windsors' London solicitor, George Allen, issued a warning to the Duchess of the dire tax consequences of US residence: virtually the total confiscation of their joint income, as well as a potential claim for tax on previous years.[8] Although this may have been an exaggeration, the high post-war tax rates in America were sufficient to deter the Windsors from settling there without some form of privileged tax status such as diplomatic exemption.[9]

Throughout the autumn and winter of 1945, Edward lobbied hard to be given diplomatic status under the auspices of the British Embassy, but to no avail. Lord Halifax, the Ambassador in Washington, thought that Edward would be an embarrassment and a security risk, while the Foreign Secretary, Ernest Bevin, was opposed to the idea because he suspected that the American government would regard the grant of diplomatic immunity as a transparent device to secure tax-exempt status for the Duke and Duchess. The Windsors' plans to settle in America thus came to nothing, together with the Duke's hopes of an official job. The couple found themselves trapped in limbo, exiled from Britain, but disbarred from the kind of public service at which Edward had excelled as Prince of Wales.[10] The ghost of King Edward VIII continued to haunt the Windsors. As Wallis wrote in her memoirs, 'while David stepped down from the throne, he could never step out of the royal family … he is immutably part of the Royal institution, fixed there for ever, like a fly in amber'.[11]

For several years after the war, the Windsors lived a rootless, itinerant life, with no real home of their own. The emptiness of their existence was obvious to anyone who met them. An acquaintance later said that they 'elevated the art of doing nothing into a ceremonial for princes'.[12] On one occasion, sitting next to the wife of an American diplomat at a dinner party in Paris, the Duke lamented his lack of purposeful occupation. 'The famous charm is still there,' she noted, 'but I never saw a man so bored.'[13] In 1947, on their tenth wedding anniversary, their plight was neatly summed up by the Associated Press columnist Cynthia Lowry, in an article syndicated throughout the United States. Titled 'The Wandering Windsors: Restless Couple Still on the Sidelines', the piece described the Duke's failure to find a job, and the difficulties the couple faced picking up the threads of their lives in Europe after returning from the Bahamas. It concluded with an accurate prediction of the Windsors' future lifestyle: 'If no job materialises, they will swing into the old circuit: Paris, Riviera, New York, Florida...'[14] In 1952 the couple did acquire two permanent homes in France: a mansion in Paris on the edge of the Bois de Boulogne, in which they kept quasi-regal state; and the Moulin de la Tuilerie, a converted mill in the countryside south-west of the capital, where the Duke did his best to recreate the atmosphere of his beloved Fort Belvedere. When in America their base was a grand apartment in Waldorf Towers in New York, where huge portraits of Hanoverian kings looked down on dinner guests.[15]

Denied the opportunity of a diplomatic role, Edward turned to writing his memoirs. Immediately after the war he began to receive offers from American publishers, and in 1947 he agreed to write four articles for *Life* magazine, covering the period of his childhood and youth up to 1918. This was relatively uncontroversial territory, but the very fact that an ex-King was publishing his personal reminiscences was sensational enough. When the articles were reproduced in Britain in the *Sunday Express*, they drew a mixed reception.[16] Nevertheless, they were a great commercial success in America, and *Life* encouraged the Duke to expand his recollections into a full-length autobiography. Motivated both by the financial reward and the desire to give his own version of the Abdication story, Edward threw himself into the task. Assisted by a ghost writer, Charles Murphy, Edward spent the next two years drafting *A King's Story*. Taster extracts were again serialized in *Life* and the *Sunday Express* in the summer of 1950, and the book itself was finally published in 1951. Significantly, it ended with the 'regicide' of King Edward in December 1936, making no attempt to cover the anti-climactic years up to 1945.[17] *A King's Story* had a winning formula, combining anecdotes of life inside the royal family with the story of the 'romance of the century', and Edward's blow-by-blow account of the Abdication. It was also revealing psychologically. With merciless accuracy the *New York Times* called it 'a character study of a well-meaning, undistinguished individual, destined from birth to a life of monumental artificiality'.[18] It was an immediate bestseller on both sides of the Atlantic, and was translated into more than twenty languages, including Japanese and Hebrew.[19] In Britain it sold 80,000 copies in the first month alone.[20] Encouraged by his success, Edward embarked on a second book, *The Crown and the People*, a short work of personal reminiscences inspired by Queen Elizabeth's coronation in 1953.[21] Not long afterwards, the Duchess also wrote her autobiography, *The Heart has its Reasons*, which was serialized in *McCall's* magazine in America before being published in 1956.[22]

The steady stream of publications in the decade after the Second World War kept the Windsors in the public eye, especially in the USA where they were frequent visitors. They enjoyed the status of minor international celebrities, reminders of a past era of glamour and elegance. Their attendance at a film premiere or fundraiser, whether in Paris, New York, or Washington, was guaranteed to attract publicity, and the events in their social life often featured in the gossip columns.[23] In America, they continued to move in the highest social and political circles. The Duke was well acquainted with all the post-war presidents, and mixed easily with leading politicians and businessmen. For example, he met President Eisenhower shortly before his inauguration in January 1953, and paid him a number of visits at the White House.[24] The esteem and affection with which Edward was regarded in America was revealed at the dinner of the Washington Gridiron Club, a prestigious association of journalists, in 1957. The club's annual dinner was (and remains) one of the set-piece events in the Washington calendar, regularly attended by the President and other prominent establishment figures. Others present that year included Earl Warren, Chief Justice of the Supreme Court, and Senators John F. Kennedy and Lyndon B. Johnson. Edward had been invited in a private capacity as a guest, but at the last minute he was asked to preside at the head of a table in place of President Eisenhower, who had fallen sick. When the president of the club welcomed the Duke, the entire room rose to give him a spontaneous standing ovation.[25] There could be no better illustration of how in America Edward had achieved the status of honoured elder statesman which had been denied to him in his native land.

By the 1960s Edward was a largely forgotten figure in Britain and the Abdication a distant historical event. Thirty years on, in 1966, there was a flurry of books on the subject, but the anniversary attracted little public interest, and the national press passed over it in silence.[26] In the US it was a different matter. The American producer Jack Le Vien turned Edward's autobiography, *A King's Story*, into a documentary film, which was shown on general release and nominated for an Academy Award. With Orson Welles as narrator, the movie mixed old newsreel footage with still photography and interviews with the Duke and Duchess at their country home in

France.[27] The *Chicago Tribune* commissioned a further set of articles from the Duke bringing his memoirs up to date, and carried them on its front page for six consecutive days, beginning on the thirtieth anniversary of the Abdication on 11 December 1966.[28] The articles contained little that was new, but did include a confession from the Duke that he had been wrong about Hitler, and had been taken in by him to believe that he did not seek war with Britain. Two years later the Windsors were interviewed at their French country home by Harry Reasoner for the CBS news magazine programme *60 Minutes*. The couple had put the house up for sale, and the Duke could not help slipping into salesman mode, showing Reasoner round the property as if he were a prospective buyer. Commenting on 1960s youth culture, Edward plaintively remarked that in their day he and the Duchess had been one of the most 'with-it' couples in the world. At one point Reasoner asked Edward how long he had been king. 'Ten months,' said the Duke. 'Is that long enough to be a king?' 'No,' replied Edward.[29]

The Windsors continued to be in demand for public events, but there were occasions when their public appearances degenerated into a cruel parody of Edward's triumphs as Prince of Wales. In May 1967, shortly before their thirtieth wedding anniversary, they attended the American movie premiere of *A King's Story*. At the end of the film, as the lights went up shortly after the famous 'woman I love' Abdication broadcast, the audience turned towards the balcony to applaud the couple. Edward had, however, disappeared from view; the woman sitting next to him had dropped her bag, and he was down on his hands and knees, helping to retrieve the contents. After the show, there was a reception, not at City Hall, but at the New York department store Bergdorf Goodman. The *New York Times* reported the scene. 'At a cocktail party among the main floor handbag, scarf and sunglass counters, the Duke stood stoically in a receiving line as hundreds of the well-to-do elbowed each other into racks of new umbrellas in an effort to greet him ... In the end it was his lot to stand by, while the Duchess gave the newspaper interviews, described her clothes, and drew raffle numbers for men's shoes and sets of Wamsutta superscale sheets.'[30]

Edward, Duke of Windsor, died in Paris on 28 May 1972, a month short of his seventy-eighth birthday. Finally, in death, the royal family and the British establishment were able to embrace the ex-King who had been such an embarrassment to them in life. His body was flown home by the RAF, and lay in state in St George's chapel, Windsor. Thousands of mourners queued for up to five hours to file past the coffin. The royal family attended the funeral service en masse, and the Queen herself accompanied the Duchess, whose attendance was in doubt until the last minute owing to illness. After the service Edward was laid to rest at the royal burial ground at Frogmore, where fourteen years later Wallis was to be buried beside him.[31] The *Times* obituary gave a dry, factual account of the Duke's extraordinary life, with the most perfunctory references to his relationship with Wallis, who was tersely referred to as 'Mrs Simpson' throughout.[32] A more rounded account appeared in the *New York Times*, focusing on the significance of his affair with Wallis, balancing his private and public lives, and weighing up the damage done to his reputation by his Nazi associations in the 1930s. President Nixon, who was in Moscow for a superpower summit meeting, offered the Duke a fitting tribute on behalf of the American people: 'He was a man of noble spirit and high ideals, for whom millions of Americans felt deep respect and affection.'[33]

The Abdication of Edward VIII had profound consequences for the future of the British Crown. When Edward came to the throne, he promised a decisive break with the cautious traditionalism of his father, George V. He consciously sought to carry on the informal, democratic approach to his royal duties which he had developed as Prince of Wales. His formative experiences had taken place during and after the First World War, when so many European monarchies had collapsed. He recognized that the House of Windsor's position could not be taken for granted: it had to be positively sold to each generation. Through his international tours he got to know many American industrialists and businessmen, and learned something of their business methods. He was an early convert to the importance of advertising at a time when British business still regarded it as beneath their dignity. He grasped intuitively that the British monarchy was a product, a 'brand' which needed to be refreshed and marketed, and soon discovered that he himself was a natural salesman. Over the years the American press christened him 'the Prince of Sales', in recognition of his abilities. As part of the rebranding process, he believed that the Crown needed to modernize if it was to survive as a relevant institution—rather than a historical relic—in twentieth-century Britain. He was keen to dispense with Victorian pageantry, to forge closer ties with ordinary people, and to engage actively with the great issues of the day.

The Abdication led the royal family to the opposite conclusion. Modernization was dangerous, pulling the monarchy in unpredictable directions, and upsetting its time-honoured place in British society. King George VI, as his name suggests, ruled in conscious imitation of his father, George V, and through him followed the royal traditions laid down a century before by Queen Victoria and Prince Albert: embodying British national identity and tradition, living a model family life within the pattern of Christian marriage, and avoiding political controversy. In many respects the history of the British monarchy in the second half of the twentieth century was an extended commentary on the events of 1936. In April 1947, on her twenty-first birthday, the future Queen Elizabeth II gave a radio broadcast from South Africa, where she was touring with the rest of the royal family. It was an explicitly anti-abdication speech, a repudiation of the idea that the burden of monarchy could be laid aside. 'I declare before you all that my whole life, whether it be long or short, shall be devoted to your service and the service of our great imperial family to which we all belong.' In addition, the nostalgic invocation of the 'imperial family', at a moment when the British Empire was on the brink of dissolution, reflected the rigidly conservative, backward-looking perspective of the post-Abdication monarchy. In 1953, in a further echo of the Abdication controversy, Queen Elizabeth refused her consent to the marriage of her sister, Princess Margaret, to a royal equerry, Peter Townsend, who had divorced his first wife. Townsend was posted overseas, and Margaret subsequently gave up her hopes of marrying him.

Edward's abdication also cast a long shadow over the life of Prince Charles, his great-nephew and successor as Prince of Wales.[34] When Charles was a young man in the 1970s, the example of 'Uncle David' was repeatedly held up to him as a dreadful warning of how the Prince of Wales should not behave. Earl Mountbatten, who had known Edward well during the 1920s, took it upon himself to act as mentor to the young Prince Charles. He was particularly concerned that he should not make the same mistake of post-poning marriage as Edward had done. On one occasion he wrote to Charles, 'I thought you were beginning on the downward slope which wrecked your Uncle David's life and led to his disgraceful Abdication and futile life ever after.'[35] In his anxiety not to follow Edward's example, Charles rushed into an ill-judged marriage with Lady Diana Spencer, with disastrous results. In the 1990s his clandestine affair with Camilla Parker Bowles, and conse-quent divorce from Diana, rocked the royal family to its foundations, and prompted comparisons with Edward's affair with Wallis Simpson.

The unhappy, and ultimately tragic, life of Princess Diana as a member of the royal family had distinct echoes of Edward's career sixty years earlier. He was the first member of the royal family to experience the full impact of the modern media, and his dysfunctional relationship with the press set the pattern for the royal family for the rest of the twentieth century. Edward once wrote of press photography 'killing the private lives of princes', and although he did not live to see the day when photography killed a princess, her fate would not have surprised him. Like Edward, and in contrast with most other members of the House of Windsor, Diana possessed exceptional personal charisma; she discovered, as Edward had done before her, that in the face of a rapacious media industry, royalty and charisma made a toxic, even fatal, mixture. Like Edward, she tried to break out of her royal status, only to find herself ostracized by the royal family and yet trapped in it, caught like a fly in amber. Even after a century of royal reporting, the parallels between Edward, Prince of Wales, and his modern counterparts remain uncannily close. Edward's *bête noire* among reporters was the Australian Keith Murdoch. In 2012 his son, Rupert Murdoch, published photographs of a naked Prince Harry partying in Las Vegas, in the modern equivalent of the riotous parties which Edward attended on Long Island in 1924.[36]

Much has been made of Edward's Nazi associations during the 1930s, and his posthumous reputation has suffered badly as a result. However, while Edward was foolish and naive, as he later admitted, he was by no means alone in adopting a sympathetic approach towards Nazi Germany during the 1930s. Far more significant and enduring was his lifelong enthusiasm for America, and his conviction that international peace and stability rested on the Anglo-American alliance. That belief was born out of his experiences at the end of the First World War, when he met US troops for the first time. As early as 1919 he wrote, 'we just must be closely allied with the USA, closer than we are now, and it must be lasting, and they are very keen about it'.[37] It was fundamental to his world view, and he consistently repeated the belief throughout his life. In 1935, with the prospect of another European war looming, he told an American journalist that the peace of the world depended on the friendly association of the two great English-speaking peoples.[38] Shortly after ascending the throne in 1936, he said much the same to the American diplomat Norman Davis, who recounted, 'he abruptly asked me when the United States and Britain would get together...He said that the only hope for us and the world was to stand together.'[39] In 1945, when offering his services as a goodwill ambassador to the USA, he wrote to his brother King George, 'I am convinced that there can be no lasting peace for mankind unless the two countries [Britain and the USA] preserve a common approach to international politics.'[40] Even after his retirement from public life, he continued to express the same sentiments. In 1951 the *New York Times* journalist Cyrus Sulzberger met the Windsors at a dinner in Paris. The Duke told him that he thought that it was vital for Britain and the USA to work together, and that this was something he had always worked for.[41]

Edward's record shows that such statements were not mere rhetoric. One of the roles he performed most energetically as Prince of Wales, perhaps because he had chosen it for himself, was the promotion of Anglo-American cooperation.[42] In the 1920s he regularly found time to attend events of the Pilgrims, the prominent British–American friendship society, at a period when his diary was choked with public engagements. He cultivated personal relationships with American diplomats, financiers, and industrialists, including key figures such as Charles Dawes, Owen Young, and Frank Kellogg, who were highly influential in negotiating the international settlement after the First World War. He was on friendly terms with US presidents—most notably Franklin Roosevelt in the crucial years before and during the Second World War. He took an informed interest in American industry and impressed business moguls such as Henry Ford with his knowledge. During the Depression, as the US retreated into isolation and protectionism, he continued to campaign vigorously for closer Anglo-American relations.[43]

Moreover, Edward's enthusiasm for America was based on more than a cold calculation of British self-interest. His affinity with American society and culture was evident from his earliest encounters with Americans. In part this was because, with their republican democratic values, Americans were less in awe of his royal status, and more inclined to deal with him on equal terms. Nor did Edward confine his contacts to the American social elites; it is striking how his friendships extended beyond politicians, diplomats, and millionaires, to entertainers and sportsmen. His rapport with the comedian Will Rogers, the golfer Walter Hagen, and the bandleader Paul Whiteman was based on a mutual liking and respect. It was in such encounters as these, and in dealings with his neighbours at the EP ranch, that Edward gained a fleeting sense of what ordinary human relationships might be like outside the straitjacket of royalty. For Edward, America truly was a 'new-found land' of opportunity, one which offered him a tantalizing glimpse of alternative possibilities. His response to his first experience of the New World was manifested most obviously in his impulsive purchase of the EP ranch in 1919. Although situated in Canada—as Prince he could not have bought property outside the empire—the ranch was the quintessential expression of the American experience, mediated for the British audience through Buffalo Bill's Wild West shows and a thousand Hollywood Westerns. The appeal of the prairie was powerful for Edward, carrying with it the promise of new beginnings in a land far removed from the devastation of post-war Europe. Equally, New York in 1919 captured the Prince's imagination, embodying the spirit of modernity and confidence in the future that Britain had lost.

America's response to Edward was equally powerful. Although he first came to the attention of the American public as the heir to the British throne, a symbol of Old World hierarchy, his personal charisma soon ensured that he transcended his royal status to become one of the first generation of authentic American media celebrities, on a par with Hollywood film stars. The US press developed an inexhaustible appetite for news and gossip about him, chronicling his love life—real or imagined—in minute detail. His Long Island vacation in 1924 attracted unprecedented newspaper coverage, foreshadowing the furore in American newspapers over his affair with Wallis Simpson twelve years later, which contributed directly to the Abdication crisis in Britain. Yet although Edward was at times hounded by the American press, he emerged from its pages as a more human, attractive figure than the princely paragon presented through the British media. America laughed at his habit of falling off horses, and thrilled at his string of American mistresses; but it also appreciated his democratic manners and admired his persuasive abilities as the chief salesman of the British Empire.

Edward's affinity with America quickly made itself felt in his personal tastes and private life. He adopted American expressions, danced to American jazz, drove American cars, chewed American gum, and surrounded himself with American friends. He found American women irresistible, at first enjoying brief encounters, but gradually forming longer-term relationships. There was a steady line of progression from his flirtation with Carolyn Granberry, the Canal Zone shopgirl, in 1920, through his holiday romance with the New York socialite Pinna Cruger in 1924, to his affair with Thelma Furness, and ultimately his lifelong passion for Wallis Simpson. Their directness and lack of deference enchanted him, breaking down the acute sense of loneliness and emotional isolation that he felt as a royal Prince.

The causes of the Abdication have long been debated, and continue to rouse controversy. Did Edward simply give up his throne for love, or was he the victim of an establishment plot to remove him? Was he temperamentally unsuited to kingship and seeking a pretext to resign the throne? Whatever the short-term causes, there can be no doubt that Edward's personal Americanization from 1919 onwards created the preconditions for his Abdication, shaping his personal relationships, transforming his attitude to monarchy, and alienating him from the rest of the royal family. The seismic events of 1936—the only voluntary abdication by a monarch in British history—were the direct result of Edward's abiding fascination with the people and culture of the USA. Long before he fell in love with Wallis, Edward had fallen in love with America; but for America, King Edward VIII would never have abdicated.

Notes

INTRODUCTION

1. Arnold Palmer was one of the Duke's golfing heroes, and at the dinner Edward took the opportunity to consult Palmer on which sort of clubs he should use: *Montgomery Advertiser,* 6 April 1970.
2. *Des Moines Register* (Iowa), 5 April 1970; *Fresno Bee* (California), 5 April 1970.
3. Edward, Duke of Windsor, *A King's Story* (London, 1951), 145.
4. Rupert Godfrey, ed., *Letters from a Prince* (London, 1998), 140.
5. Frazier Hunt, *The Bachelor Prince* (New York, 1935), 230.
6. Compton Mackenzie, *The Windsor Tapestry* (London, 1938), 144: 'That night (11 November 1919) he made his first speech in the United States at a Washington banquet. His future wife was at that time living in Washington. He did not meet her; but he fell in love with America'.
7. For the cultural background to the impact of America on Europe in the twentieth century, see David Ellwood, *The Shock of America: Europe and the Challenge of the Century* (Oxford, 2012).
8. David Dimbleby and David Reynolds, *An Ocean Apart* (London, 1988), 106; Ellwood, *Shock of America,* 114.
9. The perceived Americanization of British society between the wars generated much anxiety and hostility, particularly among the political and intellectual elites. See Dimbleby and Reynolds, *An Ocean Apart,* 106–7. For a hostile cultural reaction, see Frank Leavis, *Mass Civilization and Minority Culture* (Cambridge, 1930).
10. See Chapter 2.
11. *LP* 122.
12. See Chapter 5.
13. *KS* 198.
14. *Brooklyn Daily Eagle,* 23 November 1919.
15. See Chapter 6.
16. *KS* 201.
17. Duff Hart-Davis, ed., *In Royal Service: Letters and Journals of Sir Alan Lascelles 1920–36* (London, 1989), 32, 37–8; *KS,* 202.
18. *KS* 200–3; Kenneth Rose, *King George V* (London, 1983), 344–5.
19. For the concept of 'inner emigration' as applied to communist Eastern Europe, see Timothy Garton Ash, 'Inner Emigration', *The Spectator* (12 October 1984), 11; Anna Funder, *Stasiland* (London, 2011), 96.

20. See Chapter 10.
21. See Chapter 8. Gloria Vanderbilt and Thelma Furness, *Double Exposure* (London, 1959).
22. Philip Ziegler, *King Edward VIII* (London, 1990), 222.
23. Frances Donaldson, *Edward VIII* (London, 1974), 196–7.
24. John Julius Norwich, ed., *Diana Cooper: Darling Monster* (London, 2013), 424.
25. Donaldson, *Edward VIII,* 323. Compare Ziegler, *Edward VIII*, 558–9.
26. Alistair Cooke, Foreword, in Robert Gray and Jane Olivier, *Edward VIII: The Man we Lost* (London, 1972). For a discussion of the historiography of the Abdication, see Frank Mort, 'Love in a Cold Climate: Letters, Public Opinion and Monarchy in the 1936 Abdication Crisis', *Twentieth Century British History*, 25/1 (2014), 30–62.
27. Mackenzie, *Windsor Tapestry*; for the role of the Archbishop of Canterbury in the Abdication, see Robert Beaken, *Cosmo Lang* (London, 2012), 86–142. Beaken argues that Lang worked closely with the Prime Minister Stanley Baldwin to secure Edward's removal.
28. *KS* 278–80.
29. Karina Urbach, *Go-Betweens for Hitler* (Oxford, 2015), 189–90.
30. John Julius Norwich, ed., *The Duff Cooper Diaries* (London, 2005), 230. See also Robert Graves and Alan Hodge, *The Long Weekend* (Harmondsworth, 1971), 105.
31. Susan Williams, *The People's King* (London, 2003); Mort, 'Love in a Cold Climate', 30–62.
32. A. J. P. Taylor, *English History, 1914–45* (Oxford, 1965), 403.
33. This interpretation of the Abdication has been influenced by the narrow focus of Edward's biographers on the recollections of the main protagonists in the drama, including Edward himself: see Ziegler, *Edward VIII*, 297–311; Donaldson, *Edward VIII*, 272–316.
34. Ellwood, *Shock of America*, 72–214
35. Mort, 'Love in a Cold Climate', 30–62.
36. See Chapter 13.

CHAPTER 1

1. Paul Kennedy, *The Rise and Fall of Great Powers* (London, 1988), 224–32.
2. Nicholas Mansergh, *The Commonwealth Experience* (London, 1969), 134.
3. Bradford Perkins, *The Great Rapprochement* (London, 1969), 31–63; Duncan Bell, *The Idea of Greater Britain* (Princeton, 2004), 254–9.
4. Perkins, *Great Rapprochement*, 78–88; Frank Prochaska, *The Eagle and the Crown* (London, 2008), 98–100.
5. Harry Peck, *Twenty Years of the Republic, 1885–1905* (New York, 1906), 557; Dimbleby and Reynolds, *An Ocean Apart,* 28; Ellwood, *Shock of America*, 23–35; Perkins, *Great Rapprochement*, 42–3.
6. Perkins, *Great Rapprochement*, 31–185; Dimbleby and Reynolds, *An Ocean Apart*, 28–33.

7. Cited in Perkins, *Great Rapprochement*, 185.

8. Harry Brittain, *Pilgrim Partners* (London, 1942), 1–34.

9. *The Review of Reviews*, 25 (1902), 90, 206.

10. William Stead, *The Americanization of the World* (New York, 1902), 396.

11. Stead, *Americanization*, 354–5.

12. Stead, *Americanization*, 329.

13. Alan Gallop, *Buffalo Bill's British Wild West* (Stroud, 2009), 67–70.

14. William Cody, *Story of the Wild West and Camp-Fire Chats* (Philadelphia, 1888), 737.

15. Robert Rydell and Rob Kroes, *Buffalo Bill in Bologna* (Chicago, 2005), 108.

16. Gallop, *Buffalo Bill's British Wild West*, 162–243. On the second tour in 1892 Queen Victoria ordered another command performance, this time at Windsor.

17. Stead, *Americanization*, 318.

18. Dimbleby and Reynolds, *An Ocean Apart*, 38; Charles Jennings, *Them and Us* (Stroud, 2007), 31–306; Gail MacColl and Carol Wallace, *To Marry an English Lord* (New York, 2012).

19. Allen Andrews, *The Follies of Edward VII* (London, 1975), 128.

20. *Oakland Tribune*, 8 May 1910.

21. Jennings, *Them and Us*, 131.

22. A. Carnegie, 'As Others See Us', *Fortnightly Review*, 23 (1882), 164.

23. *Los Angeles Times*, 24 January 1901; Perkins, *Great Rapprochement*, 116; Prochaska, *The Eagle and the Crown,* 107.

24. E.g. *New York Sun*, 24 June 1894; *Salt Lake Herald*, 24 June 1894; *San Francisco Call*, 24 June 1894.

25. *New York Sun*, 24 June 1894.

26. *New York Times*, 7 August 1894; *New York Tribune*, 12 August 1894.

27. For Edward's childhood, see Ziegler, *Edward VIII*, 1–47.

28. J. S. Ellis, 'Reconciling the Celt: British National Identity, Empire and the 1911 Investiture of the Prince of Wales', *Journal of British Studies*, 37 (1998), 391–418.

29. *KS* 78–9.

30. *Charlotte News*, 9 July 1911; *Salt Lake Tribune*, 8 March 1914.

31. *Brooklyn Daily Eagle*, 2 July 1911; *New York Sun*, 31 December 1911.

32. *Salt Lake Tribune*, 11 July 1911.

33. Helen Rappaport, *Four Sisters* (London, 2015), 168–9; *The Tennessean*, 21 July 1911; *Oregon Daily Journal*, 6 August 1911.

34. Ziegler, *Edward VIII*, 43–4.

35. *Washington Herald*, 16 July 1911; *Oregon Daily Journal*, 2 July 1911.

36. Rose, *George V*, 303–4.

37. Ziegler, *Edward VIII*, 72.

38. *The Times*, 18 November 1914.

39. Donaldson, *Edward VIII*, 69. The 1967 documentary film, *A King's Story*, includes this newsreel clip.

40. *The Times*, 15 June 1914.

41. *KS* 106.

42. Heather Jones, 'A Prince in the Trenches? Edward VIII and the First World War', in Frank Lorenz Müller and Heidi Mehrkens, eds, *Sons and Heirs* (London, 2015), 229–46. See my Chapter 10.

43. Harold Nicolson, *King George V* (London, 1952), 252.

44. Rose, *George V*, 173–4.

45. *The Times*, 11 April 1916; *New York Times*, 13 April 1916.

46. *Indianapolis Star*, 13 November 1916. In the early twentieth century Indianapolis had a substantial German-American population.

47. Ziegler, *Edward VIII*, 103.

48. Rose, *George V*, 173–5; Nicolson, *George V,* 308–10.

49. *The Times*, 21 April 1917.

50. *Washington Herald*, 22 April 1917.

51. Nicolson, *George V*, 307–9; Frank Prochaska, *Royal Bounty: The Making of a Welfare Monarchy* (New Haven, 1995), 182.

52. Prochaska, *Royal Bounty*, 184.

53. D.Williams, *The Prince of Wales* (London, 1915).

54. *KS* 115–16.

55. Jones, 'A Prince in the Trenches?', 240–1.

56. *Wichita Beacon*, 6 March 1918.

57. *The Times*, 22 February, 5 and 13 March 1918.

58. *KS* 123–4.

59. *Boston Post*, 27 March 1918; Brittain, *Pilgrim Partners*, 116–19.

60. John Pershing, *My Experiences in the World War* (New York, 1931), i. 45–8.

61. Sara Jeannette Duncan, *His Royal Happiness* (London, 1915), 309.

62. See Chapter 2.

CHAPTER 2

1. Martin Gilbert, *First World War* (London, 1994), 408; Pershing, *My Experiences in the World War*, i. 355.

2. Pershing, *My Experiences in the World War*, i. 364–5.

3. *The Times*, 19 July 1919.

4. David Stevenson, *With our Backs to the Wall* (London, 2011), 73.

5. Vera Brittain, *Testament of Youth* (London, 1979), 420–1.

6. Gilbert, *First World War*, 429.

7. Brittain, *Pilgrim Partners*, 115–19.

8. *The Times*, 5 July 1918.

9. *The Times*, 5 July 1918.

10. Jim Leeke, 'Royal Match: The Army–Navy Service Game, July 4, 1918', *NINE: A Journal of Baseball History and Culture*, 20/2 (Spring 2012), 15–26. The ball is now in the Woodrow Wilson House in Washington, DC.

11. *The Times*, 5 July 1918.

12. Imperial War Museum, Docs 6992/7.

13. *LP* 57.

14. *LP* 69.

15. Gilbert, *First World War*, 376.

16. *LP* 85.

17. *LP* 94.

18. *LP* 109–10.

19. *LP* 117–18.

20. Ziegler, *Edward VIII*, 84.

21. *New York Tribune*, 17 December 1918.

22. *The Times*, 27 December 1918.

23. Rose, *George V*, 232; *The Times*, 30 December 1919.

24. Zara Steiner, *The Lights that Failed* (Oxford, 2005), 33–4.

25. *New York Tribune*, 7 December 1918; *The True Democrat* (Louisiana), 7 December 1918; *The Times*, 7 December 1918.

26. *Daily Express*, 1 January 1919.

27. *Daily Ardmoreite* (Oklahoma), 29 January 1919; *Evening World Magazine*, 3 January 1919; *Wichita Daily Eagle*, 6 March 1919.

28. *The Times*, 6 January 1919.

29. *New York Times*, 13 January 1919.

30. *The Sun*, 14 January 1919.

31. *Wichita Daily Eagle*, 14 January 1919.

32. *Emporia Gazette* (Kansas), 12 March 1919; *Leavenworth Times* (Kansas), 26 March 1919.

33. Ziegler, *Edward VIII*, 85.

34. *Fort Scott Daily Tribune* (Kansas), 21 March 1919.

35. Ziegler, *Edward VIII*, 67.

36. *KS* 124.

37. *LP* 141.

38. *Richmond Times-Despatch*, 1 August 1920.

39. *LP* 140–1; *New York Times*, 19 February 1919.

40. *KS* 415.

41. *The Times*, 30 May 1919; Genevieve Parkhurst, *A King in the Making* (London, 1925), 153–4.

42. *LP* 134.

43. Ziegler, *Edward VIII*, 114.

44. *Richmond Times-Despatch*, 19 January 1919.

45. *The Times*, 28 February 1919.

46. *KS* 134.

47. Described in Parkhurst, *A King in the Making*, 163–6.

48. *The Times*, 2 July 1919; *KS* 136.

49. *LP* 151–5; *KS* 135.

50. *The Times*, 1 January, 5 February 1919.

51. Graham Wallace, *The Flight of Alcock and Brown* (London, 1955), 63–4.

52. *The Times*, 2 June 1919.

53. *The Times*, 6 June 1919.

54. *The Times*, 29 May 1919.
55. *The Times*, 23 June 1919.
56. *The Times*, 21 June 1919.
57. *The Times*, 14 and 16 July 1919.
58. *LP* 123.
59. A. Cunningham Reid, *Planes and Personalities* (London, 1920), 104–6.
60. Wayne Ralph, *Barker VC* (London, 1999), 180.
61. *KS* 240.
62. Martin Gilbert, ed., *Churchill Documents*, ix (Hilldale, MI, 1977), 746–7.
63. *The Times*, 19 July 1919.
64. *New York Tribune*, 20 July 1919.
65. *LP* 161.
66. *The Times*, 21 July 1919; *LP* 162; *KS* 135.
67. *LP* 142.
68. *LP* 143–4.
69. *LP* 146; Robert Wainwright, *Sheila* (London, 2014), 57–83.
70. *LP* 156–9.
71. *New York Times*, 24 July 1919.
72. *LP* 167.
73. Log of HMS *Renown* for 5 August 1919: <http://naval-history.net>.

CHAPTER 3

1. *KS* 209–10.
2. *KS* 132.
3. *The Times*, 7 June 1919; Ziegler, *Edward VIII*, 114–15.
4. Leo Amery, *My Political Life* (London, 1953), ii. 197.
5. Parliamentary Archives, Houses of Parliament, Lloyd George Papers, LG/F/29/3/40.
6. See Parliamentary Archives, LG/F/29/4/19, for reports on the Prince's health while on tour in Australia in 1920.
7. Parliamentary Archives, LG/F/29/3/40. The suggestion had been made by the press magnate Lord Rothermere.
8. *KS* 138.
9. *LP* 175; *KS* 138–40.
10. *LP* 177.
11. Donaldson, *Edward VIII*, 69; *LP* 228.
12. *St John Evening Times Star*, 15 August 1919.
13. Parliamentary Archives, LG/F/29/5/1.
14. *LP* 172.
15. Simon Evans, *Prince Charming Goes West* (Calgary, 1993), 10–11.
16. *KS* 140.
17. *The Times*, 1 September 1919.
18. Amery, *My Political Life*, ii. 197.

19. Parkhurst, *A King in the Making*, 170–1.

20. *KS* 143.

21. *Winnipeg Tribune*, 9 September 1919; *Vancouver Daily World*, 23 September 1919.

22. *San Bernardino County Sun*, 26 September 1919.

23. *New York Evening World*, 17 November 1919.

24. *LP* 212.

25. *Vancouver Daily World*, 16 and 23 September 1919: 'Miss Beatrice Buckman Rogers, daughter of Colonel Maynard Rogers, superintendent of Jasper Park, had the honor of dancing twice with the Prince of Wales at the ball given by His Honor the Lieutenant-Governor of Alberta at the Parliament Buildings Edmonton.'

26. *LP* 212–13.

27. *LP* 181.

28. Luke McKernan, *Topical Budget: The Great British News Film* (London, 1992), 64, 118.

29. 'Two Score in Prince's Party': *Vancouver Daily World*, 19 September 1919.

30. *The Times*, 10 December 1919.

31. Evans, *Prince Charming Goes West*, 11.

32. In his memoirs Edward confirmed that it was Wallis's favourite photograph of him.

33. Parliamentary Archives, LG/F/29/5/1: Grigg to Lloyd George 16 August 1919. See e.g. the Prince's speech at St John New Brunswick. 'I want Canada to look on me as a Canadian, if not actually by birth, yet certainly in mind and spirit': *New Brunswick Evening Times-Star*, 15 August 1919. Ziegler, *Edward VIII*, 119–20.

34. *The Times*, 1 September 1919.

35. *KS* 139.

36. For Churchill's assistance with the Prince's early speeches, see Chapter 2.

37. This report was widely syndicated in the USA: see e.g. *Indiana Evening Gazette*, 13 September 1919; *Bisbee Daily Review* (Arizona), 14 September 1919; *Great Bend Tribune* (Kansas), 24 September 1919.

38. W. Douglas Newton, *Westward with the Prince of Wales* (London, 1920), 183–4.

39. *LP* 190.

40. *LP* 189–92; Alfred Shaughnessy, ed., *Sarah: Letters and Diaries of a Courtier's Wife 1906–36* (London, 1989), 113.

41. Evans, *Prince Charming Goes West*, 19–21; Newton, *Westward with the Prince*, 196.

42. See Chapter 6.

43. *Winnipeg Tribune*, 13 October 1919; *KS* 150.

44. *Calgary Herald*, 18 September 1919.

45. *The Times*, 19 September 1919.

46. Newton, *Westward with the Prince*, 201–3.

47. *LP* 194.

48. *Punch*, 1 October 1919.

49. Shaughnessy, ed., *Sarah*, 116; *LP* 195–9.

50. Shaughnessy, ed., *Sarah*, 130.

51. By comparison, the Duke and Duchess of Cambridge's tour of Australia in 2014 lasted ten days.

52. *Brooklyn Daily Eagle*, 18 August 1919, 16.

53. *Parsons Daily Sun* (Kansas), 4 September 1919: 'The Prince of Wales, who tried out democracy in the dances of the doughboys, wants more of it.'

54. *Brooklyn Daily Eagle*, 3 August 1919.

55. *North Platte Review*, 2 September 1919; *Atlanta Constitution*, 7 September 1919: 'Proud society mammas are setting their caps for the Prince of Wales, soon to visit Newport'. Ziegler, *Edward VIII*, 121.

56. Adam Tooze, *The Deluge: The Great War, America, and the Remaking of the Global Order* (London, 2014), 334–5.

57. *New York Evening World*, 9 September 1919.

58. Parliamentary Archives, LG/F/12/1/49.

59. *LP* 207–8; *The Times*, 8 September 1919.

60. *LP* 208.

61. *LP* 215.

62. Rose, *George V*, 344.

63. *LP* 212–13.

64. Newton, *Westward with the Prince of Wales*, 291–2.

65. Parkhurst, *A King in the Making*, 173; *The Times*, 12 November 1919.

66. *Washington Times*, 11 November 1919.

67. Will Rogers, *Wit and Philosophy from the Radio Talks of America's Humorist* (New York, 1930), 25.

68. Donaldson, *Edward VIII*, 72–4.

69. *KS* 415. In his correspondence with Freda, Edward frequently distinguished himself as an individual from 'the Prince of Wales', e.g. *LP* 180, 183, 188, 196, 208, 216.

70. *New York Sun,* 16 November 1919.

71. *KS* 145–7.

72. *New York Tribune,* 15 November 1919.

73. *The Times,* 17 November 1919.

74. *Speeches by HRH The Prince of Wales, 1912–26* (London, 1926), 22–7.

75. Newton, *Westward with the Prince*, 295–7.

76. *Washington Herald*, 12 November 1919.

77. *Washington Post*, 12 November 1919; *New York Tribune*, 15 November 1919.

78. *Washington Times*, 2 November 1919; Rose, *George V*, 304; Edward had paid Jusserand a gracious compliment in one of his Washington speeches: *Speeches by the Prince of Wales*, 22.

79. Ziegler, *Edward VIII*, 120–1.

80. *New York Sun*, 16 November 1919. Leiter, a wealthy industrialist, was the brother-in-law of British Foreign Secretary Lord Curzon.

81. Donaldson, *Edward VIII*, 72.

82. Michael Minden and Holger Bachmann, *Fritz Lang's Metropolis* (Woodbridge, 2002), 4.

83. *KS* 148.

84. *KS* 148–9; *New York Sun*, 19 November 1919.

85. Irish-American groups boycotted the Prince's visit.

86. *KS* 149; *New York Sun*, 19 November 1919, 6.

87. *Aren't We Lucky? The Magazine of HMS Renown, August to December 1919*, 120.

88. *Aren't We Lucky*, 88.

89. *Aren't We Lucky*, 51.

90. *New York Evening World*, 17 November 1919.

91. *Sandusky Register* (Ohio), 25 September 1919.

92. Newton, *Westward with the Prince*, 317–18; *New York Sun*, 19 November 1919.

93. *Aren't We Lucky*, 119.

94. Newton, *Westward with the Prince*, 332–3.

95. Newton, *Westward with the Prince*, 323–4.

96. *New York Times*, 22 November 1919.

97. *Brooklyn Daily Eagle*, 23 November 1919.

98. *Aren't We Lucky*, 85.

99. *The Times*, 4 December 1919.

100. Ziegler, *Edward VIII*, 123.

101. See p. 61. *KS* 144.

102. *KS* 136–9; Ziegler, *Edward VIII*, 106.

103. See the inscription on the Statue of Liberty, '"Keep, ancient lands, your storied pomp!" cries she / With silent lips. "Give me your tired, your poor, / Your huddled masses yearning to breathe free".'

CHAPTER 4

1. *The Times*, 10 December 1919.

2. *The Times*, 11 December 1919.

3. *The Times*, 2 December 1919.

4. Parliamentary Archives, LG/F/29/3/40.

5. *LP* 227.

6. *LP* 230. He wrote a very similar letter to Godfrey Thomas on the same day: Ziegler, *Edward VIII*, 122.

7. *LP* 246.

8. Parliamentary Archives, LG/F/29/4/2; Churchill Archives, Cambridge, Amery Papers AMEL 1/3/42.

9. Ziegler, *Mountbatten: The Official Biography* (London, 1985), 57; Shaughnessy, ed., *Sarah*, 122. Mountbatten's father, Prince Louis of Battenberg, had been forced to resign as First Sea Lord in October 1914 on a swell of anti-German sentiment.

10. Churchill Archives Centre, AMEL 1/3/42.

11. J. Greene, *The Canal Builders: Making America's Empire at the Panama Canal* (London, 2009), 2.

12. Churchill Archives Centre, AMEL 1/3/42.

13. Tooze, *The Deluge*, 44.
14. Parliamentary Archives, LG/F/29/3/40; Hunt, *Bachelor Prince*, 153–4.
15. Churchill Archives Centre, AMEL 1/3/42.
16. Guy Schofield, *The Visit of His Royal Highness the Prince of Wales to New Zealand* (Wellington, 1926), p. iv.
17. Donaldson, *Edward VIII*, 78; *LP* 251–3.
18. Rose, *George V*, 303–4.
19. Philip Ziegler, ed., *The Diaries of Lord Louis Mountbatten, 1920–1922* (London, 1987), 20; *LP* 259.
20. Ziegler, ed., *Diaries of Mountbatten*, 21; *LP* 255, 257.
21. Parkhurst, *King in the Making*, 181–2; Everard Cotes, *Down Under with the Prince* (London, 1921), 14.
22. *LP* 261.
23. Greene, *Canal Builders*, 1–2, 30–1, 341–2.
24. Cotes, *Down Under with the Prince*, 17; Ziegler, ed., *Diaries of Mountbatten*, 22; *LP* 263.
25. *Fitchburg Sentinel* (Massachusetts), 31 March 1920; *LP* 263.
26. Cotes, *Down Under with the Prince*, 22.
27. *Washington Times*, 20 April 1920; Hunt, *Bachelor Prince*, 154–5.
28. Ziegler, *Edward VIII*, 125.
29. *LP* 264.
30. *LP* 263–5.
31. *Washington Times*, 20 April 1920; see also the *Melbourne Age*, 3 April 1920.
32. *New York Times*, 25 April 1920.
33. *Washington Times*, 20 April 1920. See also *Sandusky Register*, 25 April 1920.
34. *New York Times*, 7 February 1931.
35. *LP* 272.
36. Richard Kurial, 'The Prince of Wales Visits San Diego: A Study in Perception', *San Diego Historical Society*, 38/3 (1992), 160–75.
37. *San Diego Union*, 8 April 1920.
38. *New York Times*, 8 April 1920, 17. Ziegler, ed., *Diaries of Mountbatten*, 25; *LP* 270.
39. *LP* 268; see p. 35.
40. *Daily Journal-Gazette* (Illinois), 9 April 1920.
41. E.g. *Wilmington Morning Star*, 8 April 1920.
42. Ziegler, ed., *Diaries of Mountbatten*, 25–6; *LP* 272.
43. C. H. Rolleston, ed., *HMS Renown in Australasia: Authentic Record and Account of the Visit of HMS 'Renown' to Australasia* (Melbourne, 1920), 98.
44. Wallis, Duchess of Windsor, *The Heart has its Reasons* (London, 1956), 84–5.
45. B. Sacks, 'The Duchess of Windsor and the Coronado Legend', *Journal of San Diego History*, 34/1 (1988), 1–15.
46. *LP* 270, 298–9. Her first letters eventually arrived on 21 and 22 May, having taken more than two months to reach him.
47. *LP* 268–74.

48. 1 April 1920.
49. *Lincoln Evening Journal*, 8 April 1920.
50. *San Diego Union*, 8 April 1920.
51. Rolleston, ed., *HMS Renown in Australasia*, 102.
52. Rolleston, ed., *HMS Renown in Australasia*, 104, 107.
53. Ziegler, ed., *Diaries of Mountbatten*, 28.
54. See the website of the Museum of British Surfing: <http:// www.museumof britishsurfing.org.uk>.
55. Ziegler, ed., *Diaries of Mountbatten*, 64–6.
56. *Euroa Advertiser* (Victoria), 28 May 1920.
57. Parliamentary Archives, LG/F/29/4/19.
58. Ziegler, ed., *Diaries of Mountbatten*, 74; *Darling Downs Gazette* (Queensland), 5 June 1920.
59. *Newcastle Sun* (New South Wales), 7 August 1920; Ziegler (ed.), *Diaries of Mountbatten*, 127.
60. *Daily Examiner* (Grafton, New South Wales), 11 August 1920.
61. *KS* 160.
62. Parliamentary Archives, LG/F/29/4/19.
63. Shaughnessy, ed., *Sarah*, 125–6.
64. *LP* 345–7.
65. Rolleston, ed., *HMS Renown in Australasia*, 143.
66. *LP* 304; Sarah Bradford, *King George VI* (London, 1989), 86.
67. *LP* 319.
68. *LP* 328–32.
69. Shaughnessy, ed., *Sarah*, 126.
70. *LP* 331–3.
71. *LP* 334.
72. Parliamentary Archives, LG/F/29/4/19.
73. Parliamentary Archives, LG/F/29/4/22.
74. Cotes, *Down Under with the Prince*, 216; *Wichita Daily Eagle*, 21 September 1920.
75. *LP* 377.
76. See Chapter 13.
77. Ziegler, ed., *Diaries of Mountbatten*, 162.
78. Ziegler, *Edward VIII*, 133.
79. *The Times*, 11 October 1920.
80. *The Times*, 12 October 1920.
81. Parliamentary Archives, LG/F/29/4/19.
82. *New York Times*, 13 October 1920.
83. *The Times*, 14 October 1920.
84. *The Times*, 19 October 1920.
85. *KS* 348–9; see below, pp. 317–18.
86. *Toronto Star*, 8 November 1920.
87. *Washington Herald*, 16 October 1920; *Boston Post*, 13 November 1920.
88. *Louisville Courier-Journal*, 31 October 1920.

89. *Santa Ana Register* (California), 14 October 1920; *Philadelphia Evening Public Ledger*, 7 October 1920; *Indianapolis Star*, 28 October 1920.
90. *Washington Times*, 11 May 1920.
91. *Brooklyn Daily Eagle*, 25 January 1921; *Billboard*, 4 December 1920.
92. *Brooklyn Daily Eagle*, 25 January 1921.
93. *LP* 301–2.
94. *LP* 171, 262, 283.
95. See below, pp. 213–14.
96. *LP* 350.
97. *LP* 394.
98. *LP* 386.
99. For Edward's anger at Bertie, see *LP* 350–2.

CHAPTER 5

1. Evans, *Prince Charming Goes West*, 19–21; Newton, *Westward with the Prince*, 195–6; *Dictionary of Canadian National Biography, 1921–30* (Toronto, 2005).
2. Simon Evans, *The Bar U* (Calgary, 2004), 301.
3. *LP* 174, 184. Freda had visited western Canada on her honeymoon in 1913. Edward's fantasy of settling there may have been inspired by her love of the country.
4. *LP* 188.
5. *LP* 191–2.
6. *LP* 189.
7. *Louisville-Courier Journal* (Kentucky), 23 September 1923.
8. Bedingfeld had come out to Alberta in the 1880s with his mother and built up a successful ranch in the years before the First World War. In 1914, at the age of 47, he enlisted in the British Army, and served as an ambulance driver in France. He returned after the war in poor health, and was eager to sell up and take his family back to England: Evans, *Prince Charming Goes West*, 49–54.
9. Glenbow Archives, Calgary, Helen Yule papers, M3973 file 16.
10. Evans, *Prince Charming*, 22; Newton, *Westward with the Prince*, 197.
11. *LP* 189.
12. *The Times*, 16 March 1903; Alan Gallop, *Buffalo Bill's British Wild West* (Stroud, 2009), 220.
13. Rogers, *Wit and Philosophy*, 28.
14. *LP* 202; Evans, *Prince Charming Goes West*, 23–4. Distantly related to the British writer and historian Thomas Carlyle, William Carlyle was Canadian by birth but had spent most of his adult life in the USA. He was an expert in animal husbandry and had held academic posts in Wisconsin, Colorado, and Oklahoma. He returned to Canada in 1917 to manage George Lane's breeding programme for Percheron horses.
15. The painting, 'When Law Dulls the Edge of Chance', is now in the Royal Collection.

16. *Vancouver Daily World*, 13 October 1919.

17. Hart-Davis, ed., *In Royal Service*, 39.

18. *KS* 150; Hart-Davis, ed., *King's Counsellor*, 107.

19. *The Day* (New London, Connecticut), 12 August 1931; *Mt Ida Chronicle* (New Zealand), 9 October 1925; *The Age* (Melbourne, Australia), 13 February 1924.

20. Duncan, *His Royal Happiness*, 154.

21. *New York Times*, 16 September 1923.

22. *Speeches by the Prince of Wales*, 169.

23. *The Times*, 21 February 1920; Evans, *Prince Charming Goes West*, 23; *KS* 119; *New York Times*, 16 September 1923.

24. *The Times*, 7 October 1921; Duncan Marshall, *Shorthorn Cattle in Canada* (Toronto, 1932), 503–12; Evans, *Prince Charming Goes West*, 63–87, 207–8.

25. Andrew Rose, *The Prince, the Princess and the Perfect Murder* (London, 2013), 49–70, 193. Marguerite was acquitted on 15 September 1923, the day before the Prince's arrival at the EP ranch.

26. *Manchester Guardian*, 14 September 1923; *High River Times*, 20 September 1923.

27. Evans, *Prince Charming Goes West*, 71–7.

28. Evans, *Prince Charming Goes West*, 90.

29. See p. 199.

30. Ziegler, *Edward VIII*, 149; Evans, *Prince Charming Goes West*, 90–4; *High River Times*, 4 October 1923.

31. *Winnipeg Tribune*, 13 September 1924; *Manchester Guardian*, 11 and 21 October 1923.

32. Ziegler, *Edward VIII*, 153.

33. Hart-Davis, ed., *In Royal Service*, 39; *New York Times*, 2 October 1924; *Winnipeg Tribune*, 2 October 1924; *High River Times*, 2 October 1924; Ziegler, *Edward VIII*, 149.

34. *New York Times*, 13 March 1920; *High River Times*, 3 September 1925.

35. *High River Times*, 14 April 1921; Gilbert, ed., *Churchill Documents*, xii. 59. Members of Edward's staff often spent holidays at the ranch: Admiral Halsey's daughter and son-in-law spent their honeymoon there in 1933.

36. *High River Times*, 25 August 1927.

37. See pp. 94–5; *The Times*, 17 February 1928, 7 April 1931.

38. The Prince had no direct involvement, but his name was used in the publicity for the film. *High River Times*, 3 December 1925; *New Castle News* (Pennsylvania), 12 November 1925: 'Exclusive pictures taken on the Prince of Wales's ranch at Calgary Alberta'. The ranch was also used as a location for the 1992 Clint Eastwood film *Unforgiven*.

39. *New York Times*, 26 February 1926.

40. See pp. 160–1.

41. A few days later Edward made amends by meeting a group of veterans from High River. *High River Times*, 11 and 18 August 1927.

42. Evans, *Prince Charming Goes West*, 111–13; Hart-Davis, ed., *In Royal Service*, 56.

43. *New York Times*, 4 September 1924; *High River Times*, 22 May 1924; *Souvenir Guide to the EP Ranch* (Calgary, c.1924).

44. For the later history of the EP ranch, see Evans, *Prince Charming Goes West*, 143–98. After his Abdication Edward made two brief visits to the ranch with Wallis, in 1941 and 1950.
45. Eric Hobsbawm, 'The American Cowboy: An International Myth?', in *Fractured Times: Culture and Society in the Twentieth Century* (London, 2013), 272–90.
46. *Louisville Courier-Journal*, 23 September 1923; *New York Times*, 7 August 1924.
47. Evans, *Prince Charming Goes West*, 70.

CHAPTER 6

1. *Speeches by the Prince of Wales,* pp. x–xii.
2. *Speeches by the Prince of Wales,* 86; *KS* 213.
3. Anne Orde, *The Eclipse of Great Britain* (Basingstoke, 1996), 77–80. Steiner, *The Lights that Failed*, 187–8. See p. 96.
4. London Metropolitan Archives, 4632/D/01/034.
5. *The Times*, 1 March 1923.
6. *The Times*, 2 March 1923.
7. <https://www.brent.gov.uk/media/387533/The%20British%20Empire%20Exhibition.pdf>.
8. *Speeches by the Prince of Wales*, 265.
9. *The Times*, 1 July 1924. Edward, as President of the RSPCA, diplomatically avoided the rodeo on his visits to the Exhibition: *Speeches by the Prince of Wales*, 272.
10. *Speeches by the Prince of Wales*, 279–82.
11. C. R. Greer, *Across with the Ad-Men* (Hamilton, OH, 1924), 41–52; *The Times*, 12 and 15 July 1924.
12. *New York Times*, 19 September 1924.
13. Greer, *Across with the Ad-Men*, 48–9.
14. *The Times,* 21 July 1924; Josephine Case and Everett Case, *Owen Young and American Enterprise* (Boston, 1982), 303.
15. *The Times*, 22 July 1924; Steiner, *The Lights that Failed*, 243.
16. Case and Case, *Owen Young and American Enterprise*, 303.
17. Cumbria Record Office, D/HW/9/55. Later in the year, when he was in New York, Edward did arrange a meeting with leading newspapermen, including two Hearst editors: see p. 108.
18. *The Times*, 8 July 1924.
19. *Ottawa Journal*, 8 July 1924; *Wilkes-Barre Record* (Pennsylvania), 12 July 1924.
20. One scene in the film has Prince Edward attempting to persuade Liddell to run on a Sunday in breach of his Christian principles, but there is no evidence that such an encounter took place. Liddell was aware of the race timetable several months before the Games.
21. *The Times*, 22 July 1924: 'Olympic Games Doomed'.
22. Greer, *Across with the Ad-Men*, 110–23.
23. *New York Times*, 8 July 1924.

24. Godfrey Thomas took advantage of the rare break from royal duties to get married: *The Times*, 12 September 1924.

25. *KS* 168, 188.

26. Ziegler, *Edward VIII*, 149–50.

27. *Lincoln Evening Journal*, 21 August 1924.

28. *New York Times*, 23 August 1924.

29. *New York Times*, 24 August 1924.

30. *New York Times*, 29 August 1924; John Julius Norwich, ed., *The Duff Cooper Diaries 1915–51* (London, 2005), 203–4.

31. Hart-Davis, ed., *In Royal Service*, 22; Duff Cooper, *Old Men Forget* (London, 1954), 131–2.

32. *New York Times*, 27 and 28 August 1924.

33. Hart-Davis, ed., *In Royal Service,* 19.

34. *New York Times*, 31 August 1924.

35. *New York Times*, 7 September 1924.

36. *New York Times*, 31 August 1924.

37. See p. 106.

38. Hart-Davis, ed., *In Royal Service*, 22.

39. *KS* 201–2; *Des Moines Register*, 30 August 1924.

40. Hart-Davis, ed., *In Royal Service*, 22.

41. *KS* 197.

42. Hart-Davis, ed., *In Royal Service*, 22.

43. *New York Times*, 31 August 1924.

44. See the start of the Introduction.

45. *New York Times*, 31 August 1924.

46. *Springfield Leader* (Missouri), 4 September 1924; *Oshkosh Daily Northwestern* (Wisconsin), 8 September 1924.

47. *Brooklyn Daily Eagle*, 1 September 1924; *Warren Tribune* (Pennsylvania), 2 September 1924.

48. *The Times*, 15 September 1924.

49. *New York Times*, 17 September 1924. *Baltimore Sun*, 17 September 1924.

50. Will Rogers was an American original. Born in Oklahoma, part Cherokee Indian, he began his career as a cowboy. He moved on to become an entertainer, performing rope tricks in vaudeville, and eventually appeared in the Ziegfeld Follies before becoming a Hollywood star. In the 1920s he wrote a nationally syndicated newspaper column which combined sharp wit with homespun wisdom: Ben Yagoda, *Will Rogers: A Biography* (New York, 1994).

51. Yagoda, *Will Rogers*, 161.

52. Hart-Davis, ed., *In Royal Service*, 26; *New York Times*, 14 September 1924; Rogers, *Wit and Philosophy*, 26.

53. *New York Times*, 19 September 1924.

54. *New York Times*, 14 September 1924.

55. Rogers, *Wit and Philosophy*, 27.

56. Will Rogers, *Letters of a Self-Made Diplomat* (New York, 1926), 101–4.

57. Ziegler, *Edward VIII*, 151–2.

58. *New York Times*, 19 September 1924.

59. Sotheby's Catalogue, London, 12 December 2003, 190–1; *Houston Post*, 19 October 1924.

60. *Springfield Republican* (Missouri), 18 October 1925: 'Pretty Pinna Sails to Meet Her Prince'; *New York Sun*, 8 February 1926.

61. Scott Fitzgerald, *The Great Gatsby* (Oxford, 1998), 7.

62. *KS* 199.

63. Matthew Bruccoli, ed., *Zelda Fitzgerald: The Collected Writings* (New York, 1992), 309–16.

64. Hart-Davis, ed., *In Royal Service*, 34–5; *Franklin News-Herald* (Philadelphia), 23 September 1924.

65. *Manitowoc Herald Times* (Wisconsin), 30 September 1924. It is possible that Virginia de Lanty was the actress and future playwright of the same name, who married Guy Bolton, the co-writer of the musical *Anything Goes*.

66. Cumbria Record Office, D/HW/9/55; Anne De Courcy, *The Viceroy's Daughters* (London, 2000), 92–3.

67. Hart-Davis, ed., *In Royal Service*, 32.

68. Hart-Davis, ed., *In Royal Service*, 17; see e.g. *Decatur Herald*, 24 September 1924.

69. Hart-Davis, ed., *In Royal Service*, 37. The meeting was arranged by Arthur Woods, the former New York Police Commissioner, who had shown Edward round Manhattan.

70. Hart-Davis, ed., *In Royal Service*, 32, 37; Ziegler, *Edward VIII*, 153.

71. Cumbria Record Office, D/HW/9/55. Howard described the author of the letter, Frederick Cunliffe-Owen, as a 'tiresome busybody': Ziegler, *Edward VIII*, 151.

72. *New York Times*, 13 September 1924; Hart-Davis, *In Royal Service*, 31–2.

73. *New York Times*, 18 and 19 September 1924.

74. Cumbria Record Office, D/HW/9/55.

75. *New York Times*, 14 October 1924.

76. Cumbria Record Office, D/HW/9/55; *LP* 213; *Detroit Free* Press, 19 October 1924.

77. *KS* 199; *New York Times*, 14 October 1924.

78. *Detroit Free* Press, 19 October 1924.

79. Hart-Davis, ed., *In Royal Service*, 36.

80. *New York Times*, 25 October 1924.

81. *The Times*, 27 October 1924, 12; Hart-Davis, ed., *In Royal Service*, 32.

83. *KS* 201.

83. *The Times*, 28 November 1924. The Wrigley Twins were the advertising symbol for Wrigley's 'Doublemint' chewing gum.

84. Hunt, *Bachelor Prince*, 47.

85. E.g. *Des Moines Register*, 27 December 1931; 23 June 1935.

86. Miguel Covarrubias, *The Prince of Wales and Other Famous Americans* (New York, 1925); Laura Mayhall, 'The Prince of Wales versus Clark Gable: Anglophone Celebrity and Citizenship between the Wars', *Cultural and Social History*, 4/4 (2007), 529-44.

CHAPTER 7

1. *KS* 358.
2. John Gunther, *Inside Europe* (New York, 1940), 296.
3. Charles Ponce de Leon, *Self-Exposure: Human Interest Journalism and the Emergence of Celebrity in America, 1890–1940* (Chapel Hill, NC, 2002), 80-1.
4. Samantha Barbas, *Movie Crazy: Fans, Stars and the Cult of Celebrity* (New York, 2001), 56; Bill Bryson, *One Summer: America 1927* (London, 2013), 412-13.
5. *Los Angeles Times*, 9 October 1924.
6. Bryson, *One Summer*, 115.
7. D. Cannadine, 'The Context, Performance and Meaning of Ritual: The British Monarchy and the "Invention of Tradition", c.1820–1977', in Eric Hobsbawm and Terence Ranger, eds, *The Invention of Tradition* (Cambridge, 1983), 101-64.
8. *Lincoln Star* (Nebraska), 14 September 1924.
9. Adrian Bingham, *Family Newspapers? Sex, Private Life and the British Popular Press, 1918–1978* (Oxford, 2009), 239-41.
10. Ziegler, *Edward VIII*, 150.
11. See Chapter 3.
12. Hart-Davis, ed., *In Royal Service*, 37.
13. See p. 103.
14. *Helena Independent Record* (Montana), 7 October 1924.
15. Newton, *Westward with the Prince of Wales*, 24, 27; Hart-Davis, ed., *In Royal Service*, 53; Edward, Duke of Windsor, *A Family Album* (London, 1960), 1. See also Ryan Linkof, 'The Photographic Attack on His Royal Highness: The Prince of Wales, Wallis Simpson and the Pre-History of the Paparazzi', *Photography and Culture*, 4/3 (November 2011), 277-92.
16. *New York Times*, 20 May 1928.
17. John Plunkett, *Queen Victoria, First Media Monarch* (Oxford, 2003), 144-98.
18. See p. 14.
19. Raymond Fielding, *American Newsreel 1911–67* (Norman, OK, 1972), 151-2. The prohibition on photographing the Prince playing sport was soon relaxed.
20. See pp. 43-4. Brooks had covered King George V's Delhi Durbar in 1911, and was the official photographer on the Western Front during the Great War: E. Brooks, 'The King and the Prince of Wales', *Strand Magazine*, 62 (1921), 204-13.
21. Ziegler, *Edward VIII*, 132.
22. Brooks, 'The King and the Prince of Wales', 212.

23. Cumbria Record Office, Howard Papers, D/HW/9/46; Shaughnessy, ed., *Sarah*, 140. The *Washington Times* was one of the Hearst chain of newspapers, which was vociferously anti-British. The *Chicago Tribune* ran a special advertisement trailing the pictures the day before publication: *Manitowoc Herald-News*, 31 October 1925. There is no evidence of how the newspaper obtained the photograph, but it was probably sold to a journalist by a member of the ship's crew.

24. *Altoona Tribune* (Pennsylvania), 31 March 1924; *Franklin News-Herald* (Pennsylvania), 27 March 1924.

25. E.g. *Yorkshire Post*, 17 March 1923.

26. McKernan, *Topical Budget*, 119.

27. McKernan, *Topical Budget*, 117–20.

28. 'The Prince and the Pictures', *Photoplay Magazine*, March 1920, 55–6. See e.g. the footage from the 1919 tour shown in the 1924 Pathé newsreel: <http://www.britishpathe.com/video/prince-of-wales-visits-usa>.

29. *The Times*, 10 December 1919.

30. McKernan, *Topical Budget*, 71, 87.

31. *Albany Democrat* (New York), 28 May 1922; *Indianapolis Star*, 9 September 1928.

32. *New York Times*, 27 June 1933.

33. *Daily Capital Journal* (Oregon), 6 February 1931. British Pathé on SS *Oropesa*, 5 February 1931: <http://streamingbritishpathe.com/hls/vod/flash>. The Prince reportedly took a great interest in the recording equipment which the cameramen used.

34. Bryson, *One Summer*, 412–13.

35. *Indianapolis News*, 10 November 1927.

36. *KS* 220; *Wilmington Evening Journal* (Delaware), 8 August 1927; *Reading Times*, 8 August 1927.

37. *Brooklyn Daily Eagle*, 8 July 1930; *The Times*, 8 July 1930: 'perhaps the British prototype of Mr Rockefeller is among us tonight'.

38. *Scranton Republican* (Pennsylvania), 14 March 193; *Detroit Free Press*, 22 May 1931.

39. *Brooklyn Daily Eagle*, 13 May 1923.

40. E.g. in discussion among Oxford undergraduates in the early 1930s (information from family reminiscences).

41. See Chapter 1.

42. *Richmond Times Despatch* (Virginia), 1 August 1920.

43. *Washington Times*, 30 June 1918; *Washington Herald*, 14 July 1920; *Bismarck Tribune* (North Dakota), 11 August 1920.

44. Occasionally there were hints in the American press of the Prince's relationship with Freda Dudley Ward: see p. 126.

45. *Washington Times*, 27 November 1921: 'The Real Secret of the Prince of Wales' Trip to India'; *St Louis Post-Dispatch*, 10 June 1923: 'What's Wrong with the Prince of Wales?'

46. *Daily Messenger*, 27 April 1923; *Huntington Herald* (Indiana), 1 May 1924.

47. *Wilmington News Journal* (Delaware), 30 January 1925; *New York Evening World*, 1 April 1922.

48. *Anniston Star* (Alabama), 23 June 1934; *Miami Daily News-Record*, 1 April 1935.

49. *Des Moines Register*, 5 May 1935.

50. *Louisville Courier-Journal* 13 April 1924.

51. For Will Rogers and the Prince, see pp. 104–5.

52. *Arizona Republic*, 24 April 1928; *Pittsburgh Press*, 17 September 1934.

53. *Pittsburgh Post-Gazette*, 17 September 1934.

54. *St Louis Post-Dispatch*, 2 September 1923: 'The Prince of Wales as a Jazzer'; *Altoona Tribune*, 3 June 1924; *Wilmington Evening Journal* (Delaware), 10 March 1927.

55. *Wilmington News-Journal* (Delaware),12 March 1935.

56. *Bismarck Tribune* (North Dakota), 5 August 1919.

57. As reflected e.g. in the syndicated 'Beaunash' column in US newspapers: *Modesto Evening News* (California), 9 September 1924; *Oakland Tribune* (California), 5 December 1924.

58. Photographs of the Prince's arrival in New York in 1924 show dozens of reporters climbing aboard the *Berengaria*, all wearing boaters.

59. *New York Times*, 17 September 1924.

60. *Detroit Free Press*, 13 October 1924. For the Prince's various identities, see pp. 149–50.

61. American consumers also responded to the 'heritage' aspect of Fair Isle knitwear, as the fashion pages in the newspapers explained the traditional methods used by the Islanders, and the rather unlikely legend of how the distinctive designs had been brought to the Shetlands by Spanish sailors wrecked in the Spanish Armada: *Cincinnati Enquirer*, 24 October 1922; *Fort Wayne Sentinel* (Indiana), 17 March 1923.

62. *Dunkirk Evening Observer*, 8 November 1924; *Brooklyn Daily Eagle*, 5 October 1924.

63. *Indianapolis Star*, 4 November 1927; *Warren Times-Mirror* (Pennsylvania), 23 October 1935. In 1925 the Prince had his portrait painted by John St Helier Lander, wearing his Fair Isle sweater.

64. *Pittsburgh Daily Post*, 23 August 1925.

65. *Literary Digest,* 11 May 1929, unpaginated.

66. *Sandusky Register,* 15 March 1931.

67. *Muscatine Journal* (Iowa), 10 February 1931.

68. G. Parkhurst, *A King in the Making: An Authentic Story of Edward, Seventeenth Prince of Wales* (New York, 1925).

69. In May 1925, two months after the publication of Parkhurst's book in the USA, Brooks was summarily deprived of his royal warrant as photographer to the King and the Prince of Wales, which he had held for fifteen years. At the same time he was stripped of his decorations, including an OBE (Officer of the British Empire) for wartime service: *The Times*, 6 May 1925, 19; *London Gazette*, 33044 (5 May 1925), 3025. No reason was given for the dismissal, but it

followed Brooks's conviction in London for indecent assault:TNA, Metropolitan Police Special Branch Files, MEPO/38/50. In America Brooks's departure was linked to Parkhurst's book: *Springfield Republican*, 28 June 1925, 21:'Why did the King Fire the Royal Photographer?'

70. Hunt, *Bachelor Prince*, 90–1.

71. Hunt, *Bachelor Prince*, 3, 229.

72. 'The Prince and the Pictures', *Photoplay Magazine*, March 1920, 55–6.

73. *New York Times*, 19 July 1931; Mayhall, 'Prince of Wales versus Clark Gable', 529–30.

74. *Vanity Fair*, September 1932, 43–4.

75. *Vanity Fair*, November 1932, 40; Mayhall, 'Prince of Wales versus Clark Gable', 529–30.

76. *New York Times*, 11 October 1925: 'Skit on Prince of Wales proves quite amusing'.

77. See p. 77.

78. *New York Times*, 22 October 1926.

79. *San Mateo Times*, 19 April 1926, Marion Davies was best known for being the mistress of press baron William Randolph Hearst.

80. *The Tennessean*, 31 December 1922, 22; *Sedalia Democrat*, 11 October 1929.

81. E.g. *New Castle News* (Pennsylvania), 12 November 1925: 'Exclusive Pictures Taken on the Prince of Wales's Ranch at Calgary Alberta'.

82. *The Times*, 22 January 1920; *Washington Herald*, 1 February 1920; *Bemidji Pioneer* (Minnesota), 3 February 1920; *Washington Post*, 8 February 1920.

83. Mort, 'Love in a Cold Climate', 41–2.

84. *Washington Times*, 1 May 1926.

85. *Winnipeg Tribune*, 1 May 1926. See pp. 217–18.

86. The compilation of such lists was a popular parlour game at the time. One example was naming ten men 'whose deaths would cause the world most excitement'. The Prince appeared on the list, alongside Stalin, Rockefeller, and the Pope.

87. *Murphysboro Daily Independent* (Illinois), 29 September 1931. This was one of a series titled 'modern dilemmas'.

88. *Reading Times*, 12 December 1933.

CHAPTER 8

1. *New York Times*, 26 November 1995. The song was written by the playwright and songwriter Herbert Farjeon. It was not well received when it was first performed, being regarded as disrespectful to the Prince: Herbert Farjeon, *Herbert Farjeon Omnibus* (London, no date), 243.

2. Diana Vreeland, *DV*, ed. G Plimpton and C. Hemphill (London, 1984), 70.

3. The quotation is attributed to George Bernard Shaw.

4. D. O. Stewart, *Perfect Behavior* (New York, 1922), 49.

5. By extraordinary coincidence, Edward first met Freda at the house of Maud Kerr-Smiley, the elder sister of Ernest Simpson.

6. Windsor, *The Heart has its Reasons*, 143.

7. Martin Gilbert, ed., *Churchill Documents*, xi. *1922–29* (Hilldale, MI, 2009), 1068; *LP* 196.

8. Donaldson, *Edward VIII*, 74.

9. *LP, passim*; Sotheby's Catalogue, New York, 20 June 2003: Fine Books and Manuscripts, lot 241.

10. *LP* 254, 262, 283; Ziegler, *Edward VIII*, 99–100.

11. E.g. in September 1922 he wrote to Freda saying that he had a meeting with his mother, Queen Mary, 'when she brought up the hackneyed old subject of my marriage which I quickly squashed'. A few weeks later he wrote that he was 'hating life without you and away from you my precious and the fact that you can't take the place in my life that I want you to and that is *yours* by right because I love you'. Sotheby's Catalogue, New York, 20 June 2003, p. 259.

12. Sotheby's Catalogue, New York, 20 June 2003, p. 259.

13. Glenda Riley, *Divorce: An American Tradition* (New York, 1991), 133; O. R. McGregor, *Divorce in England* (London, 1957), 38; A. J. P. Taylor, *English History 1914–1945* (Oxford, 1965), 170.

14. *LP* 89, 90.

15. *LP* 94.

16. See p. 29.

17. *Sandusky Register* (Ohio), 25 September 1919; *LP* 193.

18. *LP* 265.

19. *Washington Times*, 8 June 1922.

20. Gary Chapman, *The Dolly Sisters: Icons of the Jazz Age* (London, 2013), 126–60, 205–6.

21. Chapman, *Dolly Sisters*, 153–4; Ziegler, *Edward VIII*, 151. The Dollies may have timed their return from Europe to New York to coincide with the Prince's visit: Chapman, *Dolly Sisters*, 151–3.

22. *Brooklyn Daily Eagle*, 31 August 1924.

23. *New York Evening World*, 3 January 1919.

24. In one account of the first meeting between Wallis and Edward, Wallis is supposed to have said, 'Sir, do you think me very like Rita Kruger [*sic*]?' Ziegler, *Edward VIII*, 227.

25. The New Woman, who emerged in Britain and the USA in the 1890s, challenged the stereotype of the submissive Victorian wife confined to the domestic sphere. She was emancipated, well educated, and socially progressive. She voiced opinions about politics and social reform, played sports like golf and tennis, and rode a bicycle. One popular incarnation of the New Woman was the Gibson Girl, created by graphic artist Charles Dana Gibson at the turn of the twentieth century. The Gibson Girl was seen as the embodiment of American female beauty, confident and independent, and meeting men on equal or even superior terms. One famous sketch shows four disdainful Gibson Girls examining a tiny kneeling man under a magnifying glass. The Gibson Girl was to be found primarily in East Coast high society and among the affluent middle classes, and

Edward would have met many of them in Washington and New York in 1919. See Martha Patterson, *Beyond the Gibson Girl* (Chicago, 2005), 1–49.

26. Trina Robbins, *Nell Brinkley and the New Woman in the Early Twentieth Century* (Jefferson, NC, 2001), 79–112.

27. Dimbleby and Reynolds, *An Ocean Apart,* 106.

28. Evelyn Waugh, *Brideshead Revisited* (Harmondsworth, 1973), 218.

29. *Indianapolis Star,* 25 May 1932; *Pittsburgh Press,* 1 June 1932.

30. Hart-Davis, ed., *King's Counsellor,* 112. Lascelles believed that Edward was obsessed with sex: 'his whole existence had been made to conform to what H. G. Wells called "the urgency of sex"...Mrs S[impson] was no isolated phenomenon, but merely the current figure in an arithmetical progression that had been robustly maintained for nearly twenty years.'

31. See Chapter 6.

32. Angela Dudley Ward sometimes played truant from school in order to go to tea with Edward at St James's Palace: Donaldson, *Edward VIII,* 120–1. The Prince bought a pony for Penelope in 1927, although Freda's father insisted on reimbursing him for it: Edward to Col. Charles Birkin, 7 February 1927, author's collection.

33. Gilbert, ed., *Churchill Documents,* xi. 1068.

34. Ziegler, *Edward VIII,* 174. Wanamaker was a great admirer of the British royal family, and Freda would have been a 'trophy' lover for him as the Prince's ex-mistress: see p. 54.

35. The relationship was through Eleanor of Castile, the wife of King Edward I of England (reigned 1272–1307).

36. E.g. *Troy Sunday Budget* (New York), 20 September 1926: 'What Next for Mrs Reggy's Lovely Sister?'

37. Vanderbilt and Furness, *Double Exposure,* 218–27; Ziegler, *Edward VIII,* 222.

38. Furness and Vanderbilt, *Double Exposure,* 265–6.

39. See p. 177.

40. Ziegler, *Edward VIII,* 223.

41. Furness and Vanderbilt, *Double Exposure,* 165, 218, 225.

42. Furness and Vanderbilt, *Double Exposure,* 278–9. The Prince's teddy bear was found in Thelma's handbag at her death in 1970.

43. Furness and Vanderbilt, *Double Exposure,* 269.

44. Furness and Vanderbilt, *Double* Exposure, 228–60.

45. Ziegler, *Edward VIIII,* 229; Furness and Vanderbilt, *Double Exposure,* 227–81.

CHAPTER 9

1. *St Louis Star and Times,* 30 December 1931; photograph in the author's collection.

2. Ziegler, *Edward VIII,* 51. It is not known whether Thelma Furness called him David.

3. *KS* 415.

4. Mackenzie, *Windsor Tapestry*, 213. Frances Donaldson made the same point in her biography of Edward: *Edward VIII*, 123.

5. *KS* 132.

6. Rose, *George V*, 34. A morganatic marriage was a marriage contracted between a husband and wife of unequal rank, where the children did not inherit the father's rank and titles. Teck's father was a member of the royal house of Württemberg in Germany, while his mother was a Hungarian countess.

7. *Decatur Daily Review*, 5 May 1927. Lascelles was a mere aristocrat and not of royal blood.

8. Windsor, *The Heart has its Reasons* (London, 1956), 202.

9. Bruno Bettelheim, *The Informed Heart* (Harmondsworth, 1986), 190. Bettelheim cited the example of the Duke of Hohenberg, the son of the assassinated Archduke Franz Ferdinand of Austria, who was imprisoned in Dachau for opposing the German annexation of Austria in 1938. The SS made the Duke clean the camp latrines.

10. Both relationships have been the subject of films starring Judi Dench as Queen Victoria.

11. Mackenzie, *Windsor Tapestry*, 125–6.

12. Ziegler, *Edward VIII*, 38, 49.

13. Hunt, *Bachelor Prince*, 62; Hart-Davis, ed., *King's Counsellor*, 110.

14. Ziegler, *Edward VIII*, 72.

15. Rose, *George V*, 303–4.

16. N. John Hall, *Max Beerbohm Caricatures* (New Haven, 1997), 135.

17. Windsor, *Family Album*, 92; Shaughnessy, ed., *Sarah*, 122–7; Hart-Davis, ed., *In Royal Service*, 104. 'Georgie's toto' caused Lascelles great amusement, because 'toto', besides being the Swahili word for boy, was also wartime slang for a louse.

18. Donaldson, *Edward VIII*, 120.

19. Windsor, *The Heart has its Reasons*, 202; Anne Sebba, *That Woman* (London, 2011), 196; Bloch, ed., *Wallis and Edward Letters*, 118–20.

20. Hart-Davis, ed., *King's Counsellor*, 110.

21. *KS* 72.

22. *KS* 78–9; John Ellis, 'Reconciling the Celt: British National Identity, Empire and the 1911 Investiture of the Prince of Wales', *Journal of British Studies*, 37 (1998), 391–418.

23. *KS* 117.

24. *KS* 131; see also <http://princeofwales.gov.uk>.

25. See e.g. *Louisville Courier-Journal*, 24 August 1924.

26. *KS* 117.

27. Heather Jones, 'A Prince in the Trenches? Edward VIII and the First World War', in Frank Lorenz Müller and Heidi Mehrkens, eds, *Sons and Heirs: Succession and Political Culture in Nineteenth-Century Europe* (London, 2016), 237, 243; Ziegler, *Edward VIII*, 71; *KS* 113.

28. Jones, 'A Prince in the Trenches?', 240–1; see p. 19.

29. Rose, *Prince, Princess and Perfect Murder*, 26–7.
30. Hunt, *Bachelor Prince*, 63–4; Jones, 'A Prince in the Trenches?', 243; Rose, *Prince, Princess and Perfect Murder*, 28–32, 53–5.
31. *LP* 128–9.
32. See p. 78.
33. Ziegler, *Mountbatten*, 55.
34. *LP* 160.
35. Ziegler, *Edward VIII*, 221, 244.
36. *LP* 196, 266.
37. *LP* 183, 266.
38. *LP* 215.
39. *LP* 229.
40. J. Bryan and Charles Murphy, *The Windsor Story* (London, 1979), 47.
41. Ziegler, *Edward VIII*, 75.
42. *LP* 222.
43. *LP* 278. If Edward had shared his suicidal thoughts with Freda before he left, she might have suggested a pact in order to ensure that he made no attempt while he was away on tour.
44. *Louisville Courier-Journal*, 24 August 1924.
45. *Philadelphia Inquirer*, 13 August 1924.
46. Ziegler, *Edward VIII*, 168; Hart-Davis, ed., *King's Counsellor*, 105.
47. For the history of the EP ranch, see Chapter 5.
48. For Edward's strategy of 'inner emigration', see Chapter 10.
49. Rose, *George V*, 106–10.
50. Cannadine, 'The Context, Performance and Meaning of Ritual', 43–100. On a more mundane level the royal family sought to justify its existence by taking part in good works and charitable activities, promoting the image of a 'welfare monarchy': Prochaska, *Royal Bounty*.
51. *KS* 136.
52. By contrast, Edward's tour of India in 1921–2 was much less successful, relying as it did on the traditional royal formulae of pageantry, formality, and remoteness: see Ziegler, *Edward VIII*, 134–47.
53. Hart-Davis, ed., *In Royal Service*, 65.
54. *Ottawa Journal*, 3 August 1927.
55. Hart-Davis, ed., *In Royal Service*, 65, 69.
56. Lascelles was so worried by the Prince's behaviour on the Canadian tour that he sought a meeting with Prime Minister Stanley Baldwin. '[I] told him directly that the Heir Apparent, in his unbridled pursuit of Wine and Women, and whatever selfish whim occupied him at the moment, was rapidly going to the devil, and unless he mended his ways would soon become no fit wearer of the British Crown.' Baldwin agreed with Lascelles's damning assessment and promised to speak to the Prince, although in the event he failed to do so: Hart-Davis, ed., *In Royal Service*, 69.
57. Prince Christopher of Greece, *Memoirs* (London, 1938), 165.

CHAPTER 10

1. *KS* 199–200.
2. *KS* 199–202. Edward did not give up hope of visiting America again during the 1920s. Speaking to a journalist late in 1926, he said he was planning a trip later in the year, and in 1928 Tommy Lascelles, writing about possible foreign trips by the Prince, referred to 'the ever-present menace of the USA': *Hamilton Daily News* (Ohio), 1 October 1926, 2; Hart-Davis, ed., *In Royal Service*, 100.
3. Timothy Garton Ash, 'Inner Emigration', *The Spectator*, 12 October 1984, 11; Funder, *Stasiland*, 193.
4. David Reynolds, *The Creation of the Anglo-American Alliance, 1937–41* (London, 1981), 12; Dimbleby and Reynolds, *An Ocean Apart*, 106.
5. *LP* 194.
6. *Marion Star* (Ohio), 25 January 1926; *Winnipeg Tribune*, 1 May 1926 *Spartanburg Herald* (South Carolina), 29 September 1926.
7. Alistair Cooke, *Six Men* (Harmondsworth, 1978), 62.
8. See pp. 112–13.
9. *Los Angeles Times*, 13 August 1927.
10. Cooke, *Six Men*, 59.
11. *The Times*, 23 June 1921.
12. *LP*. 138; Cooke, *Six Men*, 61–2.
13. Chapman, *Dolly Sisters*, 147–9; Case and Case, *Owen D. Young*, 302–3; *Reno Gazette Journal* (Nevada), 1 September 1926: 'Prince of Wales Hurries to Play Golf with Yankee'.
14. See pp. 194–5.
15. Vanderbilt and Furness, *Double Exposure*, 181; *Philadelphia Inquirer*, 29 August 1925.
16. Windsor, *The Heart has its Reasons*, 166–8; *Pittsburgh Press*, 21 January 1932.
17. An estimated 100,000 people turned out to watch Lindbergh land at Croydon Aerodrome; the crowd broke through the fences surrounding the airfield, so that he had to circle several times to allow the police to clear the runway: Bryson, *One Summer*, 119.
18. Wainwright, *Sheila*, 191–5.
19. Joyce Milton, *Loss of Eden: A Biography of Charles and Anne Lindbergh* (New York, 1993). Lindbergh's celebrity took a terrible toll on his personal life. In 1932 his infant son was kidnapped and murdered, and in 1935 he fled the USA for England to escape the press and protect his family. The two men kept up their acquaintance over the years. In 1936 Lindbergh and his wife attended the dinner at which Edward introduced Wallis Simpson to Prime Minister Baldwin, and Lindbergh was also a guest at the Nixons' dinner for the Windsors at the White House in 1970: see p. 1.
20. His golf handicap was said to be 16 in 1929: *Sydney Morning Herald*, 20 May 1929.
21. Tom Clavin, *Sir Walter* (London, 2005), 251–2. The story may be apocryphal, but it is consistent with the Prince's democratic instincts and dislike of snobbery. A similar story is told about the Royal and Ancient Club in St Andrews.

22. *Palm Beach Post*, 9 May 1930.

23. The four championships consisted of the British Open, the British Amateur, the US Open, and the US Amateur. Edward's prediction was correct: Jones's achievement has never been repeated.

24. *The Times*, 28 November 1930.

25. *The Times*, 15 March 1919.

26. *The Times*, 5 September 1923; Genevieve Abravanel, *Americanizing Britain* (Oxford 2012), 63.

27. 'Jazz History: Paul Whiteman, George Gershwin, and the Stale Bread Orchestra', *Saturday Evening Post*, 4 April 2016.

28. Joshua Berrett, *Louis Armstrong and Paul Whiteman* (New Haven, 2004), 55–6; 'The Musicians' Union: A Social History, 1921–30', <https:// www.muhistory. com>. The arrangement worked out through the Prince's intervention, later known as 'the Whiteman Clause', became an industry standard during the inter-war period. Whiteman was scathing about the British musicians he hired, finding them arrogant and unwilling to learn the new jazz techniques.

29. *St Louis Post-Despatch*, 2 September 1923: 'The Prince as a Jazzer'.

30. Berrett, *Armstrong and Whiteman*, 56–67; see pp. 104–5.

31. A. H. Lawrence, *Duke Ellington and his World* (London, 2001), 215.

32. Jeffrey Jackson, *Making Jazz French* (Durham, NC, 2003), 74–8.

33. Jean-Claude Baker and Chris Chase, *Josephine Baker: The Hungry Heart* (New York, 2001), 59.

34. Chapman, *Dolly Sisters*, 148.

35. Jed Kiley, *Hemingway: A Title Fight in Ten Rounds* (London, 1965), pp. vii–xii, 115; Basil Woon, *The Paris that's Not in the Guide Books* (New York, 1926), 247–56; *Pittsburgh Press*, 23 May 1924. Kiley was a friend and patron of Ernest Hemingway's, publishing early pieces by him in the *Boulevardier*, a literary journal he edited which was published in Paris in the 1920s. Kiley also tried to set up an ice cream business, which foundered when he discovered that the French did not eat ice cream in the winter.

36. Jackson, *Making Jazz French*, 63–70; *Pittsburgh Courier*, 22 June 1929; <http:// brbl-archive.library.yale.edu/exhibitions/cvvpw/gallery/bricktop.html>. Cole Porter is reputed to have written the song 'Miss Otis Regrets' for Bricktop. Scott Fitzgerald mentioned Bricktop's in his 1931 short story 'Babylon Revisited'.

37. *KS* 211.

38. Hart-Davis, ed., *In Royal Service*, 99–100.

39. Ziegler, *Edward VIII*, 192–3; Rose, *George V*, 357.

40. Kiki Preston was a member of the Vanderbilt family, and had been part of the decadent Happy Valley set in Kenya. She became notorious as 'the girl with the silver syringe'.

41. Ziegler, *Edward VIII*, 200–1.

42. *KS* 235; Jane Roberts, *Royal Landscape: The Gardens and Parks of Windsor* (London, 1997), 455–6.

43. *KS* 235–8; Windsor, *The Heart has its Reasons*, 179–88.

44. David Oliver, *Hendon Aerodrome: A History* (Shrewsbury, 1994), 85–97.

45. The airfield is now the site of the Guards' Polo Club.

46. *KS* 237; Roberts, *Royal Landscape*, 455.

47. Windsor, *The Heart has its Reasons*, 179–88.

48. Entries in the Fort's Visitors' Book for 1935–6 are printed in Michael Bloch, ed., *Wallis and Edward Letters, 1931–1937* (London, 1986), appendix 2.

49. Windsor, *Family Album*, 103.

CHAPTER II

1. *Cohocton Tribune* (Ohio), 10 March 1925.

2. *The Times*, 16 March 1925.

3. *The Spectator*, 17 October 1925.

4. Alfred Gardiner, *Certain People of Importance* (London, 1929), 60–5. For the reference to the Prince dressed as a girl, see Chapter 7.

5. *Hamilton Daily News* (Ohio), 1 October 1926.

6. *The Times*, 27 December 1928; 8 and 25 January 1929. Edward's radio broadcast may have inspired King George to make annual Christmas broadcasts, which began in 1932.

7. *KS* 227–8.

8. *The Times*, 31 January 1929.

9. Ziegler, *Edward VIII*, 185–6.

10. *The Times*, 12 and 27 February 1929.

11. *The Times*, 19 February 1929.

12. *Winnipeg Tribune*, 11 July 1929.

13. *Radio Times*, 24 January 1936.

14. See p. 205.

15. *The Times*, 28 January 1932; *San Bernardino Sun*, 31 January 1929: 'Pathetic Scenes of Starvation and Suffering Confront Wales'.

16. Brasnett, *Voluntary Social Action*, 70.

17. *The Times*, 25 February 1932.

18. Brasnett, *Voluntary Social Action*, 76.

19. See p. 178.

20. Kingsley Martin, *The Crown and the Establishment* (London, 1962), 87.

21. Kirkwood, *My Life of Revolt*, 259–60. The Prime Minister, Ramsay MacDonald, was present at Lady Astor's reception for Mellon, and Edward may have spoken to him after his conversation with Kirkwood.

22. One of his first functions as king was a visit to the *Queen Mary* in Glasgow before she sailed to Southampton for her maiden voyage to New York: *The Times*, 6 March 1936.

23. *KS* 249.

24. *Collier's Magazine*, 30 September 1933, 40: 'The Prince Sees Red'. The magazine did not print the expletive, but the context makes clear that this was the word Edward used.

25. *KS* 250; *The Times*, 26 May 1919.

26. *Collier's Magazine*, 30 September 1933, 16, 40–1.

27. *The Times*, 18 May 1933; *Chicago Tribune*, 18 May 1933; *Los Angeles Times*, 18 May 1932.

28. *KS* 250–1.

29. *The Times*, 28 January 1932.

30. Michael Hogan, *Informal Entente: The Private Structure of Co-operation in Anglo-American Economic Diplomacy, 1918–1928* (New York, 1977), 218–24; Reynolds, *Anglo-American Alliance*, 7–16.

31. *Los Angeles Times*, 16 May 1929.

32. *KS* 230–4.

33. *The Times*, 28 November 1930.

34. *The Times*, 15 April 1932.

35. *Winnipeg Tribune*, 11 July 1929.

36. *The Times*, 1 May 1929, 13. On Eastman's 75th birthday later in the year, Edward sent him the silver trowel which he had used at the ceremony.

37. *The Times*, 3 August 1929; *Rochester Democrat and Chronicle* (New York), 23 August 1929. 'Boondoggle' acquired its modern meaning, as an unnecessary or wasteful public project, as the result of work creation projects during the Depression in which the unemployed were set to work making boondoggles: *Oxford English Dictionary*.

38. *The Times*, 25 April 1932; *Indianapolis Star*, 24 April 1932. On the same day, the Folger Shakespeare Library was opened in Washington, DC, in the presence of President Hoover.

39. Dimbleby and Reynolds, *An Ocean Apart*, 97.

40. See pp. 64–5.

41. *Brooklyn Daily Eagle*, 7 February 1931; *Harrisburg Evening News*, 10 February 1931.

42. Edward had been coached in Spanish by Thelma Furness, whose mother was Chilean: Furness and Vanderbilt, *Double Exposure*, 283–4.

43. *KS* 241; *The Times*, 16 March 1931; *Los Angeles Times*, 15 March 1931; *Scranton Republican*, 14 March 1931; *Clovis News-Journal* (New Mexico), 15 May 1931.

44. *The Times*, 12 and 13 May 1931; *Klamath Falls Evening Herald* (Oregon), 12 May 1931; *KS* 242–3.

45. *The Times*, 31 May 1933. The speech was widely praised in the American press. Edward's hopes were soon dashed, however. At the London World Economic Conference a few weeks later, Roosevelt refused to agree any measures which would restrict his freedom to revive the US economy. After a month the Conference broke up acrimoniously and without agreement, and attempts to secure economic cooperation in Europe collapsed.

46. Edgar Nixon, ed., *Franklin D. Roosevelt and Foreign Affairs* (Cambridge, MA, 1969), ii. 79.

47. Ziegler, *Edward VIII*, 213.

48. See pp. 128–9.

49. In 2007 the car sold at auction for £100,000: Bonhams, Sale of Important Collectors' Motor Cars, London, 3 December 2007, lot 706. Windsor, *Family Album*, 76–7.

CHAPTER 12

1. Windsor, *The Heart has its Reasons*, 17–26.
2. D. G. Felder, *A Century of Women* (New York, 1999), 108.
3. Windsor, *The Heart has its Reasons*, 50–69.
4. Bloch, ed., *Wallis and Edward Letters*, 9–11.
5. Bloch, ed., *Wallis and Edward Letters*, 29–51.
6. Furness and Vanderbilt, *Double Exposure*, 274.
7. Before they became friendly with the Prince, the Simpsons were invited several times to Knole in Kent, the country house of Baron Sackville and his American wife, Anne, who had been a chorus girl in the Ziegfeld Follies.
8. Bloch, ed., *Wallis and Edward Letters*, 64–6.
9. Bloch, ed., *Wallis and Edward Letters*, 89.
10. Bloch, ed., *Wallis and Edward Letters*, 69.
11. Bloch, ed., *Wallis and Edward Letters*, 73.
12. Bloch, ed., *Wallis and Edward Letters*, 72–4; Windsor, *The Heart has its Reasons*, 189–90.
13. Furness and Vanderbilt, *Double Exposure*, 290–1.
14. Donaldson, *Edward VIII*, 170.
15. KS 256; Windsor, *The Heart has its Reasons*, 192–3.
16. Furness and Vanderbilt, *Double Exposure*, 293–5.
17. Furness and Vanderbilt, *Double Exposure*, 298–8; Windsor, *The Heart has its Reasons,* 194.
18. Bloch, ed., *Wallis and Edward Letters*, 92.
19. Sotheby's Sale, Geneva, 2–3 April 1987: The Jewels of the Duchess of Windsor, pp. 39–41.
20. Donaldson, *Edward VIII*, 170–1.
21. Windsor, *The Heart has its Reasons*, 195–200; *Detroit Free Press*, 2 August 1934; *Reading Times* (Pennsylvania), 10 August 1934; *St Louis Post-Dispatch*, 17 September 1934; *Florence Morning News* (South Carolina), 27 August 1934.
22. Ziegler, *Edward VIII*, 230–1.
23. E.g. *Albuquerque Journal* (New Mexico), 2 December 1934. The other prince was Thelma's latest lover, Aly Khan.
24. *Pittsburgh Post-Gazette*, 14 August 1935.
25. The best summary remains Ziegler, *Edward VIII*, 236–9.
26. Sebba, *That Woman*, 112.
27. KS 256.
28. Windsor, *The Heart has its Reasons*, 201.
29. Windsor, *The Heart has its Reasons*, 192.
30. Wallis made this clear in her memoirs: *The Heart has its Reasons*, 201–2.

31. Ziegler, *Edward VIII*, 238. By 1936 Edward had settled enough money on her to make her financially independent, a factor which must have been important in her decision to divorce Ernest. At the time Edward's staff understandably thought that Wallis and Ernest were conspiring to milk Edward financially.

32. See pp. 147–8.

33. Ziegler, *Edward VIII*, 218–19.

34. *St Louis Post-Dispatch*, 27 August 1935; *Salt Lake Tribune*, 27 August 1935; *Des Moines Register*, 11 September 1935.

35. Ziegler, *Edward VIII*, 218–21. King George died before Halsey and Thomas were able to submit their remonstrance to Edward.

36. Bloch, ed., *Wallis and Edward Letters*, 137.

37. KS 257–64.

CHAPTER 13

1. In the movie of *Gone With the Wind*, Ashley Wilkes was played by Leslie Howard, whose resemblance to Edward was well known: see p. 77.

2. *Time's* first Man of the Year had been Charles Lindbergh in 1927. The British magazine *Cavalcade*, modelled on *Time*, rather more dubiously made the ex-King Edward VIII its Man of the Year for 1936.

3. *Time*, 4 January 1937.

4. Cooke, *Six Men*, 73.

5. KS 254; Windsor, *The Heart has its Reasons*, 219; Ziegler, *Edward VIII*, 241.

6. Piers Brendon, *The Uncrowned King* (London, 2016), 49–50.

7. E.g. *Logan Daily News* (Ohio), 22 January 1936; *Idaho Post-Register*, 22 January 1936.

8. *Decatur Review* (Georgia), 4 March 1936; *Des Moines Register* (Iowa), 8 March 1936.

9. *St Louis Star and Times*, 5 March 1936.

10. KS 187–8, 292.

11. Lord Birkenhead, *Walter Monckton* (London, 1969), 127.

12. KS 285; *The Times*, 2 March 1936.

13. As far as Edward was concerned, his father's court retained a Victorian flavour. 'I had come to look on it as at least sexagenarian in composition and outlook': KS 278.

14. Philip Williamson, *Stanley Baldwin: Conservative Leadership and National Values* (Cambridge, 1999), 327.

15. Gabriel Gorodetsky, ed., *The Maisky Diaries: Red Ambassador to the Court of St James's 1932–43* (New Haven and London, 2015), 20.

16. George Ward Price, *Extra-Special Correspondent* (London, 1957), 185. By contrast, he thought that Labour MPs, many of whom were themselves working-class, were more in tune with their constituents.

17. Ward Price was a right-wing journalist who later became an enthusiastic supporter of Oswald Mosley and an admirer of Hitler.

18. Ward Price, *Extra-Special Correspondent*, 185–6.

19. *KS* 218.

20. See pp. 182–3; *Documents of German Foreign Policy*, series CIV, 1024; Urbach, *Go-Betweens for Hitler*, 189–90.

21. *Documents of German Foreign Policy*, series CIV, 1017.

22. See e.g. his belief that the differences between Britain and America could be sorted out over a round of golf: Chapter 11.

23. *Cavalcade*, 21 November 1936.

24. *KS* 282–93; Donaldson, *Edward VIII*, 197–8.

25. Birkenhead, *Walter Monckton*, 127.

26. Ziegler, *Edward VIII*, 273.

27. The Act had been passed in the reign of George III to prevent the King's seven sons from making unsuitable marriages. It failed in its intention, as they simply refused to marry and instead lived with their mistresses. The Act contained a technical provision allowing a member of the royal family over the age of 25 to marry without the monarch's consent provided Parliament agreed. However, the procedure had never been invoked and would not have been a practical option for Edward.

28. Under the Act of Settlement of 1701, a member of the royal family who married a Catholic was barred from the line of succession to the throne.

29. Hart-Davis, ed., *King's Counsellor*, 110; Keith Middlemas and John Barnes, *Baldwin: A Biography*, (London, 1969), 985.

30. Graves and Hodge, *The Long Weekend*, 105.

31. Windsor, *The Heart has its Reasons*, 226. Edward appears to have formulated his plan within a few days of coming to the throne. Early in February 1936, Baldwin received reports that Ernest Simpson had confided to a friend that the King wanted to marry his wife. At the time, Baldwin dismissed them as clumsy attempts at blackmail by the Simpsons: Ziegler, *Edward VIII*, 278.

32. Bloch, ed., *Wallis and Edward Letters*, 176, 223; Adrian Phillips, *The King Who Had to Go: Edward VIII, Mrs Simpson and the Hidden Politics of the Abdication Crisis* (London, 2016), 84. See p. 215.

33. *KS* 258.

34. Bloch, ed., *Wallis and Edward Letters*, 177. Ernest's affair with Mary appears to have begun when he visited America in 1935.

35. Birkenhead, *Walter Monckton*, 123.

36. Windsor, *The Heart has its Reasons*, 237.

37. *The Times*, 28 May 1936; Nigel Nicolson, ed., *Harold Nicolson: Diaries and Letters, 1930–39* (London, 1966), 255, 263; *Baltimore Sun*, 28 May 1936; *Pittsburgh Press*, 28 May 1936: 'Beauty and Eminence Mingle at Dinner'.

38. G. M. Young, *Stanley Baldwin* (London, 1952), 233; Middlemas and Barnes, *Baldwin*, 981.

39. Ziegler, *Edward VIII*, 281.

40. *The Times*, 10 July 1936.

41. *Time*, 20 July 1936.

42. *Pittsburgh Press*, 27 October 1936. 'Buttercup Kennedy' was probably Mary Raffray: see Bloch, ed., *Wallis and Edward Letters*, 186.

43. E.g. the *Baltimore Sun* reported on 5 July 1936 that Edward's choice of bride had narrowed to Princess Alexandrine-Louise of Denmark and Princess Frederica-Louise of Brunswick.

44. *KS* 320.

45. Linkof, 'The Photographic Attack on His Royal Highness', 282–3.

46. *Time*, 31 August 1936.

47. *Time*, 17 August 1936; Stanley Devon, *Glorious: The Life Story of Stanley Devon* (London, 1957), 102.

48. Windsor, *The Heart has its Reasons*, 231–2.

49. *Time*, 14 September 1936.

50. E.g. *St Louis Post-Despatch*, 4 September 1936; *Des Moines Register* (Iowa), 6 September 1936. The couple were on their way to see King George of Greece, who lived openly with his English mistress, Joyce Batten-Jones.

51. *Philadelphia Inquirer*, 30 September 1936; Ziegler, *Edward VIII*, 238, 310.

52. *Detroit Free Press*, 21 September 1936; V. D. Volkan and N. Itzkowitz, *The Immortal Ataturk* (Chicago, 1984), 326–7.

53. Bloch, ed., *Wallis and Edward Letters*, 193–4; Windsor, *The Heart has its Reasons*, 172, 237.

54. Ziegler, *Edward VIII*, 287–8; Bloch, ed., *Wallis and Edward Letters*, 196.

55. Bloch, ed., *Wallis and Edward Letters*, 186; *Brooklyn Daily Eagle*, 26 September 1936. *Cincinnati Enquirer*, 27 September 1936; Middlemas and Barnes, *Baldwin*, 982.

56. *Philadelphia Inquirer*, 30 September 1936.

57. Lord Beaverbrook, *The Abdication of King Edward VIII* (London, 1966), 29.

58. *Chicago Daily News*, 14 October 1936; Bloch, ed., *Wallis and Edward Letters*, 200.

59. *Washington Post*, 17 October 1936.

60. Phillips, *The King Who Had to Go*, 69–74.

61. Middlemas and Barnes, *Baldwin*, 983–6; Phillips, *The King Who Had to Go*, 78–80.

62. *Gettysburg Times* (Pennsylvania), 15 October 1936.

63. Windsor, *The Heart has its Reasons*, 237; Bloch, ed., *Wallis and Edward Letters*, 200.

64. Beaverbrook, *Abdication*, 30–1; *Time*, 26 October 1936.

65. Inglis, *Abdication*, 193–4; Alexis Schwarzenbach, 'Love, Marriage and Divorce: American and European Reactions to the Abdication of Edward VIII', in Luisa Passerini, Liliana Ellena, and Alexander Geppert, eds, *New Dangerous Liaisons: Discourses on Europe and Love in the Twentieth Century* (Oxford, 2010), 140–1.

66. Phillips, *King Who Had to Go*, 125–6.

67. Schwarzenbach, 'Love, Marriage and Divorce', 140–1; Inglis, *Abdication*, 194.

68. Inglis, *Abdication*, 197.

69. *Time*, 26 October 1936.

70. *Time*, 23 November 1936.

71. *New York Times*, 21 and 24 October 1936.

72. Inglis, *Abdication*, 192; Linkof, 'The Photographic Attack on His Royal Highness'; *Pittsburgh Press*, 27 October 1936; *Reno Gazette* (Nevada), 27 October 1936.

73. *Pittsburgh Press*, 27 October 1936; *Reno Gazette* (Nevada), 27 October 1936; *New York Times*, 28 October 1936.

74. *The Times*, 28 October 1936.

75. *Time*, 26 October 1936.

76. *Time*, 26 October 1936, 23 November 1936; *New York Times*, 18 October 1936; Inglis, *Abdication*, 263.

77. Evelyn Wrench, *Geoffrey Dawson and our Times* (London, 1955), 340–2.

78. Inglis, *Abdication*, 196–201.

79. Windsor, *The Heart has its Reasons*, 244–5; Inglis, *Abdication*, 209.

80. Inglis, *Abdication*, 211–14; Edward told members of his family the same evening.

81. Michele Holmes, *Network Nations: A Transnational History of British and American Broadcasting* (London, 2012), 71.

82. Cooke, *Six Men*, 70–2. After the broadcast, Cooke was berated by an apoplectic BBC announcer for denigrating the King to a foreign audience.

83. Cooke, *Six Men*, 73.

84. Rostow later became a distinguished economist and served as President Johnson's National Security Adviser during the Vietnam War.

85. Cooke, *Six Men*, 73.

86. E.g. *Altoona Tribune* (Pennsylvania), 11 December 1936.

87. *Oshkosh Daily Northwestern* (Wisconsin), 12 December 1936; *Times Herald* (Michigan), 12 December 1936. See p. 2.

88. *Daily Mirror*, 7 December 1936. The attack was picked up in the US press: see *Danville Morning News* (Virginia), 7 December 1936.

89. *The Times*, 11 December 1936.

90. *Time*, 26 October 1936.

91. *Time*, 4 January 1937.

92. Donaldson, *Edward VIII*, 303.

93. *KS* 415: 'it was here that I had begun to fit myself for life in the real world—the world which by my own free will I had chosen'.

CHAPTER 14

1. Bloch, ed., *Wallis and Edward Letters,* 253.

2. Ziegler, *Edward VIII*, 336–65.

3. Windsor, *The Heart has its Reasons*, 289. *Burke's Peerage, Baronetage and Knightage 1938* (London, 1938), Table of Royal Pedigree; Ziegler, *Edward VIII*, 484–7.

4. Nicolson, *Diaries and Letters, 1930–39*, 230.

5. Hart-Davis, ed., *In Royal Service*, 65.

6. Sarah Bradford, *King George VI* (London, 1989), 444.

7. Edward also lost his domestic staff, valets, and drivers, some of whom had served him for many years: Ziegler, *Edward VIII*, 333.

8. Bloch, ed., *Wallis and Edward Letters*, 248.

9. *Daily Telegraph*, 27 January 2001: obituary of Sir Dudley Forwood.

10. Thomas became private secretary to Edward's brother, Henry, Duke of Gloucester, while Legh became Master of the Royal Household under George VI.

11. See Chapter 12.

12. Osbert Sitwell, *Rat Week* (London, 1986).

13. Sebba, *That Woman*, 192. Brookman published the book under the pseudonym Edwina Wilson. The book was based on a series of articles that Brookman had written for US newspapers in October 1936: e.g. *Scranton Republican*, 14 October 1936. The British edition was titled *The Duchess of Windsor*.

14. Bloch, ed., *Wallis and Edward Letters*, 246.

15. Bloch, ed., *Wallis and Edward Letters*, 209, 236–8, 260. See e.g. *McCall's Magazine*, March 1937, 13.

16. *Des Moines Register*, 17 January 1937.

17. Bloch, ed., *Wallis and Edward Letters*, 260.

18. Mackenzie, *Windsor Tapestry*.

19. *Time*, 21 December 1936.

20. *Lincoln Star*, 17 February 1937.

21. < https:// Yankeedollar.wordpress.com/2009/11/11/caresser-in-canada>: Lord Caresser's real name was Rufus Callender. The most well-known version of the song is the recording by Harry Belafonte on his 1956 album *Calypso*.

22. *Minneapolis Star*, 6 December 1937. Also in the band were Albert Einstein on the saxophone and Bernard Shaw on triangle.

23. E.g. *The Idaho Falls Register*, 12 February 1937.

24. Phillips's column 'The Once Over' was widely syndicated: e.g. *Harrisburg Evening News*, 26 February 1937.

25. Bloch, ed., *Wallis and Edward Letters*, 227–37.

26. Michael Bloch, *The Duke of Windsor's War* (London, 1982), 155; Michael Bloch, *The Secret File of the Duke of Windsor* (London, 1988), 136–8.

27. Bloch, ed., *Wallis and Edward Letters*, 230; Windsor, *The Heart has its Reasons*, 289–92.

28. Jim Christy, *The Price of Power* (New York, 1984), 181.

29. *Time*, 8 November 1937; P. Glading, *How Bédaux Works* (London, 1932); *Pittsburgh Press*, 6 November 1937.

30. Windsor, *The Heart has its Reasons*, 302.

31. *Time*, 15 November 1937; Bloch, *Secret File*, 111–19.

32. *New York Times*, 23 October 1937.

33. Bloch, *Secret File*, 115–16.

34. Ziegler, *Edward VIII*, 386–401.

35. *New York Times*, 13 October 1937; *Time*, 25 October 1937.

36. *New York Times*, 29 October 1937; Bloch, *Secret File*, 118–19.

37. *Los Angeles Times*, 16 October 1937.

38. E.g. *Great Falls Tribune* (Montana), 8 November 1937.

39. *Time*, 15 November 1937; *Louisville Courier-Journal*, 5 November 1937.

40. *Time*, 15 November 1937.

41. *The Times*, 6 November 1937.

42. Windsor, *The Heart has its Reasons*, 204.

43. Christy, *Price of Power*, 182–5. During the Second World War, Bédaux was suspected of collaborating with the Nazis on behalf of the Vichy government in France. He was arrested in North Africa in 1943, and extradited to the USA, where he committed suicide while awaiting trial for treason: Deborah Cadbury, *Princes at War* (London, 2016), 285–8.

44. *Lansing State Journal*, 27 April 1939; Bloch, *Secret File*, 136.

45. *New York Times*, 8 May 1939; *Pittsburgh Press*, 8 May 1939.

46. Donaldson, *Edward VIII*, 365; the full text was printed in *The Times*, 9 May 1939, 11, which pointedly reported that the speech was not being broadcast in Britain or Canada; see also Bloch, *Secret File*, appendix III.

47. Bloch, *Secret File*, 138.

48. Ziegler, *Edward VIII*, 402–19; Bloch, *Duke of Windsor's War*, 27–75.

49. Ziegler, *Edward VIII*, 421–5.

50. The events of June and July 1940 remain the most controversial of Edward's life: at best, he was defeatist about Britain's prospects in the war; at worst he has been accused of collaborating with the Nazis, although the evidence is circumstantial. The affair has been examined in detail by all three of Edward's leading biographers, Frances Donaldson, Philip Ziegler, and Michael Bloch, all of whom acquit Edward of collaboration.

51. Ziegler, *Edward VIII*, 426–9.

52. See Chapter 4.

53. Elliott Roosevelt, *A Rendezvous with Destiny* (London, 1977), 149.

54. Beaverbrook, *Abdication*, 108.

55. Ziegler, *Edward VIII*, 397.

56. *Pittsburgh Post-Gazette*, 23 July 1937; *Jackson Clarion-Ledger* (Mississippi), 14 May 1939.

57. Bloch, *Duke of Windsor's War*, 119–21; *Bridgewater Courier-News* (New Jersey), 19 August 1940.

58. E.g. the *Syracuse Herald-American*, and the *Indianapolis Star*, 17–30 November 1940.

59. Bloch, *Duke of Windsor's War*, 126.

60. Bloch, *Duke of Windsor's War*, 164–6. Roosevelt was inspecting potential sites for US naval bases in the British West Indies.

61. *New York Times*, 10 December 1940.

62. *New York Times*, 11 December 1940. Bloch, *Duke of Windsor's War*, 166–70.

63. *New York Times*, 13 and 15 December 1940; *Fort-Myers News Press* (Florida), 15 December 1940.

64. *New York Times*, 14 December 1940.

65. Bloch, *Duke of Windsor's War*, 175.

66. *New York Times*, 26 December 1940; Edward expressed almost identical sentiments in a speech to the New York Pilgrims on 21 November 1919: *Speeches by HRH The Prince of Wales*, 26.

67. *Liberty*, 22 March 1941: interview with Fulton Oursler; Piers Brendon, *Edward VIII* (London, 2016), 85–7.

68. Bloch, *Secret File*, 185–91.

69. *Winnipeg Tribune*, 2 October 1941.

70. Bloch, *Duke of Windsor's War*, 202–22.

71. Ziegler, *Edward VIII*, 466–7; René MacColl, *Deadline and Dateline* (London, 1956), 122.

72. *New York Times*, 26 September 1941.

73. *Kingsport Times* (Tennessee), 28 September 1941.

74. *Time*, 6 October 1941.

75. *Green Bay Press Gazette* (Wisconsin), 27 September 1941; *Indiana Gazette* (Pennsylvania), 27 September 1941.

76. *DeKalb Daily Chronicle* (Illinois), 27 September 1941.

77. *Minneapolis Star*, 28 September 1941.

78. Bloch, *Duke of Windsor's War*, 211.

79. Evans, *Prince Charming Goes West*, 155.

80. *Winnipeg Tribune*, 2 October 1941.

81. Evans, *Prince Charming Goes West*, 157.

82. Evans, *Prince Charming Goes West*, 155–60; Bloch, *Duke of Windsor's War*, 213–15.

83. *Baltimore Sun*, 12 and 14 October 1941.

84. *Baltimore Sun*, 17 and 18 October 1941.

85. Bloch, *Duke of Windsor's War*, 216.

86. *New York Times*, 23 October 1941.

87. *New York Times*, 25 and 30 October 1941.

88. Bloch, *Duke of Windsor's War*, 220–2. When Halifax did visit Detroit, he was pelted with eggs and tomatoes by isolationist demonstrators.

89. *Detroit Free Press*, 31 October 1941.

90. Bloch, *Duke of Windsor's War*, 221. Edward and Ford had previously met in 1924, when Ford formed a very favourable view of the Prince: see Chapter 5.

91. E.g. on the train from Chicago to St Paul, the Windsors gave an interview to Catherine Quealy of the *Minneapolis Star*. 27 September 1941.

92. MacColl, *Deadline and Dateline*, 130–2.

93. *Time*, 6 October 1941.

94. Hitler declared war on the USA a few days after Pearl Harbor.

95. Kenneth Davis, *FDR, War President, 1940–43* (New York, 2000), 498.

96. *Chicago Daily Tribune*, 16 June 1942.

97. *Philadelphia Daily News*, 16 December 1966 (article on the thirtieth anniversary of the Abdication).

98. Bloch, *Duke of Windsor's War*, 317.

99. Bloch, *Duke of Windsor's War*, 293; *New York Times*, 20 May 1943; *St Louis Star*, 18 May 1943.

100. Ziegler, *Edward VIII*, 496–513.

101. Bloch, *Duke of Windsor's War*, 356.

EPILOGUE

1. Bloch, *Duke of Windsor's War*, 364–5.
2. Bloch, *Duke of Windsor's War*, 360.
3. *New York Times*, 20 June 1945.
4. *Ogden Standard-Examiner* (Utah), 26 July 1947; *Pittsburgh Press*, 1 August 1945.
5. See Chapter 2.
6. Ziegler, *Edward VIII*, 503–4.
7. Phillip Hall, *Royal Fortune: Tax, Money and the Monarchy* (London, 1992), 70–9; Bloch, *Secret File*, 220.
8. Ziegler, *Edward VIII*, 491.
9. From the 1940s to the 1960s the highest rate of US income tax was 91%: T. Piketty, 'The Rise of Bernie Sanders', *The Guardian*, 16 February 2016.
10. Ziegler, *Edward VIII*, 506–8; Norwich, ed., *Duff Cooper Diaries*, 394–5. *Baltimore Sun*, 2 November 1946.
11. Windsor, *The Heart has its Reasons*, 365.
12. *New York Times*, 29 May 1972.
13. Susan Alsop, *From Paris to Marietta* (London, 1976), 54.
14. *Detroit Free Press*, 1 June 1947.
15. Ziegler, *Edward VIII*, 518, 534–5.
16. *Pittsburgh Press*, 5 December 1947. Ziegler, *Edward VIII*, 521–55.
17. *A King's Story* ends with Edward's late-night drive from Fort Belvedere to Portsmouth on 11 December 1936, as he departed to begin his new life: p. 415.
18. *New York Times*, 16 April 1951.
19. Sotheby's Sale 7000, New York, 11–19 September 1997, lots 419–28.
20. Ziegler, *Edward VIII*, 527.
21. Edward, duke of Windsor, *The Crown and the People* (New York and London, 1953).
22. E.g. *Lubbock Morning Avalanche* (Texas), 21 February 1956.
23. *New York Times*, 29 May 1972 (obituary of the Duke of Windsor); Stephen Gundle, *Glamour: A History* (Oxford, 2008), 223–4, 302.
24. Ziegler, *Edward VIII*, 546; *Odessa American* (Texas), 4 January 1947; *Richmond Times-Despatch*, *San Mateo Times* (California), 8 January 1953; *Chester Times* (Pennsylvania), 14 January 1955.
25. *Lincoln Star*, 7 March 1957.
26. *Troy Record* (New York), 12 December 1966: 'British Papers Ignore Edward's Abdication'. Brian Inglis, *Abdication* (London, 1966); Beaverbrook, *Abdication*.
27. The film premiered in Paris in February 1966: *Tallahassee Democrat*, 9 February 1966.
28. *Chicago Tribune*, 11 December 1966.
29. Douglas Daniel, *Harry Reasoner: A Life in the News* (Austin, TX, 2007), 112–13.
30. *New York Times*, 29 May 1972.
31. *The Times*, 2 June 1972; Ziegler, *Edward VIII*, 557–8.

32. *The Times*, 29 May 1972. The obituary had been drafted as early as 1943, when it was reviewed by Tommy Lascelles. It is clear from Lascelles's comments that the version which finally appeared was very similar to the original: Hart-Davis, ed., *King's Counsellor*, 105–11.

33. *New York Times*, 29 May 1972.

34. The Duke was still alive at the time of Charles's investiture as Prince of Wales at Caernarvon in 1969, but declined an invitation to attend the ceremony because Wallis was not included.

35. Ziegler, *Mountbatten: The Official Biography* (London, 1985), 686.

36. *The Sun*, 23 August 2012.

37. *LP* 140.

38. Hunt, *Bachelor Prince*, 230; see p. 3.

39. Nixon, ed., *Franklin D. Roosevelt and Foreign Affairs*, iii. 183–4.

40. Bloch, *Duke of Windsor's War*, 364.

41. Charles Sulzberger, *A Long Row of Candles: Memoirs and Diaries, 1934–1954* (New York, 1969), 588.

42. See pp. 92–3.

43. See pp. 186–9.

Bibliography

ABBREVIATIONS

KS   Edward, Duke of Windsor, *A King's Story* (London, 1951)
LP   Rupert Godfrey, ed., *Letters from a Prince* (London, 1998)

ARCHIVE SOURCES

Churchill Archives Centre (Churchill College, Cambridge), Amery Papers
Cumbria Record Office, Howard Papers
Glenbow Archives, Calgary, Helen Yule papers
Imperial War Museum (London), Docs 6992/7
London Metropolitan Archives, Pilgrims Papers
The National Archives (TNA) Metropolitan Police Special Branch Files, MEPO 38
Parliamentary Archives (London), Lloyd George Papers

PRINTED SOURCES

Abravanel, Genevieve, *Americanizing Britain* (Oxford, 2012)
Aitken, Jonathan, *Nixon: A Life* (London, 1993)
Alsop, Susan, *From Paris to Marietta* (London, 1976)
Amery, Leo, *My Political Life* (London, 1953)
Andrews, Allen, *The Follies of Edward VII* (London, 1975)
Aren't We Lucky? The Magazine of HMS Renown, August to December 1919 (privately
    printed, 1920)
Baker, Jean-Claude, and Chase Chris, *Josephine Baker: The Hungry Heart* (New York,
    2001)
Barbas, Samantha, *Movie Crazy: Fans, Stars and the Cult of Celebrity* (New York, 2001)
Beaken, Robert, *Cosmo Lang* (London, 2012)
Beaverbrook, Lord, *The Abdication of King Edward VIII* (London, 1966)
Bell, Duncan, *The Idea of Greater Britain* (Princeton, 2004)
Berrett, Joshua, *Louis Armstrong and Paul Whiteman* (New Haven, 2004)
Bettelheim, Bruno, *The Informed Heart* (Harmondsworth, 1986)
Bingham, Adrian, *Family Newspapers? Sex, Private Life and the British Popular Press
    1918–78* (Oxford, 2009)
Birkenhead, Lord, *Walter Monckton* (London, 1969)

Bloch, Michael, *The Duke of Windsor's War* (London, 1982)

Bloch, Michael, ed., *Wallis and Edward Letters, 1931–1937* (London, 1986)

Bloch, Michael, *The Secret File of the Duke of Windsor* (London, 1988)

Bradford, Sarah, *King George VI* (London, 1989)

Brasnett, Margaret, *Voluntary Social Action: A History of the National Council of Social Service* (London, 1969)

Brendon, Piers, *Edward VIII: The Uncrowned King* (London, 2016)

Brittain, Harry, *Pilgrim Partners* (London, 1942)

Brittain, Vera, *Testament of Youth* (London, 1979)

Brooks, Ernest, 'The King and the Prince of Wales', *Strand Magazine*, 62 (1921), 204–13

Bruccoli, Matthew, ed., *Zelda Fitzgerald: The Collected Writings* (New York, 1992)

Bryan, J., and Charles Murphy, *The Windsor Story* (London, 1979)

Bryson, Bill, *One Summer: America 1927* (London, 2013)

Burke's Peerage, Baronetage and Knightage 1938 (London, 1938)

Cadbury, Deborah, *Princes at War* (London, 2016)

Cannadine, David, 'The Context, Performance and Meaning of Ritual: The British Monarchy and the "Invention of Tradition", c.1820–1977', in Eric Hobsbawm and Terence Ranger, eds, *The Invention of Tradition* (Cambridge, 1983), 43–100

Carnegie, Andrew, 'As Others See Us', *Fortnightly Review*, 37 (Feb. 1882)

Case, Josephine, and Everett Case, *Owen Young and American Enterprise* (Boston, 1982)

Chapman, Gary, *The Dolly Sisters: Icons of the Jazz Age* (London, 2013)

Christopher of Greece, Prince, *Memoirs* (London, 1938)

Christy, Jim, *The Price of Power* (New York, 1984)

Clavin, Tom, *Sir Walter* (London, 2005)

Cody, William, *Story of the Wild West and Camp-Fire Chats* (Philadelphia, 1888)

Cooke, Alistair, *Six Men* (Harmondsworth, 1978)

Cooper, Duff, *Old Men Forget* (London, 1954)

Covarrubias, Miguel, *The Prince of Wales and Other Famous Americans* (New York, 1925)

Daniel, Douglass, *Harry Reasoner: A Life in the News* (Austin, TX, 2007)

Davis, Kenneth, *FDR, War President, 1940–43* (New York, 2000)

De Courcy, Anne, *The Viceroy's Daughters* (London, 2000)

Devon, Stanley, *Glorious: The Life Story of Stanley Devon* (London, 1957)

Dimbleby, David, and David Reynolds, *An Ocean Apart* (London, 1988)

Donaldson, Frances, *Edward VIII* (London, 1974)

Duncan, Sara, *His Royal Happiness* (London, 1915)

Ellis, John, 'Reconciling the Celt: British National Identity, Empire and the 1911 Investiture of the Prince of Wales', *Journal of British Studies*, 37 (1998), 391–418

Ellwood, David, *The Shock of America: Europe and the Challenge of the Century* (Oxford, 2012)

Evans, Simon, *Prince Charming Goes West* (Calgary, 1993)

Evans, Simon, *The Bar U* (Calgary, 2004)

Felder, D. G., *A Century of Women* (New York, 1999)

Fielding, Raymond, *American Newsreel 1911–67* (Norman, OK, 1972)

Funder, Anna, *Stasiland* (London, 2011)

Gallop, Alan, *Buffalo Bill's British Wild West* (Stroud, 2009)

Gardiner, Alfred, *Certain People of Importance* (London, 1929)

Garton Ash, Timothy, 'Inner Emigration', *The Spectator* (12 Oct. 1984), 11

Gilbert, Martin, ed., *Churchill Documents*, vol. ix (Hilldale, MI, 1977)

Gilbert, Martin, *First World War* (London, 1994)

Gilbert, Martin, ed., *Churchill Documents*, vol. xi (Michigan, 2009)

Glading, P., *How Bédaux Works* (London, 1932)

Godfrey, Rupert, ed., *Letters from a Prince* (London, 1998)

Gorodetsky, Gabriel, ed., *The Maisky Diaries: Red Ambassador to the Court of St James's 1932–43* (New Haven and London, 2015)

Graves, Robert, and Alan Hodge, *The Long Weekend* (Harmondsworth, 1971)

Gray, Robert, and Jane Olivier, *Edward VIII: The Man we Lost* (London, 1972)

Greene, Julie, *The Canal Builders: Making America's Empire at the Panama Canal* (London, 2009)

Greer, Carl, *Across with the Ad-Men* (Hamilton, OH, 1924)

Gundle, Stephen, *Glamour: A History* (Oxford, 2008)

Gunther, John, *Inside Europe* (New York, 1940)

Hall, N. John, *Max Beerbohm Caricatures* (New Haven, 1997)

Hall, Phillip, *Royal Fortune: Tax, Money and the Monarchy* (London, 1992)

Hart-Davis, Duff, ed., *In Royal Service: Letters and Journals of Sir Alan Lascelles 1920–36* (London, 1989)

Hart-Davis, Duff, ed., *King's Counsellor: Abdication and War* (London, 2007)

Hobsbawm, Eric, 'The American Cowboy: An International Myth?', in Eric Hobsbawm, *Fractured Times: Culture and Society in the Twentieth Century* (London, 2013), 272–90

Hogan, Michael, *Informal Entente: The Private Structure of Co-operation in Anglo-American Economic Diplomacy, 1918–1928* (New York, 1977)

Holmes, Michele, *Network Nations: A Transnational History of British and American Broadcasting* (London, 2012)

Hunt, Frazier, *The Bachelor Prince* (New York, 1935)

Inglis, Brian, *Abdication* (London, 1966)

Jackson, Jeffrey, *Making Jazz French* (Durham, NC, 2003)

Jennings, Charles, *Them and Us* (Stroud, 2007)

Jones, Heather, 'A Prince in the Trenches? Edward VIII and the First World War', in Frank Lorenz Müller and Heidi Mehrkens, eds, *Sons and Heirs* (London, 2015), 229–46.

Kennedy, Paul, *The Rise and Fall of Great Powers* (London, 1988)

Kiley, Jed, *Hemingway: A Title Fight in Ten Rounds* (London, 1965)

Kirkwood, David, *My Life of Revolt* (London, 1935)

Kurial, Richard, 'The Prince of Wales Visits San Diego: A Study in Perception', *San Diego Historical Society*, 38/3 (1992), 160–75

Lawrence, A. H., *Duke Ellington and his World* (London, 2001)

Leavis, Frank, *Mass Civilization and Minority Culture* (Cambridge, 1930)

Leeke, Jim, 'Royal Match: The Army–Navy Service Game, July 4, 1918', *NINE: A Journal of Baseball History and Culture,* 20/2 (Spring 2012), 15–26

Linkof, Ryan, 'The Photographic Attack on His Royal Highness: The Prince of Wales, Wallis Simpson and the Pre-History of the Paparazzi', *Photography and Culture,* 4/3 (Nov. 2011), 277–92

MacColl, Gail, and Carol Wallace, *To Marry an English Lord* (New York, 2012)

MacColl, René, *Deadline and Dateline* (London, 1956)

McGregor, O. R., *Divorce in England* (London, 1957)

Mackenzie, Compton, *The Windsor Tapestry* (London, 1938)

McKernan, Luke, *Topical Budget: The Great British News Film* (London, 1992)

Mansergh, Nicholas, *The Commonwealth Experience* (London, 1969)

Marshall, Duncan, *Shorthorn Cattle in Canada* (Toronto, 1932)

Martin, Kingsley, *The Crown and the Establishment* (London, 1962)

Mayhall, Laura, 'The Prince of Wales versus Clark Gable: Anglophone Celebrity and Citizenship between the Wars', *Cultural and Social History,* 4/4 (2007), 529–44

Middlemas, Keith, and John Barnes, *Baldwin: A Biography* (London, 1969)

Milton, Joyce, *Loss of Eden: A Biography of Charles and Anne Lindbergh* (New York, 1993)

Minden, Michael, and Holger Bachmann, *Fritz Lang's Metropolis* (Woodbridge, 2002)

Mort, Frank, 'Love in a Cold Climate: Letters, Public Opinion and Monarchy in the 1936 Abdication Crisis', *Twentieth Century British History,* 25/1 (2014), 30–62

Newton, W. Douglas, *Westward with the Prince of Wales* (London, 1920)

Nicolson, Harold, *King George V* (London, 1952)

Nixon, Edgar, ed., *Franklin D. Roosevelt and Foreign Affairs* (Cambridge, MA, 1969), vol. iii

Norwich, John Julius, ed., *The Duff Cooper Diaries* (London, 2005)

Norwich, John Julius, ed., *Diana Cooper: Darling Monster* (London, 2013)

Oliver, David, *Hendon Aerodrome: A History* (Shrewsbury, 1994)

Orde, Anne, *The Eclipse of Great Britain* (Basingstoke, 1996)

Parkhurst, Genevieve, *A King in the Making* (London, 1925)

Patterson, Martha, *Beyond the Gibson Girl* (Chicago, 2005)

Peck, Harry, *Twenty Years of the Republic, 1885–1905* (New York, 1906)

Perkins, Bradford, *The Great Rapprochement* (London, 1969)

Pershing, John, *My Experiences in the World War* (New York, 1931)

Phillips, Adrian, *The King Who Had to Go: Edward VIII, Mrs Simpson and the Hidden Politics of the Abdication Crisis* (London, 2016)

Plunkett, John, *Queen Victoria: First Media Monarch* (Oxford, 2003)

Ponce de Leon, Charles, *Self-Exposure: Human Interest Journalism and the Emergence of Celebrity in America, 1890–1940* (Chapel Hill, NC, 2002)

Prochaska, Frank, *Royal Bounty: The Making of a Welfare Monarchy* (New Haven, 1995)

Prochaska, Frank, *The Eagle and the Crown* (London, 2008)

Ralph, Wayne, *Barker VC* (London, 1999)

Rappaport, Helen, *Four Sisters* (London, 2015)

Reid, A. Cunningham, *Planes and Personalities* (London, 1920)

Reynolds, David, *The Creation of the Anglo-American Alliance, 1937–41* (London, 1981)

Riley, Glenda, *Divorce: An American Tradition* (New York, 1991)

Robbins, Trina, *Nell Brinkley and the New Woman in the Early Twentieth Century* (Jefferson, NC, 2001)

Roberts, Jane, *Royal Landscape: The Gardens and Parks of Windsor* (London, 1997)

Rogers, Will, *Letters of a Self-Made Diplomat* (New York, 1926)

Rogers, Will, *Wit and Philosophy from the Radio Talks of America's Humorist* (New York, 1930)

Rolleston, C. H., ed., *HMS Renown in Australasia: Authentic Record and Account of the Visit of HMS 'Renown' to Australasia* (Melbourne, 1920)

Roosevelt, Elliott, *A Rendezvous with Destiny* (London, 1977)

Rose, Andrew, *The Prince, the Princess and the Perfect Murder* (London, 2013)

Rose, Kenneth, *King George V* (London, 1983)

Sacks, Benjamin, 'The Duchess of Windsor and the Coronado Legend', *Journal of San Diego History,* 34/1 (1988), 1–15

Schofield, Guy, *The Visit of His Royal Highness the Prince of Wales to New Zealand* (Wellington, 1926)

Sebba, Anne, *That Woman* (London, 2011)

Shaughnessy, Alfred, ed., *Sarah: Letters and Diaries of a Courtier's Wife 1906–36* (London, 1989)

Sitwell, Osbert, *Rat Week* (London, 1986)

Sotheby's Catalogue, Geneva, 2–3 April 1987: The Jewels of the Duchess of Windsor

Sotheby's Catalogue, New York, 20 June 2003: Fine Books and Manuscripts

Souvenir Guide to the EP Ranch (Calgary, c. 1924)

Speeches by HRH The Prince of Wales, 1912–26 (London, 1926)

Stead, William, *The Americanization of the World* (New York, 1902)

Steiner, Zara, *The Lights that Failed* (Oxford, 2005)

Stevenson, David, *With our Backs to the Wall* (London, 2011)

Stewart, D. O., *Perfect Behavior* (New York, 1922)

Sulzberger, Charles, *A Long Row of Candles: Memoirs and Diaries, 1934–1954* (New York, 1969)

Taylor, A. J. P., *English History 1914–1945* (Oxford, 1965)

Tooze, Adam, *The Deluge: The Great War, America, and the Remaking of the Global Order* (London, 2014)

Urbach, Karina, *Go Betweens for Hitler* (Oxford, 2015)

Vanderbilt, Gloria, and Thelma Furness, *Double Exposure* (London, 1959)

Volkan, V. D., and N. Itzkowitz, *The Immortal Ataturk* (Chicago, 1984)

Vreeland, Diana, *DV*, ed. G Plimpton and C. Hemphill (London, 1984)

Wainwright, Robert, *Sheila* (London, 2014)

Wallace, Graham, *The Flight of Alcock and Brown* (London, 1955)

Ward Price, George, *Extra-Special Correspondent* (London, 1957)
Waugh, Evelyn, *Brideshead Revisited* (Harmondsworth, 1973)
Williams, David, *The Prince of Wales* (London, 1915)
Williams, Susan, *The People's King* (London, 2003)
Williamson, Philip, *Stanley Baldwin: Conservative Leadership and National Values* (Cambridge, 1999)
Windsor, Edward, Duke of, *A King's Story* (London, 1951)
Windsor, Edward, Duke of, *The Crown and the People* (New York and London, 1953)
Windsor, Edward, Duke of, *A Family Album* (London, 1960)
Windsor, Wallis, duchess of, *The Heart has its Reasons* (London, 1956)
Woon, Basil, *The Paris that's Not in the Guide Books* (New York, 1926)
Wrench, Evelyn, *Geoffrey Dawson and our Times* (London, 1955)
Yagoda, Ben, *Will Rogers: A Biography* (New York, 1994)
Young, G. M., *Stanley Baldwin* (London, 1952)
Ziegler, Philip, *Mountbatten: The Official Biography* (London, 1985)
Ziegler, Philip, ed., *The Diaries of Lord Louis Mountbatten, 1920–1922* (London, 1987)
Ziegler, Philip, *King Edward VIII* (London, 1991)

WEBSITES

London Borough of Brent http://www.brent.gov.uk/media.
Pathé Newsreel http://www.britishpathe.com/video/prince-of-wales-visits-usa.
'The Musicians' Union: a Social History: 1921–30' https://www.muhistory.com.
Prince of Wales http://princeofwales.gov.uk.

NEWSPAPERS AND MAGAZINES

Australia

Daily Examiner (Grafton, New South Wales)
Darling Downs Gazette (Queensland)
Euroa Advertiser (Victoria)
Melbourne Age (Victoria)
Newcastle Sun (New South Wales)

Canada

Calgary Herald
High River Times (Alberta)
New Brunswick Evening Times-Star
Ottawa Journal
St John Evening Times Star
Toronto Star
Vancouver Daily World
Winnipeg Tribune

New Zealand

Mt Ida Chronicle

United Kingdom

Cavalcade
Daily Express
Daily Mirror
Daily Telegraph
Manchester Guardian
Punch
Radio Times
The Spectator
The Times
Yorkshire Post

USA

Albany Democrat (New York)
Albuquerque Journal (New Mexico)
Altoona Tribune (Pennsylvania)
Anniston Star (Alabama)
Arizona Republic
Atlanta Constitution
Baltimore Sun
Bemidji Pioneer (Minnesota)
Billboard
Bisbee Daily Review (Arizona)
Bismarck Tribune (North Dakota)
Bridgewater Courier-News (New Jersey)
Brooklyn Daily Eagle
Chester Times (Pennsylvania)
Chicago Tribune
Cincinnati Enquirer (Ohio)
Clovis News-Journal, (New Mexico)
Cohocton Tribune (Ohio)
Collier's Magazine
Daily Ardmoreite (Oklahoma)
Daily Capital Journal (Oregon)
Daily Journal-Gazette (Illinois)
Daily Messenger
The Day (New London, Connecticut)
Decatur Daily Review (Georgia)
Decatur Herald (Georgia)
DeKalb Daily Chronicle (Illinois)

Des Moines Register (Iowa)
Detroit Free Press
Dunkirk Evening Observer (New York)
Emporia Gazette (Kansas)
Evening World Magazine
Fitchburg Sentinel (Massachusetts)
Florence Morning News (South Carolina)
Fort-Myers News Press (Florida)
Fort Scott Daily Tribune (Kansas)
Franklin News-Herald (Pennsylvania)
Gettysburg Times (Pennsylvania)
Great Bend Tribune (Kansas)
Great Falls Tribune (Montana)
Green Bay Press Gazette (Wisconsin)
Hamilton Daily News (Ohio)
Harrisburg Evening News (Pennsylvania)
Helena Independent Record (Montana)
Houston Post
Huntington Herald (Indiana)
The Idaho Falls Register
Idaho Post-Register
Indiana Gazette (Pennsylvania)
Indianapolis News
Indianapolis Star
Jackson Clarion-Ledger (Mississippi)
Kingsport Times (Tennessee)
Klamath Falls Evening Herald (Oregon)
Lansing State Journal (Michigan)
Leavenworth Times (Kansas)
Liberty
Lincoln Evening Journal (Nebraska)
Lincoln Star (Nebraska)
Literary Digest
Logan Daily News (Ohio)
Los Angeles Times
Louisville Courier-Journal
Lubbock Morning Avalanche (Texas)
Manitowoc Herald Times (Wisconsin)
McCall's Magazine
Marion Star (Ohio)
Miami Daily News-Record
Minneapolis Star
Modesto Evening News (California)
Muscatine Journal (Iowa)

New Castle News (Pennsylvania)
New York Evening World
New York Sun
New York Times
New York Tribune
North Platte Review (Nebraska)
Oakland Tribune (California)
Odessa American (Texas)
Ogden Standard-Examiner (Utah)
Oshkosh Daily Northwestern (Wisconsin)
Palm Beach Post (Florida)
Parsons Daily Sun (Kansas)
Philadelphia Daily News
Philadelphia Evening Public Ledger
Philadelphia Inquirer
Photoplay Magazine
Pittsburgh Daily Post
Pittsburgh Post-Gazette
Pittsburgh Press
Reading Times (Pennsylvania)
Reno Gazette Journal (Nevada)
Richmond Times-Despatch (Virginia)
Rochester Democrat and Chronicle (New York)
St Louis Post-Dispatch
St Louis Star
San Bernardino County Sun (California)
San Diego Union
Sandusky Register (Ohio)
San Mateo Times (California)
Santa Ana Register (California)
Scranton Republican (Pennsylvania)
Sedalia Democrat (Missouri)
Spartanburg Herald (South Carolina)
Springfield Leader (Missouri)
Springfield Republican (Missouri)
Syracuse Herald-American (New York)
Tallahassee Democrat (Florida)
The Tennessean
Time
Troy Record (New York)
Troy Sunday Budget (New York)
True Democrat (Louisiana)
Warren Times-Mirror (Pennsylvania)
Warren Tribune (Pennsylvania)

Washington Herald
Washington Post
Washington Times
Wichita Daily Eagle (Kansas)
Wilkes-Barre Record (Pennsylvania)
Wilmington Evening Journal (Delaware)
Wilmington Morning Star (Delaware)
Wilmington News Journal (Delaware)

Picture Acknowledgements

0.1 Everett Collection Inc / Alamy Stock Photo

1.1 Photograph, author's collection

2.1 Topical Press Agency/Getty Images

3.1 Photograph, author's collection

3.2 The Print Collector/Print Collector/Getty Images

3.3 The Print Collector/Heritage Image/age fotostock

3.4 *Punch*, October 1919

4.1 Photograph, author's collection

4.2 Photo by kind permission of the Museum of British Surfing

5.1 Photograph, author's collection

5.2 Photo ©: The Glenbow Museum, Glenbow Archives (NA-2626-11)

6.1 Photograph, author's collection

6.2 Photograph, author's collection

6.3 Photograph, author's collection

6.4 Photograph, author's collection

6.5 Hulton Archive/Getty Images

6.6 'frontispiece' from *Prince of Wales* by Miguel Covarrubias, copyright 1925 by Alfred A. Knopf, Inc., copyright renewed © 1953 by Miguel Covarrubias. Used by permission of Alfred A. Knopf, an imprint of the Knopf Doubleday Publishing Group, a division of Penguin Random House LLC. All rights reserved.

7.1 Popperfoto/Getty Images

7.2 George W. Price, *Extra-special correspondent*, 1957

7.3 Popperfoto/Getty Images

7.4 Topical Press Agency/Hulton Archive/Getty Images

7.5 Portrait of HRH The Prince of Wales, 1925 (oil on canvas), Lander, John St. Helier (1869–1944) / Leeds Museums and Galleries (Lotherton Hall) U.K. / Bridgeman Images

7.6 *The Literary Digest*, 1929

7.7 *Impossible Interviews:* Clark Gable and Edward, *the Prince of Wales* (gouache
     on paper), Covarrubias, Miguel (1904–57) / Private Collection /
     Photo © Christie's Images / Bridgeman Images

8.1 Freda Dudley Ward, 1919 (b/w photo), English Photographer,
     (20th century) / The Illustrated London News Picture Library, London,
     UK / Bridgeman Images

8.2 J. H, Gardner Soper, *The Ladies Home Journal*, 1919

8.3 Photo ©: TopFoto.co.uk

8.4 Paul Fearn / Alamy Stock Photo

10.1 Popperfoto/Getty Images

10.2 Glasshouse Images / Alamy Stock Photo

10.3 Photograph, author's collection

12.1 Wallis Simpson, 1936 (b/w photo), English Photographer, (20th century) /
     The Illustrated London News Picture Library, London, UK / Bridgeman
     Images

The publisher and author apologize for any errors or omissions in the above list.
If contacted they will be pleased to rectify these at the earliest opportunity.

Text Acknowledgements

Winnipeg Tribune, 11 July, 1929, pp. 3, 7. Used under the Creative Commons Attribution-NonCommercial 4.0 International license (https://creativecommons. org/licenses/by-nc/4.0/).

Extracts from the Howard Papers, held in the Cumbria Record Office, appear by kind permission of Lord Howard.

Extracts from the Lloyd George Papers appear by kind permission of the Senior Archivist of the Parliamentary Archives.

Extracts from Alfred Shaughnessy, ed., Sarah: Letters and Diairies of a Courtier's Wife (London, 1989), appear by kind permission of Peter Owen publishers.

Whilst every effort has been made to secure permissions, we may have failed in a few cases to trace the copyright holders. We apologise for any apparent negligence. Should the copyright holders wish to contact us after publication, we would be happy to include an acknowledgement in subsequent reprints.

Index

Note: (f) following a locator indicates a figure.